Moving towards 6G Wireless Technologies

Moving towards 6G Wireless Technologies

Editors

Alessandro Raschellà
Michael Mackay

Basel • Beijing • Wuhan • Barcelona • Belgrade • Novi Sad • Cluj • Manchester

Editors
Alessandro Raschellà
Liverpool John Moores University
Liverpool
UK

Michael Mackay
Liverpool John Moores University
Liverpool
UK

Editorial Office
MDPI AG
Grosspeteranlage 5
4052 Basel, Switzerland

This is a reprint of articles from the Special Issue published online in the open access journal *Future Internet* (ISSN 1999-5903) (available at: https://www.mdpi.com/journal/futureinternet/special_issues/MT_6G_WT).

For citation purposes, cite each article independently as indicated on the article page online and as indicated below:

Lastname, A.A.; Lastname, B.B. Article Title. *Journal Name* **Year**, *Volume Number*, Page Range.

ISBN 978-3-7258-2599-8 (Hbk)
ISBN 978-3-7258-2600-1 (PDF)
doi.org/10.3390/books978-3-7258-2600-1

© 2024 by the authors. Articles in this book are Open Access and distributed under the Creative Commons Attribution (CC BY) license. The book as a whole is distributed by MDPI under the terms and conditions of the Creative Commons Attribution-NonCommercial-NoDerivs (CC BY-NC-ND) license.

Contents

About the Editors vii

Alessandro Raschella and Michael Mackay
Editorial for the Special Issue on Moving Towards 6G Wireless Technologies
Reprinted from: *Future Internet* **2024**, *16*, 400, doi:10.3390/fi16110400 1

Chiara Suraci, Sara Pizzi, Federico Montori, Marco Di Felice and Giuseppe Araniti
6G to Take the Digital Divide by Storm: Key Technologies and Trends to Bridge the Gap
Reprinted from: *Future Internet* **2022**, *14*, 189, doi:10.3390/fi14060189 4

Faycal Bouhafs, Alessandro Raschellà, Michael Mackay and Frank den Hartog
A Spectrum Management Platform Architecture to Enable a Sharing Economy in 6G
Reprinted from: *Future Internet* **2022**, *14*, 309, doi:10.3390/fi14110309 17

Leonardo Militano, Adriana Arteaga, Giovanni Toffetti and Nathalie Mitton
The Cloud-to-Edge-to-IoT Continuum as an Enabler for Search and Rescue Operations
Reprinted from: *Future Internet* **2023**, *15*, 55, doi:10.3390/fi15020055 30

Maziar Nekovee and Ferheen Ayaz
Vision, Enabling Technologies, and Scenarios for a 6G-Enabled Internet of Verticals (6G-IoV)
Reprinted from: *Future Internet* **2023**, *15*, 57, doi:10.3390/fi15020057 48

Sang-Yoon Chang, Kyungmin Park, Jonghyun Kim and Jinoh Kim
Securing UAV Flying Base Station for Mobile Networking: A Review
Reprinted from: *Future Internet* **2023**, *15*, 176, doi:10.3390/fi15050176 58

Vinoth Babu Kumaravelu, Agbotiname Lucky Imoize, Francisco R. Castillo Soria, Periyakarupan Gurusamy Sivabalan Velmurugan, Sundarrajan Jayaraman Thiruvengadam, Dinh-Thuan Do, et al.
RIS-Assisted Fixed NOMA: Outage Probability Analysis and Transmit Power Optimization
Reprinted from: *Future Internet* **2023**, *15*, 249, doi:10.3390/fi15080249 72

Carlos Serôdio, José Cunha, Guillermo Candela, Santiago Rodriguez, Xosé Ramón Sousa and Frederico Branco
The 6G Ecosystem as Support for IoE and Private Networks: Vision, Requirements, and Challenges
Reprinted from: *Future Internet* **2023**, *15*, 348, doi:10.3390/fi15110348 90

Lidong Liu, Shidang Li, Mingsheng Wei, Jinsong Xu and Bencheng Yu
Joint Beam-Forming Optimization for Active-RIS-Assisted Internet-of-Things Networks with SWIPT
Reprinted from: *Future Internet* **2024**, *16*, 20, doi:10.3390/fi16010020 122

Véronique Georlette, Anne-Carole Honfoga, Michel Dossou and Véronique Moeyaert
Exploring Universal Filtered Multi Carrier Waveform for Last Meter Connectivity in 6G: A Street-Lighting-Driven Approach with Enhanced Simulator for IoT Application Dimensioning
Reprinted from: *Future Internet* **2024**, *16*, 112, doi:10.3390/fi16040112 143

Mira M. Zarie, Abdelhamied A. Ateya, Mohammed S. Sayed, Mohammed ElAffendi and Mohammad Mahmoud Abdellatif
Microservice-Based Vehicular Network for Seamless and Ultra-Reliable Communications of Connected Vehicles
Reprinted from: *Future Internet* **2024**, *16*, 257, doi:10.3390/fi16070257 157

About the Editors

Alessandro Raschellà

Alessandro Raschellà received B.Sc. and M.Sc. degrees in telecommunications engineering from the University Mediterranea of Reggio Calabria (UNIRC), Italy, in 2004 and 2007, respectively, and a PhD degree in wireless communications from Universitat Politècnica de Catalunya (UPC), Barcelona, Spain, in 2015. From 2007 to 2009, he was a Research Assistant with UNIRC. He joined the School of Computer Science and Mathematics, Liverpool John Moores University (LJMU), U.K., in 2015, working as a Research Fellow, where he is currently a Senior Lecturer. His research interests include wireless network optimization, software-defined networking, cognitive radio, the IoT, and heterogeneous networks.

Michael Mackay

Michael Mackay received a B.Sc. degree in computer science and a PhD degree from Lancaster University, in 2000 and 2005, respectively. He is currently a Reader in wireless and edge systems at Liverpool John Moores University (LJMU) and leads the Networking and Distributed Systems Research Group. He joined LJMU as a Senior Lecturer in 2010. His current research interests include networking protocols and beyond 5G and 6G wireless systems. He is also widely published in a range of research areas focused around networking technologies, including IPv6, IP mobility, QoS and CDNs, grid networking, and, more recently, cloud and edge computing and the Internet of Things.

Editorial

Editorial for the Special Issue on Moving Towards 6G Wireless Technologies

Alessandro Raschella * and Michael Mackay *

School of Computer Science and Mathematics, Liverpool John Moores University, Byrom Street, Liverpool L3 3AF, UK
* Correspondence: a.raschella@ljmu.ac.uk (A.R.); m.i.mackay@ljmu.ac.uk (M.M.)

Citation: Raschella, A.; Mackay, M. Editorial for the Special Issue on Moving Towards 6G Wireless Technologies. *Future Internet* **2024**, *16*, 400. https://doi.org/10.3390/fi16110400

Received: 9 October 2024
Accepted: 11 October 2024
Published: 31 October 2024

Copyright: © 2024 by the authors. Licensee MDPI, Basel, Switzerland. This article is an open access article distributed under the terms and conditions of the Creative Commons Attribution (CC BY) license (https://creativecommons.org/licenses/by/4.0/).

Fifth-generation (5G) wireless networks have been a key enabler for information societies over the last few years. Now, sixth-generation (6G) wireless networks are under development, and the research community is preparing for the intelligent information societies of 2030 and beyond, targeting even more ambitious performance targets, such as peak data rates from 1 Tb/s, enhanced spectrum and energy efficiency, and extremely low latency communications. This Special Issue of *Future Internet* titled "Moving towards 6G Wireless Technologies" focuses on the design, development, testing, and evaluation of 6G-enabling solutions to meet these ambitious goals. We have published a total of ten papers covering a range of topics including, but not limited to, IoT applications, vehicular networks, 6G-Enabled Internet of Verticals (6G-IoV), and spectrum sharing.

In the first paper [1], the authors investigate how the problem of the digital divide, which became clearer in the COVID-19 pandemic, can be mitigated by looking to 6G and other emerging technologies, the latter being not just a mere exploration of more spectra at high-frequency bands but a new paradigm for ubiquitous, pervasive, and high-speed internet connectivity, which can remedy actual limitations in the realization of a truly digital world. Specifically, the authors first introduce several key 6G technologies, such as non-terrestrial networks and Terahertz (THz) frequencies, for bridging the digital gap and then illustrate how these can work in two use cases of particular importance, namely eHealth and education. In [2], the authors encourage further research and development of Unmanned Aerial Vehicle (UAV) flying base station operations, which could also play a significant role in 6G networking. In fact, one of the main goals of 6G networking is reliable connectivity with high-performance communication channels even in rural regions. The authors discuss the unique properties of UAV flying base stations while describing the main properties of its component technologies and functionalities, including traditional telecommunications networking, UAV drones, authentication, and distributed networking. In [3], the authors present HODNET (Heterogeneous on Demand NETwork resource negotiation), an open platform based on the Software-Defined Wireless Network (SDWN) which is able to realize a novel vision to trade and allocate wireless spectra in 6G communication networks inspired by the concept of the sharing economy. Moreover, they analyzed the benefits of the platform with a use case of massive IoT deployment showing a significant improvement in resource utilization with respect to a standard 5G deployment. In [4], the authors discuss how the cloud-to-edge-to-IoT compute continuum can support Search and Rescue (SAR) operations in cases of natural and human disasters. A detailed analysis of current challenges with respect to the technology used in SAR operations is presented with an overview of the advanced solutions that may be adopted in these scenarios. In [5], the authors have reviewed key architecture, networking, and technology components, which are considered critical to the successful expansion of 5G connectivity services and platforms into vertical sectors in the 6G era. While 5G is primarily aimed at the connectivity requirements of specific verticals, such as manufacturing, automotives, and energy, the authors discuss how, in the longer term, the expansion of wide-area cellular connectivity to these sectors will pave the way for a transformation to a new Internet of Verticals (IoV) in the 6G era, which they call 6G-IoV. They also discuss possible use cases of 6G-IoV, which include distributed and over-the-top cloud manufacturing as a service, the Internet of Robotics (IoR), and the Internet of Smart Energy Grids.

In [6], the authors analyze the outage probability expressions for smart Reconfigurable Intelligent Surface (RIS)-assisted Fixed Non-Orthogonal Multiple Access (FNOMA). This is considered one of the primary potential components of 6G networks, taking into account the instances of RIS as a Smart Reflector (SR) and an Access Point (AP). According to simulations, their results show that RIS-assisted FNOMA surpasses FNOMA by 62% in terms of outage and sum capacity. The authors in [7] discuss the essential parameters of 6G technology, exploring the substantial challenges that will have to be surmounted to realize the desired benchmarks and fulfill the envisioned potential. Wireless networks based on 6G promise, in fact, to deliver a substantial increase in the Quality of Service (QoS) while also emphasizing sustainability. The authors discuss how this assurance is underpinned by a new architectural paradigm shift around existing and emerging spectrum technologies such as THz, Visible Light Communication (VLC), and molecular and quantum communication. This paradigm also encompasses integrating terrestrial and non-terrestrial networks, fostering intelligent connections made possible by pervasive AI, and bolstering the network's protocol stack framework. In [8], the authors investigate how to solve the problem of the shortage of energy harvested by users in communication systems using the Active RIS (A-RIS)-assisted Simultaneous Wireless Information and Power Transfer (SWIPT) technique. The problem of maximizing the sum of energy harvested by the users has been established under the constraints of the minimum signal-to-dry-noise ratio required by the user, the maximum power of A-RIS, the maximum power of the base station, and the Power Splitting (PS) ratio. The numerical values have demonstrated an efficient convergence of the proposed algorithm. In [9], the authors contribute to the understanding and optimization of VLC systems for IoT, which they consider crucial in the 6G era for their application versatility in various scenarios. Specifically, they highlight the growing efficiency of lighting LEDs in infrastructure, facilitating the seamless integration of VLC. Then, they analyze VLC's robustness in outdoor settings, demonstrating effective communication up to 10 m. Finally, the authors delve into multi-carrier modulation schemes, Orthogonal Frequency-Division Multiplexing (OFDM) and Universal Filtered Multi Carrier (UFMC), exploring the adaptations for UFMC in VLC, revealing a superior performance compared to OFDM. Finally, in [10], the authors investigate the major challenges presented by the demanding needs of Vehicular Ad Hoc Networks (VANETs) in the Beyond 5G (B5G) and 6G eras, including extremely low latency, exceptional reliability, and seamless communications at high mobilities. Their paper introduces a novel structure for VANETs based on fog computing, Mobile Edge Computing (MEC), and a microservices architecture. The authors demonstrate how utilizing this approach can improve the network's capacity to handle computational activities and maintain minimal latency effectively.

In conclusion, this Special Issue presents a range of papers that explore the development and evaluation of key 6G-enabling solutions currently addressed in the research community and that can help meet the ambitious goals of upcoming 6G networks. We would like to thank all of the authors for their submissions to this Special Issue. We would also like to acknowledge all of the reviewers for their careful and timely reviews that have helped to improve the quality of this Special Issue.

Conflicts of Interest: The authors declare no conflict of interest.

References

1. Suraci, C.; Pizzi, S.; Montori, F.; Di Felice, M.; Araniti, G. 6G to Take the Digital Divide by Storm: Key Technologies and Trends to Bridge the Gap. *Future Internet* **2022**, *14*, 189. [CrossRef]
2. Chang, S.-Y.; Park, K.; Kim, J.; Kim, J. Securing UAV Flying Base Station for Mobile Networking: A Review. *Future Internet* **2023**, *15*, 176. [CrossRef]

3. Bouhafs, F.; Raschellà, A.; Mackay, M.; Hartog, F.D. A Spectrum Management Platform Architecture to Enable a Sharing Economy in 6G. *Future Internet* **2022**, *14*, 309. [CrossRef]
4. Militano, L.; Arteaga, A.; Toffetti, G.; Mitton, N. The Cloud-to-Edge-to-IoT Continuum as an Enabler for Search and Rescue Operations. *Future Internet* **2023**, *15*, 55. [CrossRef]
5. Nekovee, M.; Ayaz, F. Vision, Enabling Technologies, and Scenarios for a 6G-Enabled Internet of Verticals (6G-IoV). *Future Internet* **2023**, *15*, 57. [CrossRef]
6. Kumaravelu, V.B.; Imoize, A.L.; Soria, F.R.C.; Velmurugan, P.G.S.; Thiruvengadam, S.J.; Do, D.-T.; Murugadass, A. RIS-Assisted Fixed NOMA: Outage Probability Analysis and Transmit Power Optimization. *Future Internet* **2023**, *15*, 249. [CrossRef]
7. Serôdio, C.; Cunha, J.; Candela, G.; Rodriguez, S.; Sousa, X.R.; Branco, F. The 6G Ecosystem as Support for IoE and Private Networks: Vision, Requirements, and Challenges. *Future Internet* **2023**, *15*, 348. [CrossRef]
8. Liu, L.; Li, S.; Wei, M.; Xu, J.; Yu, B. Joint Beam-Forming Optimization for Active-RIS-Assisted Internet-of-Things Networks with SWIPT. *Future Internet* **2024**, *16*, 20. [CrossRef]
9. Georlette, V.; Honfoga, A.-C.; Dossou, M.; Moeyaert, V. Exploring Universal Filtered Multi Carrier Waveform for Last Meter Connectivity in 6G: A Street-Lighting-Driven Approach with Enhanced Simulator for IoT Application Dimensioning. *Future Internet* **2024**, *16*, 112. [CrossRef]
10. Zarie, M.M.; Ateya, A.A.; Sayed, M.S.; ElAffendi, M.; Abdellatif, M.M. Microservice-Based Vehicular Network for Seamless and Ultra-Reliable Communications of Connected Vehicles. *Future Internet* **2024**, *16*, 257. [CrossRef]

Disclaimer/Publisher's Note: The statements, opinions and data contained in all publications are solely those of the individual author(s) and contributor(s) and not of MDPI and/or the editor(s). MDPI and/or the editor(s) disclaim responsibility for any injury to people or property resulting from any ideas, methods, instructions or products referred to in the content.

 *future internet*

Review

6G to Take the Digital Divide by Storm: Key Technologies and Trends to Bridge the Gap

Chiara Suraci [1], Sara Pizzi [1,*], Federico Montori [2], Marco Di Felice [2] and Giuseppe Araniti [1]

[1] Department of Information Engineering, Infrastructure and Sustainable Energy (DIIES), University Mediterranea of Reggio Calabria, 89100 Reggio Calabria, Italy; chiara.suraci@unirc.it (C.S.); araniti@unirc.it (G.A.)

[2] Department of Computer Science and Engineering (DISI), University of Bologna, 40127 Bologna, Italy; federico.montori2@unibo.it (F.M.); marco.difelice3@unibo.it (M.D.F.)

* Correspondence: sara.pizzi@unirc.it

Abstract: The pandemic caused by COVID-19 has shed light on the urgency of bridging the digital divide to guarantee equity in the fruition of different services by all citizens. The inability to access the digital world may be due to a lack of network infrastructure, which we refer to as *service-delivery divide*, or to the physical conditions, handicaps, age, or digital illiteracy of the citizens, that is mentioned as *service-fruition divide*. In this paper, we discuss the way how future sixth-generation (6G) systems can remedy actual limitations in the realization of a truly digital world. Hence, we introduce the key technologies for bridging the digital gap and show how they can work in two use cases of particular importance, namely eHealth and education, where digital inequalities have been dramatically augmented by the pandemic. Finally, considerations about the socio-economical impacts of future 6G solutions are drawn.

Keywords: 6G; digital divide; NTNs; AI; XR; MEC; affective computing; BCI; D2D; use cases

Citation: Suraci, C.; Pizzi, S.; Montori, F.; Di Felice, M.; Araniti, G. 6G to Take the Digital Divide by Storm: Key Technologies and Trends to Bridge the Gap. *Future Internet* 2022, 14, 189. https://doi.org/10.3390/fi14060189

Academic Editor: Vincenzo Eramo

Received: 17 May 2022
Accepted: 16 June 2022
Published: 19 June 2022

Publisher's Note: MDPI stays neutral with regard to jurisdictional claims in published maps and institutional affiliations.

Copyright: © 2022 by the authors. Licensee MDPI, Basel, Switzerland. This article is an open access article distributed under the terms and conditions of the Creative Commons Attribution (CC BY) license (https://creativecommons.org/licenses/by/4.0/).

1. Introduction

The digital divide has existed since access to the Internet began to spread among the worldwide population. This phenomenon consists of the gap between people who have access to the digital world and those who have not, for various reasons, such as geographical location, economic status, level of education, and general interests. Nonetheless, the health emergency triggered by the COVID-19 propagation has opened our eyes to the difficulties related to a life far from the digital world. Among others, Nokia collects some statistics relating to the inclusivity in distance teaching activities, undertaken during the lockdowns caused by the pandemic, pointing out that, according to UNICEF, 31% of the school children in the world were unable to access remote learning [1]. From a different perspective, Ericsson provided some data on the impact of the pandemic in the U.S. wireless communications industry, reporting a 19.6% increase in data traffic, 24.3% in voice traffic, and 25% in texting; moreover, the authors state that the COVID-19 spread has highlighted the true face of the digital gap, which is not only an access problem but, more generally, it is caused by lacks in affordability, quality of coverage, and technical skills [2]. This thesis is supported even by Huawei which emphasizes the fact that 50% of our planet has no Internet access and, thus, presents the TECH4ALL project, aimed at expanding the granting of digital rights by acting on three core fronts: technologies, applications, and skills [3]. The Cisco Annual Internet Report claims that about 2/3 of the worldwide population will have access to the Internet by 2023, with an estimate of almost four devices per capita [4]. Bridging the gap must not be considered only a cost: the forecasts from Vodafone in [5] mention that the cumulative additional contribution to the GDP of new digital technologies could amount to 2.2 trillion euros in the EU by 2030. Furthermore, this report highlights the benefits obtainable through the application of a digital-by-design approach in the recovery plan for Europe following the COVID-19 crisis: enhanced quality of life for citizens, long-term economic growth, lower resource consumption, increased resilience and fairness of society.

Statistics and forecasts are shown in Figure 1 prove that the digital divide problem is very striking and multi-dimensional. Indeed, the likelihood that people have access to the Internet is influenced by the level of economic and cultural development of the country in which they live; besides, the generation gap impacts the digital divide; even the gender is a factor of diversity when looking at the number of people open to digitization. Whatever the reason that causes the impossibility or unwillingness of some people to *live connected*, today, the digital divide represents a real obstacle to the recovery that the world needs following the COVID-19 pandemic, which has befallen the global population some time ago and which is still conditioning our lives. Although some countries were more digitized than others, similar disparities in Internet access for households with a higher level of poverty and rural areas were reported worldwide and even before the pandemic began [6]. This led us to consider the reassessment of numerous aspects concerning the enforcement of information and communications technologies (ICT) in various areas of society, including work, education, and health. Unfortunately, none of the existing solutions has been proved to be an effective response to the digital divide problem, being too focused on specific demand or introducing high costs for its development. For this reason, in this paper, we investigate how the problem of the digital divide can be mitigated by looking to the future, specifically to the sixth generation (6G) and rising technologies, being the latter not just a mere exploration of more spectrum at high-frequency bands [7] rather a new paradigm for ubiquitous, pervasive and high-speed Internet connectivity. Furthermore, 6G could represent the turning point as it will allow the achievement of a high level of automation in the execution of various services and the extension of coverage of cellular networks. This is the reason why this work refers to 6G technologies, classified as *evolutionary* and *revolutionary*, wherein the former has already emerged with the fifth generation (5G), but is not yet widespread on the market [8]. In more detail, we provide three main contributions to this study. First, in Section 2 we discuss the evolution of the digital divide concept and the challenges that can be addressed by the technological development; differently from [9], which focuses on the specific issue of coverage of remote areas, our study proposes a multi-dimensional discussion, by further distinguishing between *service-delivery divide*, from a network-oriented perspective, and *service-fruition divide*, from an individual-oriented perspective. Second, in Sections 3 and 4, we discuss how the future 6G network is expected to overcome both the issues, by identifying trending technologies that should be further developed and be part of the upcoming specifications. The role of Artificial Intelligence (AI) and big-data collection and analytics via Machine Learning (ML) techniques is transversal to service delivery and fruition and for this reason is discussed apart in Section 5. Third, in Section 6, we describe selected use cases (e.g., eHealth and education) where digital inequalities have been dramatically augmented by the COVID-19 pandemic, and how the aforementioned 6G technologies could be effective in bridging the gaps. Considerations about the socio-economical impacts of future 6G solutions are drawn in Section 7.

2/3
of the worldwide population will have access to the Internet by 2023

50%
of our planet has not Internet access

31%
of the world's school children were unable to access to remote learning during lockdowns

+€2.2 trillion
is the cumulative additional contribution of new digital technologies to the GDP by 2030

Impact of COVID-19 in the U.S. wireless communications industry:

+19.6% in data traffic
+24.3% in voice traffic
+25% in texting

Figure 1. Some numbers on the Digital Divide.

2. The Evolution of the Digital Divide

The origin of the digital divide dates back to the mid-nineties when, in the U.S., through the publication of some reports, the differences between people with access to the Internet ("haves") and those without ("have-nots") began to be analyzed. The phenomenon of the digital divide has evolved over time, passing from the *first-level*, related to the problems of access and connectivity, to the *second-level*, consisting in the lack of the necessary skills to properly exploit ICT, and finally to the *third-level*, concerning the differences in the outcomes and consequences obtained by using the Internet [10].

According to this, we classify the different types of digital divide into two major categories: the *service-delivery divide* and the *service-fruition divide*. The former concerns the digital exclusion caused by the absence of network infrastructures necessary for Internet access and digital services delivery; the latter can be considered related to a person-specific divide, since an insufficient level of digital literacy or a set of physical inabilities could prevent people from enjoying the benefits deriving from the fruition of digital services.

The existence of these conditions not only affects the origin and the past of the digital divide phenomenon, but also concerns the current time. As a matter of fact, the state of health emergency we are still experiencing has exacerbated the digital gap. In the enterprise context, the resilience of companies has been enabled only for those that invested in technological innovation. This has represented a lifeline for the operational continuity of the businesses that had the readiness to carry out the *digital metamorphosis* path, necessary for survival in the period of COVID-19. Similarly, receiving the provision of numerous services in telematic and innovative modalities has proved to be straightforward only for the part of the population inclined to use ICT; all the others encountered not a few difficulties in adapting to the new set-up imposed by the measures implemented to limit the pandemic. Even in light of the reports cited in Section 1, we can state that the digital exclusion corresponds to exclusion from access to services. Indeed, going through the pandemic caused by COVID-19, we have realized how important technology is as a means of keeping people in contact with the outside world by digitally receiving different types of services. This is the reason why we define a service-based classification to group the causes of the digital divide.

Regarding the future evolution of the digital gap phenomenon, *normalization* and *stratification* are the two contradictory predictions that have been defined in the literature [11]. According to the first, over time the differences that cause the gap will gradually disappear until they reach saturation; it relies on the belief that government institutions will succeed in promoting and facilitating Internet access in the long run. Conversely, the second promotes the idea that the digital divide will unavoidably grow, owing to a continuing tightening of disparities within societies. This perspective appears to be more realistic, since some opinions exist according to which the evolution of mobile wireless networks could worsen the digital divide. For example, the very fact that, in this first phase of release, the 5G standard has been unevenly distributed in different countries of the world, led to the establishment of a further gap between areas that receive state-of-the-art network coverage and those that don't. Again in [11], it is stated that *connectivity does not end the digital divide, skills do* to emphasize that, anyway, increasing network coverage alone may not suffice to bridge the digital divide, instead, technology ought to be exploited to bring people closer to the digital world.

The described evolution path is represented in Figure 2.

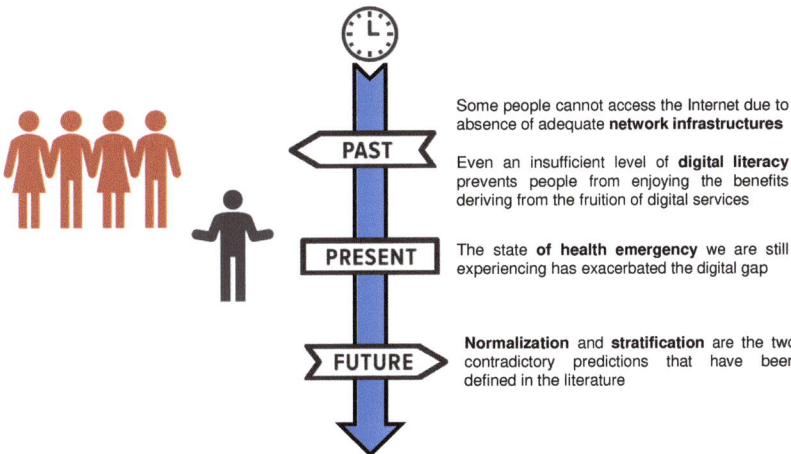

Figure 2. The evolution of the Digital Divide.

3. The Technologies for Bridging the Service-Delivery Divide

In this section, we examine the possible implementations of technologies that can be considered powerful tools to face and govern the problem of the service-delivery divide, as they would be able to offer Internet access even where traditional network infrastructures fall short. Some of the technologies that will be mentioned belong to the evolutionary category (see Section 1) as they have been already considered promising for the deployment of 5G but they are not yet suitably widespread.

3.1. Non-Terrestrial Networks

Service continuity and scalability are two prerogatives of ubiquitous connectivity that can be fostered, in 5G and beyond systems, with the integration of terrestrial and non-terrestrial networks (NTN) [12]. NTNs encompass spaceborne and airborne systems. Satellites may be either geostationary (i.e., GEO) or orbit around the Earth at low or medium orbits (i.e., LEO and MEO). Among LEO satellites, a growing interest has risen towards CubeSats, a new class of miniaturized satellites known for their very small dimension and low cost, hence enabling their deployment in mega-constellations to provide global connectivity and large throughput. Equally interesting are Unmanned Aerial Vehicles (UAVs) that may be deployed in swarms to provide an on-demand aerial infrastructure where needed [13]. Based on these features, NTNs can come into play to mitigate the digital gap, by ensuring connectivity to a massive number of Internet of Everything (IoE) devices where terrestrial networks can fail, therefore in disadvantaged areas, in emergency scenarios, and highly crowded environments.

3.2. Exploiting Higher Frequencies

To truly bridge the digital divide, ultra-high-speed communications required to deliver 6G services need to be enabled. A very promising solution in this direction is to exploit new portions of the spectrum [14]. While the millimeter-wave band has been already considered in 5G mobile networks, now the interest is moving towards TeraHertz and even optical bands, motivated by the very recent advances in electronics and photonics that enabled the manufacturing of portable equipment operating at such frequencies. However, signal propagation becomes critical due to severe path loss, high molecular absorption, and the requirement for very precise antenna pointing. Coverage extension may be achieved by means of Intelligent Reflecting Surfaces (IRS) [15] that allow us to realize a virtual line-of-sight (LoS) link by smartly reconfiguring the wireless propagation environment [16]. Mainly, IRSs exploit massive low-cost passive reflecting elements integrated on a planar surface that independently reflect the incident signal by controlling its amplitude and/or phase and thus collaboratively achieve fine-grained three-dimensional (3D) passive beamforming for directional signal enhancement. The service-delivery divide could benefit from the use of higher frequencies in application scenarios that span from indoor coverage to Earth-to-ground communications.

3.3. Device-to-Device

Although technologies such as Software-Defined Networking (SDN) have emerged as enablers in the evolution process of 5G networks [17], the trend to evaluate distributed networking approaches to extend the network coverage and scalability has gained great momentum. On the eve of 6G, this still represents a key solution to boost the access to connectivity, therefore, also bridging the digital divide. Particularly, Device-to-Device (D2D) communications could be harnessed to master the problem of the limited distance that the higher frequency waves exploited in future 6G networks can cover [18]. Actually, relay nodes could be exploited to forward the signal through the establishment of direct communications, thus extending network coverage and facilitating access to services even to devices outside the antenna's LoS. D2D communications are characterized by high speed and low latency thanks to the proximity between end-devices [19], hence they are entirely in line with the requirements of the upcoming 6G networks.

3.4. Multi-Access Edge Computing

In the vein of the previous discussion on the shifting to distributed networking paradigm, also the Multi-access Edge Computing (MEC) is increasingly catching the eye, since it allows to improve the delivery of services in several respects. First of all, the resources of MEC servers can be provided, through virtualization, to limited-resources consumers based on the most appropriate service model (Infrastructure as a Service—IaaS, Platform as a Service—PaaS, Software as a Service—SaaS) [20]. Then, the proximity of the MEC to users enables various benefits, including low latency and context-awareness, which allows us to customize the service delivery to the needs of the consumers. The authors of [21] cite the efficacy of MEC in providing support to communication, computing, and storage, thus improving the Quality of Service (QoS) provided to users. This can be considered a plus in bridging the digital gap as poor QoS is seen as an impediment to the effective delivery of bandwidth-intensive services.

4. The Technologies for Bridging the Service-Fruition Divide

Over the past couple of years, the presence of a pandemic has accentuated the problem of the service-fruition divide, affecting those who have inabilities to access digital services, not because of infrastructural issues, but rather of their physical conditions, handicaps, age, or digital illiteracy. Applications revolving around 6G are proposing to support a set of digital interfaces at a large scale, not only in localized and specialized environments. This is possible for the first time in history, as these interfaces, while promoting ease of use and human centrality, have requirements in terms of latency and reliability that are too stringent to overcome with legacy technologies. The most debated solutions are presented in this section.

4.1. Extended Reality

Extended Reality (XR), which encompasses key terms such as Virtual Reality (VR), Mixed Reality (MR), and Augmented Reality (AR), is believed to drive several killer applications in the 6G era. 5G requirements fall short in supporting such applications, which need ultra-reliable low latency communications and cannot rely on mobile broadband [7]. In particular, XR pervasive applications will depend not only on the networking constraints, but also on the perceptual and sensory ones, which should be aligned with the above (i.e., tolerate delays that are imperceptible to human senses). The data rate is one of the major obstacles as, even now, many of the existing XR applications struggle in moving from wired to wireless, in particular for WAVAR (Wide Area VR, AR, MR) which aims to provide ubiquitous wireless services for XR [22]. WAVAR demand 6G technologies for ultimate application—as opposed to their local counterpart, LAVAR—in terms of data rate requirements (1Tbps peak rate), which cannot be satisfied by current 5G deployments [23]. If requirements are met, even digital illiterates would be able to interact with a controlled digital world through actions and perceptions that leverage all five senses (haptic, gestures, sound and speech, virtual sight, etc.). Over the past years, XR has been proposed in a variety of use cases connected to teaching activities [24] and aiding people with disorders [25], however, these use cases are typically experimental or extremely localized. It is evident how the potential of overcoming the service-fruition divide may dramatically increase if these technologies become pervasive. Challenges rise now in designing unique metrics capable of capturing both network requirements and the physical experience of users.

4.2. Brain-Computer Interfaces

Brain-Computer Interfaces (BCI) have been used extensively in assisting elderly or disabled people. While wired BCIs have been active for years, wireless BCIs are less supported due to their stringent QoS and Quality of Experience (QoE) requirements [26]. Over the last years, we can observe a handful of wireless BCIs implemented through short-range communication technologies in LANs, for use cases like home automation and digital healthcare [27]. However, these technologies are far from bridging the service-fruition divide, as their pervasiveness is limited to localized areas and hardcoded functions (e.g., switching on and off smart bulbs, etc.). With the perspective of 6G, requirements for deploying BCIs at large could be met and the deployment of a set of compelling applications in, for instance, urban environments could become a reality. Just like (and probably more than) XR, BCIs may be the new frontier of Human-Computer Interaction, involving Internet of Things (IoT) devices that will pervade our urban realities and will enable 6G ultra-low-latency connections. This also involves applications in healthcare that have, so far, only been conducted in controlled environments [28]. Such a giant leap in overcoming the service-fruition divide is envisioned to mark the end of the smartphone era, in a decade from now. Using wireless Brain-Computer Interaction technologies instead of smartphones, people will interact with their environment and other people using discrete devices, some worn, some implanted, and some embedded in the world around them.

4.3. Affective Computing

Affective computing encompasses a set of use cases that will be particularly enhanced by 6G technologies. It refers primarily to devices that can adapt their service provisioning schemes according to the mood and the emotions of the final user [29]. The first studies on the concept were presented a couple of decades ago, while recently it experienced a revamp due to its natural applicability on smartphones [30]. Now, 6G brings a set of concepts to the table that will change the way in which service provisioning takes place. One such is Human-Centric Services (HCS), a set of services that put the final user in the foreground and match her or his requirements to network performances, making affective computing potentially more pervasive than ever [7]. This is specially tailored to the educational use case, for instance in enhancing the relationship between teacher and student in online classes through online automatic learning processes fed by physical parameters (e.g., posture, speech, and expression) [31]. This results in involving more individuals who would instead be cut out due to e.g., lack of attention.

Table 1 shows a classification based on the possible employment of each technology described in Sections 3 and 4 for the resolution of the major categories of digital divide (i.e., service-delivery and service-fruition).

Table 1. Classification of technologies based on the mastered type of Digital Divide.

Technology	Service-Delivery	Service-Fruition
Affective Computing	✗	✓
Artificial Intelligence (AI)	✓	✓
Brain-Computer Interface (BCI)	✗	✓
Device-to-Device (D2D)	✓	✗
Exploiting Higher Frequencies	✓	✗
Extended Reality (XR)	✗	✓
Multi-access Edge Computing (MEC)	✓	✗
Non-Terrestrial Networks (NTN)	✓	✗

5. Artificial Intelligence: The Ultimate Breakthrough?

AI plays a role of paramount importance in the evolution process that wireless networks are experiencing. Its use can enhance the performance of many applications by providing a wide range of beneficial properties. In particular, ML is a branch of AI that is considered a top solution in many tricky 6G applications [32]. The ML technology allows us to train systems that, by the processing of collected data, can learn patterns by experience and, consequently, improve the performance and quality of the offered services. In particular, following the recent progress in deep learning as well as the advent of smart devices that are capable of processing ML algorithms on the edge, the wireless community has gained a renewed and huge interest in such technologies, which can now be leveraged in use cases that were unable to support them before. Now, with edge AI and ML we can envision networks of heterogeneous objects that are self-organizing and can meet high KPIs even in harsh scenarios via, e.g., reinforcement learning [7]. In this context, we are witnessing the shift of AI and ML components closer and closer to the edge, to the point that ML is projected to be an actual part of 6G technologies, rather than something that builds on top of them as it was with previous generations. Another remark is that this transition is expected to take place transversely, which means that potentially all 6G technologies will be affected at once.

This section aims to bring forth the potential achievable by applying AI to the purpose of lowering the gap brought by the digital divide. Current trends suggest that both the service-delivery gap and the service-fruition gap would greatly benefit from embedding AI into shared resources. In such a context, any single node of the network will produce data about connectivity, environment, and such, and the collection of big data from IoT scenarios is a key enabler to better understand the challenges of various nature in Internet access. Specifically, data is then analyzed through ML to create more inclusive and scalable networks. For example, data could be gathered and investigated to comprehend which categories of people make better use of the benefits provided by ICT and which ones find difficulties in doing so. In [10], a predictive ML technique is implemented to analyze the primary socioeconomic factors that cause the digital gap in Spain. According to [33], ML can improve the network performance through the undertaking of *adaptive network optimization actions*, enabled by the ability to learn from the wireless environment that ML provides to the network infrastructure. In such a sense, there are a lot of potential usages that meet the purpose of bridging the digital divide. Certain types of network traffic, if their nature is well understood by an AI engine, could be privileged (e.g., remote health diagnosis, online lectures) in contrast to others (e.g., entertaining). Historical network parameters observed by edge nodes can also feed a fog/edge ML model so that the distribution of network resources could be locally automated. Moreover, *planning* capabilities could be introduced to lower the risks of shortages under normal resource usage. This is also crucial to coordinate with mobile and on-demand network resources, as in NTNs, forming a real "collective network intelligence" [7] to overcome the service-delivery gap and bring resources where and when they are most needed. On the other hand, AI is also a powerful tool for improving the accessibility of innovative digital services for people with a low level of digital literacy, notably the elderly, people with disabilities, and people living in underdeveloped areas. Usages in this direction are often mentioned in the literature, for example, in [34], where authors survey some works concerning the application of technology to the provision of accessible cultural heritage sites experiences, also highlighting the importance of the role of AI in adapting the offered experiences to the target audience. Moreover, most of the technologies that we presented for bridging the service-fruition gap rely on AI and ML as their core enablers. This entails that AI could be a powerful tool for overcoming the digital cultural and cognitive gap, as it could be used to support those who would otherwise remain "digitally excluded".

In Table 2 we match the major AI trends to the 6G driving technologies to show that AI is by now an orthogonal trend that embraces all of them in different guises.

Table 2. AI candidates for the 6G technologies.

6G Technology	AI Candidates
Sensor Networks and Edge Systems	Reinforcement Learning, Unimodal & Multimodal Classification, Autoregressive Models
SDN & D2D	(Deep) Reinforcement Learning, Multimodal Classification, Deep Neural Networks
Drone Swarms	Reinforcement Learning, Unsupervised Learning, Agent-based models
Extended Reality	Computer Vision, Autoregressive models
Brain-Computer Interfaces	Recurrent Neural Networks, Autoregressive Models, Continual Learning
Affective Computing	Convolutional Neural Networks, Multimodal Classification, Natural Language Processing

6. The 6G Services to "Connect" People

In this section, we describe two use cases for which leaps and bounds need to be made in the area of digitization: eHealth and education. The main weaknesses of the current digitization status of these services are highlighted, to demonstrate that, in these fields, existing access difficulties for some categories may be overcome by the aforementioned 6G technologies.

6.1. The eHealth Case

6G will mark a turning point in the digitization process of the healthcare sector and the application of new paradigms can help in achieving a *fully digital and connected world* [35]. This represents an important step forward in overcoming the problem of the digital divide. Thanks to the provision of telemedicine services, the physical barriers of separation between patients and health professionals can be surpassed and the delivery of health services can be remotely guaranteed to many people, wherever they are whatever their condition. Indeed to integrate telemedicine into the health systems of the different countries of the world training courses should be taught to medical personnel and inclusive solutions should be designed to allow access to digital services even for people culturally far away from the technological world.

Figure 3 depicts the eHealth scenario consisting of the caring @home of a patient residing in a rural/critical area. Internet access to the patient premises may be provided by means of either spaceborne or airborne vehicles to enable its health monitoring by means of Medical Things (IoMT) devices, possibly exploiting D2D communications among them to extend indoor coverage. Due to the likely impossibility/inability of the patient to interact with the eHealth devices, AI and BCI can come to the rescue for contriving the fittest remedies. For example, IoMT devices that can obey voice commands and execute precise instructions can be delivered to the patients to allow them to remotely manage simple monitoring operations of health parameters. Furthermore, MEC servers can be installed close to the IoMT devices clusters (i.e., on the UAVs) to lighten their workload through computation offloading and reduce the data-gathering delay.

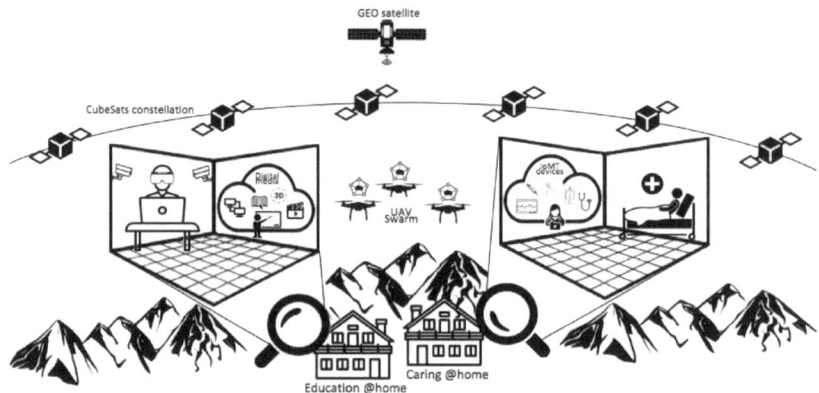

Figure 3. The analyzed use cases where 6G can bridge the digital divide: caring and education @home in rural areas.

Remote monitoring and assistance of patients are just some of the eHealth services that can be efficiently managed thanks to mobile wireless networks and that could benefit a lot from the advantages offered by 6G technologies. For example, specialist teleconsultation between doctors operating in different parts of the world is a very important application that would allow to break down the geographical boundaries of knowledge, making the experience and skills of medical luminaries available everywhere. Remote surgery, which can be defined as the telehealthcare service thanks to which a doctor can perform surgery at long distances from the patient [36], is an example of an application that asks for stringent requirements in terms of latency, security, and reliability in order to be widely diffused and that, therefore, would greatly enjoy the support of future 6G networks. A different use of technology in support of healthcare is shown in [37], where the benefits of applying VR for motor rehabilitation are deeply described. There are also numerous research proposals that introduce the use of potentially key technologies of 6G for eHealth services related to COVID-19, such as [38–40].

6.2. Education

The COVID-19 pandemic has demonstrated the crucial role played by ICT in the education sector, specifically in the support of remote learning. Recent studies like [6] revealed that during school closures, teachers faced challenges related to student engagement and students' lack of Internet access, and that the challenges were more prominent in high-poverty schools and rural areas. Approximately 43% of teachers reported concerns related to communication with students and student participation, while teachers in higher-poverty schools were more likely to indicate that their students did not have Internet access at home. It is not difficult to imagine how the technologies presented in Sections 3 and 4 could help bridge such gaps. In Figure 3, NTN solutions, such as GEO/LEO satellites or UAVs, may serve as space/aerial access points providing internet access to schools as well as to students' houses located in remote or critical areas. As a matter of fact, UAVs and other aerial appliances have always played the role of Internet carriers in poorly connected areas, such as for disaster recovery. However, many studies also consider them as a means for bridging the digital divide in education [41]. A pilot experiment was conducted by Google through its Project Loon [42], which aims to bring connectivity to millions of people that are offline in rural New Zealand, or Facebook Aquila (https://engineering.fb.com/2018/06/27/connectivity/high-altitude-connectivity-the-next-chapter/, accessed on 15 June 2022). Moreover, within each school building, smart antennas and intelligent surfaces can enable dynamic resource allocation policies, so that the bandwidth is allocated to different indoor locations/rooms in a fine-grained way based on the activities being performed. In the same way, service-fruition 6G technologies can result in increased effectiveness of remote/in-presence teaching, higher student engagement, and customized experiences based on the students' needs. Affective computing constitutes one of the most active research topics in education via the integration of visual and textual channels according to the survey in [31]. It can also help in detecting abnormal situations with the scholars at early stages, such as Attention Deficit and Hyperactivity Disorder [43] that otherwise would cause students to easily detach from the learning environment. Educational scenarios could also take advantage of XR. In particular, seminal XR-based solutions have been implied in education, mostly for medical purposes [44], with successful outcomes. However, it is in pedagogical use that XR technologies arguably unleash their most significant outcome: their ability to enhance active and experiential learning [45]. With such technology at hand, even scholars that are not physically collocated can share experiences and collaboration. This can transform the way educational content is delivered to students, encouraging creativity and bringing abstract concepts to life.

Figure 4 shows a comparison of the two analyzed use cases in terms of importance level of the technologies discussed in Sections 3 and 4 for their realization.

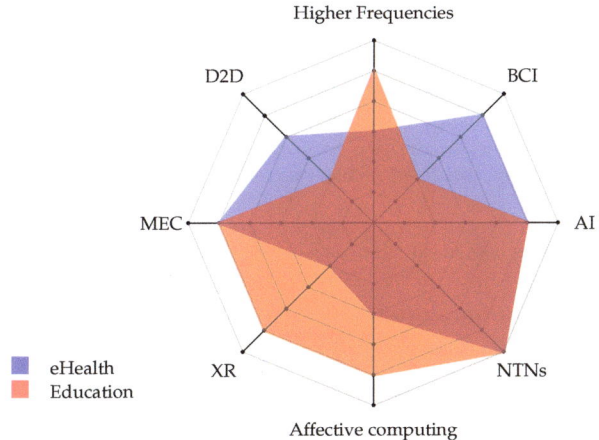

Figure 4. Relevance of the 6G technologies on the two use cases.

7. Discussion and Conclusions

The 6G is foreseen to support ground-breaking requirements. Top-notch technologies will have to be exploited by the future generation networks to foster high-performance management of the new expected use cases, including those that arose during the health emergency caused by COVID-19. Due to the lockdowns imposed by the pandemic, work organization, education, and other daily-life habits have been *contaminated* by technology in ways that cannot be defined as temporary. We could state that the acceleration experienced by the digitization process, in the last year, represents the silver lining of COVID-19. Indeed, the pandemic has shifted the attention of worldwide researchers and government institutions to the importance of technological progress and, consequently, even to the problem of the digital divide, which affects people who have been excluded from the progress achieved thanks to the stimulus for improvement favored by the health emergency and investments in the ICT sector. At the same time, although digital transformation may represent a lifeline in many cases, opinions exist for which it could represent an additional cause of exclusion for the so-called *have-nots*. Considering the evolution of wireless mobile networks, 6G could exacerbate the digital divide, given that already the 5G standard has been unevenly distributed in different countries of the world in the first phase of release, thus leading to the creation of a further gap between the areas that receive state-of-the-art network coverage and those that do not. As we also stated in Section 2, there are contradictory opinions according to which technological evolution could solve or, on the contrary, aggravate the phenomenon of the digital divide; however, COVID-19 has put the spotlight on the problems relating to the profound inequalities in access to information and communication technologies, thus triggering various world institutions to conduct studies on the impact of the pandemic also on the economic field. For example, the report released by United Nations University (UNU) and United Nations Institute for Training and Research (UNITAR) highlights the exacerbation of the digital divide caused by COVID-19, reporting a 30% fall in sales of electronic and electrical equipment in the low- and middle-income countries, and only 5% in high-income countries [46]. This argues that the pandemic has hurt the worldwide economy but the poorest countries harder, testifying to the fact that at the root of the problem of the digital divide there are also significant economic disparities, the solution of which is outside the scope of this paper. In fact, this work aims to illustrate the evolution of the digital divide phenomenon and place it in the context of the future 6G, providing an overview of technologies and applications that telecommunications companies could exploit to help in bridging this gap, which has existed since technology began to spread among the people. In the vein of the decentralization trend described in Section 3, also 6G business models are expected to be decentralized to support the new use cases. The birth of the telecom virtual operators (MVNO) or the network sharing business model are concrete examples of how business dynamics are increasingly moving away from the classic model of centralization of resources at the mobile network operator (MNO) [47]. This can bring benefits in terms of extension of network coverage and enhancement of the provided services. For example, the newly-introduced micro operators can manage the requests of specific target users by offering higher-quality localized connectivity customized to the consumer's needs.

Author Contributions: Conceptualization, C.S. and S.P.; writing—original draft preparation, C.S., S.P., F.M. and M.D.F.; writing—review and editing, C.S., S.P., F.M., M.D.F. and G.A. All authors have read and agreed to the published version of the manuscript.

Funding: This research received no external funding.

Informed Consent Statement: Not applicable.

Data Availability Statement: Not applicable.

Conflicts of Interest: The authors declare no conflict of interest.

References

1. Nokia. *How Do We Create Inclusivity in a Digital Future? Building a Better World with Broadband Technologies*; Technical Report, White Paper; Nokia: Espoo, Finland, 2020.
2. Ericsson. *Bridging the Digital Divide for an Inclusive Digital Economy*; Technical Report, White Paper; Ericsson: Stockholm, Sweden, 2021.

3. Huawei. *TECH4ALL: Leaving No One behind in the Digital World*; Technical Report; Huawei: Shenzhen, China, 2021.
4. Cisco. *Annual Internet Report (2018–2023)*; Technical Report, White Paper; Cisco: San Jose, CA, USA, 2020.
5. Vodafone. *Digital for Europe: Collaboration, Innovation, Transformation*; Technical Report, White Paper; Vodafone: Berkshire, UK, 2021.
6. Stelitano, L.; Doan, S.; Woo, A.; Diliberti, M.K.; Kaufman, J.H.; Henry, D. *The Digital Divide and COVID-19: Teachers' Perceptions of Inequities in Students' Internet Access and Participation in Remote Learning*; RAND Corporation: Santa Monica, CA, USA, 2020. [CrossRef]
7. Saad, W.; Bennis, M.; Chen, M. A vision of 6G wireless systems: Applications, trends, technologies, and open research problems. *IEEE Netw.* **2019**, *34*, 134–142. [CrossRef]
8. Suraci, C.; Pizzi, S.; Molinaro, A.; Araniti, G. MEC and D2D as Enabling Technologies for a Secure and Lightweight 6G eHealth System. *IEEE Internet Things J.* **2022**, *9*, 11524–11532. [CrossRef]
9. Chaoub, A.; Giordani, M.; Lall, B.; Bhatia, V.; Kliks, A.; Mendes, L.; Rabie, K.; Saarnisaari, H.; Singhal, A.; Zhang, N.; et al. 6G for Bridging the Digital Divide: Wireless Connectivity to Remote Areas. *IEEE Wirel. Commun.* **2022**, *69*, 160–168. [CrossRef]
10. Hidalgo, A.; Gabaly, S.; Morales-Alonso, G.; Urueña, A. The digital divide in light of sustainable development: An approach through advanced machine learning techniques. *Technol. Forecast. Soc. Chang.* **2020**, *150*, 119754. [CrossRef]
11. Van Dijk, J.A. Digital divide: Impact of access. In *The International Encyclopedia of Media Effects*; Wiley: Hoboken, NJ, USA, 2017; pp. 1–11.
12. Rinaldi, F.; Maattanen, H.L.; Torsner, J.; Pizzi, S.; Andreev, S.; Iera, A.; Koucheryavy, Y.; Araniti, G. Non-Terrestrial Networks in 5G & Beyond: A Survey. *IEEE Access* **2020**, *8*, 165178–165200.
13. Dao, N.N.; Pham, Q.V.; Tu, N.H.; Thanh, T.T.; Bao, V.N.Q.; Lakew, D.S.; Cho, S. Survey on aerial radio access networks: Toward a comprehensive 6G access infrastructure. *IEEE Commun. Surv. Tutor.* **2021**, *23*, 1193–1225. [CrossRef]
14. Polese, M.; Jornet, J.M.; Melodia, T.; Zorzi, M. Toward end-to-end, full-stack 6G terahertz networks. *IEEE Commun. Mag.* **2020**, *58*, 48–54. [CrossRef]
15. Wu, Q.; Zhang, R. Towards smart and reconfigurable environment: Intelligent reflecting surface aided wireless network. *IEEE Commun. Mag.* **2019**, *58*, 106–112. [CrossRef]
16. Mu, X.; Liu, Y.; Guo, L.; Lin, J.; Poor, H.V. Intelligent reflecting surface enhanced multi-UAV NOMA networks. *IEEE J. Sel. Areas Commun.* **2021**, *39*, 3051–3066. [CrossRef]
17. Zaidi, Z.; Friderikos, V.; Yousaf, Z.; Fletcher, S.; Dohler, M.; Aghvami, H. Will SDN be part of 5G? *IEEE Commun. Surv. Tutor.* **2018**, *20*, 3220–3258. [CrossRef]
18. Zhang, S.; Liu, J.; Guo, H.; Qi, M.; Kato, N. Envisioning device-to-device communications in 6G. *IEEE Netw.* **2020**, *34*, 86–91. [CrossRef]
19. Jameel, F.; Hamid, Z.; Jabeen, F.; Zeadally, S.; Javed, M.A. A survey of device-to-device communications: Research issues and challenges. *IEEE Commun. Surv. Tutor.* **2018**, *20*, 2133–2168. [CrossRef]
20. Taleb, T.; Samdanis, K.; Mada, B.; Flinck, H.; Dutta, S.; Sabella, D. On multi-access edge computing: A survey of the emerging 5G network edge cloud architecture and orchestration. *IEEE Commun. Surv. Tutor.* **2017**, *19*, 1657–1681. [CrossRef]
21. Saarnisaari, H.; Dixit, S.; Alouini, M.S.; Chaoub, A.; Giordani, M.; Kliks, A.; Matinmikko-Blue, M.; Zhang, N.; Agrawal, A.; Andersson, M.; et al. A 6G white paper on connectivity for remote areas. *arXiv* **2020**, arXiv:2004.14699.
22. Akyildiz, I.F.; Guo, H. Wireless Extended Reality (XR): Challenges and New Research Directions. *ITU J. Future Evol. Technol.* **2022**, *3*.
23. Narayanan, A.; Ramadan, E.; Carpenter, J.; Liu, Q.; Liu, Y.; Qian, F.; Zhang, Z.L. A first look at commercial 5G performance on smartphones. In Proceedings of the Web Conference 2020, New York, NY, USA, 20–24 April 2020; pp. 894–905.
24. Oleksiuk, V.P.; Oleksiuk, O.R. Exploring the Potential of Augmented Reality for Teaching School Computer Science. In Proceedings of the 3rd International Workshop on Augmented Reality in Education, Kryvyi Rih, Ukraine, 13 May 2020.
25. Chen, Y.; Zhou, Z.; Cao, M.; Liu, M.; Lin, Z.; Yang, W.; Yang, X.; Dhaidhai, D.; Xiong, P. Extended Reality (XR) and Telehealth Interventions for Children or Adolescents with Autism Spectrum Disorder: Systematic Review of Qualitative and Quantitative Studies. *Neurosci. Biobehav. Rev.* **2022**, *138*, 104683. [CrossRef]
26. Mahmoud, H.H.H.; Amer, A.A.; Ismail, T. 6G: A comprehensive survey on technologies, applications, challenges, and research problems. *Trans. Emerg. Telecommun. Technol.* **2021**, *32*, e4233. [CrossRef]
27. Jafri, S.R.A.; Hamid, T.; Mahmood, R.; Alam, M.A.; Rafi, T.; Haque, M.Z.U.; Munir, M.W. Wireless brain computer interface for smart home and medical system. *Wirel. Pers. Commun.* **2019**, *106*, 2163–2177. [CrossRef]
28. Anitha, T.; Shanthi, N.; Sathiyasheelan, R.; Emayavaramban, G.; Rajendran, T. Brain-computer interface for persons with motor disabilities—A review. *Open Biomed. Eng. J.* **2019**, *13*, 127–133. [CrossRef]
29. Picard, R.W. *Affective Computing*; MIT Press: Cambridge, MA, USA, 2000.
30. Politou, E.; Alepis, E.; Patsakis, C. A survey on mobile affective computing. *Comput. Sci. Rev.* **2017**, *25*, 79–100. [CrossRef]
31. Yadegaridehkordi, E.; Noor, N.F.B.M.; Ayub, M.N.B.; Affal, H.B.; Hussin, N.B. Affective computing in education: A systematic review and future research. *Comput. Educ.* **2019**, *142*, 103649. [CrossRef]
32. Kato, N.; Mao, B.; Tang, F.; Kawamoto, Y.; Liu, J. Ten challenges in advancing machine learning technologies toward 6G. *IEEE Wirel. Commun.* **2020**, *27*, 96–103. [CrossRef]
33. Chen, M.; Challita, U.; Saad, W.; Yin, C.; Debbah, M. Artificial neural networks-based machine learning for wireless networks: A tutorial. *IEEE Commun. Surv. Tutor.* **2019**, *21*, 3039–3071. [CrossRef]

34. Pisoni, G.; Díaz-Rodríguez, N.; Gijlers, H.; Tonolli, L. Human-centred artificial intelligence for designing accessible cultural heritage. *Appl. Sci.* **2021**, *11*, 870. [CrossRef]
35. Giordani, M.; Polese, M.; Mezzavilla, M.; Rangan, S.; Zorzi, M. Toward 6G networks: Use cases and technologies. *IEEE Commun. Mag.* **2020**, *58*, 55–61. [CrossRef]
36. Senk, S.; Ulbricht, M.; Tsokalo, I.; Rischke, J.; Li, S.C.; Speidel, S.; Nguyen, G.T.; Seeling, P.; Fitzek, F.H. Healing Hands: The Tactile Internet in Future Tele-Healthcare. *Sensors* **2022**, *22*, 1404. [CrossRef]
37. Wang, L.; Huang, M.; Yang, R.; Liang, H.N.; Han, J.; Sun, Y. Survey of Movement Reproduction in Immersive Virtual Rehabilitation. *IEEE Trans. Vis. Comput. Graph.* **2022**. [CrossRef]
38. El-Sherif, D.M.; Abouzid, M.; Elzarif, M.T.; Ahmed, A.A.; Albakri, A.; Alshehri, M.M. Telehealth and Artificial Intelligence insights into healthcare during the COVID-19 pandemic. *Healthcare* **2022**, *10*, 385. [CrossRef]
39. Alrubei, S.M.; Ball, E.; Rigelsford, J.M. A Secure Blockchain Platform for Supporting AI-Enabled IoT Applications at the Edge Layer. *IEEE Access* **2022**, *10*, 18583–18595. [CrossRef]
40. Nasser, N.; Fadlullah, Z.M.; Fouda, M.M.; Ali, A.; Imran, M. A lightweight federated learning based privacy preserving B5G pandemic response network using unmanned aerial vehicles: A proof-of-concept. *Comput. Netw.* **2022**, *205*, 108672. [CrossRef]
41. West, D.M. Digital divide: Improving Internet access in the developing world through affordable services and diverse content. *Cent. Technol. Innov. Brookings* **2015**, 1–30.
42. Nagpal, L.; Samdani, K. Project Loon: Innovating the connectivity worldwide. In Proceedings of the 2017 2nd IEEE International Conference on Recent Trends in Electronics, Information & Communication Technology (RTEICT), Bangalore, India, 19–20 May 2017; IEEE: Piscataway, NJ, USA, 2017; pp. 1778–1784.
43. Martínez, F.; Barraza, C.; González, N.; González, J. KAPEAN: Understanding affective states of children with ADHD. *J. Educ. Technol. Soc.* **2016**, *19*, 18–28.
44. Zweifach, S.M.; Triola, M.M. Extended reality in medical education: Driving adoption through provider-centered design. *Digit. Biomarkers* **2019**, *3*, 14–21. [CrossRef] [PubMed]
45. Pomerantz, J. Teaching and learning with extended reality technology. In *Information and Technology Transforming Lives: Connection, Interaction, Innovation*; University of Osijek: Osijek, Croatia, 2019; pp. 137–157.
46. Baldé, C.; Kuehr, R. *The Impact of the COVID-19 Pandemic on One-Waste in the First Three Quarters of 2020*; Technical Report; United Nations University (UNU)/United Nations Institute for Training and Research (UNITAR): Bonn, Germany, 2020.
47. Yrjölä, S. Decentralized 6G Business Models. In Proceedings of the 6G Wireless Summit, Levi, Finland, 26 April 2019.

Article

A Spectrum Management Platform Architecture to Enable a Sharing Economy in 6G

Faycal Bouhafs [1], Alessandro Raschellà [2,*], Michael Mackay [2] and Frank den Hartog [1]

[1] School of Engineering and IT, University of New South Wales, Canberra, ACT 2600, Australia
[2] School of Computer Science and Mathematics, Liverpool John Moores University (LJMU), Liverpool L3 3AF, UK
* Correspondence: a.raschella@ljmu.ac.uk

Abstract: We propose a novel vision to trade and allocate wireless spectrum in 6G communication networks inspired by the concept of the sharing economy. We argue that such an approach will help ease the surge in demands for wireless spectrum that will characterise the 6G world. We also introduce HODNET (Heterogeneous on Demand NETwork resource negotiation), an open platform that is able to realise this new spectrum-sharing model. To demonstrate the benefits of spectrum trading and allocation in this new paradigm, we considered the use-case of massive Internet of Things (IoT) on a local scale. We simulated a large IoT deployment and evaluated the spectral efficiency of the system when managed using HODNET compared with a standard 5G deployment. Our experiments show that HODNET can indeed offer better allocation, based on our spectrum sharing model, of spectrum resources compared with standard allocation approaches.

Keywords: Beyond 5G; 6G; spectrum sharing; software-defined network; massive IoT

1. Introduction

The number of mobile phones and tablets in use has now significantly outgrown fixed phones and wired devices. Besides phones and tablets, billions of other devices are now also wirelessly connected to the Internet, including personal devices, cars, cameras, health devices, garbage bins, traffic lights, and various industrial sensors and actuators. This emergence of the Internet of Things (IoT) has resulted in a surge in data traffic over wireless mediums. According to Cisco [1], this traffic grew by 63% in comparison to 2015, reaching an average of 7.2 exabytes per month. The fifth generation of mobile networks (5G) represents a significant part of the latest development in wireless communications and is expected to support this massive growth in wireless IoT and ultra-high-resolution video streaming. This will fuel wireless data traffic to increase even further, by at least a factor of 5 by 2024 [2].

The telecommunication industry and regulators are facing a major challenge in satisfying these ever-increasing demands for wireless bandwidth. Spectral resources have always been scarce and will become even more so in the future. The current spectrum allocation strategy, which is still based on the static allocation of frequency bands, is considered by many as wasteful. Several contributions have been made to alleviate spectrum congestion using high radiofrequency bands and visible light communications. However, it is widely agreed that carrier frequencies below 6 GHz are mostly needed for wireless communications, including 5G, due to their more suitable propagation properties. Given this usable spectrum, two types of solutions are being discussed. One is to allocate more spectrum to communications, which inevitably means recovering blocks of low and medium frequencies. This solution, often called spectrum reframing or refarming, is too limited when facing such high radio spectrum demands.

The second type of solutions are various forms of spectrum sharing. Spectrum sharing has received a lot of attention over the last few years and is promoted as an alternative to

the fixed licence model that has been used for nearly a century. Three spectrum frameworks are commonly discussed regarding 5G [3] and include Citizens Broadband Radio Service (CBRS) approaches, Licensed Shared Access (LSA), and Concurrent Shared Access (CSA), which are discussed in more detail in the next section. The key observation however is that all these models still rely on a major licence holder (an entity or a club of entities) which has primary rights and may allow other parties to use spectrum which the major holder is not using, in an only quasi-dynamic way.

There are frequency bands where allocation (either administrative or market-based) does not apply. Such bands, commonly known as unlicensed frequency bands, are not owned by any entity and can be used freely by stakeholders for a variety of applications [4]. The most well-known frequency band in this class is 2.4 GHz, which is widely used for Wi-Fi, Bluetooth, and many other communication technologies. Here, the spectrum is shared by protocol design but will eventually lead to the complete depletion of the band [5].

In this article, we propose a new way of sharing spectrum, which is completely based on the dynamic matching of offer and demand of network resources. It is based on the principles of the sharing economy paradigm. The remainder of this paper is structured as follows. Section 2 provides a detailed analysis of the state of the art on spectrum sharing and our novel contributions. Then, in Section 3, we build the case for a new form of spectrum sharing, based on the principles of the sharing economy, and in Section 4, we propose the system architecture with which this can be achieved. We illustrate the benefits of this approach with a use case revolving around massive IoT deployment in Section 5. Final conclusions and significant aspects to explore further are given in Section 6.

2. Literature Review

2.1. Traditional Spectrum Allocation and Sharing

Currently, spectrum allocation is still dominated by administrative allocation controlled by national regulators. These regulators also stipulate static conditions on how operators can utilise the allocated spectrum, expressed in offered capacity, coverage, etc although these conditions do not always reflect the real requirements of wireless users [6].

An alternative approach is to apply the laws of the market to incentivise a fairer and more consumer-oriented allocation of the spectrum resource. Here, the right to operate blocks of radio frequency will be granted to operators who value this spectrum the most, for instance as determined by auctions. This approach has been very successful in the 3G, 4G, and 5G eras. In LSA [7], market-based allocations allow an operator to lease some of its frequencies to a third party, thus introducing more flexibility in the dynamic of spectrum allocation.

A variety of LSA is CSA [3]. Here, multiple operators share access to the same block of the spectrum but in a coordinated and managed way. An example is club licencing: A licence is given to a club of operators. An operator can use the whole block if it is the sole provider in an area. When another club member wants to operate in that area too, it has the right to a fair share of the block. This is a form of dynamic spectrum sharing, but time scales are measured in weeks or months rather than minutes or hours. CBRS has also recently been authorised for use in the United States. Here, a three-tiered spectrum authorisation framework accommodates various commercial models simultaneously for the 3.5 GHz band [8]. The highest tier is Incumbent Access, which reserves a part of the band for radar operation, similar to administrative allocation. In the second tier, Priority Access, sub-bands of 10 MHz are licenced commercially, such as market-oriented allocation. In the General Authorised Access, users are permitted to use any portion of the band not assigned to higher tier users but still need to acquire a temporary low-cost license for use of the spectrum in, e.g., a single building.

A commonality between these spectrum-sharing models is that they rely on spectrum uniquely allocated to a major licence holder which has primary rights to it in a semi-static way, regardless of whether that spectrum is actually used or not. This inevitably leads to spectrum waste, where the demand is low, and spectrum congestion, where the demand is high, and unnecessary costs either way. The only alternative able to address this problem is to use the so-called unlicensed bands. Here, everybody has the fundamental right to access the spectrum anytime and anywhere but must accept possible interference from other users. Most protocols using these bands typically have "listen-before-talk", "clear channel assessment" and "duty-cycle muting" mechanisms included to allow other devices to access the medium too [9–11], but when congestion becomes eminent, they all apply the law of the jungle resulting in only losers [4]. Moreover, works in [12,13] illustrate how multiple systems that coexist in unlicensed bands interfere with each other due to asymmetries and selfish system behaviour. The authors then propose punishment strategies based on game theory which allow for fair and efficient use of the band. However, the solutions are not evaluated in realistic scenarios involving wireless technologies.

2.2. Spectrum Sharing Platforms

Several articles in the literature propose platforms to address the problem of spectrum resource scarcity for next-generation networks. The work in [14] presents a survey on spectrum sharing for next-generation networks discussing how several methods can be implemented in a general architecture. Moreover, the authors discuss techniques for spectrum sensing, network selection, channel allocation, and power optimisation in spectrum sharing together with the corresponding security issues. The authors in [15] present a survey on recent spectrum-sharing solutions for 5G networks and 5G-enabling technologies. Spectrum-sharing methods are presented in terms of network architecture, spectrum allocation, and spectrum access solutions. Furthermore, they provide a survey on cognitive radio (CR) technology for spectrum sharing in 5G networks. Additionally, the work in [16] proposes a solution based on CR in 5G networks. Specifically, it proposes the integration of non-orthogonal multiple access (NOMA) with CR into a holistic system, namely a cognitive NOMA network, for intelligent spectrum sharing. In [17] authors present a survey on spectrum-sharing solutions, interference models, and interference management for IoT technology. Work in [18] presents a green spectrum-sharing framework targeting Beyond 5G networks with the aim to improve spectrum utilisation through a cost-efficiency approach for IoT devices.

Moreover, note that communication networks have recently witnessed a paradigm shift in the way data traffic and spectrum resources are managed. The introduction of novel softwarisation techniques such as Software Defined Networking (SDN) [19] and Network Function Virtualisation (NFV) [20] has enabled more scalable and efficient management of these networks. Although initially limited to wired networks, such techniques are now also used for wireless communications. The rise of Software Defined Wireless Networking (SDWN) [21] represents an extension of SDN specifically in this context. Spectrum programming [22] extends this concept further, from managing data traffic right down to the radio resources themselves. In this context, the Wi-5 spectrum programming architecture in [22] presents a system to manage radio resources for Wi-Fi networks.

2.3. Our Motivations and Novel Contributions

The efficient use of the spectrum will be a crucial problem in 6G and will face further challenges in comparison with current wireless technologies, mainly due to the targeted multi-Gigabit data rates and a broader set of potential spectrum bands and spectrum management strategies. Therefore, 6G will need novel and intelligent spectrum allocation and sharing models [23]. The introduction of virtualisation, softwarisation, and programmability technologies, including Artificial Intelligence (AI), will undoubtedly help address these challenges. This trend has already started in 5G, for example with the introduction of SDN and NFV in the core as we have previously mentioned, which made concepts such as Mobile Edge Computing (MEC) and network slicing possible. In this context, we believe that the spectrum-sharing mechanisms and platforms for 5G illustrated in Sections 2.1 and 2.2 present key limitations that make them unsuitable for upcoming 6G networks. These limitations can be summarised as follows:

- Current spectrum-sharing mechanisms and platforms only acknowledge operators as service providers, thus eliminating other entities that own or manage a wireless network and that could offer wireless spectrum access;
- They lack flexibility as reflected in the architecture of current wireless systems and their radio access and allocation protocols, which are too elementary and do not consider the characteristics of the wireless devices and their data traffic requirements. For instance, an IoT device will always try to connect to its operator's base station although there may be closer Radio Access Nodes (RANs) which could save them energy.

Therefore, in this paper, our aim is to address these limitations by proposing a novel spectrum-sharing model, applicable to 6G networks, which is completely based on the dynamic matching of offer and demand of network resources. It is based on the principles of the sharing economy paradigm. In this model, any entity that owns or manages a wireless device (mobile phones, Wi-Fi Access Points, etc.) can offer wireless spectrum access and hence could contribute to connecting wireless devices.

3. Trading and Allocating Spectrum as Part of a Sharing Economy in 6G

3.1. Principles and Definitions

In this section, we introduce a new way of sharing the spectrum, based on the principles of the sharing economy paradigm, and its foundation in the dynamic and distributed matching of offer and demand of spectrum resources. The sharing economy is defined as creating a business model allowing consumers to be paid for providing a service similar to what they receive. It is currently considered among the most innovative and efficient sharing economic models. The strength of this concept comes from its ability to bypass traditional intermediaries and use Internet platforms to connect consumers to suppliers of goods and services. It has helped to increase the capacity of markets, bring down prices and enhance the reliability of services.

The concept is strongly rooted in the observation that many economic resources are more and more provided by the consumers themselves (hence the popular term "prosumers") instead of by large incumbent operators. We also see such a trend with wireless communications. With the arrival of private picocells and the ability of most Wi-Fi end-user devices to provide hotspot services to other devices, many users not only have a demand for wireless capacity but are also able to offer it to others. Our aim, therefore, is to design a spectrum-trading platform that matches offer and demand locally and dynamically, provides broker deals, and aids business partners in executing, securing, validating, and verifying these deals. Of course, similar wireless spectrum-trading platforms can already be found in the literature [24] and there is an established discussion on so-called 'Spectrum as a Service' approaches [25,26] but our novelty as outlined in the previous section, is the inclusion of any potential connectivity provider in our system and the flexibility to cover a broad range of technologies and use cases.

Our vision is, therefore, to allow any entity that owns or manages a wireless network (which we call an "operator" in the remainder of this paper) to trade its spectrum resource with any user in a range that requires it. A wireless network can be licenced or unlicenced, including both Wi-Fi and IoT deployments and cellular networks. In its extreme, such a trading platform would make the current market-oriented licencing a system of the past and, while this may sound controversial, it is a normal cause of things in economics: after demand is created by rolling out services by government-owned or -regulated monopolistic industry, a deregulated and distributed market can take over. We are currently witnessing this with taxi rides, power generation, public transport, space exploration, etc. As illustrated by the example in Figure 1, our vision is to make radio resources universally available for trading and sharing between any operator and 6G users. Moreover, note that we apply the following definitions:

- Spectrum Trading is the act of voluntary matching of offer and demand of spectral resources between parties acting in a common geographical space in which spectral

resources are scarce and contended. The parties are treated as economic actors and trading may or may not result in consensus and a joint agreement. Trading may or may not be galvanised by a broker;
- Spectrum Allocation is the act of allocating spectral resources offered by one or more parties to parties who demand spectral resources. Ideally, the allocation follows from the consensus resulting from the previous step of trading and correctly executes the joint agreement;
- Spectrum Sharing is the most likely result of Spectrum Allocation: parties are sharing the spectral resources as agreed upon. Alternatively, the spectrum is not shared, and one party consumes it all.

While a radio resource management approach that makes our vision possible will be presented in Section 5, in the remainder of this section, we explore the requirements and potential technical approaches to achieve this.

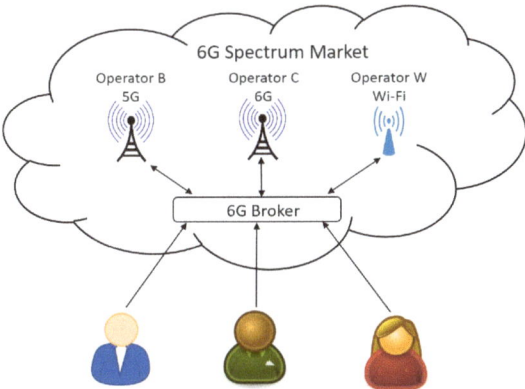

Figure 1. Vision of spectrum trading and allocating as part of a sharing economy in 6G with an online broker.

3.2. Requirements of the Spectrum Trading Platform

Realising this vision requires the functionality of wireless devices and Radio Access Networks (RANs) to be enhanced such that resources become discoverable, sharable, and accessible almost in real time. The key functionality required for a spectrum-sharing economy platform is, therefore:

1. Providing Connectivity. This is the ability to offer connectivity to wireless devices at (at least) the same or (preferably) better quality and efficiency (e.g., energy consumption) than existing radio access schemes. In other words, the platform should be able to connect to every device offering and/or demanding resources and should have access to fine-grained radio- and link-control functionality in order to offer the optimal (i.e., agreed) connectivity;
2. Scalability. The platform needs to support the anticipated scale and density of networks and devices in both current and future deployments, and maximise their capacity based on new and existing Radio Access Technologies (RATs). In other words, dynamic spectrum trading is particularly important when multiple devices vie for resources, and the platform should be able to deal with this, and in near real time: deals may have to be renewed within minutes, with changing offers and demand of devices in range;
3. Heterogeneous Access. This is the ability to offer suitable network access to devices that are heterogeneous in terms of capabilities, requirements, and limitations. Particularly in unlicensed networks, devices sporting different RATs (e.g., Wi-Fi or Bluetooth)

may compete for the same spectral resources. The platform should be able to deal with that.

3.3. Spectrum Trading with Spectrum Programming

As introduced in Section 2, SDN and SDWN are commonly used to enable more scalable and efficient management of wireless networks. In this context, the Wi-5 spectrum programming architecture based on SDWN presented in [22] is a solution to manage radio resources for Wi-Fi networks and we see this platform as a precursor for spectrum sharing and trading as we envision here. The architecture is illustrated in Figure 2. Specifically, we can find the following entities: the Wi-5 Controller (operated by the Wi-5 System Operator) which resides in the control plane, and the Brokering Platform, which is operated by a separate Spectrum Broker. This approach allows having radio parameters programmable through an open Southbound API to the wireless Access Points (APs), and an open Northbound API. Intelligent algorithms can then use these interfaces to obtain certain objectives set by policies that are sent to the Wi-5 Controller by the Brokering Platform. Moreover, the Wi-5 Controller has a Flow and Network Monitoring Module (FNMM, not illustrated in the figure), which performs measurements from the APs, monitors the new flows in the network and communicates this information to the management algorithms.

To our knowledge, this architecture was the first of its kind to treat the wireless spectrum as a resource that can be traded among different service providers [24]. The developers demonstrated the scalability of a single Wi-5 controller in a dense Wi-Fi deployment and explored hierarchical multi-operator/controller approaches which could serve as the basis for req. 2 above. The suitability of the Wi-5 architecture is a key motivation for us to adopt this novel approach for spectrum sharing. However, we need to extend the Wi-5 architecture to support heterogeneous radio access that goes beyond a single RAT (req. 3). Moreover, Wi-5 currently does not address req. 1 as it assumes the Wi-5 controller to be deployed as a physical entity accessible to all devices and service providers.

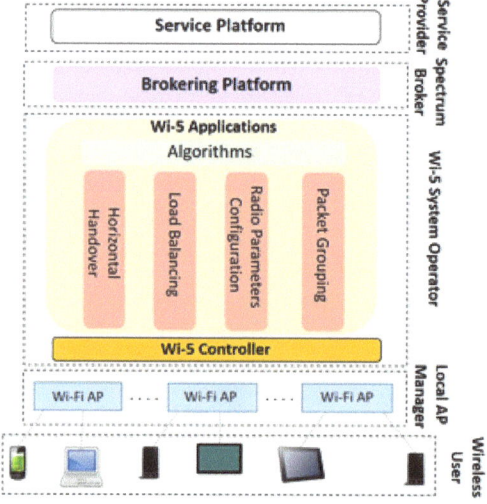

Figure 2. The Wi-5 spectrum programming architecture based on Software-Defined Wireless Networking.

4. HODNET Architecture

Based on the Wi-5 spectrum programming architecture we now propose Heterogeneous On Demand NETwork (HODNET), a spectrum trading architecture for 6G networks. A high-level description of this architecture is presented in Figure 3a. All entities will negotiate through HODNET's Brokering Interface provided. To enforce our concept, operators may dynamically join and leave the system in the same way that drivers in a taxi-sharing service are available at different times as it suits them, and operators can 'charge' more for offering connectivity during busy times but less when demand is low. The Controller is a centralised entity that populates the Brokering Interface with information related to the underlying RANs that have resources on offer in a given area. It also takes the outcome of the negotiation between the entities from the Brokering Interface, i.e., the operators of each RAN, and implements it. To maintain its scalability, HODNET adopts the SDWN model as described above (req. 2) but adopts a heterogeneous spectrum programming approach that allows it to manage multiple radio access networks seamlessly (req. 3).

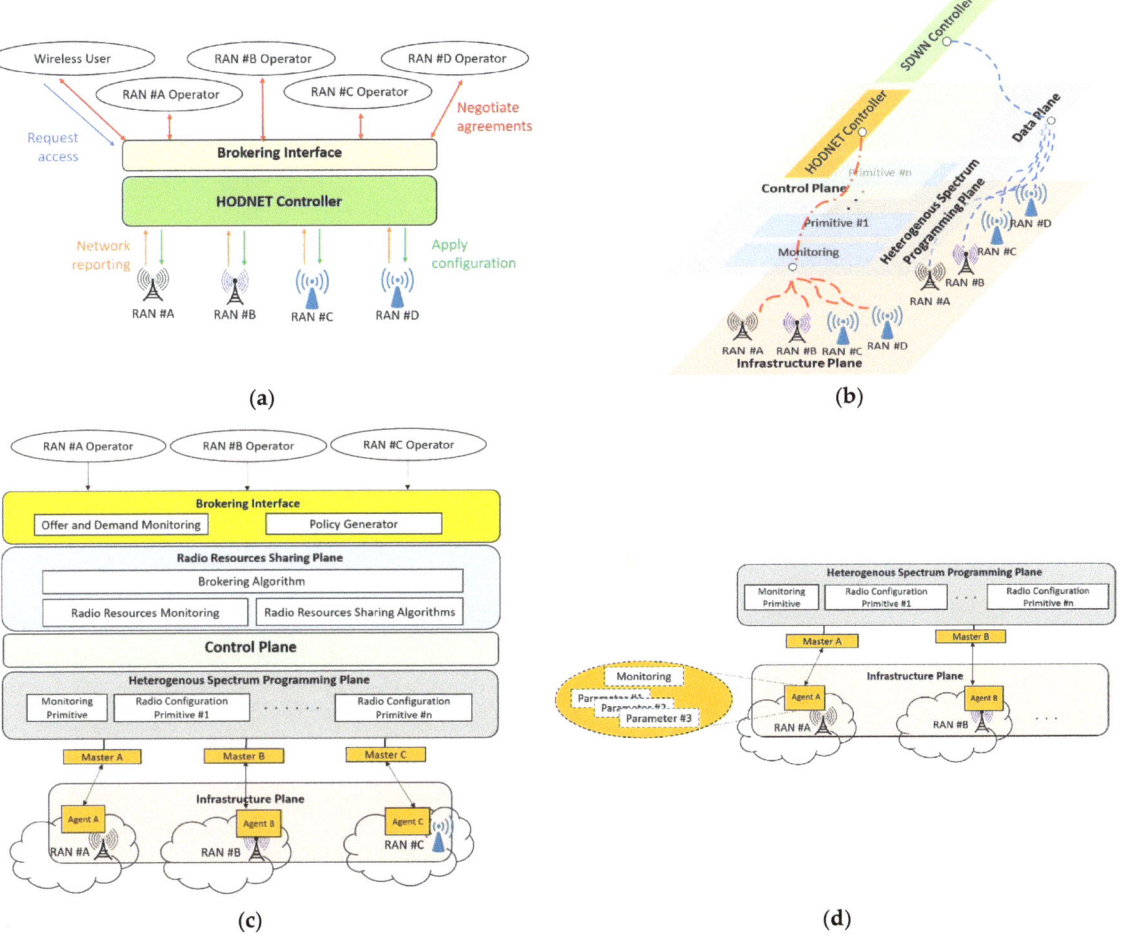

Figure 3. Description of HODNET architecture: (**a**) high-level description of HODNET architecture; (**b**) illustration of the difference between HODNET and SDWN control paths; (**c**) planes in HODNET architecture; (**d**) Interaction between Agent and Master in HODNET architecture.

4.1. Description of HODNET Planes

The HODNET architecture defines a set of planes that facilitate the low-level programmability necessary to achieve scalable, logically centralised spectrum trading as depicted in Figure 3c. While Wi-5 only considered a single centralised physical controller for a specific scenario, HODNET can be deployed in a distributed manner, making use of dynamic Edge Computing platforms, and partly being implemented through NFV and Service Function Chaining architectures to facilitate multi-operator deployments. This will further reinforce the scalability aspects of HODNET (req. 2) and address the availability issues discussed above (req. 1). The planes presented in Figure 3c can be described as follows:

- Infrastructure Plane. This plane includes the nodes through which the radio resources of each RAN can be accessed and shared, such as 5G Base Stations (gNBs) or Wi-Fi APs. The nodes each run software agents which expose the parameters to configure these nodes, such as transmission power, transmission and reception channel, coding scheme, and the number of connected devices.
- Heterogeneous Spectrum Programming Plane. This plane defines the primitives that enable access to and configuration of the RAN parameters. The configurations are applied to the nodes via a Master/Agent system which translates them to be specific to the underlying technology (e.g., 802.11 channel and transmission strength) and also includes a monitoring primitive that gathers information related to the radio resources available at each RAN.
- Control Plane. This plane includes the HODNET controller as well as the SDWN controller. The difference between the roles of each controller is depicted in Figure 3b. The SDWN controller is responsible for managing the data path, depicted by a blue dashed line. The HODNET controller is responsible for managing the spectrum path (depicted by a red dashed line), i.e., the radio configuration of the access nodes. The control plane will, for example, coordinate vertical handovers between operators and technologies via the SDWN Controller but manage interference using the HODNET Controller.
- Radio Resources Sharing Plane. This plane implements a variety of Radio Resource Management (RRM) algorithms and monitoring mechanisms, communicating with the available RANs about their resources via the control plane. The algorithms use the collected monitoring information and apply heterogeneous RRM techniques such as cell aggregation. Note that the techniques used to manage the heterogeneous radio resource will be limited to the RATs accessed by the controller through the Heterogeneous Spectrum Programming Plane.
- Brokering Interface. This is the interface between the Radio Resources Sharing Plane and the various operators. It automates the negotiation process, in which the RANs and offers are each represented by agents. The agents then barter a deal, e.g., using a negotiating algorithm as described in [13]. While an in-depth analysis of this functionality is beyond the scope of this paper, an example of what the architecture for such a Brokering Platform could look like has been published in [27].

4.2. Interaction between HODNET Planes

The lower two HODNET planes interact through Master and Agent components. Figure 3d illustrates how an Agent in the Infrastructure Plane exposes all the parameters required to configure the RAN from the Master. It also operates a monitoring function that gathers information related to the RAN such as its status and the quality of the channel. The configuration and monitoring information gathered by the Agent is accessed by the Radio Configuration and Monitoring Primitives in the Heterogeneous Spectrum Programming Plane through the Master. The Master also allows a radio configuration to be applied back to the RAN via the Agent. Note that there will be one Master-Agent pair associated with each RAN. This will enable the controller to configure each node separately and according to the nature and specifics of the RAT it operates on.

The Radio Resource Sharing plane enables the implementation of different algorithms that could be applied to marshal the radio resources necessary to satisfy the requirements of the IoT network. Several approaches have been proposed in the literature to achieve this goal [28,29] depending on the available RATs. These algorithms are implemented here via the northbound API of the HODNET controller, as illustrated in Figure 3c, and can be configured to optimise various aspects of the operation of the managed networks. The controller will execute these algorithms using the primitives exposed by the Heterogeneous Spectrum Programming Plane as described above.

It is worth noting that, as we have mentioned in Section 4, HODNET is based on the Wi-5 architecture which does not introduce significant overhead to real-time operation through the execution of algorithms for spectrum sharing and RAT selection [22]. On the other hand, if HODNET is implemented on limited computing and networking resources, the trading, brokering, and allocation may take some time, and the ambition of "real-time" dynamic sharing may be difficult to achieve. However, it will nevertheless be a significant improvement over the current static mechanisms deployed in 5G.

5. Use Case: Spectrum Access in Massive IoT

To illustrate how significant the benefits can be of deploying spectrum through an architecture such as HODNET, we analyse the following use case of massively deployed wireless IoT devices within a limited area. It is expected that over the next ten years the number of IoT devices will reach densities of several million devices per square kilometre. Current radio access models, including both grant-based and grant-free models have not been designed to guarantee wireless connectivity on this scale. This is because operators cannot currently provide enough spectrum capacity to satisfy the demands of these devices [30]. In this use case, HODNET will act as the platform linking IoT networks to entities offering wireless spectrum and connectivity. We envisage that a RAN operator initially manages its wireless network independently (i.e., in the traditional way), resulting in inadequate spectrum access. By introducing HODNET as a brokering and control entity, other operators could be invited to trade spectrum access and alleviate each other's burden based on the new spectrum-sharing paradigm. HODNET coordinates with the operators to optimise the spectrum usage through the monitoring and sharing functionality in the Radio Resources Sharing Plane and, as such, increases usable capacity.

For our analysis, we focus on two performance metrics:

- Signal to Interference plus Noise Ratio (SINR): this is the average SINR experienced by all IoT devices in the network;
- Probability of denying connectivity: this is the percentage of devices that cannot achieve their bit rate requirements.

We used MATLAB to simulate a dense deployment of IoT devices served by a set of RANs that belong to different network operators, all deployed in an open-air area of 250 m × 250 m. We then introduce HODNET and assess how both approaches (with and without HODNET) can provide connectivity to IoT devices while optimising network capacity, and how they then perform as the number of devices increases. Each RAN can be either a 5G Base Station (gNB) or a Wi-Fi 802.11ah Access Point (AP). Specifically, the 5G connectivity is provided by 4 gNBs and the Wi-Fi connectivity is offered by 16 802.11ah APs. Furthermore, the 20 nodes belong to 4 different operators, with each one managing 5 nodes. We assume that each node offers a 5 MHz uplink channel operating on the 880–915 MHz and a 4 MHz uplink channel on 900–928 MHz frequency bands in the case of the gNBs and Wi-Fi APs, respectively. We also assume that the IoT devices have transmission power capabilities varying between 1 and 10 dBm and data rates varying between 8 kbps and 128 kbps. The selected settings are representative of a dense environment [31], and follow 3GPP and IEEE specifications. Note that the aim of this implementation is to demonstrate the benefits of our novel spectrum-sharing paradigm that we envision for next-generation 6G networks, through the massive IoT use case involving technologies currently available in the market, i.e., Wi-Fi and 5G. As we will demonstrate in the rest of this section, these results will encourage further investigation to extend our approach into next-generation 6G-based technologies.

Moreover, for the sake of comparison, we consider a simplified version of 5G that connects each IoT device to the closest of its 5 available nodes and does not have access to the connectivity offered by other operators, whereas the HODNET Controller can utilise the whole environment. For this, HODNET implements a Sharing-Economy-based Smart Connectivity algorithm on its Radio Resource Sharing Plane based on information gathered from the Infrastructure Plane. This information includes the Received Signal Strength Indicator (RSSI) monitored by the RANs from each IoT device and the number of devices connected to each RAN. This algorithm connects dynamically each IoT device to the RAN belonging to any RAN operator that has the smallest number of connections, and which provides a sufficient RSSI based on the data rate requirements. This is indeed a very simple trading paradigm, but the following figures show that even such an uncomplicated scheme can produce a significant improvement in resource utilisation.

Figure 4 shows the performance results in terms of SINR for different numbers of IoT devices distributed in the deployed area. The upper and lower edges of the plotted boxes are the 25th and 75th percentile of the values. The median values are indicated by the central red lines. The whiskers extend the SINR values to the most extreme points still not considered an outlier, while the values which we considered as outliers are indicated by red dots. The figure shows that our approach results in better performance in terms of SINR compared with regular 5G operation regardless of how many IoT devices are connected to the network. Specifically, the figure illustrates how: (1) the median value is always higher for our approach; and (2) although the standard method has an extensive range of SINR, most of these values are below the median value achieved by the proposed approach.

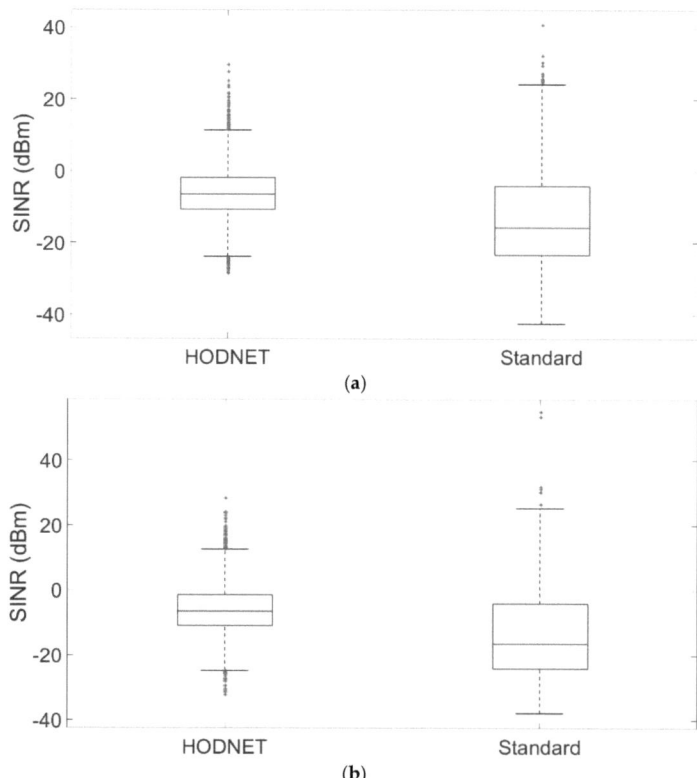

Figure 4. *Cont.*

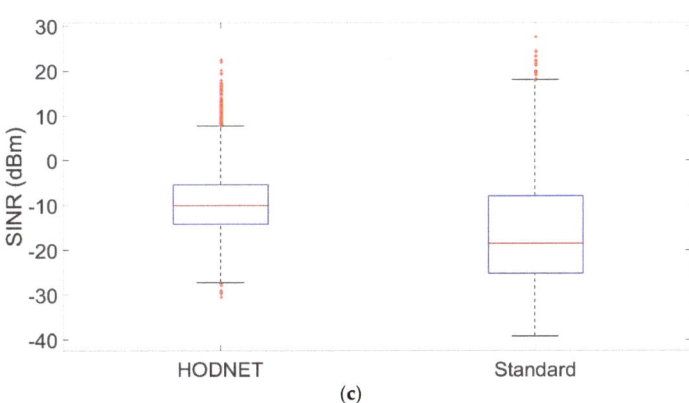

(c)

Figure 4. Measured SINR under both access models for different numbers of IoT devices: (**a**) SINR in case of 1000 IoT devices; (**b**) SINR in case of 2000 IoT devices; (**c**) SINR in case of 3000 IoT devices.

Figure 5 illustrates how this overall increase in SINR leads to improved overall connectivity. It shows that the probability of denying connectivity decreases by 76%, and 16%. and 13%, for 1000, 2000, and 3000 IoT devices, respectively, when HODNET is applied compared with a standard 5G connectivity scenario. However, while with HODNET the blocking probability is always lower than in a standard 5G scenario regardless of the number of devices, it is also clear from Figure 5 that the network is reaching over-saturation when going well above 1000 devices. There is, of course, an absolute maximum to the available capacity and HODNET does not provide extra capacity but instead optimises the effectiveness with which these resources are used by the devices. As such, while this problem may only be solved by the development of more efficient RATs and the addition of usable frequency bands, HODNET can help to maximise the available resources.

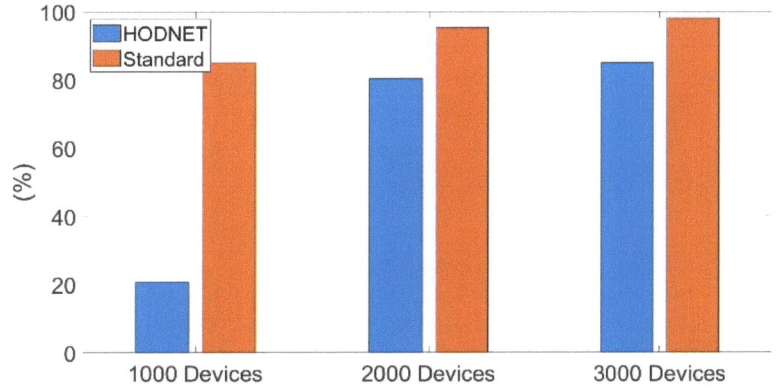

Figure 5. Probability of denying connectivity for different numbers of IoT devices.

6. Conclusions

Current spectrum allocation models for 5G are still based on relatively static frequency band allocation and centralised licencing, with the only alternative provided by unlicensed bands. In either case, unnecessary congestion is observed when the demand is high, due to the suboptimal spectrum management that these models allow for. In this article, we proposed a new vision for spectrum sharing in wireless and mobile networks, based on the recent developments in economic models around sharing of common goods. This vision of trading and allocating spectrum as part of a sharing economy in 6G centres around the ability to automate the matching of locally offered and demanded spectral resources, incentivising stakeholders to share their resources and, therefore, help in easing the demand for this scarce resource.

We also introduced the system architecture of HODNET, an open platform that is capable of realising this new sharing model. HODNET is based on spectrum trading between operators to optimise efficiency and scalability on a high level and builds on the concept of spectrum programming down to the individual radio primitives to enforce fine-grained protocol control.

To demonstrate the benefits of this novel spectrum-sharing paradigm, we considered the use case of massive IoT on a local scale. We simulated a large IoT deployment and evaluated the spectral efficiency of the system when managed using HODNET and compared the results with a standard 5G deployment. We only looked at a very simple trading scheme, in which each IoT device's demand is matched by having it connected to the RAN that has the smallest number of connections, and which provides a sufficient RSSI based on the data rate requirements. Even with such an uncomplicated scheme, a significant improvement in resource utilisation was observed.

Significant aspects to explore further include the wider application of the platform to optimise other metrics, such as efficiency, security, and quality of service. Other important areas to investigate are the upper planes of the platform and the inter-operator spectrum broking system. Key questions include how the good to be traded should be mathematically defined (i.e., the utility function), how dynamic the trading can be executed (we expect in the order of minutes or maybe faster), how deals can be secured, verified, and validated, how the platform can be implemented in a distributed fashion, how participation in the trading can remain voluntary but still effective, and how this concept can be extended to other types of network resources. We, therefore, conclude that the concept of enabling a sharing economy in the 6G spectrum has sufficient merit to warrant further investigation and it represents a fascinating step forward for research in this relatively new area of massive automated heterogeneous spectrum trading and allocation.

Author Contributions: Conceptualisation, F.B. and F.d.H.; methodology, F.B., M.M., A.R. and F.d.H.; software, A.R.; validation, A.R.; formal analysis, F.B., M.M., A.R. and F.d.H.; investigation, F.B., M.M., A.R. and F.d.H.; writing—original draft preparation, F.B., A.R. and M.M.; writing—review and editing, F.d.H.; visualisation, A.R.; supervision, F.B. and M.M. All authors have read and agreed to the published version of the manuscript.

Funding: This research received no external funding.

Data Availability Statement: Not applicable.

Conflicts of Interest: The authors declare no conflict of interest.

References

1. Cisco Annual Internet Report. 2020. Available online: https://www.cisco.com/c/en/us/solutions/collateral/executive-perspectives/annual-internet-report/white-paper-c11-741490.html (accessed on 26 October 2022).
2. Ericsson Mobility Report. 2020. Available online: https://www.ericsson.com/en/mobility-report/reports/november-2020 (accessed on 26 October 2022).
3. Spectrum Sharing: GSMA Public Policy Position. 2019. Available online: https://www.gsma.com/spectrum/wp-content/uploads/2019/09/Spectrum-Sharing-PPP.pdf (accessed on 26 October 2022).
4. Bazelon, C. Licensed or unlicensed: The economic considerations in incremental spectrum allocations. *IEEE Commun. Mag.* **2009**, *47*, 110–116. [CrossRef]
5. den Hartog, F.; Raschella, A.; Bouhafs, F.; Kempker, P.; Boltjes, B.; Seyedebrahimi, M. A pathway to solving the Wi-Fi tragedy of the commons in apartment blocks. In Proceedings of the 27th International Telecommunication Networks and Applications Conference (ITNAC), Melbourne, Australia, 22–24 November 2017; pp. 1–6.
6. Anker, P. From spectrum management to spectrum governance. *Telecommun. Policy* **2017**, *41*, 486–497. [CrossRef]
7. Mustonen, M.; Matinmikko, M.; Palola, M.; Yrjölä, S.; Horneman, K. An evolution toward cognitive cellular systems: Licensed shared access for network optimization. *IEEE Commun. Mag.* **2015**, *53*, 68–74. [CrossRef]
8. Grissa, M.; Yavuz, A.A.; Hamdaoui, B.; Tirupathi, C. Anonymous Dynamic Spectrum Access and Sharing Mechanisms for the CBRS Band. *IEEE Access* **2021**, *9*, 33860–33879. [CrossRef]

9. Ali, R.; Kim, B.; Kim, S.; Kim, H.; Ishmanov, F. (ReLBT): A Reinforcement learning-enabled listen before talk mechanism for LTE-LAA and Wi-Fi coexistence in IoT. *Comput. Commun.* **2020**, *150*, 498–505. [CrossRef]
10. Zhang, J.; Liu, S.; Yin, R.; Yu, G.; Jin, X. Coexistence algorithms for LTE and WiFi networks in unlicensed spectrum: Performance optimization and comparison. *Wirel. Netw.* **2021**, *27*, 1875–1885. [CrossRef]
11. Qin, Z.; Li, A.; Wang, H. Modeling and Performance Analysis of LTE Coexisting with Wi-Fi. In Proceedings of the International Conference on Information, Communication and Networks (ICICN), Xi'an, China, 22–25 August 2020.
12. Etkin, R.; Parekh, A.; Tse, D. Spectrum Sharing for Unlicensed Bands. *IEEE J. Sel. Areas Commun.* **2007**, *25*, 517–528. [CrossRef]
13. Van Heesch, M.; Wissink, P.L.J.; Ranji, R.; Nobakht, M.; Den Hartog, F. Combining Cooperative with Non-Cooperative Game Theory to Model Wi-Fi Congestion in Apartment Blocks. *IEEE Access* **2020**, *8*, 64603–64616. [CrossRef]
14. Koura, H.; Jhaa, R.K.; Jain, S. A comprehensive survey on spectrum sharing: Architecture, energy efficiency and security issues. *Elsevier J. Netw. Comput. Appl.* **2018**, *103*, 29–57. [CrossRef]
15. Ahmad, W.S.H.M.W.; Radzi, N.A.M.; Samidi, F.S.; Ismail, A.; Abdullah, F.; Jamaludin, M.Z.; Zakaria, M.N. 5G Technology: Towards Dynamic Spectrum Sharing Using Cognitive Radio Networks. *IEEE Access* **2020**, *8*, 14460–14488. [CrossRef]
16. Lv, L.; Chen, J.; Ni, Q.; Ding, Z.; Jiang, H. Cognitive Non-Orthogonal Multiple Access with Cooperative Relaying: A New Wireless Frontier for 5G Spectrum Sharing. *IEEE Commun. Mag.* **2018**, *56*, 188–195. [CrossRef]
17. Zhang, L.; Liang, Y.-C.; Xiao, M. Spectrum Sharing for Internet of Things: A Survey. *IEEE Wirel. Commun.* **2019**, *26*, 132–139. [CrossRef]
18. Wang, X.; Umehira, M.; Akimoto, M.; Han, B.; Zhou, H. Green spectrum sharing framework in B5G era by exploiting crowdsensing. *IEEE Trans. Green Commun. Netw. Early Access* **2022**, 1. [CrossRef]
19. Bera, S.; Misra, S.; Vasilakos, A.V. Software-Defined Networking for Internet of Things: A Survey. *IEEE Internet Things J.* **2017**, *4*, 1994–2008. [CrossRef]
20. López, L.I.B.; Caraguay, L.V.; Villalba, L.J.G.; López, D. Trends on virtualisation with software defined networking and network function virtualisation. *IET Netw.* **2015**, *4*, 255–263. [CrossRef]
21. Rawat, D.B.; Reddy, S. Recent advances on Software Defined Wireless Networking. In Proceedings of the SoutheastCon 2016, Norfolk, VA, USA, 30 March–3 April 2016; pp. 1–8.
22. Bouhafs, F.; Mackay, M.; Raschella, A.; Shi, Q.; Hartog, F.D.; Saldana, J.; Munilla, R.; Ruiz-Mas, J.; Fernandez-Navajas, J.; Almodovar, J.; et al. Wi-5: A Programming Architecture for Unlicensed Frequency Bands. *IEEE Commun. Mag.* **2018**, *56*, 178–185. [CrossRef]
23. Matinmikko-Blue, M.; Yrjola, S.; Ahokangas, P. Spectrum Management in the 6G Era: The Role of Regulation and Spectrum Sharing. In Proceedings of the 2nd 6G Wireless Summit (6G SUMMIT), Levi, Finland, 17–20 March 2020.
24. Qin, Q.; Choi, N.; Rahman, M.R.; Thottan, M.; Tassiulas, L. Network Slicing in Heterogeneous Software-defined RANs. In Proceedings of the IEEE International Conference on Computer Communications (INFOCOM), Toronto, ON, Canada, 6–9 July 2020.
25. El-Refaey, M.; Magdi, N.; Abd El-Megeed, H. Cloud-assisted spectrum management system with trading engine. In Proceedings of the International Wireless Communications and Mobile Computing Conference (IWCMC), Nicosia, Cyprus, 4–8 August 2014.
26. Teng, F.; Guo, D.; Honig, M.L. Sharing of Unlicensed Spectrum by Strategic Operators. *IEEE J. Sel. Areas Commun.* **2017**, *35*, 668–679. [CrossRef]
27. den Hartog, F.; Bouhafs, F.; Shi, Q. Toward secure trading of unlicensed spectrum in cyber-physical systems. In Proceedings of the 16th IEEE Annual Consumer Communications & Networking Conference (CCNC), Las Vegas, NV, USA, 11–14 January 2019; pp. 1–4.
28. Kan, S.; Chen, H.; Zhu, Y.; Li, W. Aggregation based Cell Selection Methods for multi-RAT HetNet. In Proceedings of the 8th International Conference on Wireless Communications & Signal Processing (WCSP), Yangzhou, China, 13–15 October 2016; pp. 1–5.
29. Peng, M.; Wang, C.; Li, J.; Xiang, H.; Lau, V. Recent advances in underlay heterogeneous networks: Interference control, resource allocation, and self-organization. *IEEE Commun. Surv. Tutor.* **2015**, *17*, 700–729. [CrossRef]
30. Chen, X.; Ng, D.W.K.; Yu, W.; Larsson, E.G.; Al-Dhahir, N.; Schober, R. Massive access for 5G and beyond. *arXiv* **2020**, arXiv:2002.03491. [CrossRef]
31. Bouhafs, F.; Seyedebrahimi, M.; Raschellà, A.; Mackay, M.; Shi, Q. Per-flow radio resource management to mitigate interference in dense IEEE 802.11 wireless LANs. *IEEE Trans. Mob. Comput.* **2019**, *19*, 1170–1183. [CrossRef]

 *future internet*

Article

The Cloud-to-Edge-to-IoT Continuum as an Enabler for Search and Rescue Operations

Leonardo Militano [1,*], Adriana Arteaga [2], Giovanni Toffetti [1] and Nathalie Mitton [2]

1 School of Engineering, ZHAW Zurich University of Applied Sciences, 8400 Winterthur, Switzerland
2 INRIA, Lille, 59650 Villeneuve d'Ascq, France
* Correspondence: leonardo.militano@zhaw.ch

Abstract: When a natural or human disaster occurs, time is critical and often of vital importance. Data from the incident area containing the information to guide search and rescue (SAR) operations and improve intervention effectiveness should be collected as quickly as possible and with the highest accuracy possible. Nowadays, rescuers are assisted by different robots able to fly, climb or crawl, and with different sensors and wireless communication means. However, the heterogeneity of devices and data together with the strong low-delay requirements cause these technologies not yet to be used at their highest potential. Cloud and Edge technologies have shown the capability to offer support to the Internet of Things (IoT), complementing it with additional resources and functionalities. Nonetheless, building a continuum from the IoT to the edge and to the cloud is still an open challenge. SAR operations would benefit strongly from such a continuum. Distributed applications and advanced resource orchestration solutions over the continuum in combination with proper software stacks reaching out to the edge of the network may enhance the response time and effective intervention for SAR operation. The challenges for SAR operations, the technologies, and solutions for the cloud-to-edge-to-IoT continuum will be discussed in this paper.

Keywords: search and rescue; robot operating system; Internet of Things; edge computing; cloud continuum; orchestration; computer vision; wireless sensor networks; cloud robotics; distributed applications

Citation: Militano, L.; Arteaga, A.; Toffetti, G.; Mitton, N. The Cloud-to-Edge-to-IoT Continuum as an Enabler for Search and Rescue Operations. *Future Internet* 2023, *15*, 55. https://doi.org/10.3390/fi15020055

Academic Editors: Alessandro Raschellà and Michael Mackay

Received: 15 December 2022
Revised: 23 January 2023
Accepted: 23 January 2023
Published: 30 January 2023

Copyright: © 2023 by the authors. Licensee MDPI, Basel, Switzerland. This article is an open access article distributed under the terms and conditions of the Creative Commons Attribution (CC BY) license (https://creativecommons.org/licenses/by/4.0/).

1. Introduction

When a natural or human disaster occurs, the first 72 hours are particularly critical to locate and rescue victims [1]. Although advanced technological solutions are being investigated by researchers and industry for search and rescue (SAR) operations, rescue teams and first responders still suffer from limited situational awareness in an emergency. The main motivation for this is a generalized lack of modern and integrated digital communication and technologies. Relying only on direct visual or verbal communication is indeed the root cause of limited situational awareness. First responders have very limited, sparse, non-integrated ways of receiving information about the evolution of an emergency and its response (e.g., team members and threat locations). A real-time visual representation of the emergency response context would greatly improve their decision accuracy and confidence on the field. "The greatest need for cutting-edge technology, across disciplines, is for devices that provide information to the first responders in real-time" [2].

Mobile robot teams comprising possibly robots with heterogeneous sensory (cameras, infrared cameras, hyperspectral cameras, light detection and ranging—LiDARs, radio detection additionally, ranging—RADARs, etc.) and mobility (land, air) capabilities have the potential of scaling up first responders' situational awareness [3]. They are, therefore, an important asset in the response to catastrophic incidents, such as wildfires, urban fires, landslides, and earthquakes as they also offer the possibility to generate 3D maps of a disaster scene with the use of cameras and sensors. However, in many cases, robots used by first responders are remotely teleoperated, or they can operate autonomously only in scenarios with good global positioning system (GPS) coverage. Furthermore, 3D maps cannot be provided in low-visibility scenarios, such as when smoke is present, in which remote operation is also very complicated. Operating robots in scenarios such as large indoor fires requires the robots to be able to navigate autonomously in environments with smoke and/or where GPS is not available.

Other advanced technologies, such as artificial intelligence (AI) and computer vision are also gaining momentum in SAR operations to fully exploit the information available through cameras and sensors and by this enable smart decision-making and enhanced mission control. On the other hand, these technologies are often very resource-demanding in time and computation. Therefore, the computational power in the cloud and at the edge of the infrastructure has shown great potential to strongly support them. Edge computing is where devices with embedded computing and "hyper-converged" infrastructures integrate and virtualize key components of information technology (IT) infrastructure such as storage, networking and computing. It is also the first step towards a computing continuum that spans from network-connected devices to remote clouds. To leverage this continuum, the seamless integration of capabilities and services is required. Advanced connectivity techniques such as 5G (fifth generation) mobile networks and software-defined networking (SDN) offer unified access to the edge and cloud from anywhere. Workloads can potentially run wherever it makes the most sense for the application to run. At the same time, the different environments along the continuum will work together to provide the right resources for the task at hand. The range of applications and workloads with unique cost, connectivity, performance, and security requirements will demand a continuum of computing and analysis at every step of the topology, from the edge to the cloud, with new approaches to orchestration, management, and security being required.

In this context, there are several open research and technological questions that need to be addressed. On the one side, there is a need to reduce the computational and storage load on the physical device to perform timely actions, but simply offloading to the edge may not improve as the edge also has limited resources. On the other side, how to use all the technologies and devices available to improve situational awareness for first responders is nontrivial due to heterogeneity in communication protocols, semantics and data formats (e.g., generating a collaborative map of the area using the information from drones and robots considering that data fusion from heterogeneous data sources is a challenging task). In this paper, we will investigate how the cloud-to-edge-to-IoT continuum can support and enable post-disaster SAR operations, and we will propose solutions for the challenges and technological/research questions introduced above. Indeed, distributed applications paired with advanced resource orchestration solutions over the continuum reaching out to the edge of the network can enhance the response time and effective intervention for SAR operation [4–6]. The challenges will be discussed, and the possible solutions will be described as part of the Horizon Europe NEPHELE project (NEPHELE project website: https://nephele-project.eu/ (accessed on 19 January 2023)). This project proposes a lightweight software stack and synergetic meta-orchestration framework for the next-generation compute continuum ranging from the IoT to the remote cloud, which perfectly matches the needs of SAR operations.

The paper is organized as follows. Section 2 reports the related work on the main related technologies in cloud computing, sensor networks, the Internet of Things (IoT), robotic applications and cloud robotics. Section 3 describes the reference use case for SAR operations, with its requirements. Section 4 describes the proposed solutions based on the approach followed in the NEPHELE project. Section 5 concludes the paper.

2. Related Work

In this section, we will go over the main technologies that we believe can and should be considered to best cope with SAR scenarios and enhance the situational awareness of first responders.

2.1. Cloud and Edge Robotics for SAR

The idea of utilizing a "remote brain" for robots can be traced back to the 90s [7,8]. Since then, attempts to adopt cloud technologies in the robotics field have seen a constantly growing momentum. The benefits deriving from the integration of networked robots and cloud computing are, among others, powerful computation, storage, and communication resources available in the cloud which can support the information sharing and processing for robotic applications. The possibility of remotely controlling robotic systems further reduces costs for the deployment, monitoring, diagnostics, and orchestration of any robotic application. This, in turn, allows for building lightweight, low-cost, and smarter robots, as the main computation and communication burden is brought to the cloud. Since 2010, when the cloud robotics term first appeared, several projects (e.g., RoboEarth [9], KnowRob [10], DAVinci [11], Robobrain [12]) investigated the field, pushing forward both research and products to appear on the market. Companies started investing in the field as they recognized the large potential of cloud robotics. This led to the first open-source cloud robotics frameworks appearing in recent years [13]. An example of this is the solution from Rapyuta Robotics (Available online: https://www.rapyuta-robotics.com/ (accessed on 19 January 2023)). Similarly, commercial solutions for developers have seen the light such as Formant (Available online: https://formant.io/ (accessed on 19 January 2023)), Robolaunch (Available online: https://www.robolaunch.io/ (accessed on 19 January 2023)) and Amazon's Robomaker [14]. Additionally, for key features such as navigation and localization in indoor environments, commercial products exist on the market. Adopting commercial solutions, however, leads to additional costs that might threaten the success of offering a low-cost product/service to the market. Open source offers customizable solutions with production and maintenance costs kept low, whereas ad hoc designed solutions allow us to deploy customized technology solutions in terms of services and features envisioned for the final product. With the advances in edge [15] and fog computing [16] in the last few years, robotics has seen an even greater potential as higher bandwidth and lower latencies can be achieved [17]. With computing and storage resources at the edge of the infrastructure, applications can be executed closer to the robotic hardware which generally improves the performance [17] and enables advanced applications that pure cloud-based robotics would not be able to support [18–20].

Multiple research and development (R&D) projects have investigated the adoption of robotic solutions in SAR operations. For instance, the SHERPA project [21] developed a mixed ground and aerial robotic platform with human–robot interaction to support search and rescue activities in real-world hostile environments; RESPOND-A [22] developed holistic solutions by bringing together 5G wireless communications, augmented and virtual reality, autonomous robot and unmanned aerial vehicle coordination, intelligent wearable sensors and smart monitoring, geovisual analytics and immersive geospatial data analysis, passive and active localization and tracking, and interactive multi-view 360-degrees video streaming. These are two examples of several projects that have investigated and demonstrated the use of robotic applications in SAR and disaster scenarios. Whereas the adoption of cloud and edge robotics for SAR has gained interest in recent years [20,23,24], how the cloud and edge computing frameworks can support SAR operations at their best is still an open challenge. Nonetheless, we believe that the cloud-to-edge-to-IoT continuum can strongly support and enable the widespread use of cloud robotics in a large set of application domains.

2.2. Cloud Continuum

With the term cloud continuum, we intend the edge computing extension of cloud services towards the network boundaries [25] reaching out to end devices (i.e., the IoT devices). Edge computing revealed itself as a valid paradigm to bring cloud computation and data storage closer to the data source of applications. On the one hand, edge computing provides better performance for delay-sensitive applications, whereas, on the other hand, applications with a high computational cost have access to more processing resources distributed along the continuum. This continuum reaches out to the IoT devices as sensors are the source of massive amounts of data that are challenging for infrastructure, data analysis, and storage. The Cloud-Edge-IoT computing continuum has been explored in various areas of research. For instance, it has been investigated to provide services and applications for autonomous vehicles [26], smart cities [27], UAV cooperative schemes [28] and Industry 4.0 [29], where most of the data require real-time processing using machine learning and artificial intelligence.

One of the main challenges of the cloud continuum is the orchestration between the components of the system, which includes computational resources, learning models, algorithms, networking capabilities and edge/IoT device mobility. Context awareness is required in the continuum to decide when and where to store data and perform computation [30]. For IoT environments, context information is generated by processing raw sensor data to make decisions in order to reduce energy consumption, reduce overall latency and message overload [31], achieve a more efficient data transmission rate in large-scale scenarios using caching [32], and store and process placement across the continuum [33,34]. The mobility-aware multi-objective IoT application placement (mMAPO) method [25] proposes an optimization model for the application placement across the continuum considering the edge device mobility to optimize the completion time, energy consumption and economic cost. Task offloading from ground IoT devices to UAV (unmanned aerial vehicle) cooperative systems to deploy edge servers is explored in [35], where authors also present an energy allocation strategy to maximize long-term performance.

The use of the cloud continuum for SAR operations has the potential to extend the capabilities and resources available and by this enhance the situational awareness of first responders. The orchestration process of the different systems, including robots and rescue teams, is a challenging aspect that might obtain support from models from industry, health and military systems [36].

2.3. Sensor Networks and IoT for SAR Operations

Sensor networks have seen broad application in areas such as healthcare, transportation, logistics, farming, and home automation, but even more in search and rescue operations. Sensors capture signals from the physical world and increase the information available to make decisions. The IoT as an extension of the sensor network includes any type of device and system such as vehicles, drones, machines, robots, human wearables or cameras with a unique identifier that can gather, exchange and process data without explicit human intervention. The use of IoT systems has been widely explored to extend the capabilities of SAR teams in disaster situations. Drone and UAV capabilities allow access to remote areas in less time, deploy communications systems, improve area visibility and transport light cargo if necessary [37]. Acoustic source location based on azimuth estimation and distance was proposed to estimate the victim's location [38,39]. Image/video resources in drone-based systems are also used for automatic person detection by applying deep convolutional neural networks and image processing tools [40]. SARDO [41] is a drone-based location system that allows locating victims by locating mobile phones in the area without any modification to the mobile phones or infrastructure support.

Collaborative multi-robots have a high impact on SAR operations. providing real-time mapping and monitoring of the area [42]. The multi-robot systems in SAR operation have been explored for urban [43], maritime [44] and wilderness [45] operational environments. Several types of robots are involved in multi-robot systems such as UAVs, unmanned surface vehicles (USVs), unmanned ground vehicles (UGVs) or unmanned underwater vehicles (UUVs). Serpentine robots are useful in narrow and complex spaces [46]. The snake robot proposed in [47] has a gripper module to remove small objects and a camera to move the eyes and look in all directions without moving the body. There are also more flexible and robust ground units with long-term autonomy and the capacity to carry aerial robots to extend the coverage area using an integrated vision system [48]. Maritime SAR operations are supported by UAVs, UUVs and USVs, where the UUV includes seafloor pressure sensors, hydrophones for tsunami detection and a sensor for measuring water conditions such as temperature, the concentration of different chemicals, depth, etc. [49].

Other fundamental elements in SAR operations are personal devices such as smartphones and wearables [23]. One of the constraints during a disaster is infrastructure failure where electricity is off or communications equipment is destroyed, damaged or saturated COPE is a solution to exploit the multi-network feature of mobile devices to provide an alert messages delivery system based on smartphones [50]. COPE considers several energy levels to use the technologies available in smartphones nowadays (Bluetooth, Wi-Fi, cellular) for alert diffusion in the disaster area. Drones are used to collect emergency messages from smartphones and take the messages to areas where there is connectivity This approach is explored in [51] to propose a collaborative data collection protocol that organizes wireless devices in multiple tiers by targeting fair energy consumption in the whole network, thereby extending the network lifetime. Wearables are also important in SAR operations because they can monitor the vital signs such as temperature, heart rate, respiration rate and blood pressure of the victims and rescuers [51]. This information can be collected by the rescuer or the robot-based system to determine the victim's status and provide a more convenient treatment depending on the conditions [52].

SAR dogs have also been involved in disaster events to locate victims even in limited vision and sound scenarios. A wearable computing system for SAR dogs is proposed in [53], where the dog uses a deep learning-assisted system in a wearable device. The system incorporates inertial sensors, such as a three-axial accelerometer and gyroscope, and a wearable microphone. The computational system collects audio and motion signals, processes the sensor signals, communicates the critical messages using the available network and determines the victim's location based on the dog's location. Incorporating IoT systems into SAR operations increases rescue teams' capabilities, saving time by receiving information in real time. The development of autonomous systems allows the integration of machines precisely and reduces the risks for victims and rescuers.

2.4. Situation Awareness and Perception with Mobile Robots

Mobile robot teams with heterogeneous sensors have the potential of scaling up first responders' situational awareness. Being able to cover wide areas, these are an important asset in the response to catastrophic incidents, such as wildfires, urban fires, landslides, and earthquakes. In their essence, robot teams make possible two key dimensions of situation awareness: space distribution and time distribution [54]. Although the former means the possibility of multiple robots perceiving simultaneously different (far) locations of the area of interest, the latter arises from the fact that multiple robots, possibly endowed with complementary sensor modalities, can visit a location at different instant times, thus coping with environments' evolution over time, i.e., with dynamic environments. Together with space and time distribution, robot teams also potentially provide efficiency, reliability, robustness and specialization [55]; efficiency because they allow building in fewer time models of wide areas, which is of utmost importance to provide situational awareness within response missions to catastrophic scenarios; reliability and robustness because the failure of individual robots in the team does not necessarily compromise the overall mission success; specialization because robots have complementary, i.e., heterogeneous, sensory and mobility capabilities, thus increasing the team's total utility.

Although distributed robot teams potentially allow for persistent, long-term perception in wide areas, i.e., they allow for cooperative perception, fulfilling this potential requires solving two fundamental scientific sub-problems [56]: (i) data integration for building and updating a consistent unified view of the situation, eventually over a large time span; (ii) multi-robot coordination to optimize the information gain in active perception [57,58]. The former sub-problem deals with space and time distribution and involves data fusion, i.e., merging partial perceptual models of individual robots into a globally consistent perceptual model, so that robots can update percepts in a spot previously visited by other robotic teammates. The latter sub-problem involves the use of partial information contained in the global perceptual model to decide where either a robot or the robot team should go next to acquire novel or more recent data to augment or update the current perceptual model, thus closing the loop between sensing and actuation. In order to optimize the collective performance and take full advantage of space distribution provided by the multi-robot system, active perception requires action coordination among robots, which usually is based on sharing some coordination data among robots (e.g., state information). In both sub-problems, devising distributed solutions that do not rely on a central point of failure [55] is a key requirement to operate in the wild, e.g., in forestry environments or in large urban areas, so that adequate resiliency and robustness are attained in harsh operational conditions, including individual robots' hardware failures and communication outages.

Cooperative perception has been studied in specific testbeds [55] or several robotics application domains, such as long-term security and care services in man-made environments [57], monitoring environmental properties [58–63], the atmospheric dispersion of pollutants monitoring [64], precision agriculture [65,66] or forest fire detection and monitoring [67,68]. However, the research problem has been only partially and sparsely solved (i.e., usually tackling only a specific dimension of cooperative perception), and it is still essentially an open research problem. Especially in field robotic applications, including robotics to aid first responders in catastrophic incidents, which involve a much wider diversity of robots in terms of sensory capabilities and mobility and strict time response constraints, a more thorough and extensive treatment is needed to encompass all the dimensions of the cooperative perception problem, thus being able to fulfill the requirements posed by those complex real scenarios.

2.5. Simultaneous Localization and Mapping

Operating robots in scenarios such as large indoor fires or collapsed buildings requires the robots to be able to navigate in environments with smoke and/or where GPS is not available. This involves using simultaneous localization and mapping (SLAM) techniques. SLAM consists of the concurrent construction of a model of the environment (the map that can be used also for navigation) and the estimation of the position of the robot moving within it and is considered a fundamental problem for robots to become truly autonomous. As such, over the years, a large variety of SLAM approaches have been developed, with methods based on different sensors (camera, LiDAR, RADAR, etc.), new data representations and consequently new types of maps [69,70]. Similarly, various estimation techniques have emerged inside the SLAM field. Nonetheless, it is still an actively researched problem in robotics, so much so that the robotics research community is only now working towards designing benchmarks and mechanisms to compare different SLAM implementations. In recent years, there has been particularly intense research into VSLAM (visual SLAM) [71]. Specifically, the focus is on using primarily visual (camera) sensors to allow robots to track and keep local maps of their relative positions also in indoor environments (where GPS-based navigation fails). Extracting key features from images, the robot can determine where it is in the local environment by comparing features to a database of images taken of the environment during prior passes by the robot. As this latter procedure quickly becomes the bottleneck for its applicability, solutions are being explored to offload the processing to the cloud [72] and to the edge [56]. Additionally, in this context, we believe the cloud-to-edge-to-IoT continuum will sustain these advanced technologies.

2.6. ROS Applications

With robots coming out of research labs to interact with the real world in several domains comes the realization that robots are but one of the many components of "robotic applications". The distributed nature of such systems (i.e., robots, edge, cloud, mobile devices), the inherent complexity of the underlying technologies (e.g., networking, artificial intelligence—AI, specialized processors, sensors and actuators, robotic fleets) and the related development practices (e.g., continuous integration/continuous development, containerization, simulation, hardware-in-the-loop testing) pose high entry barriers for any actor wishing to develop such applications. With new features and robotic capabilities being constantly developed in all main five elements of modern advanced robotics (i.e., perception, modeling, cognition, behavior and control) and AI solutions expanding what is possible each day, software updates will become frequent across all involved devices, requiring development and operation (DevOps) practices to be adapted to the specific nature of robotic applications and their lifecycle (e.g., mobile robots, frequent disconnections, over-the-air updates, safety).

ROS (robot operating system) is an open-source framework for writing robotic software that was conceived with the specific purpose of fostering collaboration. In its relatively short existence (slightly more than ten years) it has managed to become the de facto standard framework for robotic software. The ROS ecosystem now consists of tens of thousands of users worldwide, working in domains ranging from tabletop hobby projects to large industrial automation systems (see Figure 1).

Figure 1. The ROS ecosystem is composed of multiple elements: (i) plumbing: a message-passing system for communication; (ii) tools: a set of development tools to accelerate and support application development; (iii) capabilities: drivers, algorithms, user interfaces as building blocks for applications; (iv) community: a large, diverse, and global community of students, hobbyists and multinational corporations and government agencies.

Open Robotics (Available online: https://www.openrobotics.org (accessed on 19 January 2023)) sponsors the development of ROS and aims to generally "support the development, distribution, and adoption of open-source software for use in robotics research, education, and product development". Currently, ROS is the most widely used framework for creating generic and universal robotics applications. It aims to create complex and robust robot behaviors across the widest possible variety of robotic platforms. ROS achieves that by allowing the reuse of robotics software packages and creating a hardware-agnostic abstraction layer. This significantly lowers the entry threshold for non-robotic-field developers who want to develop robotic applications.

On the other hand, from the architectural point of view, ROS still treats the robot as a central point of the system and relies on local computation. This limitation makes the task of creating large-scale and advanced robotics applications much harder to achieve. The current state of cloud platforms does not support the actual robotic application needs off the shelf [13–17]. It includes bi-directional data flow, multi-process applications or exposing sockets outside the cloud environment. These hurdles make them less accessible for robotics application developers. By creating a cloud-to-edge-to-IoT continuum which provides the needs of such robotic environments, we can lower the hurdle for an application developer to use or extend robots' capabilities.

3. Challenges for Risk Assessment and Mission Control in SAR Operations in Post-Disaster Scenarios

When a natural or human disaster occurs, the main objective is to rescue as many victims as possible in the shortest possible time. To this aim, the rescue team needs to (1) locate and identify victims, (2) assess the victims' injuries and (3) assess the damages and comprehend the remaining risks to prioritize rescue operations. All these actions are complementary and require a different part of the data collected in the area. On the data coming from sensors, cameras and other devices, image recognition, AI-powered decision-making, path planning and other technological solutions can be implemented to support the rescue teams in enhancing their situational awareness. Today, only part of the available data can be collected, and robots, although a great support, are not fully autonomous and just act as relays to the rescuers. The main technical challenges are linked to the heterogeneity of devices and strict time requirements. Data should be filtered and processed at different levels of the continuum to guarantee short delays while maintaining full knowledge of the situation. Devices are heterogeneous in terms of CPU, memory, sensors and energy capacities. Some of the hardware and software components are very specific to the situation (use-case specific), whereas others are common to multiple scenarios. Different complementary applications can be run on top of the same devices but exploit different sets of data, potentially incomplete. The network is dynamic because of link fluctuations, the energy depletion of devices and device mobility (which can also be exploited when controllable).

The high-level goal for this scenario is to enhance situational awareness for first responders. Sensor data fusion built on ROS can help provide precise 3D representations of emergency scenarios in real time, integrating the inputs from multiple sensors, pieces of equipment and actors. Furthermore, collecting and visually presenting aggregated and processed data from heterogeneous devices and prioritizing selected information based on the scenario is an additional objective. All the information that is being collected should improve the efficiency of decision-making and responses and increase safety and coordination.

Robotic platforms have features that are highly appreciated by first responders, such as the possibility to generate 3D maps of a disaster scene in a short time. Open-source technologies (i.e., ROS) offer the tools to aggregate sensor data from different coordinate frameworks. To achieve this, precise localization and mapping solutions in disaster scenarios are needed, together with advanced sensor data fusion algorithms. The envisaged real-time situation awareness is only possible through substantial research advancement with respect to the state of the art in localization, mapping, and cooperative perception in emergency environments. The ability to provide information from a single specialized device (e.g., drone streaming) has been demonstrated, whereas correctly integrating multiple heterogeneous moving data sources with imprecise localization in real-time is still an open challenge. We can summarize the main technical requirements and challenges as follows:

1. **Dynamic multi-robot mapping and fleet management**: the coordination, monitoring and optimization of the task allocation for mobile robots that work together in building a map of unknown environments;
2. **Computer vision for information extraction**: AI and computer vision enable people detection, position detection and localization from image and video data;
3. **Smart data filtering/aggregation/compression**: a large amount of data is collected from sensors, robots, and cameras in the intervention area for several services (e.g., map building, scene and action replay). Some of them can be filtered, and others can be downsampled or aggregated before sending them to the edge/cloud. Smart policies should be defined to also tackle the high degree of data heterogeneity;
4. **Device Management**: some application functionalities can be pre-deployed on the devices or at the edge. The device management should also enable bootstrapping and self-configuration, support hardware heterogeneity and guarantee the self-healing of software components;
5. **Orchestration of software components**: given the SAR application graph, a dynamic placement of software components should be enabled based on service requirements and resource availability. This will require performance and resource monitoring at the various levels of the continuum and dynamic component redeployment;
6. **Low latency communication**: communication networks to/from disaster areas towards the edge and cloud should guarantee low delays for a fast response in locating and rescuing people under mobility conditions and possible disconnections.

4. Nephele Project as Enabler for SAR Operations

NEPHELE (NEPHELE project website: https://nephele-project.eu/ (accessed on 19 January 2023)) is a research and innovation action (RIA) project funded by the Horizon Europe program under the topic "Future European platforms for the Edge: Meta Operating Systems" for the duration of three years (September 2022–August 2025). Its vision is to enable the efficient, reliable and secure end-to-end orchestration of hyper-distributed applications over a programmable infrastructure that is spanning across the compute continuum from IoT to edge to cloud. In doing this, it aims at removing the existing openness and interoperability barriers in the convergence of IoT technologies against cloud and edge computing orchestration platforms and introducing automation and decentralized intelligence mechanisms powered by 5G and distributed AI technologies. To reach this overall objective, the NEPHELE project aims to introduce two core innovations, namely:

1. An **IoT and edge computing software stack** for leveraging the virtualization of IoT devices at the edge part of the infrastructure and supporting openness and interoperability aspects in a device-independent way. Through this software stack, the management of a wide range of IoT devices and platforms can be realized in a unified way, avoiding the usage of middleware platforms, whereas edge computing functionalities can be offered on demand to efficiently support IoT applications' operations. The concept of the virtual object (VO) is introduced, where the VO is considered the virtual counterpart of an IoT device. The VO significantly extends the notion of a digital twin as it provides a set of abstractions for managing any type of IoT device through a virtualized instance while augmenting the supported functionalities through the hosting of a multi-layer software stack, called a virtual object stack (VOStack). The VOStack is specifically conceived to provide VOs with edge computing and IoT functions, such as, among others, distributed data management and analysis based on machine learning (ML) and digital twinning techniques, authorization, security and trust based on security protocols and blockchain mechanisms, autonomic networking and time-triggered IoT functions taking advantage of ad hoc group management techniques, service discovery and load balancing mechanisms. Furthermore, IoT functions similar to the ones usually supported by digital twins will be offered by the VOStack;

2. A **synergetic meta-orchestration framework** for managing the coordination between cloud and edge computing orchestration platforms, through high-level scheduling supervision and definition. Technological advances in the areas of 5G and beyond networks, AI and cybersecurity are going to be considered and integrated as additional pluggable systems in the proposed synergetic meta-orchestration framework. To support modularity, openness and interoperability with emerging orchestration platforms and IoT technologies, a microservices-based approach is adopted where cloud-native applications are represented in the form of an application graph. The application graph is composed of independently deployable application components that can be orchestrated. Such components regard application components that can be deployed at the cloud or the edge part of the continuum, VOs and IoT-specific virtualized functions that are offered by the VOs. Each component in the application graph is also accompanied by a sidecar -based on a service-mesh approach for supporting generic/supportive functions that can be activated on demand. The meta-orchestrator is responsible for activating the appropriate orchestration modules to efficiently manage the deployment of the application components across the continuum. It includes a set of modules for federated resources management, the control of cloud and edge computing cluster managers, end-to-end network management across the continuum and AI-assisted orchestration. The interplay among VOs and IoT devices will allow for exploitation functions even at the device level in a flexible and opportunistic fashion. The synergetic meta-orchestrator (SMO) interacts with a set of further components for both computational resources management (federated resources manager—FRM) and network management across the continuum, by taking advantage of emerging net-

work technologies. The SMO makes use of the hyper-distributed applications (HDA) repository, where a set of application graphs, application components, virtualized IoT functions and VOs are made available to/by application developers (see Figure 2).

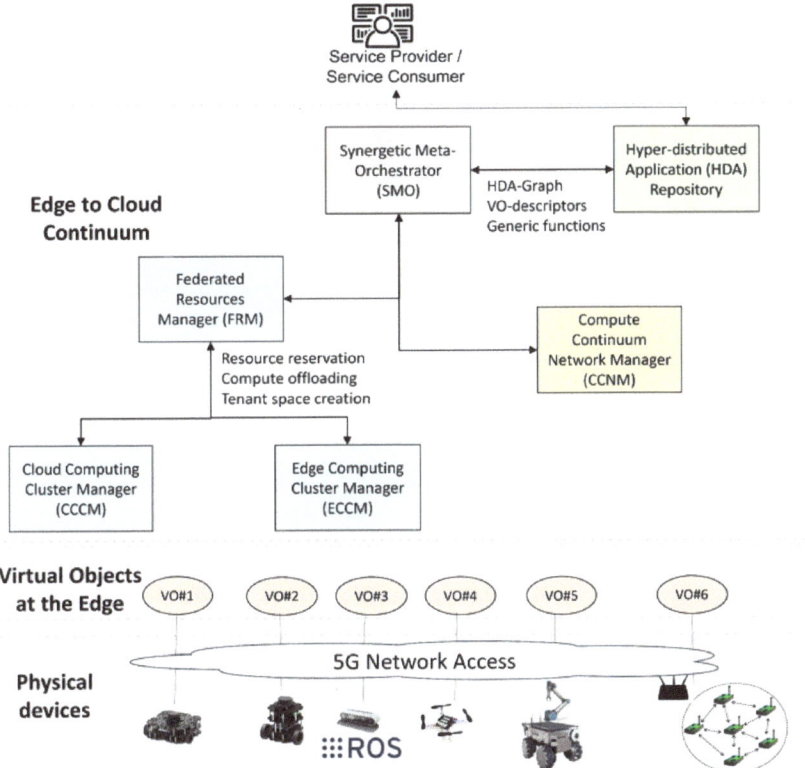

Figure 2. NEPHELE's high-level architecture. Three layers are foreseen: a physical devices layer, with all the IoT devices (e.g., robots, drones, and sensors) connected over a wireless network to the platform; a virtual objects layer at the edge, with the virtual representation of the physical devices as a VO; edge-to-cloud continuum with a set of logic blocks for cloud and networking resource management and the orchestration of the application components.

The NEPHELE outcomes are going to be demonstrated, validated and evaluated in a set of use cases across various vertical industries, including areas such as disaster management as presented in this paper, logistic operations in ports, energy management in smart buildings and remote healthcare services.

4.1. The Search and Rescue Use Case in NEPHELE

For the specific use case discussed in this paper, we foresee a service provider which defines the logic of a SAR application to be deployed and executed over the NEPHELE platform. The application logic is represented as an HDA graph which will be available on the NEPHELE HDA repository (see Figure 2). The application logic will define the high-level goal and the key performance indicator (KPI) requirements for the application. To run and deploy the HDA represented by the graph, some input parameters will be given, such as the time, zone, and area to be covered. The application graph will foresee the use of one or more VOs as representative of IoT devices such as robots or sensors and one or more generic functions to support the application (see Figure 3). This latter will support the SAR operations with movement, sensing and mapping capabilities and may be provided through the service mesh approach that enables managed, observable and secure communication across the involved microservices. The VO description required by the SAR HDA graph to be deployed at the edge of the infrastructure will also be available on the NEPHELE repository. In Figure 3, we also see highlighted the different levels of the VOStack and their matching to the SAR application components/microservices.

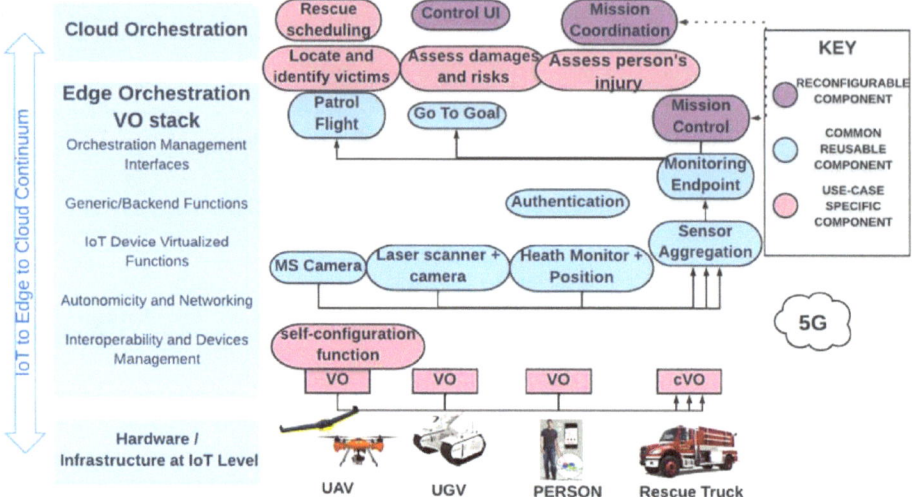

Figure 3. VOStack mapping to SAR application scenarios. Hyperdistributed applications are formed of multiple components that are either use-case specific or generic or reconfigurable. These components are placed on different levels of the IoT-to-edge-to-cloud continuum and based on their functionalities are part of the different layers of the VOStack.

We foresee a service consumer (e.g., a firefighter brigade) owning a set of physical devices (robots, drones and sensors). These devices are ready to be used with some basic software components running and connected to a local network, e.g., a 5G access point. As for the software components already deployed on the robots, we foresee the ROS environment correctly set up, with some basic ROS components already running. The sensors can be either pre-deployed in the area or carried by firefighter personnel. When a SAR mission is started, the Service Consumer connects to the NEPHELE HDA repository and looks for the HDA to deploy and provides the input data that are required. Then, the following operations will have to be initiated by the NEPHELE platform (see Figure 2 for reference of the building blocks):

1. The synergetic meta-orchestrator (SMO) receives the HDA graph, the set of parameters for the specific instance of the SAR application, the VO descriptors needed for the application and a descriptor of the supportive functions to be deployed in the continuum. The supportive functions are provided by the VOStack and can be, for instance, risk assessments, mission control with task prioritization and optimized planning, health monitoring based on AI and computer vision, predictions of dangerous events, the localization and identification of victims, and so on. The SMO will interact with the federated resources manager and the compute continuum network manager to deploy the networking, computing and storage resource over the continuum according to the requirements derived from the HDA graph, the VO descriptors and the input parameters given by the service consumer;

    a. The federated resources manager (FRM) orchestrator will ensure that the application components will be deployed either on the edge or on the cloud based on the computational and storage resources needed for the application components and the overall resource availability. For instance, large data amounts used to replay some actions from robots paired with depth images of the surroundings (e.g., using rosbags) can be stored on the remote cloud. On the other hand, maps to be navigated by the robot could be stored at the edge for further action planning. Similarly, computation can be performed on the edge for identifying imminent danger situations or planning a robotic arm movement so that low delay is guaranteed, whereas complex mission optimization and prioritization computations can be performed in the cloud, and the needed resources should be allocated. The FRM will produce a deployment plan that will be provided to the compute continuum network manager;

    i. The cloud computing cluster manager (CCCM) is responsible for the cloud deployments and interaction with the edge computing cluster manager (ECCM) (e.g., reserve resources, create tenant spaces at the edge and compute offloading mechanisms);

    ii. The edge computing cluster manager (ECCM) is responsible for the edge deployments, providing feedback on the application component and resource status; it receives inputs for compute offloading. Moreover, the ECCM will orchestrate the VOs that are part of the HDA graph and synchronize the device updates from IoT devices to edge nodes and vice versa.

  b. The compute continuum network manager (CCNM) will receive the deployment plan from the FRM to set up the network resources needed for the different application components for end-to-end network connectivity and meet the networking requirements for the application across the compute continuum. Exploiting 5G technologies, a network slice based on the bandwidth requirements for each robotic device will be the output of the CCNM. Each network slice will ensure it meets the QoS requirements and service level agreements for the given application.

2. Once the VOs are deployed, a southbound interface for VO-to-IoT device interactions will be used to interoperate with the physical devices (i.e., robots, drones and sensor gateways). The VO will have knowledge on how to communicate with the IoT devices (i.e., robots, sensor gateways), as this will be stored and available on the VO storage. We assume the IoT devices to be up and running with their basic services and to be connected to the network;

3. Physical robots and sensor networks will communicate with each other through the corresponding VOs using a peer interface, whereas the application component that will use the data stream from the VOs will use the Northbound interface. Application components such as map merging, decision-making, health monitoring, etc., will interact with the VOs to exchange relative information;

4. The deployed VOs will use the Northbound interface to interact with the orchestrator for monitoring and scaling requests when, for instance, more robots are needed to cover a given area.

The SAR HDA application will have a classic three-tier architecture with a presentation tier, an application tier and a data tier all implemented with a service mesh approach for the on-demand activation of generic/supportive functions for the hyper-distributed application.

Presentation tier: the application will foresee a frontend for visualization and mission control by the end-user. A mission-specific dashboard will provide real-time situational awareness (i.e., a 3D map with the location of robots, rescue team members, victims and threats) to take well-informed confident decisions. The dashboard integrates data coming from heterogeneous sensors and equipment (e.g., drones, mobile robots). This will be accessible through a web browser or a graphical user interface (GUI) remotely and enable the service consumer to interact with the application tier to take mission decisions, trigger tasks that have been suggested by the automized application tier and analyze historic data for further information collection and situational awareness.

Application tier: the inputs and requests coming from the presentation tier are collected and the application components are activated to execute mission tasks. All application components for supporting the application logic are foreseen and run on the different layers of the continuum. As an example, localization functions and camera streaming will run directly on the robots/drones. Three-dimensional SLAM solutions and video analysis will run on the edge in cases where the IoT devices (i.e., robots and drones) do not have the required resources. Other more advanced and computationally demanding functions and components will instead run on the cloud (or edge) through VO-supportive functions. Examples of these are AI algorithms for mission control, risk assessment, danger prediction, optimization problems for path planning, and so on. In all of these components, new data can be produced, and old data can be accessed from the data tier.

Data tier: this foresees a storage element for storing processed images or historical data about the SAR mission. The data produced by the IoT devices (drones, robots, sensors) will be compressed, downsampled and/or secured before being stored for future use by the application tier. These functions on the data will be running, if possible, on the drones and robots themselves, to reduce the data transmissions. Data analysis and complex information extraction will be offered by support functions from the VO. The data can be either stored on the VO data storage or on remotely distributed storage.

4.2. NEPHELE's Added Value

The implementation of the described use case will demonstrate several benefits obtained with the NEPHELE innovation and research activities. Most importantly, they will help in coping with the identified challenges for the SAR operations and take important steps in meeting the overall high-level goal of improving situational awareness for first responders in cases of natural or human disasters. The benefits deriving from the solutions proposed in NEPHELE can be summarized in the following points.

1. **Reduced delay in time-critical missions**: by exploiting compute and storage resources at the edge of the networks, with the possibility of the dynamic adaptation of the application components deployment over the continuum, lower delays will be expected for computationally demanding tasks on a large amount of data. This will be of high importance as it will strongly enhance first responders' effectiveness and security in their operations;
2. **Efficient data management**: a large amount of data available and collected by sensors, drones and robots will be filtered, compressed and analyzed by exploiting supportive functions made available by the VOStack in NEPHELE. Only a subset of the produced data will be stored for future reuse based on data importance. This will reduce the bandwidth needed for communications from the incident area to the applications layers that introduce intelligence into the application and by this reduce the delay in communication and the risk of starvation in terms of networking resources;
3. **Robot fleet management and trajectory optimization**: exploiting the IoT-to-edge-to-cloud compute continuum, smart decisions will be taken and advanced algorithms will be provided for optimal robot and drone trajectory planning in multi-robot environments. Solutions will rely on AI techniques able to learn from what fleets robots see in their environment and enable semantic navigation with time-optimized trajectories;
4. **Rescue operations prioritization**: AI techniques and optimization algorithms can elaborate the high amount of data and information collected from the intervention area to support rescue teams in giving priorities to the intervention tasks. The compute continuum will enable computationally heavy and complex decisions in a dynamic environment where risk prediction and assessment, victims' health monitoring and victim identification may produce new information continuously and new decisions should be triggered;

5. **HW-agnostic deployment**: the introduction of the VO concept and the multilevel meta-orchestration open for device-independent deployment and bootstrapping using generic HW. Different software components of an HDA can be deployed at every level of the IoT-to-edge-to-cloud continuum, which reduces the HW requirements (e.g., in computation and storage) at the IoT level for enabling a given application;
6. **AI for computer vision and image processing**: advanced AI algorithms can be deployed as part of the supportive functions made available through the VOSstack innovation from NEPHELE. These can then be enabled on demand and deployed over the compute continuum for image and analysis and computer vision to locate and identify victims and perform risk assessments and predictions;
7. **End-to-end security**: IoT devices and HDA users will benefit from the security and authentication, authorization, and accounting (AAA) functionalities offered by the NEPHELE framework. These functions will be offered as support functions for the VOs representing the IoT devices and will help in controlling access to the services, authorization, enforcing policies and identifying users and devices;
8. **Optimal network resource orchestration**: based on the HDA requirements, an optimized network resource allocation policy will be enforced over the IoT-to-edge-to-cloud continuum. Here, the experience in network slicing and software-defined networking (SDN) will be exploited to be able to support time-critical applications such as the SAR operations presented in this paper.

To summarize, the NEPHELE framework will enable and support the integration of different technologies and solutions over the cloud-to-edge-to-IoT continuum. Indeed, combining all these elements into a single framework represents a breakthrough advance in the cloud-to-edge-to-IoT continuum-based applications. Better performance and enhanced situational awareness in SAR operations are nicely paired with advanced technological solutions offering smart decision-making and optimization techniques for mission control and robotic applications in mobile environments.

5. Conclusions

In this paper, it has been discussed how the cloud-to-edge-to-IoT compute continuum can support SAR operations in cases of natural and human disasters. Augmented computing, networking, and storage resources from the "remote brain" in the edge/cloud can strongly enhance the situational awareness of the first responders. An analysis of current challenges with respect to the technology used in SAR operations has been presented with an overview of advanced solutions that may be adopted in these scenarios. The NEPHELE project and its main concepts were introduced as an enabler for cloud/edge robotics applications with low delay requirements and mission control to enhance the situational awareness of first responders. With the proposed solutions, network, storage, and computation resources can be dynamically allocated through advanced techniques such as network slicing. The orchestration and smart placement of application components exploiting AI models will enable adaptation to current status and dynamics factors. The VOStack in the NEPHELE project will enable the elaboration of data effectively and efficiently with supportive functions tailored to the specific use-case requirement.

Our future work will consist of the implementation of a hyper-distributed application that demonstrates the benefits described in the paper for a post-earthquake scenario in a port. In such a scenario, we can imagine that the network infrastructure is down, the map of the port is not reliable due to collapsed infrastructure and buildings and several dangerous factors (e.g., containers with dangerous materials or at risk of collapsing) are of high risk for the SAR operations. It will be an ROS application for multiple robots and drones that enables the dynamic mapping of an unknown area. AI and computer vision models will be used for object detection and victim identification in the area and to update the map of the post-disaster scenario. Advanced data aggregation solutions will be investigated including consensus-based solutions as proposed, e.g., in [73] to extract information from a wide set of different sources in an efficient and effective manner. The extracted information will be used for mission control purposes, for priority definition in the SAR tasks and the assessment of risks and the health of victims. For integration with the NEPHELE framework, virtualization techniques and cloud-native technologies will be adopted.

Author Contributions: Conceptualization, L.M., G.T. and N.M.; writing—original draft preparation, L.M. and A.A.; writing—review and editing, L.M., A.A., G.T. and N.M.; funding acquisition, L.M., N.M. and G.T. All authors have read and agreed to the published version of the manuscript.

Funding: This research was funded by the European Union's Horizon Europe research and innovation program under grant agreement No 101070487. Views and opinions expressed are however those of the authors only and do not necessarily reflect those of the European Union. The European Union cannot be held responsible for them.

Data Availability Statement: Not applicable.

Conflicts of Interest: The authors declare no conflict of interest.

References

1. Ochoa, S.F.; Santos, R. Human-Centric Wireless Sensor Networks to Improve Information Availability during Urban Search and Rescue Activities. *Inf. Fusion* **2015**, *22*, 71–84. [CrossRef]
2. Choong, Y.Y.; Dawkins, S.T.; Furman, S.M.; Greene, K.; Prettyman, S.S.; Theofanos, M.F. *Voices of First Responders—Identifying Public Safety Communication Problems: Findings from User-Centered Interviews*; National Institute of Standards and Technology: Gaithersburg, MD, USA, 2018; Volume 1.
3. Saffre, F.; Hildmann, H.; Karvonen, H.; Lind, T. Self-swarming for multi-robot systems deployed for situational awareness. In *New Developments and Environmental Applications of Drones*; Springer: Cham, Switzerland, 2022; pp. 51–72.
4. Queralta, J.P.; Raitoharju, J.; Gia, T.N.; Passalis, N.; Westerlund, T. Autosos: Towards multi-uav systems supporting maritime search and rescue with lightweight ai and edge computing. *arXiv* **2020**, arXiv:2005.03409.
5. Al-Khafajiy, M.; Baker, T.; Hussien, A.; Cotgrave, A. UAV and fog computing for IoE-based systems: A case study on environment disasters prediction and recovery plans. In *Unmanned Aerial Vehicles in Smart Cities*; Springer: Cham, Switzerland, 2020; pp. 133–152.
6. Alsamhi, S.H.; Almalki, F.A.; AL-Dois, H.; Shvetsov, A.V.; Ansari, M.S.; Hawbani, A.; Gupta, S.K.; Lee, B. Multi-Drone Edge Intelligence and SAR Smart Wearable Devices for Emergency Communication. *Wirel. Commun. Mob. Comput.* **2021**, 1–12. [CrossRef]
7. Goldberg, K.; Siegwart, R. *Beyond Webcams: An Introduction to Online Robots*; MIT Press: Cambridge, MA, USA, 2002.
8. Inaba, M.; Kagami, S.; Kanehiro, F.; Hoshino, Y.; Inoue, H. A Platform for Robotics Research Based on the Remote-Brained Robot Approach. *Int. J. Robot. Res.* **2000**, *19*, 933–954. [CrossRef]
9. Waibel, M.; Beetz, M.; Civera, J.; D'Andrea, R.; Elfring, J.; Gálvez-López, D.; Haussermann, K.; Janssen, R.; Montiel, J.; Perzylo, A.; et al. Roboearth. *IEEE Robot. Autom. Mag.* **2011**, *18*, 69–82.
10. Tenorth, M.; Beetz, M. KnowRob: A knowledge processing infrastructure for cognition-enabled robots. *Int. J. Robot. Res.* **2013**, *32*, 566–590. [CrossRef]
11. Arumugam, R.; Enti, V.R.; Bingbing, L.; Xiaojun, W.; Baskaran, V.; Kong, F.F.; Kumar, A.S.; Meng, K.D.; Kit, G.W. DAvinCi: A Cloud Computing Framework for Service Robots. In Proceedings of the 2010 IEEE International Conference on Robotics and Automation, Anchorage, AK, USA, 3–7 May 2010; pp. 3084–3089.
12. Saxena, A.; Jain, A.; Sener, O.; Jami, A.; Misra, D.K.; Koppula, H.S. Robobrain: Large-scale Knowledge Engine for Robots. *arXiv* **2014**, arXiv:1412.0691.
13. Ichnowski, J.; Chen, K.; Dharmarajan, K.; Adebola, S.; Danielczuk, M.; Mayoral-Vilches, V.; Zhan, H.; Xu, D.; Kubiatowicz, J.; Stoica, I.; et al. FogROS 2: An Adaptive and Extensible Platform for Cloud and Fog Robotics Using ROS 2. *arXiv* **2022**, arXiv:2205.09778.
14. Amazon RoboMaker. Available online: https://aws.amazon.com/robomaker/ (accessed on 29 November 2018).
15. Shi, W.; Cao, J.; Zhang, Q.; Li, Y.; Xu, L. Edge Computing: Vision and Challenges. *IEEE Internet Things J.* **2016**, *3*, 637–646. [CrossRef]
16. Mouradian, C.; Naboulsi, D.; Yangui, S.; Glitho, R.H.; Morrow, M.J.; Polakos, P.A. A Comprehensive Survey on Fog Computing: State-of-the-Art and Research Challenges. *IEEE Commun. Surv. Tutor.* **2017**, *20*, 416–464.
17. Groshev, M.; Baldoni, G.; Cominardi, L.; De la Oliva, A.; Gazda, R. Edge Robotics: Are We Ready? An Experimental Evaluation of Current Vision and Future Directions. *Digit. Commun. Netw.* **2022**, *in press*. [CrossRef]
18. Huang, P.; Zeng, L.; Chen, X.; Luo, K.; Zhou, Z.; Yu, S. Edge Robotics: Edge-Computing-Accelerated Multi-Robot Simultaneous Localization and Mapping. *IEEE Internet Things J.* **2022**, *9*, 14087–14102. [CrossRef]
19. Xu, J.; Cao, H.; Li, D.; Huang, K.; Qian, H.; Shangguan, L.; Yang, Z. Edge Assisted Mobile Semantic Visual SLAM. In Proceedings of the IEEE INFOCOM 2020—IEEE Conference on Computer Communications, Toronto, ON, Canada, 6–9 July 2020; pp. 1828–1837.

20. McEnroe, P.; Wang, S.; Liyanage, M. A Survey on the Convergence of Edge Computing and AI for UAVs: Opportunities and Challenges. *IEEE Internet Things J.* **2022**, *9*, 15435–15459. [CrossRef]
21. SHERPA. Available online: http://www.sherpa-fp7-project.eu/ (accessed on 19 January 2023).
22. RESPOND-A. Available online: https://robotnik.eu/projects/respond-a-en/ (accessed on 19 January 2023).
23. Delmerico, J.; Mintchev, S.; Giusti, A.; Gromov, B.; Melo, K.; Horvat, T.; Cadena, C.; Hutter, M.; Ijspeert, A.; Floreano, D.; et al. The Current State and Future Outlook of Rescue Robotics. *J. Field Robot.* **2019**, *36*, 1171–1191. [CrossRef]
24. Bravo-Arrabal, J.; Toscano-Moreno, M.; Fernandez-Lozano, J.; Mandow, A.; Gomez-Ruiz, A.J.; García-Cerezo, A. The Internet of Cooperative Agents Architecture (X-IoCA) for Robots, Hybrid Sensor Networks, and MEC Centers in Complex Environments: A Search and Rescue Case Study. *Sensors* **2021**, *21*, 7843. [CrossRef] [PubMed]
25. Kimovski, D.; Mehran, N.; Kerth, C.E.; Prodan, R. Mobility-Aware IoT Applications Placement in the Cloud Edge Continuum. *IEEE Trans. Serv. Comput.* **2022**, *15*, 3358–3371. [CrossRef]
26. Peltonen, E.; Sojan, A.; Paivarinta, T. Towards Real-time Learning for Edge-Cloud Continuum with Vehicular Computing. In Proceedings of the 2021 IEEE 7th World Forum on Internet of Things (WF-IoT), New Orleans, LA, USA, 14 June–31 July 2021; pp. 921–926.
27. Mygdalis, V.; Carnevale, L.; Martinez-De-Dios, J.R.; Shutin, D.; Aiello, G.; Villari, M.; Pitas, I. OTE: Optimal Trustworthy EdgeAI Solutions for Smart Cities. In Proceedings of the 2022 22nd IEEE International Symposium on Cluster, Cloud and Internet Computing (CCGrid), Taormina, Italy, 16–19 May 2022; pp. 842–850.
28. Hu, X.; Wong, K.; Zhang, Y. Wireless-Powered Edge Computing with Cooperative UAV: Task, Time Scheduling and Trajectory Design. *IEEE Trans. Wirel. Commun.* **2020**, *19*, 8083–8098. [CrossRef]
29. Bacchiani, L.; De Palma, G.; Sciullo, L.; Bravetti, M.; Di Felice, M.; Gabbrielli, M.; Zavattaro, G.; Della Penna, R. Low-Latency Anomaly Detection on the Edge-Cloud Continuum for Industry 4.0 Applications: The SEAWALL Case Study. *IEEE Internet Things Mag.* **2022**, *5*, 32–37. [CrossRef]
30. Wang, N.; Varghese, B. Context-aware distribution of fog applications using deep reinforcement learning. *J. Netw. Comput. Appl.* **2022**, *203*, 103354–103368. [CrossRef]
31. Dobrescu, R.; Merezeanu, D.; Mocanu, S. Context-aware control and monitoring system with IoT and cloud support. *Comput. Electron. Agric.* **2019**, *160*, 91–99. [CrossRef]
32. Zhao, X.; Yuan, P.; Li, H.; Tang, S. Collaborative Edge Caching in Context-Aware Device-to-Device Networks. *IEEE Trans. Veh. Technol.* **2018**, *67*, 9583–9596. [CrossRef]
33. Tran, T.X.; Hajisami, A.; Pandey, P.; Pompili, D. Collaborative Mobile Edge Computing in 5G Networks: New Paradigms, Scenarios, and Challenges. *IEEE Commun. Mag.* **2017**, *55*, 54–61. [CrossRef]
34. Lee, J.; Lee, J. Hierarchical Mobile Edge Computing Architecture Based on Context Awareness. *Appl. Sci.* **2018**, *8*, 1160. [CrossRef]
35. Cheng, Z.; Gao, Z.; Liwang, M.; Huang, L.; Du, X.; Guizani, M. Intelligent Task Offloading and Energy Allocation in the UAV-Aided Mobile Edge-Cloud Continuum. *IEEE Netw.* **2021**, *35*, 42–49. [CrossRef]
36. Rosenberger, P.; Gerhard, D. Context-awareness in Industrial Applications: Definition, Classification and Use Case. In Proceedings of the 51st Conference on Manufacturing Systems (CIRP), Stockholm, Sweden, 16–18 May 2018; pp. 1172–1177.
37. Waharte, S.; Trigoni, N. Supporting Search and Rescue Operations with UAVs. In Proceedings of the 2010 International Conference on Emerging Security Technologies, Canterbury, UK, 6–7 September 2010; pp. 142–147.
38. Sibanyoni, S.V.; Ramotsoela, D.T.; Silva, B.J.; Hancke, G.P. A 2-D Acoustic Source Localization System for Drones in Search and Rescue Missions. *IEEE Sens. J.* **2018**, *19*, 332–341. [CrossRef]
39. Manamperi, W.; Abhayapala, T.D.; Zhang, J.; Samarasinghe, P.N. Drone Audition: Sound Source Localization Using On-Board Microphones. *IEEE/ACM Trans. Audio Speech Lang. Process.* **2022**, *30*, 508–519. [CrossRef]
40. Sambolek, S.; Ivasic-Kos, M. Automatic Person Detection in Search and Rescue Operations Using Deep CNN Detectors. *IEEE Access* **2021**, *9*, 37905–37922. [CrossRef]
41. Albanese, A.; Sciancalepore, V.; Costa-Perez, X. SARDO: An Automated Search-and-Rescue Drone-Based Solution for Victims Localization. *IEEE Trans. Mob. Comput.* **2021**, *21*, 3312–3325. [CrossRef]
42. Queralta, J.P.; Taipalmaa, J.; Can Pullinen, B.; Sarker, V.K.; Nguyen Gia, T.; Tenhunen, H.; Gabbouj, M.; Raitoharju, J.; Westerlund, T. Collaborative Multi-Robot Search and Rescue: Planning, Coordination, Perception, and Active Vision. *IEEE Access* **2020**, *8*, 191617–191643. [CrossRef]
43. Chen, X.; Zhang, H.; Lu, H.; Xiao, J.; Qiu, Q.; Li, Y. Robust SLAM System Based on Monocular Vision and LiDAR for Robotic Urban Search and Rescue. In Proceedings of the 2017 IEEE International Symposium on Safety, Security and Rescue Robotics (SSRR), Shanghai, China, 11–13 October 2017; pp. 41–47.
44. Murphy, R.; Dreger, K.; Newsome, S.; Rodocker, J.; Slaughter, B.; Smith, R.; Steimle, E.; Kimura, T.; Makabe, K.; Kon, K.; et al. Marine Heterogeneous Multi-Robot Systems at the Great Eastern Japan Tsunami Recovery. *J. Field Robot.* **2012**, *29*, 819–831. [CrossRef]
45. Silvagni, M.; Tonoli, A.; Zenerino, E.; Chiaberge, M. Multipurpose UAV for search and rescue operations in mountain avalanche events. *Geomat. Nat. Hazards Risk* **2016**, *8*, 18–33. [CrossRef]
46. Konyo, M. Impact-TRC Thin Serpentine Robot Platform for Urban Search and Rescue. In *Disaster Robotics*; Springer: Cham, Switzerland, 2019; pp. 25–76.

47. Han, S.; Chon, S.; Kim, J.; Seo, J.; Shin, D.G.; Park, S.; Kim, J.T.; Kim, J.; Jin, M.; Cho, J. Snake Robot Gripper Module for Search and Rescue in Narrow Spaces. *IEEE Robot. Autom. Lett.* **2022**, *7*, 1667–1673. [CrossRef]
48. Liu, K.; Zhou, X.; Zhao, B.; Ou, H.; Chen, B.M. An Integrated Visual System for Unmanned Aerial Vehicles Following Ground Vehicles: Simulations and Experiments. In Proceedings of the 2022 IEEE 17th International Conference on Control & Automation (ICCA), Naples, Italy, 27–30 June 2022; pp. 593–598.
49. Jorge, V.A.M.; Granada, R.; Maidana, R.G.; Jurak, D.A.; Heck, G.; Negreiros, A.P.F.; dos Santos, D.H.; Gonçalves, L.M.G.; Amory, A.M. A Survey on Unmanned Surface Vehicles for Disaster Robotics: Main Challenges and Directions. *Sensors* **2019**, *19*, 702. [CrossRef] [PubMed]
50. Mezghani, F.; Mitton, N. Opportunistic disaster recovery. *Internet Technol. Lett.* **2018**, *1*, e29. [CrossRef]
51. Mezghani, F.; Kortoci, P.; Mitton, N.; Di Francesco, M. A Multi-tier Communication Scheme for Drone-assisted Disaster Recovery Scenarios. In Proceedings of the 2019 IEEE 30th Annual International Symposium on Personal, Indoor and Mobile Radio Communications (PIMRC), Istanbul, Turkey, 8–11 September 2019; pp. 1–7.
52. Jeong, I.C.; Bychkov, D.; Searson, P.C. Wearable Devices for Precision Medicine and Health State Monitoring. *IEEE Trans. Biomed. Eng.* **2018**, *66*, 1242–1258. [CrossRef]
53. Kasnesis, P.; Doulgerakis, V.; Uzunidis, D.; Kogias, D.; Funcia, S.; González, M.; Giannousis, C.; Patrikakis, C. Deep Learning Empowered Wearable-Based Behavior Recognition for Search and Rescue Dogs. *Sensors* **2022**, *22*, 993. [CrossRef]
54. Arkin, R.; Balch, T. Cooperative Multiagent Robotic Systems. In *Artificial Intelligence and Mobile Robots*; Kortenkamp, D., Bonasso, R.P., Murphy, R., Eds.; MIT Press: Cambridge, MA, USA, 1998.
55. Rocha, R.; Dias, J.; Carvalho, A. Cooperative multi-robot systems: A study of vision-based 3-D mapping using information theory. *Robot. Auton. Syst.* **2005**, *53*, 282–311. [CrossRef]
56. Singh, A.; Krause, A.; Guestrin, C.; Kaiser, W.J. Efficient Informative Sensing using Multiple Robots. *J. Artif. Intell. Res.* **2009**, *34*, 707–755. [CrossRef]
57. Schmid, L.M.; Pantic, M.; Khanna, R.; Ott, L.; Siegwart, R.; Nieto, J. An Efficient Sampling-Based Method for Online Informative Path Planning in Unknown Environments. *IEEE Robot. Autom. Lett.* **2020**, *5*, 1500–1507. [CrossRef]
58. Fung, N.; Rogers, J.; Nieto, C.; Christensen, H.; Kemna, S.; Sukhatme, G. Coordinating Multi-Robot Systems Through Environment Partitioning for Adaptive Informative Sampling. In Proceedings of the 2019 International Conference on Robotics and Automation (ICRA), Montreal, QC, Canada, 20–24 May 2019.
59. Hawes, N.; Burbridge, C.; Jovan, F.; Kunze, L.; Lacerda, B.; Mudrova, L.; Young, J.; Wyatt, J.; Hebesberger, D.; Kortner, T.; et al. The STRANDS Project: Long-Term Autonomy in Everyday Environments. *IEEE Robot. Autom. Mag.* **2017**, *24*, 146–156.
60. Singh, A.; Krause, A.; Guestrin, C.; Kaiser, W.; Batalin, M. Efficient Planning of Informative Paths for Multiple Robots. In Proceedings of the 20th International Joint Conference on Artificial Intelligence, Hyderabad, India, 6–12 January 2007.
61. Ma, K.; Ma, Z.; Liu, L.; Sukhatme, G.S. Multi-robot Informative and Adaptive Planning for Persistent Environmental Monitoring. In Proceedings of the 13th International Symposium on Distributed Autonomous Robotic Systems, DARS, Montbéliard, France, 28–30 November 2016.
62. Manjanna, S.; Dudek, G. Data-driven selective sampling for marine vehicles using multi-scale paths. In Proceedings of the 2017 IEEE/RSJ International Conference on Intelligent Robots and Systems (IROS), Vancouver, BC, Canada, 24–28 September 2017.
63. Salam, T.; Hsieh, M.A. Adaptive Sampling and Reduced-Order Modeling of Dynamic Processes by Robot Teams. *IEEE Robot. Autom. Lett.* **2019**, *4*, 477–484. [CrossRef]
64. Euler, J.; Von Stryk, O. Optimized Vehicle-Specific Trajectories for Cooperative Process Estimation by Sensor-Equipped UAVs. In Proceedings of the 2017 IEEE International Conference on Robotics and Automation (ICRA), Singapore, 29 May 2017–3 June 2017.
65. Gonzalez-De-Santos, P.; Ribeiro, A.; Fernandez-Quintanilla, C.; Lopez-Granados, F.; Brandstoetter, M.; Tomic, S.; Pedrazzi, S.; Peruzzi, A.; Pajares, G.; Kaplanis, G.; et al. Fleets of robots for environmentally-safe pest control in agriculture. *Precis. Agric.* **2016**, *18*, 574–614. [CrossRef]
66. Tourrette, T.; Deremetz, M.; Naud, O.; Lenain, R.; Laneurit, J.; De Rudnicki, V. Close Coordination of Mobile Robots Using Radio Beacons: A New Concept Aimed at Smart Spraying in Agriculture. In Proceedings of the IEEE/RSJ International Conference on Intelligent Robots and Systems (IROS), Madrid, Spain, 1–5 October 2018; pp. 7727–7734.
67. Merino, L.; Caballero, F.; Martinez-de-Dios, J.R.; Maza, I.; Ollero, A. An Unmanned Aerial System for Automatic Forest Fire Monitoring and Measurement. *J. Intell. Robot. Syst.* **2012**, *65*, 533–548. [CrossRef]
68. Haksar, R.N.; Trimpe, S.; Schwager, M. Spatial Scheduling of Informative Meetings for Multi-Agent Persistent Coverage. *IEEE Robot. Autom. Lett.* **2020**, *5*, 3027–3034. [CrossRef]
69. Cadena, C.; Carlone, L.; Carrillo, H.; Latif, Y.; Scaramuzza, D.; Neira, J.; Reid, I.; Leonard, J.J. Past, Present, and Future of Simultaneous Localization and Mapping: Toward the Robust-Perception Age. *IEEE Trans. Robot.* **2016**, *32*, 1309–1332. [CrossRef]
70. Bresson, G.; Alsayed, Z.; Yu, L.; Glaser, S. Simultaneous Localization and Mapping: A Survey of Current Trends in Autonomous Driving. *IEEE Trans. Intell. Veh.* **2017**, *2*, 194–220. [CrossRef]
71. De Jesus, K.J.; Kobs, H.J.; Cukla, A.R.; De Souza Leite Cuadros, M.A.; Tello Gamarra, D.F. Comparison of Visual SLAM Algorithms ORB-SLAM2, RTAB-Map and SPTAM in Internal and External Environments with ROS. In Proceedings of the 2021 Latin American Robotics Symposium (LARS), 2021 Brazilian Symposium on Robotics (SBR), and 2021 Workshop on Robotics in Education (WRE), Natal, Brazil, 11–15 October 2021.

72. Benavidez, P.; Muppidi, M.; Rad, P.; Prevost, J.J.; Jamshidi, M.; Brown, L. Cloud-based Real Time Robotic Visual SLAM. In Proceedings of the 2015 Annual IEEE Systems Conference (SysCon) Proceedings, Vancouver, BC, Canada, 13–16 April 2015.
73. Wu, J.; Wang, S.; Chiclana, F.; Herrera-Viedma, E. Two-Fold Personalized Feedback Mechanism for Social Network Consensus by Uninorm Interval Trust Propagation. *IEEE Trans. Cybern.* **2022**, *52*, 11081–11092. [CrossRef]

Disclaimer/Publisher's Note: The statements, opinions and data contained in all publications are solely those of the individual author(s) and contributor(s) and not of MDPI and/or the editor(s). MDPI and/or the editor(s) disclaim responsibility for any injury to people or property resulting from any ideas, methods, instructions or products referred to in the content.

 *future internet*

Article

Vision, Enabling Technologies, and Scenarios for a 6G-Enabled Internet of Verticals (6G-IoV)

Maziar Nekovee * and Ferheen Ayaz

6G Lab, Centre for Advanced Communications, Mobile Technology and IoT,
School of Engineering and Informatics, University of Sussex, Brighton BN1 9RH, UK
* Correspondence: m.nekovee@sussex.ac.uk

Abstract: 5G is the critical mobile infrastructure required to both enable and accelerate the full digital transformation of vertical sectors. While the 5G for vertical sectors is aiming at connectivity requirements of specific verticals, such as manufacturing, automotive and energy, we envisage that in the longer term the expansion of wide area cellular connectivity to these sectors will pave the way for a transformation to a new Internet of Verticals (IoV) in the 6G era, which we call 6G-IoV. In this paper, we describe our vision of 6G-IoV and examine its emerging and future architectural and networking enablers. We then illustrate our vision by describing a number of future scenarios of the 6G-IoV, namely the Internet of Cloud Manufacturing accounting for around 25% of digital services and products, the Internet of Robotics to cater the challenges of the growing number of robotics and expected 7% increase in usage over the coming years and the Internet of Smart Energy Grids for net-zero energy balance and shifting to 100% dependence on the renewables of energy generation.

Keywords: 5G; 6G; IP communication; determinism networking; reliability; semantic communications; non-terrestrial networks; artificial intelligence; internet of verticals; cloud manufacturing; robotics; smart energy grids; semantic communications; internet of space

Citation: Nekovee, M.; Ayaz, F. Vision, Enabling Technologies, and Scenarios for a 6G-Enabled Internet of Verticals (6G-IoV). *Future Internet* 2023, 15, 57. https://doi.org/10.3390/fi15020057

Academic Editors: Alessandro Raschellà and Michael Mackay

Received: 19 December 2022
Revised: 20 January 2023
Accepted: 23 January 2023
Published: 30 January 2023

Copyright: © 2023 by the authors. Licensee MDPI, Basel, Switzerland. This article is an open access article distributed under the terms and conditions of the Creative Commons Attribution (CC BY) license (https://creativecommons.org/licenses/by/4.0/).

1. Introduction

The 5G in conjunction with IoT, AI and Cloud technologies will drive a significant digital transformation to fulfill the requirements of the fully connected, digitalized carbon-neutral society and industries [1]. Unlike the previous generations, 5G is offering not only ultrafast (20 Gbps peak data-rates) but also ultra-reliable, ultra-low-latency (1 ms) and massive connectivity capabilities. In comparison with the previous generations, 5G also comes with significant architectural innovations including network slicing, private networks, and edge computing/edge-AI [1]. The 5G-enabled, AI-assisted IoT has the capability of connecting both digital and physical entities, giving rise to fruitful applications including smart cities, smart homes, industry 4.0 and society 5.0 [2]. Enabled by network slicing, in the 5G era, communication services are transitioning from mass connectivity provisioning to per service level and vertical customization. Edge solutions and private networks help to overcome network performance limits, e.g., in terms of latency and deterministic delivery. Local data processing enabled by 5G private networks help to achieve the stringent security and privacy requirements of vertical sectors.

Armed with the above features, 5G is proving successful as the first generation of mobile communication systems to achieve the long-anticipated expansion of operators' connectivity services into vertical sectors, enabling new types of usage and new Business-to-Business (B2B) opportunities and communities [3–5]. Prominent success story examples of 5G for verticals include smart manufacturing, industrial automation and smart grids. There is already a rapidly growing literature on requirements, challenges and solutions and achievements, both from a technology and business perspective, of 5G services expanding into vertical sectors.

5G indeed made a significant contribution towards developing low-latency networks by providing new frequency bands, such as the millimeter-wave (mmWave) spectrum, advanced spectrum usage and management in licensed and unlicensed bands and a complete redesign of the core network. However, the rapidly growing IoT networks require a data rate on the order of terabits per second, which may exceed even the capacities of the existing 5G systems. The 6G systems are being designed to meet the demands of a seamless connectivity and ubiquitous intelligence. The current research focuses on enabling communication technologies, network architectures and integrating intelligence into the 6G networks [6]. Table 1 lists the 5G and 6G research trends from 2018 to 2030, as defined in [7]. There has been very little research, however, on taking a more "transversal" view in terms of the longer-term implications in the 6G era, which will enable the transformation of multiple verticals into new services and businesses, and its impact on the vertical digital ecosystem as a whole.

Table 1. The 5G and 6G research trends from 2018 to 2030.

Year	Research Trends
2018	5G evolution
2020	6G structure and framing, 6G technology components, 6G requirements
2022	
2024	6G systemization of research
2026	
2028	6G technical standardisation
2030	6G evolution, 6G commercialisation

The purpose of this paper is to take the first step in filling this important gap. In particular, we envisage that in the longer term the convergence of 6G "networkization" of vertical sectors with their continued digitalization, and integration with AI and cloud/edge computing will pave the way for a new type of Internet, which virtualizes orchestrates and federates entire vertical entities and services, hence ushering in the era of the 6G "Internet of Verticals" (IoV). The main contributions of the paper are as follows:

1. We provide an overview of the key 5G and 6G architectural enablers that will underpin our vison of 6G IoV.
2. We describe a number of prominent IoV transformation scenarios, namely the Internet of Cloud Manufacturing, the Internet of Robotics and the Internet of Smart Energy Grids.

The rest of this paper is organized as follows. In Section 2, reviewing key architectural and networking innovations is required to support the IoV vision. We describe key IoV applications scenarios in Section 3, and conclude the paper in Section 4.

2. Technology Enablers for the Internet of Verticals

In this section, we review key technologies that undelay the architecture for our vision of the IoV. A number of these technologies are currently being developed under the umbrella of 3GPP's 5G standards, while others, with a focus on the wide area and IP networking, are in their early stages and are being made multiple standardization bodies, including 3GPP, IETF, ETSI and the ITU, as well as the research community.

2.1. Network Slicing

Network slicing [8,9] is an innovative architectural solution in 5G networks which, thanks to virtualization, allows an operator to provide multiple services with different performance characteristics. It is defined in the 3GPP Release 15 specifications. Further enhancements to network slicing are occurring in successive releases. Each network slice operates as an independent, virtualized version of the network designed to serve a defined business purpose or customer. Thus, each slice consists of all the network resources required to address the specific need. For a given application, the network slice is the only network that the application sees. The other slices, to which the application is not subscribed, are invisible and inaccessible. GSMA [9] has identified the following vertical sectors as ones that will benefit from network slicing: Augmented Reality and Virtual Reality, Automotive, Energy, Healthcare Manufacturing, Internet of Things, Public Safety, and Smart Cities.

The standardization for statically provisioned network slices has already been completed in 3GPP. However, more work is being carried out [8] to enable dynamically provisioned network slices in an SDN-type approach. A combination of specialized applications plus 5G Network Slicing and Virtual Private Network (VPN)/Virtual Routing and Forwarding (VRF) technologies could be deployed to create large extranets that would connect and federate multiple vertical slices, hence paving the way for the IoV.

Towards the 6G era, the parallel streams of Open RAN (O-RAN) and Centralized RAN (C-RAN) will be fully realized, as well as the Cell Free architecture, hence allowing RAN resources to also be fully virtualized and software-controlled. Consequently, in the 6G era, we will see full (core, transport, and RAN) slicing of mobile networks, hence enabling end-to-end slicing of the network per (vertical) service. There is a need for orchestration solutions for the networking resources associated to each slice, so they can be dynamically coordinated to meet the performance requirements of services. Several AI approaches, including Deep Reinforcement Learning (DRL), are used for automated resource orchestration. Moreover, federated learning-based DRL solutions for 6G RAN slice orchestration are proposed in the literature [10]. Network slicing is also expected to complement digital twins-based 6G systems along with other enabling technologies, such as blockchain [11].

2.2. Private (Non-Public) Networks

In the shorter term, 5G private networks can fulfil many of the requirements of Network Slicing for verticals, as well as offering additional security that cannot be provided by public networks. Private 5G networks comprise Radio Access Networks (RAN) and core elements. The 5G base station (gNB) can scale from low to high capacity and power output according to needs. They connect to private core networks (in contract to operator's public core) that provides security, authentication, session management and QoS-control. The private 5G core network could be deployed on edge compute nodes, installed locally on premises to ensure high reliability, enable low-latency, ultra-security, and privacy, or be virtualized and reside on cloud servers. In the longer term, 5G private networks may coexist with Network Slicing or they may be entirely overtaken by slicing. Global companies are quickly recognizing the potential afforded in private 5G networks, and the additional revenue streams it offers. Deloitte expects more than 200 mobile network operators investing in 5G standalone networks in 2023, which is at least double from 2022 [12]. Early adopters for private 5G networks will be large seaports, airports and other logistical hubs. The 5G Private networks are very likely to spawn the first wave of IoV with multiple private networks belonging to different verticals, and/or enterprises are linked and orchestrated together thanks to ultra-reliable, ultra-secure, and deterministic wide area networks.

2.3. Edge Computing/Edge AI

ETSI is standardizing Multi-access Edge Computing (MEC) [13], previously known as Mobile-Edge Computing, a technology that empowers a programmable application environment at the edge of the network, within the RAN. The benefits are reduced latency, more efficient network operation for certain applications, and an improved user experience.

For many vertical applications, latency will determine how close the edge servers need to be to user devices. The 5G networks are striving for 1 msec latency (round-trip time) within the network. Light travels 300 km per millisecond, so designers will need to plan their applications accordingly. Latency is critical in vehicular edge applications, specifically [14]. Moreover, a robotic controller can tolerate around four milliseconds latency (round trip) and therefore, allowing for fluctuations and processing time, MEC need to be placed as close as possible to the controller. The other consideration is the amount of data that needs transportation to MEC. For example, a factory performing AI-based video analytics of its assembly line operation may wish to conduct such calculations on a MEC at the factories' location rather than backhauling a huge amount of data to a more central operator location. The 5G standalone network architecture provides access to user data in a local environment via a distributed User Plane Function (UPF), thus enabling local data breakout and facilitating edge computing applications.

Variations of distributed AI, such as federated learning, are expected to be evolved in the future [15,16]. In the 6G era, we will see MEC integrating increasingly more secure, low-latency AI and data analytics services at the edge of the network to a host of verticals.

2.4. Wide Area Deterministic Networks

When a network can provide end-to-end ultra-reliable packet transmission with bounded small values of latency/jitter, it is said to be a deterministic network. This concept is illustrated in Figure 1. In some industry applications, the deterministic networks are also required to provide precise end-to-end time synchronization. One of the most important features of 5G is Ultra Reliable Ultra Low Latency (URLLC) communications, e.g., for smart and fully automated manufacturing. As an example, consider mobile robots such as Automatic Guided Vehicles (AGVs), which have numerous applications in the future factories. They are usually monitored and controlled by a guidance control system. The mobile network is the most promising communication technology due to the large-scale mobility of the vehicles. The communication in some mobile robot applications may require the transmission latency to be between 1 to 10 msec and jitter to be less than 50% of latency. Furthermore, the reliability is required to be above six nines (99, 9999%). Another yet more stringent example in industry is the motion control, which is responsible for controlling the moving and/or rotating parts of the machines in a critical manner.

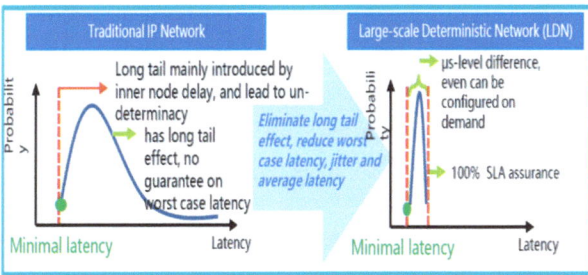

Figure 1. Latency performance of the traditional IP networks (**left**) is contrasted with the performance of future wide area/large-scale deterministic networks (**right**).

With respect to the 5G mobile networks operating on top of the TCP/IP suit of protocols, the application scenarios described above can only be realized for localized networks. The queuing in forwarding nodes may introduce large latency and jitter. The theoretical reliability of a single device is usually below six nines, which, even without packet loss, cannot meet the required reliability of the end-to-end path. For URLLC local area networking (e.g., inside a single factory plant) the Time Sensitive Networking standardized in IEEE 802.1 [17] and industrial Ethernet technologies can be used. Furthermore, staring with the Release 16, the 3GPP is progressing a new study on the NR Industrial Internet of things (IIoT), targeting the integration of the 5G and TSN networks.

However, the wide area deterministic networking for evolved vertical applications, including the distributed cloud manufacturing and wide-area smart grids, would require expanding the capabilities of TCP/IP [18,19]. The ITU-T Focus Group Technologies for Network 2030 (FG NET-2030) [18] and The ETSI Industry Specification Group on the Non-IP Networking (NIN) [19] have identified key technical issues with the current TCP/IP-based networking, which prevent it from delivering the required levels of deterministic services in a wide area and mobile networks, and are currently developing the approaches of TCP/IP evolution to address these.

2.5. Non-Terrestial Networks

From 3GPP Release 17 onwards, the 5G network architecture includes the Non-Terrestrial Networks (NTN), which include GEO, LEO and HAPS. The focus is currently on non-transparent architecture where satellites or HAPS act as "dumb" relays in the space/sky for 5G, but from Release 19 (2025) onwards, we can expect a full integration, where a satellite or HAPS will have a full gNB on board. In the 6G era, this will bring a massive change to the architecture of mobile networks with new "mobile infrastructure in the space" carried by satellites and HAPS. This will open up the extension of mobile Internet to space in the 6G era, built on a multi-tier network infrastructure architecture in the space reminiscent of Macro (GEO), Small (LEO, Femto (HAPS) networks. Besides providing ubiquitous coverage for a host of vertical applications, e.g., in areas such as transportation, supply-chain and logistics, 6G NTN will enable new "Internet of Space" applications, such as the remote command and control of spacecrafts, space robots and the Internet of Space Things, e.g., for assets in space, health and security monitoring in space and space engineering.

2.6. Semantic Communications

Semantic communication, widely regarded as a potential breakthrough in the 6G era beyond the Shannon paradigm, aims at the successful transmission of semantic information conveyed by the source rather than the accurate reception of each single symbol or bit regardless of its meaning. In contrast to the Shannon paradigm, semantic communications only transmit necessary information relevant to the specific task at the receiver. This can empower a truly intelligent and autonomous system with significant reduction in data traffic. For many vertical applications in the age of 6G empowered by artificial intelligence (AI), the agent, such as smart terminals, robot, and smart surveillance, is able to understand the scene and executes the instruction automatically using semantic communication. Hence, the technology will be widely used in the Industrial Internet, connected and autonomous driving and vehicles, and, as we describe further, for robotic communications.

3. Future Scenarios for the Internet of Verticals

3.1. The Internet of Cloud Manufactoring

Cloud manufacturing (CMfg) is an emerging manufacturing paradigm developed from existing advanced manufacturing models and enterprise information technologies with the support of cloud computing, service-oriented technologies, and advanced computing technologies. It transforms manufacturing resources and manufacturing capabilities into manufacturing services, which can be managed and operated in an intelligent and unified way to enable the full sharing and re-use of manufacturing resources and manufacturing capabilities. CMfg can provide safe and reliable, high quality, cheap and on-demand manufacturing as services. The growing use of CMfg can be realized from the fact that cloud as a digital service accounts for around 25% of the total involvements that go into complete manufactured products [20]. In the CMfg system [21], various manufacturing resources and abilities can be intelligently sensed and connected through wide area networks, and automatically managed and controlled using IoT and AI technologies. Subsequently, as is shown in Figure 2, the manufacturing resources and abilities are virtualized and encapsulated into different manufacturing cloud services that can be accessed, invoked, and deployed based on knowledge by using virtualization technologies, service-oriented technologies, and cloud computing technologies. End- users can search and invoke the qualified Manufacturing Cloud Services (MCSs) from the related manufacturing cloud according to their needs and assemble them to be a virtual manufacturing environment or solution to complete their manufacturing task involved in the whole life cycle of manufacturing processes. This means replacing high capital expenditures with pay-as-you-go manufacturing services and through-life support, which radically transforms the economics of the new product information, volume manufacturing, and lifecycle management.

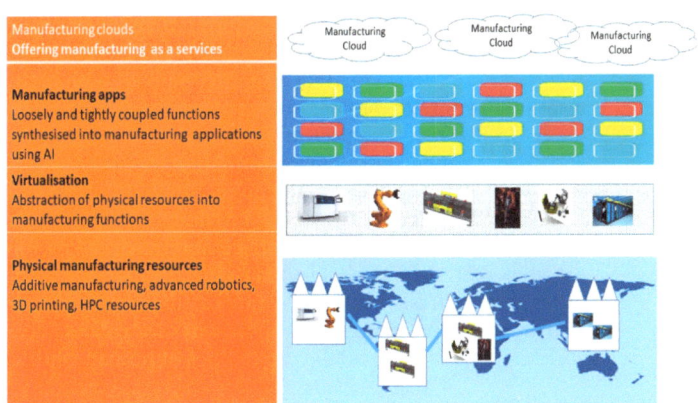

Figure 2. The transformation from CMfg to an Internet of Manufacturing enabled by 5G Wide Area Deterministic Networks.

We envisage that 5G and beyond-5G wide area networking will enable the distributed network architecture for CMfg and new Over The Top (OTT) players in the manufacturing sector (Mf-OTT). This model builds in analogy with the how the internet together with cloud computing has enabled the emergence of OTTs such as Uber for the transport sector. As shown in Figure 2, it introduces three layers: manufacturing service providers, Mf-OTTs and end-users. A layer of manufacturing service providers consists of manufacturing, computational, and AI clouds. Manufacturing clouds are formed by 5G/beyond-5G interconnected manufacturing service providers. The Mf-OTTs use intelligent search mechanism analogous to Internet search engines endowed with new AI capabilities for dynamic manufacturing service composition based on end-user requirements, and the search mechanism propagates manufacturing service inquiries through the decentralized network. Software and AI tools supporting the search process are accessible to Mf-OTTs providers in computation and AI clouds.

3.2. The Internet of Robotics

Robotics is a rapidly growing general-purpose technology with many new applications appearing in the market every day. Furthermore, with rapid advances in AI and Cloud technologies, we are seeing a rise of intelligent and cloud-based robotics in many industry sectors. A robot is a complex intelligent machine composed of mechanical, electronics, computing, embedded intelligence, sensors and connectivity technologies. Major economies in the world have the development of this technology as one of the key pillars of their national strategy. According to a recent report from the International Federation of Robots (IFR), robot installations hit new record level in 2021 with a 31% increase, and an average of 7% increase is predicted until 2025 [22]. The largest projected market for robotics currently is in the manufacturing sector, with the highest level of development being in automotive and electronic industries [23].

Robots endowed with Artificial Intelligence, rich sensorial capabilities and mobility will require communicating in a variety of scenarios, with a variety of other "actors" and for a range of reasons. Furthermore, while Human–Robot Communications will be limited by the sensory and processing capabilities of humans (which is a limiting factor in both in the nature and the rate of communications), entirely new sensory and much richer ways of communication may emerge among intelligent robots. For example, robots may use various forms of multi-sensory/multi-modal communications, which could include 3D images and videos, sound and ultra-sound, temperature and haptics to share situational information with other robots. Or they may develop new forms of speech or multi-layer vision perception for their communications, which are unrecognizable by humans. For example, a robot could layer together an image of its environment which may contain not only visible light reflection data but also infrared, radio frequency and ultrasound data all fused together. Cloud robotics are a paradigm that leverages the powerful computation, storage and resources of modern data centers combined with high speed and low-latency communication to enhance the capabilities of robots. Cloud robots are controlled by a "brain" in the cloud that may constitute a data center, a shared knowledge base, artificial intelligence and deep learning algorithms, information processing, task planners, environment models, etc. Cloud Robotics open up the possibility of *robot virtualization*, where all or the majority of Robotic intelligence as well as low-level control functions are virtualized and run on cloud or edge cloud servers. Table 2 summarizes key robotic communication scenarios together with their projected data-rates. Semantic communications will be essential in order to both drastically reduce data requirements for future robotic communications but also allow for the emergence of new ways for robots to communicate among themselves, which will go far beyond the capabilities of human-centric communications.

Table 2. Future scenarios and communication requirements of robotic networks.

Scenario	Purpose	Expected Communication Rate
Robot-environment Communications Robot–Things Communications	Control of and adaption to environment /exchange of sensory data with environment	Mbps/Gbps
Robot–Human Communications	Control, cooperation/coordination, information and context sharing, problem solving	Up to Gbps
Robot–Robot Communications (voice, video, data, VR/AR, Holographic, Multi-modal/Multi-sensory l)	Control, cooperation/coordination, information and context, sharing, problem solving	Up to Tbps

Besides the above communications scenarios, with the advancement of robot intelligence, new forms of communication scenarios can emerge [24], which will be mediated with a next generation-wide area network capable of supporting the "Internet of Robotics" (IoR), through which robots can share sensory and situational data, information and knowledge to collaborate and orchestrate their activities, collectively solve problems, learn from each other and even create their own social networks. As illustrated in Figure 3, the IoR combined with robotic visualization will pave the way for the transformation of robotic technology from specialized verticals to horizontal and virtualized robotic service platforms, and the emergence of robotic apps.

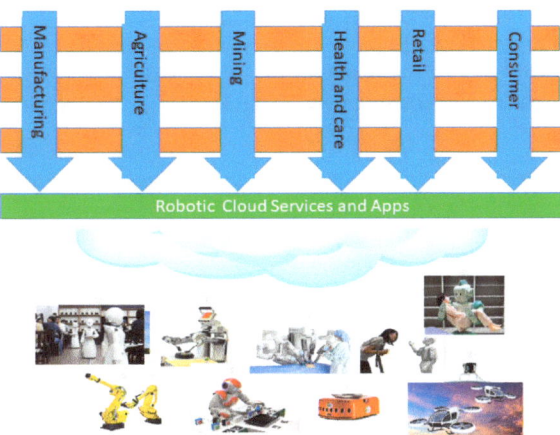

Figure 3. Transformation of robotics from specialized verticals to horizontal and virtualised robotic service platforms enabled by the IOR, and the emergence of a robotic apps ecosystem.

3.3. The Internet of Smart Energy Grids

The United Nations progress report on Sustainable Development Goals (SDGs) states that since 2012, the growth of renewables (has) outpaced the growth of total energy consumption [25], and this trend has been accelerated during the COVID-19 pandemic, i.e., we can find further evidence in relation to COVID-19. While there was a 3.8% decrease in energy demand during the first quarter of 2020 due to the lockdown, renewables were the only energy sources that posted a growth in demand, driven by larger installed capacity and priority dispatch. Hence, society as a whole is moving towards the use of renewable and sustainable energy sources. Consequently, the increase in energy demand will not be manageable unless the traditional electricity grid evolves. The convergence of the ICT infrastructure with the electricity domain, the Smart Grid (SG), has enabled new services and business opportunities, including customer-side generation and real-time energy consumption, which are guiding a significant revolution in the energy landscape.

The SG is also underpinning the emergences of new actors and entities in the energy ecosystem. In particular, the future energy user does not only consume energy but performs a crucial role as an energy Prosumer (energy producers and energy consumers) as well as providing distributed platform for renewables' energy storage, e.g., electric vehicles. These new actors are going to play a crucial role in the transition of the energy sector towards 100% renewables as well as a disruption of the entire energy value chain, resulting in the emergence of new aggregator/retailer in addition to Energy Services Companies (ESCOs), Virtual Power Plants (VPPs), Microgrids (MGs) and Prosumer Consumer Group (PCGs), which are also new components in the energy market value chain [26]. The growth in end-use consumption results in electricity generation increasing 79% between 2018 and 2050. Electricity use grows in the residential sector as rising population and standards of living in non-OECD countries increase the demand for appliances and personal equipment. Electricity use also increases in the industry and business sectors as well as demonstrating a steep rise in transportation sector as plug-in electric vehicles (EVs) enter the fleet and electricity use for the rail expands. Consequently, besides the residential sector, industry and enterprise verticals can be expected to become a key component of energy prosumer by 2050, while EVs are expected to play a major role in both prosumer and energy storage for future smart grids. Due to their energy intensity, industrial prosumers are important players in the energy transition.

Distributed Energy Resources (DERs) onsite (e.g., renewables, storage) can further help their business case. In recent years, there has been an exponential growth in offshore wind power turbines as a key renewable energy technology towards achieving carbon neutrality by 2050, and there is great interest recently in floating wind power turbines, as they can be reconfigured based on wind speed, water depth and distance to shore. Finally, the Vehicle to Grid technology (V2G) enables energy stored in Electric Vehicles to be fed back into the electricity network (grid) to help supply energy at times of peak demand and is considered a key component of future smart grids.

In order to provide monitoring and control in real time and integrate these emerging energy and storage system into the smart grid, a unified, high stability and ultra-reliable wireless communication infrastructure is required, which also support high-bandwidth, low-latency and mobility requirements. Network slicing also seems to be a promising and optimal solution for the diverse performance requirements of smart grids. It can offer virtualized and scalable communication architecture for a customized communication service expected by future smart distribution grids [27]. Consequently, the above evolving landscape in smart grids necessitate the availability of the 6G network infrastructure supporting the often-stringent requirements (in terms of latency, reliability and security) for both wide area connectivity and mobility for management of an Internet of Smart Energy Grids (IoSG).

4. Conclusions and Outlook

In this paper, we reviewed key architecture, networking and technology components, which are underpinning the successful expansion of 5G connectivity services and platforms into vertical sectors in the 6G era, as well as providing an overview of the worldwide progress by the public, and while 5G for verticals is aiming at the 5G native connectivity for specific verticals sectors in the longer term, these anticipate the emergence of entirely new horizontal entities and services across enabled by wide area 5G connectivity, which will the pave the way for a 6G-enabled Internet of Verticals (6G-IoV). Prominent use cases of 6G-IoV include distributed and over-the-top cloud manufacturing and manufacturing as a service, and the Internet of Robotics (IoR) and the Internet of Smart Energy Grids were described. In terms of timelines, we expect that by 2027 we will see 5G-native connectivity to be fully deployed in key verticals such as manufacturing automotive electricity grids, after which we will witness the initial instances of 6G-IoVs with the worldwide Internet of Verticals fully emerging in the mature era of 6G, i.e., beyond 2035.

Author Contributions: Conceptualization, M.N.; Formal analysis, M.N.; Funding acquisition, M.N.; Investigation, M.N.; Project administration, M.N.; Supervision, M.N.; Writing—original draft, M.N.; Methodology, F.A; Visualization, F.A; Writing—review & editing, F.A. All authors have read and agreed to the published version of the manuscript.

Funding: The research leading to this publication was partially funded by the UKRI/EPSRC Network Plus "A Green Connected and Prosperous Britain".

Conflicts of Interest: The authors declare no conflict of interest.

References

1. 5G White Paper 2, NGMN Alliance, 27 July 2020. Available online: https://www.ngmn.org/work-programme/5g-white-paper-2.html (accessed on 29 November 2020).
2. Zhang, W.E.; Sheng, Q.; Mahmood, A.; Tran, D.H.; Zaib, M.; Hamad, S.A.; Aljubairy, A.; Alhazmi, A.A.F.; Sagar, S.; Ma, C. The 10 Research Topics in the Internet of Things. In Proceedings of the IEEE 6th International Conference on Collaboration and Internet Computing (CIC), Atlanta, GA, USA, 1–3 December 2020.
3. ETSI Non IP Networking ISG. Available online: https://www.etsi.org/committee/nin (accessed on 29 November 2020).
4. Empowering Vertical Industries through 5G Networks—Current Status and Future Trends; 5GPPP Technology Board and 5G IA Vertical Task Force, 20 August 2020. Available online: https://5g-ppp.eu/wp-content/uploads/2020/09/5GPPP-VerticalsWhitePaper-2020-Final.pdf (accessed on 29 November 2020).
5. 5G Use Cases for Verticals China 2020, GSMA and CAICT. 2020. Available online: https://www.gsma.com/greater-china/wpcontent/uploads/2020/03/5G-Use-Cases-for-Verticals-China-2020.pdf (accessed on 29 November 2020).
6. Giordani, M.; Polese, M.; Mezzavilla, M.; Rangan, S.; Zorzi, M. Toward 6G Networks: Use Cases and Technologies. *IEEE Commun. Mag.* **2020**, *58*, 3. [CrossRef]

7. Uusitalo, M.A.; Rugeland, P.; Boldi, M.R.; Strinati, E.C.; Demestichas, P.; Ericson, M.; Fettweis, G.P.; Filippou, M.C.; Gati, A.; Hamon, M.-H.; et al. 6G Vision, Value, Use Cases and Technologies From European 6G Flagship Project Hexa-X. *IEEE Access* **2021**, *9*, 160004–160020. [CrossRef]
8. 3GPP, System Architecture for the 5G System, Table 5.15.2.2-1, 3GPP TS 23.501 V16.4.0. 2020. Available online: https://www.etsi.org/deliver/etsi_ts/123500_123599/123501/16.06.00_60/ts_123501v160600p.pdf (accessed on 29 November 2020).
9. GSMA. Network Slicing, Use Case Requirements, April 2018. Available online: https://www.gsma.com/futurenetworks/wpcontent/uploads/2018/04/NS-Final.pdf (accessed on 29 November 2020).
10. Rezazadeh, F.; Zanzi, L.; Devoti, F.; Chergui, H.; Costa-Pérez, X.; Verikoukis, C. On the Specialization of FDRL Agents for Scalable and Distributed 6G RAN Slicing Orchestration. *IEEE Trans. Veh. Technol.* **2022**, 1–15. [CrossRef]
11. Khan, L.U.; Saad, W.; Niyato, D.; Han, Z.; Hong, C. Digital-Twin-Enabled 6G: Vision, Architectural Trends, and Future Directions. *IEEE Commun. Mag.* **2022**, *60*, 1. [CrossRef]
12. Deloitte. 5G's Promised Land Finally Arrives: 5G Standalone Networks Can Transform Enterprise Connectivity. Available online: https://www2.deloitte.com/uk/en/insights/industry/technology/technology-media-and-telecom-predictions/2023/technology-media-and-telecom-predictions-standalone-5g.html (accessed on 18 January 2023).
13. ETSI, Multi-Access Edge Computing (MEC); Framework and Reference Architecture ETSI GS MEC 003V2.1.1 (2019-01). Available online: https://www.etsi.org/deliver/etsi_gs/MEC/001_099/003/02.01.01_60/gs_MEC003v020101p.pdf (accessed on 29 November 2020).
14. Ayaz, F.; Sheng, Z.; Tian, D.; Guan, Y. A Proof-of-Quality-Factor (PoQF)-Based Blockchain and Edge Computing for Vehicular Message Dissemination. *IEEE Internet Things J.* **2021**, *8*, 4. [CrossRef]
15. Ayaz, F.; Sheng, Z.; Tian, D.; Guan, Y. A Blockchain Based Federated Learning for Message Dissemination in Vehicular Networks. *IEEE Trans. Veh. Technol.* **2022**, *71*, 2.
16. Ayaz, F.; Sheng, Z.; Tian, D.; Nekovee, M.; Saeed, N. Blockchain-Empowered AI for 6G-Enabled Internet of Vehicles. *Electronics* **2022**, *11*, 3339. [CrossRef]
17. IETF. Deterministic Networking Working Group. Available online: https://datatracker.ietf.org/wg/detnet/about/ (accessed on 29 November 2020).
18. ITU. Focus Group on Technologies for Network 2030. Available online: www.itu.int/en/ITUT/focusgroups/net2030/Pages/default.aspx (accessed on 29 November 2020).
19. 5G Communications for Automation in Vertical Domains, 5G Americas, November 2018. Available online: https://www.5gamericas.org/wp-content/uploads/2019/07/5G_Americas_White_Paper_Communications_for_Automation_in_Vertical_Domains_November_2018.pdf (accessed on 29 November 2020).
20. Haghnegahdar, L.; Joshi, S.; Dahotre, N. From IoT-based Cloud Manufacturing Approach to Intelligent Additive Manufacturing: Industrial Internet of Things—An Overview. *Int. J. Adv. Manuf. Technol.* **2022**, *119*, 1461–1478. [CrossRef]
21. Ghomi, E.J.; Rahmani, A.M.; Qader, N.N. Cloud Manufacturing: Challenges, Recent Advances, Open Research Issues, and Future Trends. *Int. J. Adv. Manuf. Technol.* **2019**, *102*, 3613–3639. [CrossRef]
22. International Federation of Robotics. World Robotics 2022. Available online: https://ifr.org/downloads/press2018/2022_WR_extended_version.pdf (accessed on 18 January 2023).
23. How Connected Robots Are Transforming Manufacturing. In *Information Paper*; International Federation of Robotics: Frankfurt, Germany, 2020.
24. Sandry, E. Re-evaluating the form and communication of social robots. *Int. J. Soc. Robot.* **2015**, *7*, 335–346. [CrossRef]
25. The Sustainable Development Goals Report 2020. Unite Nations. Available online: https://unstats.un.org/sdgs/report/2020/ (accessed on 29 November 2020).
26. Caballero, V.; Vernetand, D.; Zaballos, A. A Heuristic to Create Prosumer Community Groups in the Social Internet of Energy. *Sensors* **2019**, *20*, 3704. [CrossRef] [PubMed]
27. Mendis, H.V.K.; Heegaard, P.; Kralevska, K. 5G Network Slicing for Smart Distribution Grid Operations. In Proceedings of the 5th International Conference on Electricity Distribution, Madrid, Spain, 3–6 June 2019.

Disclaimer/Publisher's Note: The statements, opinions and data contained in all publications are solely those of the individual author(s) and contributor(s) and not of MDPI and/or the editor(s). MDPI and/or the editor(s) disclaim responsibility for any injury to people or property resulting from any ideas, methods, instructions or products referred to in the content.

Review

Securing UAV Flying Base Station for Mobile Networking: A Review

Sang-Yoon Chang [1,*], Kyungmin Park [2], Jonghyun Kim [2] and Jinoh Kim [3]

[1] Computer Science Department, University of Colorado Colorado Springs, Colorado Springs, CO 80918, USA
[2] Electronics and Telecommunications Research Institute, Daejeon 34129, Republic of Korea; kmpark@etri.re.kr (K.P.); jhk@etri.re.kr (J.K.)
[3] Computer Science Department, Texas A&M University-Commerce, Commerce, TX 75428, USA; jinoh.kim@tamuc.edu
* Correspondence: schang2@uccs.edu

Abstract: A flying base station based on an unmanned aerial vehicle (UAV) uses its mobility to extend its connectivity coverage and improve its communication channel quality to achieve a greater communication rate and latency performances. While UAV flying base stations have been used in emergency events in 5G networking (sporadic and temporary), their use will significantly increase in 6G networking, as 6G expects reliable connectivity even in rural regions and requires high-performance communication channels and line-of-sight channels for millimeter wave (mmWave) communications. Securing the integrity and availability of the base station operations is critical because of the users' increasing reliance on the connectivity provided by the base stations, e.g., the mobile user loses connectivity if the base station operation gets disrupted. This paper identifies the security issues and research gaps of flying base stations, focusing on their unique properties, while building on the existing research in wireless communications for stationary ground base stations and embedded control for UAV drones. More specifically, the flying base station's user-dependent positioning, its battery-constrained power, and the dynamic and distributed operations cause vulnerabilities that are distinct from those in 5G and previous-generation mobile networking with stationary ground base stations. This paper reviews the relevant security research from the perspectives of communications (mobile computing, 5G networking, and distributed computing) and embedded/control systems (UAV vehicular positioning and battery control) and then identifies the security gaps and new issues emerging for flying base stations. Through this review paper, we inform readers of flying base station research, development, and standardization for future mobile and 6G networking.

Keywords: security; telecommunications networking; 5G networking; 6G networking; base station; UAV drone; distributed networking

Citation: Chang, S.-Y.; Park, K.; Kim, J.; Kim, J. Securing UAV Flying Base Station for Mobile Networking: A Review. *Future Internet* **2023**, *15*, 176. https://doi.org/10.3390/fi15050176

Academic Editors: Alessandro Raschellà and Michael Mackay

Received: 16 April 2023
Revised: 4 May 2023
Accepted: 5 May 2023
Published: 9 May 2023

Copyright: © 2023 by the authors. Licensee MDPI, Basel, Switzerland. This article is an open access article distributed under the terms and conditions of the Creative Commons Attribution (CC BY) license (https://creativecommons.org/licenses/by/4.0/).

1. Introduction

Mobility has traditionally been implemented and enabled for the mobile user. However, recent research and proposals introduce mobility to the telecommunications network service provider infrastructure. The unmanned aerial vehicle (UAV) drone-based flying base station (called UxNB in 3rd Generation Partnership Project or 3GPP [1,2]) improves the telecommunications connectivity provision. While the traditional stationary terrestrial base station has a fixed cell for its connectivity coverage, the flying base station's mobility and its strategic location for connectivity enable more flexible, dynamic, and adaptive connectivity coverage. The flying base station can also improve the channel quality to the mobile user by approaching or securing the line-of-sight path to the mobile user (which is especially important for mmWave communications, which do not penetrate physical barriers as well as lower-band communications). The improved connectivity coverage and communication channels enable greater bandwidth/data rates and reduced latency for the next-generation wireless applications, including sensor applications (e.g., surveillance, personal, body, and environmental monitoring) and those based on holographic and haptic operations (e.g., virtual reality/VR or augmented reality/AR).

Securing a UAV flying base station is critical because it is a part of the cellular service provider infrastructure and the mobile users rely on it for connectivity. Its disruption and manipulation represent high security risks, as our everyday lives increasingly depend on reliable connectivity. In addition, the advancements and developments in wireless/mobile implementations, including software-defined radio (SDR) and open-source mobile networking softwares such as srsRAN, reduce the threat implementation barrier and increase the attack feasibility (even though these enabler tools and technologies provide longer-term benefits in securing the system, including improving the transparency, vendor interoperability, and security awareness). We therefore treat the networking provider infrastructure as a critical infrastructure and focus on the integrity of flying base station operations (execution is as designed, and the unauthorized attackers cannot manipulate or change the protocol execution) and availability (the connectivity is provided when needed and requested).

The UAV drone flying base station system combines a telecommunications base station (for its application and purpose of connectivity provision) and UAV drone (for mobility implementation and control). While there has been research and development to secure the component technologies of the flying base station system (communications for base station, embedded control for UAV drone, and distributed computing for the base station's coexistence with other base stations and the rest of the infrastructure), research and developments taking a systems approach to secure the flying base station as a system have been lacking. In this review paper, we therefore identify the unique properties of a flying base station distinct from its component technologies, review the related research in the component technologies (based on which we can draw the initial reference designs for the security solutions before adapting and advancing them for flying base station), and discuss future work directions. We envision that this paper will inform, encourage, and facilitate further research to advance the security of flying base stations.

This review paper surveys the existing research literature on UAV flying base station security, identifies research gaps for the flying base station system built on its component technologies, and informs readers about future research directions. To the best of our knowledge, this is the first review paper focusing on the security of UAV flying base stations. Wang et al. [3] use UAV to enable physical-layer security but lack the systems approach, i.e., they do not consider the flying base station system aspects of UAV/drone control, battery, and digital security. Other survey or review papers focus on the individual component technology or lack a security focus, e.g., UAV/drone sensing and monitoring (e.g., [4,5]), communications to enable UAV/drone operations (e.g., [6,7]), the security of UAV drones (e.g., [8–11]), security of wireless communications, and security of wireless and mobile applications (e.g., [12,13]).

The rest of the paper is organized as follows. Section 2 describes the telecommunications networking background involving base stations focusing on the most recent 5G New Radio (NR) standardized protocol. Our treatment of the background information on telecommunications is brief and of a high level as we describe those factors needed for flying base station research as opposed to providing significantly longer and more detailed coverage of the 5G NR protocol. Section 3 discusses the unique properties of a UAV flying base station distinct from its component technologies of a stationary ground base station and UAV drone, which establishes the focuses of this review paper. Based on the unique properties and the component technologies of the stationary ground base station and UAV drone, Section 4 reviews the security research in base station control communication security, authentication and cryptography (the digital security mechanisms), mobility control security (traditionally been studied in embedded, cyber-physical, and vehicular systems), battery integrity security, and distributed network security. Section 5 discusses future work to facilitate and encourage future research and development to secure flying base stations. Section 6 concludes this paper.

2. Mobile Networking Background

This paper focuses on the most recent 5G New Radio protocol as standardized and specified by the Third Generation Partnership Project (3GPP) [14–16]. 3GPP standardizes and specifies the technologies for the radio access, backend core network, and service capabilities for mobile telecommunications, thus guiding mobile networking research and development and enabling interoperability between the different cellular service provider services. While 6G's protocol design and standardization are currently ongoing, 5G will provide a building base for 6G as 6G will inherit most of the existing technologies, including those described in this section.

Section 2.1 provides a high-level overview of the current mobile networking focusing on 5G, including the different protocol steps for the wireless/RF communication channel setup vs. the digital setup and the critical messages and identifiers/credentials used for the channel setup (which can become the targets for security protection in future security research). Building on the 5G architecture, Section 2.2 describes the incorporation of the UAV flying base station to the 5G architecture.

2.1. Existing Telecommunications Networking Protocol: 3GPP Standardization Protocol and User vs. Base Station vs. Core Network

The connectivity provider infrastructure to provide connectivity to the mobile user includes the base station, the core network, and the intermediate routers/switches (which forward the networking packets across the physical distances after the base station). The lower row in Figure 1 depicts these entities from the user (left) to the cloud (right), where those between the base station and the core network are within the cellular service provider infrastructure. Beyond the core network is outside of the cellular service provider infrastructure and relies on the collaborations and agreements with other service provider entities.

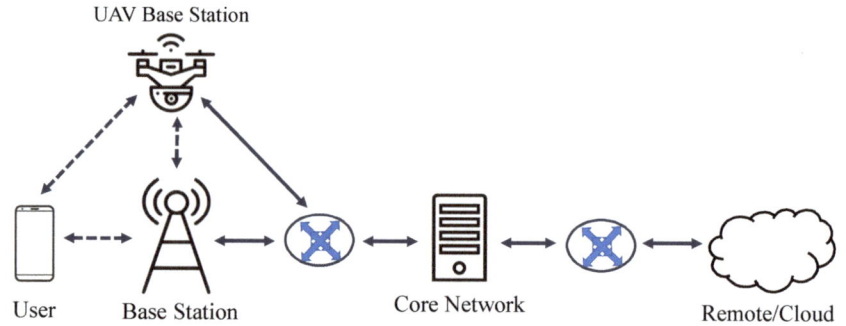

Figure 1. Telecommunications networking architecture and entities, including the UAV flying base station in the upper row.

The base station connects to the mobile user wirelessly and serves as the bridge gateway to transition to the wireless communications for the mobile users in telecommunications networking. Because the mobile user uses a wireless communication link, while the networking from the base station to the internet and cloud are in the form of wired communications, the base station serves as the gateway between wireless vs. wired networking. The user and the base station communicate via radio-frequency (RF) wireless communications, while communication from the base station to the core network and then to the cloud is via wired communications involving other nodes such as routers and switches. Therefore, the base station is the first and the last hop to the mobile users communicating in RF. Beyond the base station, the core network is responsible for much of the digital processing to set up the connectivity services to the mobile user, including user registration, security setup, and service as well as access control. The communications and packets from the user are processed by the core network before it leaves, e.g., to the public internet.

Figure 2 describes the logical interactions for the control communications between the user, base station, and core network. The brief description abstracts from the telecommunications implementations and details from [14–16] and focuses on the information needed to understand this review paper. The user and the base station require radio resource control (RRC) and a wireless channel for setting up the RF wireless communications, where the communication resources are shared with multiple other users coexisting in the nearby air medium. The RRC begins with the broadcasting messages by the base stations, including the master information block (MIB) and system information block (SIB). The MIB and SIB messages are publicly broadcasted and advertised as the base station is a public entity for serving the cellular connectivity, often serving a large number of mobile users freely entering and exiting the cell. Receiving and decoding the MIB and SIB enable the mobile user to attach to the base station and set up a communication channel, resulting in the user-dedicated cell radio network temporary identifier (C-RNTI). This wireless channel setup is followed by digital control including the registration and authentication verification as well as the security setup between the user and the core network. From the user and (universal) subscriber identity module (SIM or USIM) registration (which occur in advance before the user activation to receive the connectivity service and not drawn in Figure 2), the core network derives the mobile subscriber identification number (MSIN) and the more temporary ID of the temporary mobile subscription identifier (TMSI) and shares that with the user and the base station. The MSIN is not communicated in plain-text and rather is processed by an encryption function E, thus exchanging $E(\text{MSIN})$. Afterward, the user can use the established RF and digital channel for data communications and networking applications.

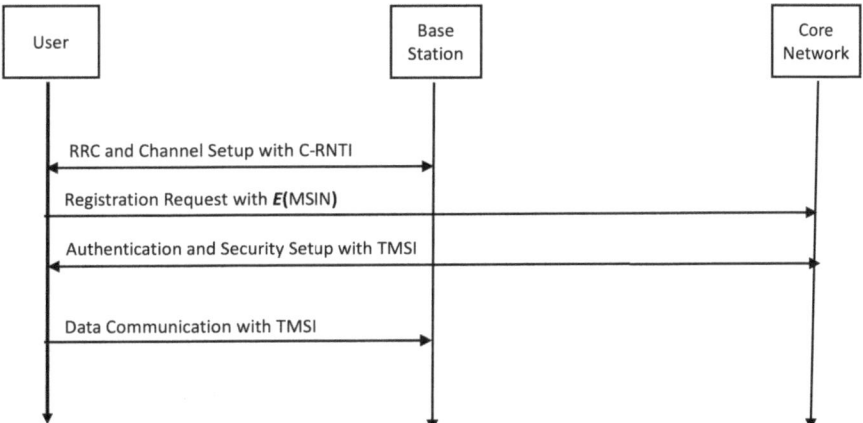

Figure 2. Control communication protocol interactions between the user, base station, and core network to set up the data channel.

2.2. Incorporating Flying Base Station

Sixth-generation networking introduces the UAV flying base stations to improve the base station coverage and the channel link qualities to mobile users. As is typical with new technologies in mobile networking, the incorporation of the flying base station to mobile networking should support backward-compatibility to the 5G networks described in Section 2.1. For example, a flying base station can provide the connectivity service even if the mobile user only supports 5G or even lower-generation telecommunications, e.g., 2G for emergency applications.

Figure 1 therefore builds on the traditional cellular/5G architecture (lower row) and introduces the flying base station (upper row). In Figure 1, the flying base station connects to the mobile user and to the stationary ground base station (to access the backend and the internet), and these communications are in wireless/RF communications, as drawn in dotted arrow lines. While mobile, the flying base station connects to the stationary ground base station to access the rest of the network. In addition, the flying base station can sometimes connect directly to the cellular provider infrastructure via a switch, e.g., when it is recharging its battery, requiring physical connections as drawn in solid arrow lines.

The flying base station can be multiple physical entities (multiple flying base stations), although drawn as one logical entity in Figure 1. These flying base stations can network with each other (forming their own network) for coordination and connectivity-provision control (involving ad hoc networking capabilities, e.g., flying ad hoc network or FANET), while maintaining the connections with the rest of the connectivity provider infrastructure including the ground base station. The collaborative network of flying base stations can extend the connectivity range by forming a relay network.

The emerging flying base station has the purpose of serving connectivity to mobile users, requiring connectivity in an on-demand basis or dynamically entering/exiting the flying base station's cellular range. To serve the public's mobile devices, the flying base station will be publicly accessible and broadcast and advertise RRC messages, similarly to the stationary terrestrial base stations described in Section 2.1. This makes the flying base station distinct from some other flying/UAV applications requiring privacy and/or having dedicated communication targets.

3. UAV Flying Base Station Properties

A UAV flying base station combines the functionalities of a base station (to provide the last-mile hop wireless communication link to the user equipment) and UAV drone (to move its location). However, a UAV flying base station is distinguishable from each of these underlying technologies and introduces novel security vulnerabilities and threats previously unseen in stationary base stations and generic UAV drones.

3.1. Controlling Mobility and Positioning

A UAV flying base station implements the mobility functionality to better serve mobile users, while the traditional base stations are stationary and have a fixed location. While this mobility presents an opportunity to better serve the user (approaching the user for greater channel reliability and data communication rate/bandwidth), it also presents unique engineering problems and risks. Because flying base station research and development is in its infancy, its user-dependent mobility control is new.

Security implications: New security risks can involve a malicious user, including those violating the integrity of the positioning control, to misplace the base station and launch a denial-of-service (DoS) of the base station's connectivity provision. The vulnerabilities for such security threats are due to the mobility capability of the flying base stations and therefore do not apply to the stationary base stations.

3.2. Operation on Battery

Because the UAV flying base station is mobile and cannot afford wired connections hindering its mobility, a UAV flying base station operates on the battery energy resource to supply the electrical power supply. The UAV flying base station requires the battery energy for both its connectivity provision (i.e., it cannot support the connectivity to the user if it does not have electrical energy) and its mobility (move and re-position its location to improve the connectivity provision to the mobile user), as depicted in Figure 3. Because of the battery's finite energy amount, the flying base station operation requires regular re-charging when the battery is running low in energy. The re-charging phases interfere with the flying base station operations because of the fixed locations of the recharging stations, reducing the flying base station to stationary base station operations.

Security implications: Such finite resources in battery energy and their direct impact on the connectivity provision lead to vulnerabilities against battery-draining DoS threats. In addition to the more traditional DoS channels focusing on networking bandwidth and processing resources, the battery energy provides a new channel for the DoS attacker to interfere with and disrupt the base station operations. Because the battery/energy resource is shared by both the base-station communication and the drone mobility, as depicted in Figure 3, there are greater DoS vulnerabilities than having either communication or mobility but not both. For example, the attacker manipulating the base station location can trigger greater power consumption for the signal transmission; requiring greater reliability and jamming resistance can incur greater bandwidth and thus power consumption, e.g., the code-division multiple access (CDMA) spread spectrum; and bogus injection messages can cause greater re-charging, disabling the optimal control of the mobility and location of the base station.

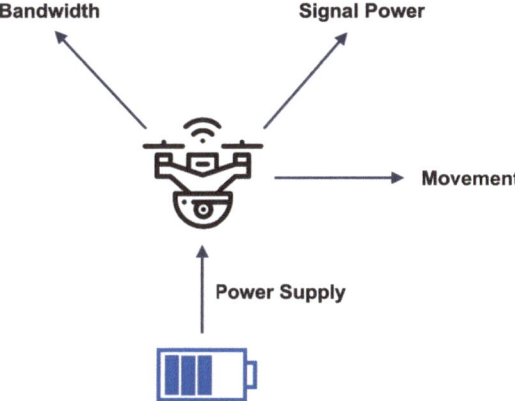

Figure 3. Flying base station control parameters affecting its power consumption. The UAV flying base station shares the power from a singular source of a battery to support multiple functionalities of the UAV drone (movement) and the base station (wireless communication).

3.3. Providing Communication and Connectivity to Users

The generic UAV drones have many applications and purposes, including sensing and collecting information and the delivery/moving of physical objects. The generic UAV drones typically use communications to facilitate and optimize their goals (communications for UAV); they are the beneficiary of communication service provider infrastructure, assuming the mobile user's role in cellular architecture. In contrast, the UAV flying base station's goal and purpose is to provide connectivity and networking to the users (UAV for communications) and is a part and enabler of the communication service provider infrastructure.

Security implications: Due to the networking application's reliance on the communications and networking provided by the cellular infrastructure (including the UAV flying base station), the flying base station has significant security risks, i.e., the integrity and availability threats on its operations have significant impacts.

3.4. Involving Distributed and Edge Computing

A UAV flying base station is inherently smaller than the stationary terrestrial base station because of its mobility and battery requirements. The smaller size and the energy constraint of a flying base station limits the number of users that a flying base station can serve, compared to a stationary terrestrial base station, which in turn increases the number of flying base stations on the edge and reduces the cell coverage size per base station. The architecture and control involving a group of base stations require greater sophistication on the networking edge and involve greater distributed computing and networking to enable dynamic, adaptive, and agile control for the improved connectivity provision of base stations. Therefore, flying base station control involves distributed networking to support the ad hoc and peer-to-peer networking, in addition to the centralized backhaul-accessible networking. Such capabilities forgoing the centralized backhaul networking can enable networking redundancy to control the flying base station operations (so that the flying base station control and operations have higher reliability) and can implement wireless relay to enable greater geographical coverage for the connectivity.

Security implications: The dynamic, flexible, and ad hoc communications to control the flying base stations' operations are high-risk communications because such operations are high-impact and mission-critical. The failure of such communications in terms of availability and integrity can disable and disrupt the cellular connectivity provision to the user. Therefore, the flying base station's communications present a higher security risk than many other UAV ad hoc communication applications.

4. Related Work

4.1. Base Station Control Communication Security

The base station provides connectivity to many users utilizing multiple-antenna/MIMO and channelization/multiplexing technologies (where the channels coexist but are separate in frequency, time, code, and/or space-direction) and the medium access control (MAC) protocol (which sets up and synchronizes such wireless channel resources to use for data communications across multiple users). Previous research secured the integrity of the MAC and control communications for the availability of data channel resources, which is especially important because the DoS on the flying base station's channel resources can disrupt and disable the channel connectivity to the other legitimate users. Such research includes securing MAC protocol and radio-control handshaking in the dynamic and sophisticated dynamic spectrum environment against the channel control against insider, credential-compromising, and dynamic jamming [17–19], against MAC injection and handshaking-manipulating threats [20,21], and against the threats on channel-state-information (CSI) feedback [22,23]. While these research use models are abstracted from the 5G protocol details and generally applicable to wireless communications, the threats apply to the concrete protocols of 5G NR RRC protocol standardized by 3GPP [24–26]. However, the research solutions for securing the specific 5G RRC protocol between the user and the base station have been lacking; rather, the 5G security research has focused on incorporating and implementing security on the backend core network beyond the base station, e.g., [27–30].

4.2. Authentication and Cryptography

Telecommunications networking, including 5G NR by 3GPP, includes digital security protection mechanisms both for key establishment and the security functionality derivations based on that. In contrast to the research in Section 4.1, these digital security mechanisms are implemented after the RRC/radio channel establishment and after the core network is involved to verify the user registration. In 5G, the USIM described in Section 2.1 includes the core network's public key in advance, i.e., when it registers for the cellular service and before the user gets activated for receiving the connectivity service. These security functionalities relying on the established public key (as the root of digital security) include the standard cryptographic techniques, including Diffie–Hellman Key Exchange to agree on the symmetric keys, the use of the symmetric key for message authentication code (MAC) for source/transmitter and message authentications, the symmetric encryption for message confidentiality, and pseudo-random number generation for random TMSI and nonces. In addition to the digital credentials for authentication, e.g., the core network's public key, previous research has suggested physical-layer and radio-based authentication credentials against malicious users [31–33].

Another threat model against base station security involves the attacker compromising or acting as the base station (as opposed to a user), hence acting as a malicious or rogue base station [34–36]. Previous research studied such malicious and rogue base station threats in the standardized cellular/telecommunications protocols, including attacks on the authentication and key agreement (AKA) [37], bidding-down to the less-secure 2G/3G protocol [38], and SMS phishing attacks [39,40]. Despite the known threats of malicious and rogue base stations, the defense solutions have been relatively lacking although recent research has proposed secure bootstrapping with a newly encountered base station based on incorporating cryptographic techniques in the 5G/4G RRC phases [41,42].

4.3. Mobility Control Security

The mobility control of a UAV flying base station relies on location and position awareness. The flying base station utilizes its component technology of a UAV/drone to provide mobility, as discussed in Section 1. For a flying base station building on a UAV drone, because of its purpose of serving the users, the mobility control depends on the flying base station's relative location to the user. For example, the flying base station moves to the line-of-sight path and closer to the user equipment to provide better wireless channel quality. Misplacing the flying base stations or the UAVs, e.g., via GPS spoofing [43–45], can disrupt the UAV flying base station's operations by triggering abnormally frequent battery re-charging [11,46]. To counter such misplacement and to defend the relative location integrity, previous research has included securing ranging to measure the distance between the nodes against signal-injection threats [47,48], including advancing distance or time-of-arrival measurements for ranging [49,50] and the detection of the distance-manipulation/DoS threats [51–53].

4.4. Battery Integrity Security

Unlike a stationary terrestrial base station, the UAV base station operates on battery energy. The battery energy introduces a unique denial-of-service (DoS) vulnerability, beyond targeting the more traditional networking and computing resources (such as those exhausting the networking bandwidth or the networking connections/states), which can be exploited by an energy-targeting DoS threat to drain the battery. Previous research includes battery-depletion DoS threat studies against drones or UAVs [11,46,54–56], which are especially related to our work in the hardware platform (flying base station is based on the UAV drone for mobility control and implementation). Because the mobility is constrained to the battery re-charging stations, disrupting the optimal connectivity provision, a DoS can disrupt the availability of the flying base station's operations. The battery-draining DoS has been more widely been studied in other wireless computing/networking contexts (wireless applications beyond the flying base station control), including in implantable medical/health devices [12,57,58], wireless charging [59,60], and standardized protocols of WiFi and Bluetooth [59–62].

4.5. Distributed Networking Security

Adding distributed, ad hoc, peer-to-peer networking capabilities beyond the centralized backend-infrastructure-accessible networking can enable greater connectivity coverage and implement redundancy in controlling the flying base stations to improve the connectivity provision reliability, as described in Section 3.4. Previous research studied the flying ad hoc network (FANET) or UAV ad hoc network to implement communications between the UAV drones, e.g., [63–65].

The Blockchain can also enable the secure dissemination of security-critical information to secure integrity and message authenticity against base-station threats. These threats are described in Section 4.2 although in a more centralized environment. The Blockchain can replace the centralized key management to enable/share the networking root of trust (from which other security functionalities and properties can be derived). Blockchain-based designs have implemented distributed key management and establishment in other computing/networking applications, e.g., general digital networking [66–69], vehicular communications [70,71], electronic voting system [72,73], and software-defined networking or SDN [74–76]. The previous research can provide initial building references for designing such solutions for the applications of securing ground/terrestrial and flying base stations. More specifically, as demonstrated by the previous research in other computing applications, the Blockchain can be used for the following security purposes: disseminating the public key while replacing the centralized-server-based public-key infrastructure (PKI) to authenticate the base station; identifying/detecting a malicious or rogue base station; and using the public-key to construct channels with message authenticity (e.g., the Blockchain can be used to securely disseminate the core network's public key, which can be used for the source integrity protection of the delivery of the core-network generated credentials, such as E(MSIN) or TMSI in Section 2.1).

5. Future Work Discussions

5.1. Systems Approach and Building on the Component Technologies

Section 4 describes the security research into the component technologies of the UAV flying base station (Section 1 surveys the review or survey articles of the component technologies to distinguish our contributions from them). While the previous research can provide the bases for securing flying base stations in principle, security solutions supporting the unique challenges and characteristics of future flying base stations require further work. This also requires a systems approach with an understanding of how the different components and requirements affect all of the security solutions. For example, an effective security solution can introduce overheads prohibitive for the flying base station system (such as delaying the RRC, introducing additional vulnerabilities for DoS, or requiring frequent re-charging of the battery) to limit its utility and practicality. Furthermore, the security challenges can be prioritized differently because of the new security impact implications introduced by the flying base station operations, e.g., a flying base station has severe and critical impact implications because of the telecommunications mobile users' reliance on the base station.

5.2. Prototype Implementation

Prototype implementation can inform and enable the systems approach described in Section 5.1. The implementation-based approach can expand our understanding of the system beyond the theoretical models and thus improve the practicality and utility of the system modeling. This is especially important for the UAV flying base station, which is a relatively novel concept and is currently undergoing engineering development, dynamically affecting our knowledge of the system.

For such research benefits, we built a UAV flying base station prototype based on a DJI Matrice 300 RTK drone for the mobility functionality and USRP B210 software-defined radio for the base station functionality. Figure 4 shows the hardwares and the corresponding simulated entities in 5G networking for our prototype. From left to right (loosely), the UAV flying base station connects to the stationary ground/terrestrial base station (the traditional base station), which in turn connects to the core network at the backend, as described in the 5G architecture in Figure 1. Our prototype also includes a monitoring system for digital networking analysis. The ground base station and the core network are connected via a switch, not shown in Figure 4. We plan to use such a prototype to better model the flying base station system and validate and test our security solutions. For example, based on a preliminary prototype-based study, for a rotor-based drone, the hovering operation dominates the lateral movements of the drone in energy, and most of the power consumption from the hovering operation is significantly larger than the marginal power consumption from adding lateral movement. We only made this observation after our prototype implementation, and the observation informed our modeling and research afterward. The observation also motivates the flying base station to land while serving as a base station as frequently as possible (as opposed to hovering in the air) and discretize and separate between the movement vs. stationary phases due to the overhead of launching itself into the air (as opposed to hovering and moving continuously).

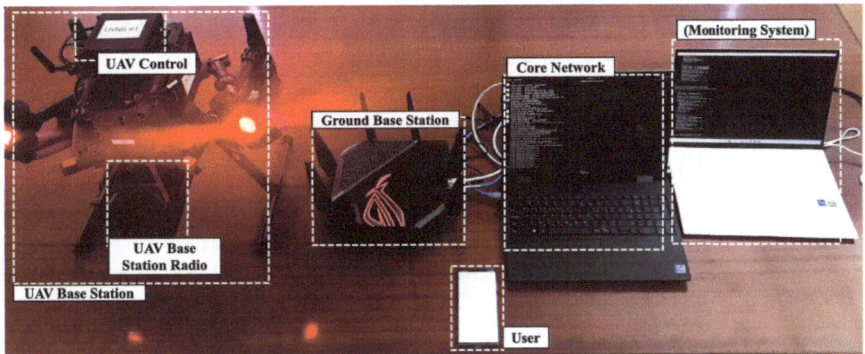

Figure 4. Our prototype implementation of UAV flying base station.

5.3. Flying Base Station for Security Opportunities

While this paper reviews the issues and gaps that challenge the security of flying base stations, flying base stations can provide unique opportunities to aid the security of base station operation. Such opportunities include advancing channel reliability and jamming resiliency by using the mobility of the flying base station, using the line-of-sight path securing to provide additional security properties (which can especially be important for mmWave communications as it gets block on the physical barriers), improving reliability by jointly processing the communications with line-of-sight sensing, and creating unique physical-layer signatures based on the mobility and the corresponding channel variations.

5.4. Hardening the Infrastructure and Ecosystem

Hardening the ecosystem including the rest of the connectivity-provision infrastructure (e.g., the backend core network, the stationary terrestrial base station, the other UAV flying base stations, the LEO satellite or HAPS base station) can improve reliability and security. The connectivity-provision infrastructure system can provide redundancy coverage and connectivity to mitigate the DoS threat and continue to provide availability/service to users by utilizing other base stations and by forming a service-provision network of base stations. For example, a mobile user can select between a flying base station and a stationary terrestrial base station, or a mobile user can have two flying base stations available.

5.5. Transition to Standardization and Practice

The telecommunications networking R&D prioritizes standardization for the implementation compatibility and interoperability across the vendors and the mobile service providers, c.f., OpenRAN. Securing the UAV flying base stations in 6G standardization facilitates the transition from security/engineering research to practice, as the standardization enables the compatibility with the systems/application requirements and drives the incorporation to the current practices and implementations. Therefore, the standardization incorporation of flying base station security research and the research community's effort to facilitate such incorporation remains an important future direction.

5.6. Security by Design

A UAV flying base station is a relatively new concept, and its prototypes and protocols are currently being developed. 3GPP introduces the notion (termed UxNB base station) and its requirements [1,2] but lacks the concrete standardization of the protocol and operations. Because the flying base station protocols are under development and a concrete and well-adopted protocol is lacking (anticipated for the upcoming 6G standardization), we encourage researchers to being addressing the misplacement threat and securing the flying base station against it. Practicing security by design and embedding security mechanisms during UAV-flying-base-station protocol design and standardization can enable security properties that would be more difficult if the protocol were already fixed and the security built as an afterthought. Security by design can also reduce the mechanisms' overheads compared to having to build modular, wrap-around security mechanisms after the rest of the functionality and performance mechanisms have been fixed. This review paper motivates such security-by-design practices as the UAV flying base stations are developed and standardized.

6. Conclusions

This paper intends to motivate and inform further research and development to secure the availability and integrity of UAV flying base station operations. We therefore identify the unique properties of the flying base station while describing and building on its component technologies, including the traditional telecommunications networking (including the stationary ground base station), UAV drone, embedded and battery control, authentication, and distributed networking. We review the related literature in securing the component technologies that would be especially useful in addressing the unique properties and the corresponding gaps for securing the flying base station. This paper ends with discussions of future works to facilitate future research and highlights important remaining challenges to secure UAV flying base stations. The future research directions highlighted in this review paper include taking a systems approach to study the security of the flying base station and its surrounding infrastructure, practicing and incorporating security-by-design as the flying base station technology is developed, using the flying base station for security opportunities, and transitioning to practice, implementations, and standardization.

Author Contributions: Conceptualization, S.-Y.C., J.K. (Jonghyun Kim) and J.K. (Jinoh Kim); methodology, S.-Y.C. and K.P.; software, K.P.; validation, S.-Y.C. and K.P.; investigation, S.-Y.C. and K.P.; writing—original draft preparation, S.-Y.C.; writing—review and editing, S.-Y.C., K.P., J.K. (Jonghyun Kim) and J.K. (Jinoh Kim); visualization, S.-Y.C. and K.P.; supervision, S.-Y.C. and J.K. (Jonghyun Kim); project administration, S.-Y.C., J.K. (Jonghyun Kim) and J.K. (Jinoh Kim); funding acquisition, S.-Y.C., J.K. (Jonghyun Kim) and J.K. (Jinoh Kim). All authors have read and agreed to the published version of the manuscript.

Funding: This work was supported by an Institute of Information and Communications Technology Planning and Evaluation (IITP) grant funded by the Korean government (MSIT) (No.2021-0-00796, Research on Foundational Technologies for 6G Autonomous Security-by-Design to Guarantee Constant Quality of Security).

Data Availability Statement: No new data were created.

Conflicts of Interest: The authors declare no conflict of interest. The funders had no role in the design of the study; in the collection, analyses, or interpretation of data; in the writing of the manuscript; or in the decision to publish the results.

References

1. 3rd Generation Partnership Project. Enhancement for Unmanned Aerial Vehicles. 2019. Available online: https://portal.3gpp.org/desktopmodules/Specifications/SpecificationDetails.aspx?specificationId=3557 (accessed on 15 April 2023).
2. 3rd Generation Partnership Project. Uncrewed Aerial System (UAS) Support in 3GPP. 2022. Available online: https://portal.3gpp.org/desktopmodules/Specifications/SpecificationDetails.aspx?specificationId=3545 (accessed on 15 April 2023).
3. Wang, H.M.; Zhang, X.; Jiang, J.C. UAV-Involved Wireless Physical-Layer Secure Communications: Overview and Research Directions. *IEEE Wirel. Commun.* **2019**, *26*, 32–39. [CrossRef]
4. Yao, H.; Qin, R.; Chen, X. Unmanned Aerial Vehicle for Remote Sensing Applications—A Review. *Remote Sens.* **2019**, *11*, 1443. [CrossRef]
5. Fascista, A. Toward Integrated Large-Scale Environmental Monitoring Using WSN/UAV/Crowdsensing: A Review of Applications, Signal Processing, and Future Perspectives. *Sensors* **2022**, *22*, 1824. [CrossRef] [PubMed]
6. Fotouhi, A.; Qiang, H.; Ding, M.; Hassan, M.; Giordano, L.G.; Garcia-Rodriguez, A.; Yuan, J. Survey on UAV Cellular Communications: Practical Aspects, Standardization Advancements, Regulation, and Security Challenges. *IEEE Commun. Surv. Tutor.* **2019**, *21*, 3417–3442. [CrossRef]
7. Shrestha, R.; Bajracharya, R.; Kim, S. 6G Enabled Unmanned Aerial Vehicle Traffic Management: A Perspective. *IEEE Access* **2021**, *9*, 91119–91136. [CrossRef]

8. Lykou, G.; Moustakas, D.; Gritzalis, D. Defending Airports from UAS: A Survey on Cyber-Attacks and Counter-Drone Sensing Technologies. *Sensors* **2020**, *20*, 3537. [CrossRef]
9. Nassi, B.; Bitton, R.; Masuoka, R.; Shabtai, A.; Elovici, Y. SoK: Security and Privacy in the Age of Commercial Drones. In Proceedings of the 2021 IEEE Symposium on Security and Privacy (SP), San Francisco, CA, USA, 24–27 May 2021; pp. 1434–1451. [CrossRef]
10. Kim, S.G.; Lee, E.; Hong, I.P.; Yook, J.G. Review of Intentional Electromagnetic Interference on UAV Sensor Modules and Experimental Study. *Sensors* **2022**, *22*, 2384. [CrossRef]
11. Tlili, F.; Fourati, L.C.; Ayed, S.; Ouni, B. Investigation on vulnerabilities, threats and attacks prohibiting UAVs charging and depleting UAVs batteries: Assessments & countermeasures. *Ad Hoc Netw.* **2022**, *129*, 102805. [CrossRef]
12. Rushanan, M.; Rubin, A.D.; Kune, D.F.; Swanson, C.M. SoK: Security and Privacy in Implantable Medical Devices and Body Area Networks. In Proceedings of the 2014 IEEE Symposium on Security and Privacy, San Jose, CA, USA, 18–21 May 2014; pp. 524–539. [CrossRef]
13. Alrawi, O.; Lever, C.; Antonakakis, M.; Monrose, F. SoK: Security Evaluation of Home-Based IoT Deployments. In Proceedings of the 2019 IEEE Symposium on Security and Privacy (SP), San Francisco, CA, USA, 19–23 May 2019; pp. 1362–1380. [CrossRef]
14. 3GPP. TS 23.003. Numbering, Addressing and Identification, 2021. Available online: https://portal.3gpp.org/desktopmodules/Specifications/SpecificationDetails.aspx?specificationId=729 (accessed on 15 April 2023).
15. 3GPP. TS 36.321. Medium Access Control (MAC) Protocol Specification. 2021. Available online: https://portal.3gpp.org/desktopmodules/Specifications/SpecificationDetails.aspx?specificationId=3194 (accessed on 15 April 2023).
16. 3GPP. TS 36.331. Evolved Universal Terrestrial Radio Access (E-UTRA); Radio Resource Control (RRC). 2021. Available online: https://portal.3gpp.org/desktopmodules/Specifications/SpecificationDetails.aspx?specificationId=2440 (accessed on 15 April 2023).
17. Chang, S.Y.; Hu, Y.C.; Laurenti, N. SimpleMAC: A jamming-resilient MAC-layer protocol for wireless channel coordination. In Proceedings of the 18th Annual International Conference on Mobile Computing and Networking, Istanbul, Turkey, 22–26 August 2012; pp. 77–88.
18. Vo-Huu, T.D.; Vo-Huu, T.D.; Noubir, G. Interleaving Jamming in Wi-Fi Networks. In Proceedings of the 9th ACM Conference on Security & Privacy in Wireless and Mobile Networks, Darmstadt, Germany, 18–20 July 2016; WiSec '16; pp. 31–42. [CrossRef]
19. Chiang, J.T.; Hu, Y.C. Cross-Layer Jamming Detection and Mitigation in Wireless Broadcast Networks. In Proceedings of the 13th Annual ACM International Conference on Mobile Computing and Networking, Montreal, QC, Canada, 9–14 September 2007; MobiCom '07; pp. 346–349. [CrossRef]
20. Kulkarni, R.V.; Venayagamoorthy, G.K. Neural network based secure media access control protocol for wireless sensor networks. In Proceedings of the 2009 International Joint Conference on Neural Networks, Atlanta, GA, USA, 14–19 June 2009; pp. 1680–1687. [CrossRef]
21. Chang, S.Y.; Hu, Y.C. SecureMAC: Securing wireless medium access control against insider denial-of-service attacks. *IEEE Trans. Mob. Comput.* **2017**, *16*, 3527–3540. [CrossRef]
22. Tung, Y.C.; Han, S.; Chen, D.; Shin, K.G. Vulnerability and Protection of Channel State Information in Multiuser MIMO Networks. In Proceedings of the 2014 ACM SIGSAC Conference on Computer and Communications Security, Scottsdale, AZ, USA, 3–7 November 2014; CCS '14; pp. 775–786. [CrossRef]
23. Hou, T.; Bi, S.; Wang, T.; Lu, Z.; Liu, Y.; Misra, S.; Sagduyu, Y. MUSTER: Subverting User Selection in MU-MIMO Networks. In Proceedings of the IEEE INFOCOM 2022-IEEE Conference on Computer Communications, Virtual Event, 2–5 May 2022; pp. 140–149. [CrossRef]
24. Hussain, S.R.; Echeverria, M.; Karim, I.; Chowdhury, O.; Bertino, E. 5GReasoner: A Property-Directed Security and Privacy Analysis Framework for 5G Cellular Network Protocol. In Proceedings of the 2019 ACM SIGSAC Conference on Computer and Communications Security, London, UK, 11–15 November 2019; CCS '19; pp. 669–684. [CrossRef]
25. Ettiane, R.; Chaoub, A.; Elkouch, R. Toward securing the control plane of 5G mobile networks against DoS threats: Attack scenarios and promising solutions. *J. Inf. Secur. Appl.* **2021**, *61*, 102943. [CrossRef]
26. Raavi, M.; Wuthier, S.; Sarker, A.; Kim, J.; Kim, J.H.; Chang, S.Y. Towards Securing Availability in 5G: Analyzing the Injection Attack Impact on Core Network. In Proceedings of the Silicon Valley Cybersecurity Conference: Second Conference, SVCC 2021, San Jose, CA, USA, 2–3 December 2021; Revised Selected Papers; Springer: Cham, Switzerland, 2022; pp. 143–154.
27. Park, S.; Kim, D.; Park, Y.; Cho, H.; Kim, D.; Kwon, S. 5G Security Threat Assessment in Real Networks. *Sensors* **2021**, *21*, 5524. [CrossRef]
28. Sarker, A.; Byun, S.; Raavi, M.; Kim, J.; Kim, J.; Chang, S.Y. Dynamic ID randomization for user privacy in mobile network. *ETRI J.* **2022**, *44*, 903–914. [CrossRef]
29. Ahmad, I.; Kumar, T.; Liyanage, M.; Okwuibe, J.; Ylianttila, M.; Gurtov, A. Overview of 5G Security Challenges and Solutions. *IEEE Commun. Stand. Mag.* **2018**, *2*, 36–43. [CrossRef]
30. Samarakoon, S.; Siriwardhana, Y.; Porambage, P.; Liyanage, M.; Chang, S.Y.; Kim, J.; Kim, J.; Ylianttila, M. 5G-NIDD: A Comprehensive Network Intrusion Detection Dataset Generated over 5G Wireless Network. *arXiv* **2022**, arXiv:2212.01298. [CrossRef]
31. Brik, V.; Banerjee, S.; Gruteser, M.; Oh, S. Wireless Device Identification with Radiometric Signatures. In Proceedings of the 14th ACM International Conference on Mobile Computing and Networking, San Francisco, CA, USA, 14–19 September 2008; MobiCom '08; pp. 116–127. [CrossRef]

32. Yu, P.L.; Baras, J.S.; Sadler, B.M. Physical-Layer Authentication. *IEEE Trans. Inf. Forensics Secur.* **2008**, *3*, 38–51. [CrossRef]
33. Wang, W.; Sun, Z.; Piao, S.; Zhu, B.; Ren, K. Wireless Physical-Layer Identification: Modeling and Validation. *IEEE Trans. Inf. Forensics Secur.* **2016**, *11*, 2091–2106. [CrossRef]
34. Shaik, A.; Borgaonkar, R.; Park, S.; Seifert, J.P. On the impact of rogue base stations in 4g/lte self organizing networks. In Proceedings of the 11th ACM Conference on Security & Privacy in Wireless and Mobile Networks, Stockholm, Sweden, 18–20 June 2018; pp. 75–86.
35. Hussain, S.; Chowdhury, O.; Mehnaz, S.; Bertino, E. LTEInspector: A systematic approach for adversarial testing of 4G LTE. In Proceedings of the Network and Distributed Systems Security (NDSS) Symposium 2018, San Diego, CA, USA, 18–21 February 2018.
36. Yang, H.; Bae, S.; Son, M.; Kim, H.; Kim, S.M.; Kim, Y. Hiding in plain signal: Physical signal overshadowing attack on {LTE}. In Proceedings of the 28th USENIX Security Symposium (USENIX Security 19), Santa Clara, CA, USA, 14–16 August 2019; pp. 55–72.
37. Kim, H.; Lee, J.; Lee, E.; Kim, Y. Touching the untouchables: Dynamic security analysis of the LTE control plane. In Proceedings of the 2019 IEEE Symposium on Security and Privacy (SP), San Francisco, CA, USA, 20–22 May 2019; pp. 1153–1168.
38. Shaik, A.; Borgaonkar, R.; Park, S.; Seifert, J.P. New vulnerabilities in 4G and 5G cellular access network protocols: Exposing device capabilities. In Proceedings of the 12th Conference on Security and Privacy in Wireless and Mobile Networks, Miami, FL, USA, 15–17 May 2019; pp. 221–231.
39. Mulliner, C.; Golde, N.; Seifert, J.P. {SMS} of Death: From Analyzing to Attacking Mobile Phones on a Large Scale. In Proceedings of the 20th USENIX Security Symposium (USENIX Security 11), San Francisco, CA, USA, 8–12 August 2011.
40. Zhang, Y.; Liu, B.; Lu, C.; Li, Z.; Duan, H.; Hao, S.; Liu, M.; Liu, Y.; Wang, D.; Li, Q. Lies in the Air: Characterizing Fake-base-station Spam Ecosystem in China. In Proceedings of the 2020 ACM SIGSAC Conference on Computer and Communications Security, Virtual Event, 9–13 November 2020; pp. 521–534.
41. Hussain, S.R.; Echeverria, M.; Singla, A.; Chowdhury, O.; Bertino, E. Insecure connection bootstrapping in cellular networks: The root of all evil. In Proceedings of the 12th Conference on Security and Privacy in Wireless and Mobile Networks, Miami, FL, USA, 15–17 May 2019; pp. 1–11.
42. Singla, A.; Behnia, R.; Hussain, S.R.; Yavuz, A.; Bertino, E. Look before you leap: Secure connection bootstrapping for 5g networks to defend against fake base-stations. In Proceedings of the 2021 ACM Asia Conference on Computer and Communications Security, Virtual Event, 7–11 June 2021; pp. 501–515.
43. Tippenhauer, N.O.; Pöpper, C.; Rasmussen, K.B.; Capkun, S. On the Requirements for Successful GPS Spoofing Attacks. In Proceedings of the 18th ACM Conference on Computer and Communications Security, Chicago, IL, USA, 17–21 October 2011; CCS '11; pp. 75–86. [CrossRef]
44. Kerns, A.J.; Shepard, D.P.; Bhatti, J.A.; Humphreys, T.E. Unmanned aircraft capture and control via GPS spoofing. *J. Field Robot.* **2014**, *31*, 617–636. [CrossRef]
45. Davidovich, B.; Nassi, B.; Elovici, Y. Towards the Detection of GPS Spoofing Attacks against Drones by Analyzing Camera's Video Stream. *Sensors* **2022**, *22*, 2608. [CrossRef]
46. Chang, S.Y.; Park, K.; Kim, J.; Kim, J. Towards Securing UAV Flying Base Station: Misplacement Impact Analyses on Battery and Power. In Proceedings of the Sixth International Workshop on Systems and Network Telemetry and Analytics (SNTA 2023), Orlando, FL, USA, 20 June 2023.
47. Poturalski, M.; Flury, M.; Papadimitratos, P.; Hubaux, J.P.; Le Boudec, J.Y. The cicada attack: Degradation and denial of service in IR ranging. In Proceedings of the 2010 IEEE International Conference on Ultra-Wideband, Nanjing, China, 20–23 September 2010; Volume 2, pp. 1–4. [CrossRef]
48. Moser, D.; Leu, P.; Lenders, V.; Ranganathan, A.; Ricciato, F.; Capkun, S. Investigation of Multi-Device Location Spoofing Attacks on Air Traffic Control and Possible Countermeasures. In Proceedings of the 22nd Annual International Conference on Mobile Computing and Networking, New York, NY, USA, 3–7 October 2016; MobiCom '16; pp. 375–386. [CrossRef]
49. Capkun, S.; Hubaux, J.P. Secure positioning of wireless devices with application to sensor networks. In Proceedings of the 24th Annual Joint Conference of the IEEE Computer and Communications Societies, Miami, FL, USA, 13–17 March 2005; Volume 3, pp. 1917–1928. [CrossRef]
50. Leu, P.; Singh, M.; Roeschlin, M.; Paterson, K.G.; Čapkun, S. Message Time of Arrival Codes: A Fundamental Primitive for Secure Distance Measurement. In Proceedings of the 2020 IEEE Symposium on Security and Privacy (SP), San Francisco, CA, USA, 18–21 May 2020; pp. 500–516. [CrossRef]
51. Singh, M.; Leu, P.; Abdou, A.; Capkun, S. UWB-ED: Distance Enlargement Attack Detection in Ultra-Wideband. In Proceedings of the 28th USENIX Security Symposium (USENIX Security 19), Santa Clara, CA, USA, 14–16 August 2019; pp. 73–88.
52. Vo-Huu, T.D.; Vo-Huu, T.D.; Noubir, G. Spectrum-Flexible Secure Broadcast Ranging. In Proceedings of the 14th ACM Conference on Security and Privacy in Wireless and Mobile Networks, Virtual Event, United Arab Emirates, 28 June–2 July 2021; WiSec '21; pp. 300–310. [CrossRef]
53. Sharma, A.; Jaekel, A. Machine Learning Approach for Detecting Location Spoofing in VANET. In Proceedings of the 2021 International Conference on Computer Communications and Networks (ICCCN), Virtual Event, 19–22 July 2021; pp. 1–6. [CrossRef]
54. Desnitsky, V.; Rudavin, N.; Kotenko, I. Modeling and evaluation of battery depletion attacks on unmanned aerial vehicles in crisis management systems. In Proceedings of the International Symposium on Intelligent and Distributed Computing, Saint-Petersburg, Russia, 7–9 October 2019; pp. 323–332.

55. Khan, M.A.; Ullah, I.; Kumar, N.; Oubbati, O.S.; Qureshi, I.M.; Noor, F.; Ullah Khanzada, F. An Efficient and Secure Certificate-Based Access Control and Key Agreement Scheme for Flying Ad-Hoc Networks. *IEEE Trans. Veh. Technol.* **2021**, *70*, 4839–4851. [CrossRef]
56. Desnitsky, V.; Kotenko, I. Simulation and assessment of battery depletion attacks on unmanned aerial vehicles for crisis management infrastructures. *Simul. Model. Pract. Theory* **2021**, *107*, 102244. [CrossRef]
57. Halperin, D.; Heydt-Benjamin, T.S.; Ransford, B.; Clark, S.S.; Defend, B.; Morgan, W.; Fu, K.; Kohno, T.; Maisel, W.H. Pacemakers and Implantable Cardiac Defibrillators: Software Radio Attacks and Zero-Power Defenses. In Proceedings of the 2008 IEEE Symposium on Security and Privacy (sp 2008), Oakland, CA, USA, 18–21 May 2008; pp. 129–142. [CrossRef]
58. Siddiqi, M.A.; Strydis, C. Towards Realistic Battery-DoS Protection of Implantable Medical Devices. In Proceedings of the 16th ACM International Conference on Computing Frontiers, Alghero, Italy, 30 April–2 May 2019; CF '19, pp. 42–49. [CrossRef]
59. Chang, S.Y.; Kumar, S.L.S.; Tran, B.A.N.; Viswanathan, S.; Park, Y.; Hu, Y.C. Power-positive networking using wireless charging: Protecting energy against battery exhaustion attacks. In Proceedings of the 10th ACM Conference on Security and Privacy in Wireless and Mobile Networks, Boston, MA, USA, 18–20 July 2017; pp. 52–57.
60. Chang, S.Y.; Kumar, S.L.S.; Hu, Y.C.; Park, Y. Power-Positive Networking: Wireless-Charging-Based Networking to Protect Energy against Battery DoS Attacks. *ACM Trans. Sen. Netw.* **2019**, *15*, 1–25. [CrossRef]
61. Moyers, B.R.; Dunning, J.P.; Marchany, R.C.; Tront, J.G. Effects of Wi-Fi and Bluetooth Battery Exhaustion Attacks on Mobile Devices. In Proceedings of the 2010 43rd Hawaii International Conference on System Sciences, Honolulu, HI, USA, 5–8 January 2010; pp. 1–9. [CrossRef]
62. Fobe, J.; Nogueira, M.; Batista, D. A New Defensive Technique Against Sleep Deprivation Attacks Driven by Battery Usage. In Proceedings of the Anais do XXII Simpósio Brasileiro em Segurança da Informação e de Sistemas Computacionais, Porto Alegre, RS, Brazil, 12–15 September 2022; pp. 85–96. [CrossRef]
63. Bekmezci, I.; Sen, I.; Erkalkan, E. Flying ad hoc networks (FANET) test bed implementation. In Proceedings of the 2015 7th International Conference on Recent Advances in Space Technologies (RAST), Istanbul, Turkey, 16–19 June 2015; pp. 665–668. [CrossRef]
64. Islam, N.; Hossain, M.K.; Ali, G.G.M.N.; Chong, P.H.J. An expedite group key establishment protocol for Flying Ad-Hoc Network(FANET). In Proceedings of the 2016 5th International Conference on Informatics, Electronics and Vision (ICIEV), Dhaka, Bangladesh, 13–14 May 2016; pp. 312–315. [CrossRef]
65. Maxa, J.A.; Ben Mahmoud, M.S.; Larrieu, N. Secure routing protocol design for UAV Ad hoc NETworks. In Proceedings of the 2015 IEEE/AIAA 34th Digital Avionics Systems Conference (DASC), Prague, Czech Republic, 13–17 September 2015; pp. 4A5-1–4A5-15. [CrossRef]
66. Matsumoto, S.; Reischuk, R.M. IKP: Turning a PKI around with decentralized automated incentives. In Proceedings of the 2017 IEEE Symposium on Security and Privacy (SP), San Jose, CA, USA, 22–26 May 2017; pp. 410–426.
67. Al-Bassam, M. SCPKI: A smart contract-based PKI and identity system. In Proceedings of the ACM Workshop on Blockchain, Cryptocurrencies and Contracts, Abu Dhabi, United Arab Emirates, 2 April 2017; pp. 35–40.
68. Yakubov, A.; Shbair, W.; Wallbom, A.; Sanda, D. A blockchain-based PKI management framework. In Proceedings of the First IEEE/IFIP International Workshop on Managing and Managed by Blockchain (Man2Block) Colocated with IEEE/IFIP NOMS 2018, Tapei, Tawain 23–27 April 2018.
69. Fan, W.; Hong, H.J.; Zhou, X.; Chang, S.Y. A Generic Blockchain Framework to Secure Decentralized Applications. In Proceedings of the ICC 2021-IEEE International Conference on Communications, Montreal, QC, Canada, 14–18 June 2021; pp. 1–7.
70. Sarker, A.; Byun, S.; Fan, W.; Chang, S.Y. Blockchain-based root of trust management in security credential management system for vehicular communications. In Proceedings of the 36th Annual ACM Symposium on Applied Computing, Virtual Event, 22–26 March 2021; pp. 223–231.
71. Didouh, A.; Labiod, H.; Hillali, Y.E.; Rivenq, A. Blockchain-Based Collaborative Certificate Revocation Systems Using Clustering. *IEEE Access* **2022**, *10*, 51487–51500. [CrossRef]
72. Sarker, A.; Byun, S.; Fan, W.; Psarakis, M.; Chang, S.Y. Voting credential management system for electronic voting privacy. In Proceedings of the 2020 IFIP Networking Conference (Networking), Virtual Event, 22–26 June 2020; pp. 589–593.
73. Alvi, S.T.; Uddin, M.N.; Islam, L.; Ahamed, S. DVTChain: A blockchain-based decentralized mechanism to ensure the security of digital voting system voting system. *J. King Saud-Univ.-Comput. Inf. Sci.* **2022**, *34*, 6855–6871. [CrossRef]
74. Fan, W.; Chang, S.Y.; Kumar, S.; Zhou, X.; Park, Y. Blockchain-based Secure Coordination for Distributed SDN Control Plane. In Proceedings of the 2021 IEEE 7th International Conference on Network Softwarization (NetSoft), Tokyo, Japan, 28 June–2 July 2021; pp. 253–257.
75. Fan, W.; Park, Y.; Kumar, S.; Ganta, P.; Zhou, X.; Chang, S.Y. Blockchain-Enabled Collaborative Intrusion Detection in Software Defined Networks. In Proceedings of the 2020 IEEE 19th International Conference on Trust, Security and Privacy in Computing and Communications (TrustCom), Guangzhou, China, 29 December–1 January 2020; pp. 967–974. [CrossRef]
76. Hameed, S.; Shah, S.A.; Saeed, Q.S.; Siddiqui, S.; Ali, I.; Vedeshin, A.; Draheim, D. A Scalable Key and Trust Management Solution for IoT Sensors Using SDN and Blockchain Technology. *IEEE Sens. J.* **2021**, *21*, 8716–8733. [CrossRef]

Disclaimer/Publisher's Note: The statements, opinions and data contained in all publications are solely those of the individual author(s) and contributor(s) and not of MDPI and/or the editor(s). MDPI and/or the editor(s) disclaim responsibility for any injury to people or property resulting from any ideas, methods, instructions or products referred to in the content.

Article

RIS-Assisted Fixed NOMA: Outage Probability Analysis and Transmit Power Optimization

Vinoth Babu Kumaravelu [1,*], Agbotiname Lucky Imoize [2,3,*], Francisco R. Castillo Soria [4], Periyakarupan Gurusamy Sivabalan Velmurugan [5], Sundarrajan Jayaraman Thiruvengadam [5], Dinh-Thuan Do [6] and Arthi Murugadass [7]

[1] Department of Communication Engineering, School of Electronics Engineering, Vellore Institute of Technology, Vellore 632014, Tamil Nadu, India
[2] Department of Electrical and Electronics Engineering, Faculty of Engineering, University of Lagos, Akoka, Lagos 100213, Nigeria
[3] Department of Electrical Engineering and Information Technology, Ruhr University, 44801 Bochum, Germany
[4] Telecommunications Department, Faculty of Science, Autonomous University of San Luis Potosí (UASLP), San Luis Potosí 78300, Mexico; ruben.soria@uaslp.mx
[5] Department of Electronics and Communication Engineering, Thiagarajar College of Engineering, Madurai 625015, Tamil Nadu, India; pgsvels@tce.edu (P.G.S.V); sjtece@tce.edu (S.J.T.)
[6] Department of Computer Science and Information Engineering, College of Information and Electrical Engineering, Asia University, Taichung 41354, Taiwan; dodinhthuan@asia.edu.tw
[7] Department of Computer Science and Engineering (AI & ML), Sreenivasa Institute of Technology and Management Studies, Chittoor 517127, Andhra Pradesh, India; arthimdas@gmail.com
* Correspondence: vinothbab@gmail.com (V.B.K.); aimoize@unilag.edu.ng (A.L.I.)

Citation: Kumaravelu, V.B.; Imoize, A.L.; Soria, F.R.C.; Velmurugan, P.G.S.; Thiruvengadam, S.J.; Do, D.-T.; Murugadass, A. RIS-Assisted Fixed NOMA: Outage Probability Analysis and Transmit Power Optimization. *Future Internet* **2023**, *15*, 249. https://doi.org/10.3390/fi15080249

Academic Editors: Alessandro Raschellà and Michael Mackay

Received: 7 July 2023
Revised: 21 July 2023
Accepted: 22 July 2023
Published: 25 July 2023

Copyright: © 2023 by the authors. Licensee MDPI, Basel, Switzerland. This article is an open access article distributed under the terms and conditions of the Creative Commons Attribution (CC BY) license (https:// creativecommons.org/licenses/by/ 4.0/).

Abstract: Reconfigurable intelligent surface (RIS)-assisted non-orthogonal multiple access (NOMA) has the ability to overcome the challenges of the wireless environment like random fluctuations, shadowing, and mobility in an energy efficient way when compared to multiple input-multiple output (MIMO)-NOMA systems. The NOMA system can deliver controlled channel gains, improved coverage, increased energy efficiency, and enhanced fairness in resource allocation with the help of RIS. RIS-assisted NOMA will be one of the primary potential components of sixth-generation (6G) networks, due to its appealing advantages. The analytical outage probability expressions for smart RIS-assisted fixed NOMA (FNOMA) are derived in this paper, taking into account the instances of RIS as a smart reflector (SR) and an access point (AP). The analytical and simulation findings are found to be extremely comparable. In order to effectively maximize the sum capacity, the formulas for optimal powers to be assigned for a two-user case are also established. According to simulations, RIS-assisted FNOMA surpasses FNOMA in terms of outage and sum capacity. With the aid of RIS and the optimal power assignment, RIS-AP-FNOMA offers ≈62% improvement in sum capacity over the FNOMA system for a signal-to-noise ratio (SNR) of 10 dB and 32 elements in RIS. A significant improvement is also brought about by the increase in reflective elements.

Keywords: fixed non-orthogonal multiple access (FNOMA); optimal power allocation; outage probability; reconfigurable intelligent surface (RIS); sixth-generation (6G); sum capacity

1. Introduction

The wireless society has begun to concentrate on connected intelligence [1]. The major focus of 6G is ultra-high rate, ultra-low latency, ultra-high dependability, and massive connectivity. The key technologies which support 6G are massive MIMO, ultra-dense networks (UDN), terahertz, and millimeter wave (mmWave) communication. The artificial intelligence (AI) and machine learning (ML)-based physical layer will pave the way for emerging applications of 6G [2]. The majority of traditional wireless research focuses on the development of algorithms, protocols, and other tools to combat the effects of radio environments. On the other hand, energy efficiency has received a lot of attention in order to secure sustainable green communication [3]. Massive MIMO employs an array of antennas at both the base station (BS) and the user equipment (UE) to provide unrivaled capacity improvements. Higher radio frequency (RF) bands, on the other hand, make electro-magnetic (EM) waves more susceptible to obstruction, particularly in metropolitan areas [4]. With today's fifth-generation (5G) wireless technologies, universal coverage and massive connectivity are not possible. As a result, new technologies are needed to enable data-intensive and energy-intensive applications.

RIS is a new emerging hardware technology that reduces energy usage, while artificially controlling and changing the propagation environment to create a superior wireless channel. The RIS is built up of a collection of low-cost, passive reflecting components that reconfigure incident EM waves [5,6]. Using RIS, the uncontrollable wireless environment is transformed into a semi-controllable wireless environment. RIS can be simply installed on a variety of surfaces, including building facades, vehicle doors, roadside billboards, indoor walls, unmanned aerial vehicles (UAVs), pedestrian clothing, and so on. Tall buildings can obstruct the line-of-sight (LoS) between BS and UEs, reducing throughput significantly. The judicious placement of RIS can create a virtual LoS between the BS and the UEs, improving the signal-to-interference plus noise ratio (SINR). RIS can passively beamform signals collected from a transmitter to a desired receiver [7]. Unlike traditional amplify-and-forward (AF) and decode-and-forward (DF) relays, power amplifiers are not required for RIS [8–10]. Further, energy sources are also not required to encode, decode, retransmit, and process RF signals [4]. As a result, RIS installation is both energy efficient and environmentally benign. RIS can be integrated with other emerging technologies, such as NOMA, simultaneous wireless information and power transfer (SWIPT), UAV-aided communication, physical layer security (PLS), cognitive radios, autonomous cars, etc., due to its appealing features [11]. Power-domain NOMA can be coupled with RIS to improve spectral efficiency and the enormous connectivity. In NOMA, the signals of different users are overlaid in the power domain so that the spectrum is exploited more efficiently. Based on the channel conditions, users are explored opportunistically. Further, it is also compatible with full-duplex relays, index modulation (IM), etc. Because of these advantages, RIS provides unlimited potential to the 6G wireless technologies.

RIS can boost cell-edge users' received signal power, while also reducing interference from nearby cells [12]. The power loss due to long haul communication can be overcome by RIS-SWIPT [13]. It helps mobile edge computing-based internet of things (IoT) networks function better in terms of latency [14]. It acts as an EM signal reflection hub, allowing the massive connectivity of device-to-device (D2D) networks [15]. It can improve PLS by intelligently canceling unauthorized transmissions using passive beamforming [16]. It can be effectively used for indoor rate-hungry applications like virtual reality (VR). The RIS-coupled visible light communications (VLC) and wireless-fidelity (Wi-Fi) ensure zero blind spots [17]. It can be utilized in vehicular ad hoc networks (VANET), autonomous vehicular networks, robotics networks [18], UAV networks [19], autonomous underwater vehicular networks, intelligent sensor networks, etc.

The following is the order in which the rest of the manuscript is presented: Related works on RIS and NOMA are discussed in Section 2. Analytical expressions for outage probability are developed in Section 3 for RIS as a smart reflector (RIS-SR)-assisted FNOMA system. Most of the traditional works integrating RIS and NOMA assume this RIS-SR-FNOMA configuration, with passive RIS installed far from the BS and UE. Because of propagation losses and shadowing, RIS may receive very weak signals and may not beamform the received signals to the intended users. As a result, RIS as an AP (RIS-AP)-assisted FNOMA configuration is proposed, in which the passive RIS is located near the AP. Analytical expressions for outage probability are developed in Section 4 for RIS-AP-FNOMA. In Section 5, analytical expressions are derived for assigning optimal powers to both the near user (NU) and far user (FU) of the NOMA system. In Section 6, extensive Monte Carlo (MC) simulations are carried through MATLAB R2023a to corroborate the developed analytical expressions. This research aimed to demonstrate that the RIS-AP-

FNOMA configuration outperforms the traditional RIS-SR-FNOMA configuration in terms of outage and sum capacity. The research findings as well as future works are described in the Conclusions.

2. Related Work

Liaskos, C. et al. developed the hypersurface tile as a prototype of RIS to realize the software-controlled wireless environment [20]. Renzo, M.D. et al. highlighted the recent research progress and key challenges in RIS-assisted communication [21]. Basar, E. et al. discussed the differences between RIS and other technologies, as well as the benefits and challenges of RIS-assisted communication [22]. Wu, Q. et al. covered the issues related to RIS-assisted communication, the optimization of passive beamforming, channel estimation, and placement design [23]. Björnson, E. et al. explored the myths and overstatements concerning the RIS that have been spread in the literature [7]. Huang, C. et al. investigated the impact of using RIS with multiple antenna BS and multiple users [3]. The transmit power and phase shifts are designed to be energy efficient such that individual link budgets of the UEs are guaranteed. Two computationally efficient approaches are explored in this article. The first technique uses fractional programming for optimal transmit power allocation and gradient descent to obtain RIS phase shift coefficients. The second approach optimizes RIS phase shifts using fractional programming. The suggested algorithms' performance is investigated in a realistic outdoor environment. When compared to typical multiple antenna AF relays, RIS-assisted resource allocation has a maximum energy efficiency improvement of 300%. Shi, W. et al. evaluated the RIS-assisted communication system under security risks [24]. The placement of RIS here is intended to increase the authorized user's secrecy probability of outage. The theoretical secrecy probability of outage expressions is constructed by considering the discrete phase shifts at RIS. It is established that increasing the RIS elements of a discrete phase shifter by 1.6 times yields a performance comparable to that of a continuous phase shifter.

Yuan, X. et al. highlighted the three important physical layer issues, such as acquiring channel state information (CSI), passive information transfer, and low-complexity design, when incorporating RIS into wireless networks [25]. Some of the prospective RIS research directions are also highlighted, such as PLS and edge intelligence. Guo, H. et al. maximized the weighted sum capacity of all UEs by jointly designing the beamforming at BS and phase shift angles at RIS [26]. On both perfect and poor CSI conditions, the suggested scheme was tested. This approach was shown to be effective, even when the channel uncertainty is less than 10%. Agarwal, A. et al. developed closed-form outage probability expressions for ordered NOMA uplink and downlink by examining generalized fading channels [27]. The authors took into account both statistical and instantaneous CSI-based ordering schemes. Singh, S. and Bansal, M. proposed NOMA-assisted cooperative relaying for reliable communication [28]. At the first and second time slots of cooperative communication, the source and relay transmits a superimposed signal. The exact analytical closed-form outage probability formulas were developed considering Rayleigh fading channel and imperfect successive cancellation decoding. The suggested scheme's outage probability was assessed and compared to that of the traditional cooperative relaying-assisted NOMA.

Yang, Y. et al. jointly optimized the power assignment from the BS to UEs and the phase shift matrix of RIS to maximize the SINR of all the UEs [29]. Ni, W. et al. maximized the sum capacity by jointly optimizing the power allocation, phase shift matrix, user association, decoding order, and channel assignment [30]. Zheng, B. et al. discussed the challenge of optimizing transmit power for a single input-single output (SISO) RIS-assisted NOMA system [31]. The theoretical performance of RIS-assisted orthogonal multiple access (OMA) and RIS-assisted NOMA was compared. All of the preceding works are based on static channel conditions. Guo, Y. et al. developed a joint optimization framework for resource allocation and deciding phase shift angles to maximize the sum capacity of SISO RIS-NOMA downlink [32]. The analysis was carried out under fading channels. To optimize beamforming vectors and phase shift matrices, Fu, M. et al. employed several convex algorithms [33]. The goal of this approach is to minimize the total transmit power for multiple input-single output (MISO) RIS-NOMA. Mu, X. et al. combined active beamforming at BS and passive beamforming at RIS to maximize the sum capacity [34]. Trigui, I. et al. developed the theoretical framework to analyze the outage performance of RIS-aided communication over generalized fading channels and in the existence of phase noise. It was demonstrated that when the fading channels are independent, RIS-aided communication achieves full diversity, even with the existence of phase noise [35].

Singh, S. and Bansal, M. proposed a cooperative cognitive radio NOMA, in which primary and secondary users share a secondary DF relay via NOMA [36]. The closed-form outage probability expressions were developed assuming imperfect CSI and successive interference cancellation (SIC). The influence of channel estimate inaccuracy, power allocated to individual users, and threshold for detection on outage probability was also investigated in this study. MC simulations were used to substantiate the accuracy of analytical outage expressions. Hemanth, A. et al. investigated the implications of hardware impairments on the reliability of RIS-assisted NOMA [37]. The closed-form analytical outage probability and throughput expressions were developed. The number of reflective components and power assignment factors were found to be important in enhancing the performance of RIS-assisted NOMA over OMA. Yang, L. and Yuan, Y. employed RIS-assisted NOMA for PLS [38]. The analytical expressions for secrecy outage probability were derived. When compared to traditional NOMA systems, it was observed that using RIS can improve secrecy performance.

Kumaravelu, V.B. et al. suggested the blind RIS-assisted FNOMA framework with SR and AP configurations for uplink transmission [39]. An optimization problem for power allocations was constructed to maximize the sum capacity of NU and FU. The analytical outage expressions were validated using extensive computer simulations. Blind RIS-SR-NOMA outperformed traditional NOMA by ≈38% for 32 reflective elements and a 20 dB SNR. Arslan, E. et al. examined the active RIS with virtual NOMA for uplink system [40]. Instead of using user-side controlling powers, the concept of power disparity was applied to achieve virtual NOMA. The end-to-end system model, analytical outage probability, and error probability expressions were developed and affirmed using computer simulations. Jadhav, H.K. and Kumaravelu, V.B. studied the downlink blind RIS-assisted framework for ordered NOMA, where channel gains determine user decoding order [41]. The closed-form outage probability and optimal powers to be assigned expressions were developed for stronger and weaker users. As there are more reflecting elements, the sum capacity increased accordingly. The suggested approach outperformed traditional FNOMA and ordered NOMA systems in terms of outage, bit error rate, and sum capacity. The suggested approach outperformed the ordered NOMA system by ≈33% for 20 dB SNR and 32 reflective elements. In this paper, the performance of RIS-assisted FNOMA is evaluated in light of these considerable benefits of RIS and NOMA.

The major contributions of this paper are threefold:
- Analytical outage probability expressions are developed for NU and FU in a RIS-SR-FNOMA and RIS-AP-FNOMA.
- Analytical expressions are developed for optimal power assignment to NU and FU in both RIS-SR-FNOMA and RIS-AP-FNOMA systems.
- Extensive MC simulations are used to corroborate the resulting analytical outage expressions. The accuracy of derived analytical expressions is proved using the strong correlation between the theoretical and simulation results.

3. Outage Probability Analysis of RIS-SR-FNOMA

The conceptual diagram of RIS-SR-FNOMA is illustrated in Figure 1. In this system, RIS with N reflecting elements acts as a smart reflector. The RIS elements are distributed evenly across the users. RIS is placed sufficiently far from the BS and the users. This results in a two-hop communication system. The BS, NU, and FU are considered to have a single antenna. In a two-user scenario, FU performs direct decoding while dealing with the NU signal as interference. The NU decodes the FU signal first, and the influence of that signal is eliminated through SIC. The resulting signal is then used to decode the NU signal.

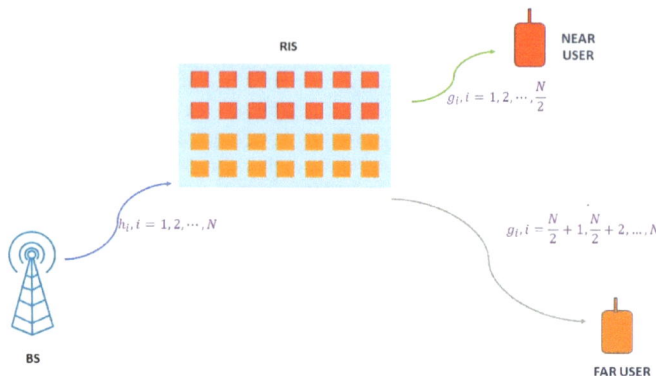

Figure 1. The conceptual diagram of RIS-SR-FNOMA system.

The superposition-coded symbol at the BS is given by [27]

$$x_s = \sqrt{\alpha_{NU} P_s}\, x_{NU} + \sqrt{\alpha_{FU} P_s}\, x_{FU}, \qquad (1)$$

where $\alpha_{NU} P_s$ and $\alpha_{FU} P_s$ are the powers allocated to NU and FU, respectively. In FNOMA, $\alpha_{NU} < \alpha_{FU}$ and $\alpha_{NU} + \alpha_{FU} = 1$. x_{NU} and x_{FU} are the transmit symbols corresponding to NU and FU, respectively. P_s is the average transmit symbol power.

The channel condition between BS to RIS and RIS to UE are modeled as $h_i = \alpha_i e^{j\theta_i}$, $h_i \sim \mathcal{CN}(0,1)$, $i = 1, 2, \ldots, N$ and $g_i = \beta_i e^{j\psi_i}$, $g_i \sim \mathcal{CN}(0,1)$, $i = 1, 2, \ldots, N$ respectively. Here, $\alpha_i = \sqrt{(Re(h_i)^2 + Im(h_i)^2)}$, $\theta_i = \tan^{-1}\left(\frac{Im(h_i)}{Re(h_i)}\right)$, $\beta_i = \sqrt{(Re(g_i)^2 + Im(g_i)^2)}$ and $\psi_i = \tan^{-1}\left(\frac{Im(g_i)}{Re(g_i)}\right)$.

The passive RIS introduces phase shift ϕ_i at each reflecting element, and it is given by

$$\phi_i = -\theta_i - \psi_i, i = 1, 2, \ldots, N. \qquad (2)$$

The signal received at the FU is [42]

$$r_{FU} = \left(\sum_{i=\frac{N}{2}+1}^{N} g_i h_i e^{j\phi_i}\right) x_s + n_{FU}, \qquad (3)$$

where n_{FU} is the additive white Gaussian noise (AWGN) at FU and $n_{FU} \in \mathcal{CN}(0, N_0)$. N_o is the noise variance. Substituting the channel conditions, the received signal at the FU is

$$r_{FU} = \left(\sum_{i=\frac{N}{2}+1}^{N} \alpha_i \beta_i\right) x_s + n_{FU}. \qquad (4)$$

Let $B = \sum_{i=\frac{N}{2}+1}^{N} \alpha_i \beta_i$ be the cumulative effect of the dual-hop channel for the FU. Substituting B and (1) in (4), the received signal at FU is

$$r_{FU} = B\sqrt{\alpha_{NU} P_s}\, x_{NU} + B\sqrt{\alpha_{FU} P_s}\, x_{FU} + n_{FU}. \qquad (5)$$

Since the cumulative dual-hop channel for the FU is weaker and α_{NU} is smaller, the first term in (5) is not more dominant than the second term. Hence, by treating the NU signal as interference, the FU signal is detected. The SINR for decoding FU signal, while treating NU signal as interference, is

$$\gamma_{FU}^{x_{FU}} = \frac{B^2 \alpha_{FU} P_s}{B^2 \alpha_{NU} P_s + N_0}. \tag{6}$$

At the desired data rate $\tilde{R}_{FU}$, the outage for FU occurs when

$$\log_2(1 + \gamma_{FU}^{x_{FU}}) \leq \tilde{R}_{FU}. \tag{7}$$

Substituting (6) in (7), the outage probability at the FU is defined as

$$P_{FU}^{o\_SR} = P\left[\log_2\left(1 + \frac{B^2 \alpha_{FU} P_s}{B^2 \alpha_{NU} P_s + N_0}\right) \leq \tilde{R}_{FU}\right]. \tag{8}$$

Simplifying (8) gives

$$P_{FU}^{o\_SR} = P\left[B^2 \leq \frac{R_{FU} N_0}{(\alpha_{FU} - \alpha_{NU} R_{FU}) P_s}\right], \tag{9}$$

where $R_{FU} = 2^{\tilde{R}_{FU}} - 1$. Since α_i and β_i are positive real, B is always positive. Hence, Equation (9) can be presented as

$$P_{FU}^{o\_SR} = P\left[B \leq \sqrt{\frac{R_{FU} N_0}{(\alpha_{FU} - \alpha_{NU} R_{FU}) P_s}}\right]. \tag{10}$$

As the number of reflecting elements allocated to FU (N_{FU}) is larger, according to the central limit theorem (CLT), B follows the Gaussian probability density function $f_B(b)$ with mean $m_B = \frac{N_{FU} \pi}{4}$ and variance $\sigma_B^2 = N_{FU}\left[1 - \frac{\pi^2}{16}\right]$. The outage probability at FU is

$$P_{FU}^{o\_SR} = \int_0^{y_{FU}} f_B(b) db, \tag{11}$$

where $y_{FU} = \sqrt{\frac{R_{FU} N_0}{(\alpha_{FU} - \alpha_{NU} R_{FU}) P_s}}$. Substituting $f_B(b)$ and integrating within the limit yields the outage probability as

$$P_{FU}^{o\_SR} = \frac{\sigma_B \left\{ erf\left(\frac{y_{FU} - m_B}{\sqrt{2}\sigma_B}\right) + erf\left(\frac{m_B}{\sqrt{2}\sigma_B}\right)\right\}}{2\sigma_B}, \tag{12}$$

where $erf(.)$ is the error function. The signal received by the NU is

$$r_{NU} = \left(\sum_{i=1}^{\frac{N}{2}} g_i h_i e^{j\phi_i}\right) x_s + n_{NU}, \tag{13}$$

where n_{NU} is the AWGN at the NU and $n_{NU} \in \mathcal{CN}(0, N_0)$. Substituting channel conditions and (2) in (13) gives

$$r_{NU} = \left(\sum_{i=1}^{\frac{N}{2}} \alpha_i \beta_i\right) x_s + n_{NU}. \tag{14}$$

Let $A = \sum_{i=1}^{\frac{N}{2}} \alpha_i \beta_i$ be the cumulative effect of the dual-hop channel for the NU. Substituting A and (1) in (14) gives

$$r_{NU} = A\sqrt{\alpha_{NU} P_s} x_{NU} + A\sqrt{\alpha_{FU} P_s} x_{FU} + n_{NU}. \tag{15}$$

Since A and α_{FU} are higher, the second term in (15) is more dominant than the first term. Hence, the FU signal is detected first by the NU. The SINR of decoding the FU signal at the NU is

$$\gamma_{NU}^{x_{FU}} = \frac{A^2 \alpha_{FU} P_s}{A^2 \alpha_{NU} P_s + N_0}. \tag{16}$$

After decoding x_{FU}, its effect is removed from r_{NU} using SIC.

$$\tilde{r}_{NU} \approx A \sqrt{\alpha_{NU} P_s} \, x_{NU} + n_{NU}. \tag{17}$$

Then, the NU signal is detected. The SNR for decoding x_{NU} at NU is given by

$$\gamma_{NU}^{x_{NU}} = \frac{A^2 \alpha_{NU} P_s}{N_0}. \tag{18}$$

The decoding of the FU signal fails at NU when

$$\log_2\left(1 + \gamma_{NU}^{x_{FU}}\right) \leq \tilde{R}_{FU}. \tag{19}$$

Substituting (16) in (19), the outage probability is given by

$$P\left[\log_2\left(1 + \frac{A^2 \alpha_{FU} P_s}{A^2 \alpha_{NU} P_s + N_0}\right)\right] \leq \tilde{R}_{FU}. \tag{20}$$

Simplifying (20) results in

$$P\left[A^2 \leq \frac{R_{FU} N_0}{(\alpha_{FU} - \alpha_{NU} R_{FU}) P_s}\right]. \tag{21}$$

Since α_i and β_i are positive real, A is always positive. Hence, Equation (21) can be written as

$$P\left[A \leq \sqrt{\frac{R_{FU} N_0}{(\alpha_{FU} - \alpha_{NU} R_{FU}) P_s}}\right]. \tag{22}$$

As the number of reflecting elements allocated to NU is larger, according to CLT, A follows Gaussian distribution $f_A(a)$ with mean $m_A = \frac{N_{NU} \pi}{4}$ and variance $\sigma_A^2 = N_{NU}\left[1 - \frac{\pi^2}{16}\right]$. At the desired rate of $\tilde{R}_{NU}$ at NU, the decoding of the NU signal fails at NU when

$$\log_2\left(1 + \gamma_{NU}^{x_{NU}}\right) \leq \tilde{R}_{NU}. \tag{23}$$

Substituting (18) in (23) gives

$$\log_2\left(1 + \frac{A^2 \alpha_{NU} P_s}{N_0}\right) \leq \tilde{R}_{NU}. \tag{24}$$

Simplifying (24), the outage probability at NU is

$$P\left[A \leq \sqrt{\frac{R_{NU} N_0}{\alpha_{NU} P_s}}\right], \tag{25}$$

where $R_{NU} = 2^{\tilde{R}_{NU}} - 1$. By combining (22) and (25), the overall condition for which decoding of NU signal fails at NU is

$$A \leq \max\left\{\sqrt{\frac{R_{FU} N_0}{(\alpha_{FU} - \alpha_{NU} R_{FU}) P_s}}, \sqrt{\frac{R_{NU} N_0}{\alpha_{NU} P_s}}\right\}. \tag{26}$$

The outage probability of NU is

$$P_{NU}^{o\_SR} = \int_0^{y_{NU}} f_A(a)\mathrm{d}a, \qquad (27)$$

where

$$y_{NU} = max\left\{\sqrt{\frac{R_{FU}N_0}{(\alpha_{FU} - \alpha_{NU}R_{FU})P_s}}, \sqrt{\frac{R_{NU}N_0}{\alpha_{NU}P_s}}\right\}. \qquad (28)$$

After mathematical simplification, the outage probability $P_{NU}^{o\_SR}$ at the NU is given by

$$P_{NU}^{o\_SR} = \frac{\sigma_A\left\{erf\left(\frac{y_{NU}-m_A}{\sqrt{2}\,\sigma_A}\right) + erf\left(\frac{m_A}{\sqrt{2}\,\sigma_A}\right)\right\}}{2\sigma_A}. \qquad (29)$$

4. Outage Probability Analysis of RIS-AP-FNOMA

Most traditional studies on passive RIS presume its deployment to be far from the BS and UE. As a result, the benefits claimed by the RIS may not be realized since RIS receives weaker signals. This makes RIS-SR-FNOMA unrealizable in practical environments. In practice, RIS is effective when it is placed near the transmitter or receiver [42]. In this system, RIS with N elements is installed nearest to BS/AP. Due to this, the effect of fading between the AP and RIS is negligible. As a result, RIS-AP and users communicate in a single hop. The conceptual diagram of RIS-AP-FNOMA is illustrated in Figure 2.

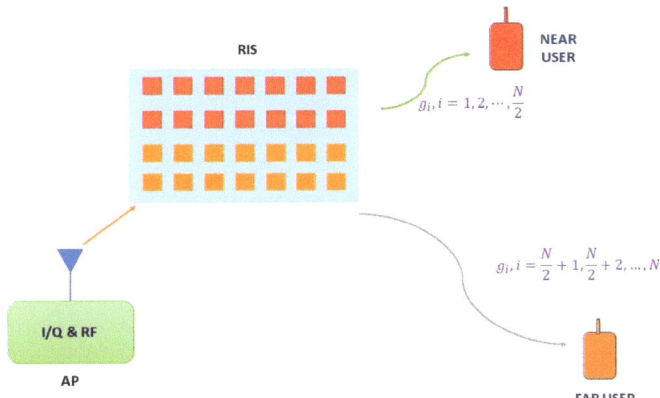

Figure 2. The conceptual diagram of RIS-AP-FNOMA system.

The signal received at the FU is

$$r_{FU} = \left(\sum_{i=\frac{N}{2}+1}^{N} g_i e^{j\phi_i}\right) x_s + n_{FU}, \qquad (30)$$

where g_i is the channel condition between the ith RIS element and UE. The passive RIS introduces phase shift ϕ_i at each reflecting element, which is

$$\phi_i = -\psi_i. \qquad (31)$$

Substituting g_i and (31) in (30), the received signal at the FU is

$$r_{FU} = \left(\sum_{i=\frac{N}{2}+1}^{N} \beta_i\right) x_s + n_{FU}. \qquad (32)$$

Let $C = \sum_{i=\frac{N}{2}+1}^{N} \beta_i$ be the cumulative channel effect between RIS and FU. Using steps similar to (5) to (11) discussed in Section 3, the outage probability of FU is determined as

$$P_{FU}^{o\_AP} = \frac{\sigma_C \left\{ erf\left(\frac{y_{FU} - m_C}{\sqrt{2}\sigma_C}\right) + erf\left(\frac{m_C}{\sqrt{2}\sigma_C}\right) \right\}}{2\sigma_C}. \tag{33}$$

where $m_C = \frac{N_{FU}\pi}{4}$ is the mean and $\sigma_C^2 = N_{FU}\left[1 - \frac{\pi^2}{16}\right]$ is the variance of C.

The signal received by the NU is

$$r_{NU} = \left(\sum_{i=1}^{\frac{N}{2}} g_i e^{j\phi_i}\right) x_s + n_{NU}. \tag{34}$$

Substituting g_i and (31) in (34), the received signal at the NU is

$$r_{NU} = \left(\sum_{i=1}^{\frac{N}{2}} \beta_i\right) x_s + n_{NU}. \tag{35}$$

Let $D = \sum_{i=1}^{\frac{N}{2}} \beta_i$ be the cumulative channel effect between RIS and NU. Using steps similar to (15) to (28) discussed in Section 3, the outage probability of NU is determined as

$$P_{NU}^{o\_AP} = \frac{\sigma_D \left\{ erf\left(\frac{y_{NU} - m_D}{\sqrt{2}\sigma_D}\right) + erf\left(\frac{m_D}{\sqrt{2}\sigma_D}\right) \right\}}{2\sigma_D}. \tag{36}$$

where $m_D = \frac{N_{NU}\pi}{4}$ is the mean, and $\sigma_D^2 = N_{NU}\left[1 - \frac{\pi^2}{16}\right]$ is the variance of D.

5. Transmit Power Optimization for Sum Capacity Maximization

In this section, optimal power allocation strategies for obtaining maximum sum capacity in RIS-SR-FNOMA and RIS-AP-NOMA systems are discussed in detail. The sum capacity of downlink RIS-SR-FNOMA for a two-user scenario is given by

$$C_{NU} + C_{FU} = \log_2\left(1 + \gamma_{NU}^{x_{NU}}\right) + \log_2\left(1 + \gamma_{FU}^{x_{FU}}\right), \tag{37}$$

where C_{NU} and C_{FU} are the capacities of NU and FU, respectively. The optimization problem for determining the power allocation factor α_{NU} and α_{FU} of both NU and FU is formulated as maximizing the sum capacity while satisfying the quality-of-service (QoS) constraints at both NU and FU. It is defined as

$$\max_{\alpha_{NU}, \alpha_{FU}} C_{NU} + C_{FU}. \tag{38}$$

Subject to

$$\log_2\left(1 + \gamma_{NU}^{x_{NU}}\right) \geq \tilde{R}_{NU}. \tag{39}$$

$$\log_2\left(1 + \gamma_{FU}^{x_{FU}}\right) \geq \tilde{R}_{FU}. \tag{40}$$

$$\alpha_{NU} + \alpha_{FU} = 1. \tag{41}$$

Substituting (6) and (18) in (37) gives

$$C_{NU} + C_{FU} = \log_2\left(1 + \frac{A^2 \alpha_{NU} P_s}{N_0}\right) + \log_2\left(1 + \frac{B^2 \alpha_{FU} P_s}{B^2 \alpha_{NU} P_s + N_0}\right). \tag{42}$$

Simplifying (42), it results in

$$C_{NU} + C_{FU} = \log_2\left(\left(1 + B^2\chi\right)\left(\frac{1 + A^2\alpha_{NU}\chi}{1 + B^2\alpha_{NU}\chi}\right)\right). \quad (43)$$

where $\chi = \frac{P_s}{N_0}$ is the received SNR. The term $(1 + B^2\chi)$ is constant. As the term $\left(\frac{1+A^2\alpha_{NU}\chi}{1+B^2\alpha_{NU}\chi}\right)$ is a monotonically increasing function of α_{NU}, the maximum sum capacity can be achieved by assigning a maximum possible value for α_{NU}. By simplifying (43), the condition for α_{NU}, which satisfies the QoS constraints, is given by

$$\underbrace{\frac{R_{NU}}{A^2\chi}}_{\alpha_{NU}^{min}} \leq \alpha_{NU} \leq \underbrace{\frac{B^2\chi - R_{FU}}{B^2\chi(1 + R_{FU})}}_{\alpha_{NU}^{max}}. \quad (44)$$

Any value between α_{NU}^{min} and α_{NU}^{max} is sub-optimal for α_{NU}. In simulations, the average of α_{NU}^{min} and α_{NU}^{max} is assumed to be α_{NU}. The sub-optimal power assigned to NU is

$$\alpha_{NU}^{sub-opt} = \frac{\left(\alpha_{NU}^{min} + \alpha_{NU}^{max}\right)}{2}. \quad (45)$$

The balance power is assigned to the FU:

$$\alpha_{FU}^{sub-opt} = 1 - \alpha_{NU}^{sub-opt}. \quad (46)$$

To find the optimal value of α_{NU}, the first threshold α_{NU}^{min} should be less than the second threshold α_{NU}^{max}

$$\frac{R_{NU}}{A^2\chi} \leq \frac{B^2\chi - R_{FU}}{B^2\chi(1 + R_{FU})}. \quad (47)$$

By solving (47), the minimal SNR demand to satisfy the QoS constraints of users is attained. This is called a feasible region:

$$\chi \geq \frac{R_{NU}}{A^2} + \frac{R_{NU}R_{FU}}{A^2} + \frac{R_{FU}}{B^2}. \quad (48)$$

If the condition in (48) is not met, then it is not possible to choose the value of α_{NU}. The largest value of α_{NU} is the optimal value of α_{NU}, which maximizes the sum capacity:

$$\alpha_{NU}^{opt} = \frac{B^2\chi - R_{FU}}{B^2\chi(1 + R_{FU})}. \quad (49)$$

The balance power is assigned to FU, which is

$$\alpha_{FU}^{opt} = 1 - \alpha_{NU}^{opt}. \quad (50)$$

In a similar way, the optimal powers to be assigned for the users of RIS-AP-FNOMA are derived. The optimal power assigned to the NU of RIS-AP-FNOMA system is given by

$$\alpha_{NU}^{opt} = \frac{C^2\chi - R_{FU}}{C^2\chi_s(1 + R_{FU})}. \quad (51)$$

The balance power is assigned to the FU as in (50). The minimal SNR demand to meet the QoS constraints of the users of RIS-AP-FNOMA is given by

$$\chi \geq \frac{R_{NU}}{D^2} + \frac{R_{NU}R_{FU}}{D^2} + \frac{R_{FU}}{C^2}. \quad (52)$$

6. Simulations and Discussion

In this section, outage, and sum capacity performances of RIS-SR-FNOMA and RIS-AP-FNOMA are simulated and analyzed using MATLAB R2023a. Table 1 lists the parameters assessed for the simulation. The results of the MC simulation are obtained by averaging the outage probability across 10^5 iterations.

Table 1. Simulation parameters.

Parameter	Typical Value
Number of RIS components (N)	32, 64, 128, 256
Number of users	2
Mean channel gain of NU	5
Mean channel gain of FU	1
Desired rate of NU ($\bar{R}_{NU}$)	1 b/s/Hz
Desired rate of FU ($\bar{R}_{FU}$)	1 b/s/Hz
Target outage probability	10^{-4}
Block length	10^5

The outage performance results are shown in Figure 3 for the FU and NU in RIS-SR-FNOMA and conventional FNOMA. It is assumed that $\alpha_{NU} = 0.1$ and $\alpha_{FU} = 0.9$. The total RIS elements of $N = 64$ with 32 elements each for NU and FU are considered. In comparison with RIS-SR-FNOMA, FNOMA without RIS has poor outage performance. In the RIS-SR-FNOMA system, the SNR requirements to procure the target probability of outage are -22 dB and -13 dB for FU and NU, respectively. Since more power is allocated to FU, the outage performance of FU is better than NU for both systems. It is shown that the MC simulation curves closely or exactly match with the analytical results.

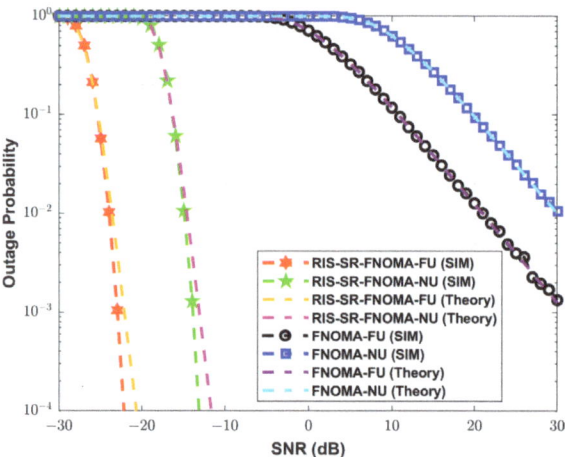

Figure 3. Analysis of outage probability between RIS-SR-FNOMA and FNOMA.

The outage performance results of the FU and NU of RIS-SR-FNOMA are indicated in Figures 4 and 5, respectively, at various numbers of reflective elements with $\alpha_{NU} = 0.2$ and $\alpha_{FU} = 0.8$. With $N = 32$, $N = 64$, $N = 128$ and $N = 256$, the FU of RIS-SR-FNOMA achieves the expected outage probability at an approximate SNR of -8 dB, -21 dB, -28 dB and -35 dB, respectively. The amount of reflecting elements in RIS is found to improve outage performance. As the CLT approximation of B holds true for higher N, at $N = 128$ and $N = 256$, a close match between MC simulation and analytical curves is observed compared to $N = 32$ and $N = 64$. On comparing the outage performance of the NU and FU in Figures 4 and 5, it is evident that the FU outage performance is superior to the NU outage performance.

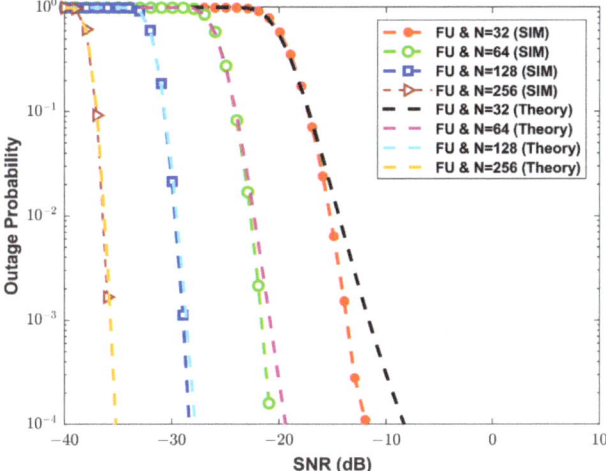

Figure 4. Comparison of RIS-SR-FNOMA FU outage probability by varying N.

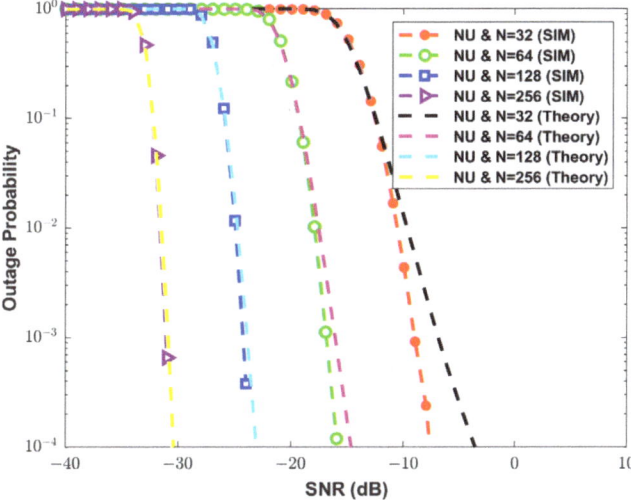

Figure 5. Comparison of RIS-SR-FNOMA NU outage probability by varying N.

The sum capacity of RIS-SR-FNOMA is shown in Figure 6 for different N. The sum capacity for all N increases as the transmit SNR increases. At SNR of -10 dB, the sum capacities are approximately 6.1 b/s/Hz, 8.1 b/s/Hz, 10.2 b/s/Hz and 12.2 b/s/Hz when $N = 32$, $N = 64$, $N = 128$ and $N = 256$ respectively. When the optimal powers are allocated, there is an improvement in the sum capacity over the sub-optimal power assignment for lower SNR. At higher SNR, the optimal and sub-optimal methods have essentially identical sum capacities.

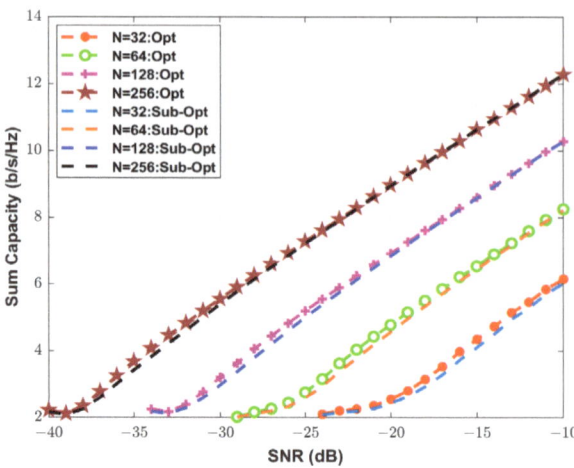

Figure 6. Sum capacity (b/s/Hz) of RIS-SR-FNOMA for optimal and sub-optimal power assignments and varying N.

The simulation parameters for the RIS-AP-FNOMA system are assumed to be the same as those given in Table 1. The outage performance results of RIS-AP-FNOMA and conventional FNOMA are shown in Figure 7. The desired rates and power for FU and NU, as well as N, are set as being similar to Figure 3. In comparison with RIS-AP-FNOMA, FNOMA without RIS has poor outage performance. In the RIS-AP-FNOMA system, the SNR requirements to achieve expected outage probability are -25 dB and -15 dB for FU and NU, respectively. Since more power is assigned to the FU, the outage performance of the FU is better than the NU for both systems. It is shown that the MC simulation curves closely or exactly match the analytical results. When comparing Figures 3 and 7, RIS-AP-FNOMA has a modest improvement over RIS-SR-FNOMA in terms of outage performance.

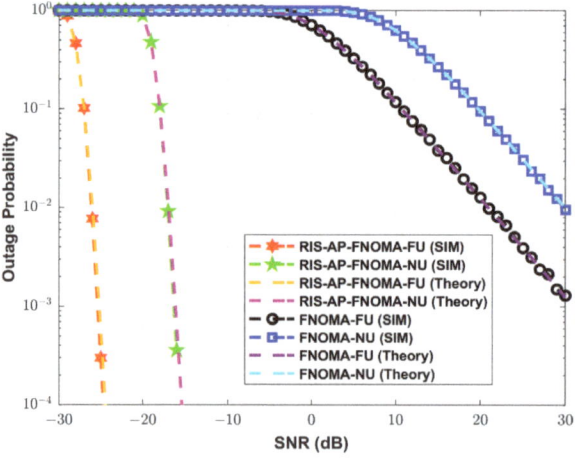

Figure 7. Analysis of outage probability between RIS-AP-FNOMA and FNOMA.

The outage performance results of the FU and NU of RIS-AP-FNOMA are shown in Figures 8 and 9, respectively, at various numbers of reflective elements with $\alpha_{NU} = 0.2$ and $\alpha_{FU} = 0.8$. With $N = 32$, $N = 64$, $N = 128$ and $N = 256$, the FU of RIS-AP-FNOMA achieves the expected outage probability at approximately -15 dB, -24 dB, -31 dB and -37 dB, respectively. It is observed that increasing N in RIS enhances the outage performance. As the CLT approximation of C holds true for higher values of N, at $N = 64$, $N = 128$ and $N = 256$, a close match between the MC simulation and analytical curves is observed compared to $N = 32$. On comparing the outage performance of the NU and FU in Figures 8 and 9, it is evident that the FU outage performance is superior to the NU outage performance. When comparing Figures 4 and 5 with Figures 8 and 9, RIS-AP-FNOMA has a modest improvement over RIS-SR-FNOMA in terms of outage performance.

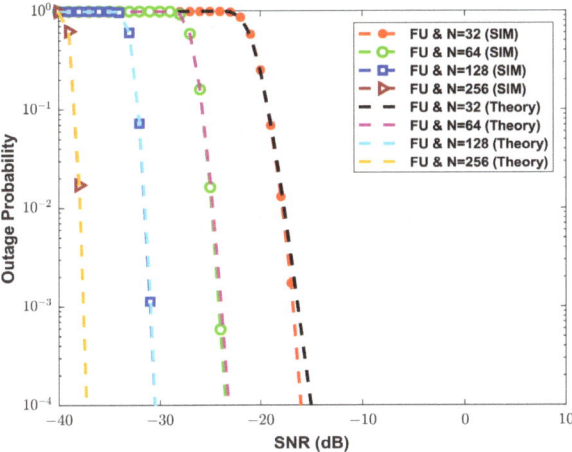

Figure 8. Comparison of RIS-AP-FNOMA FU outage probability by varying N.

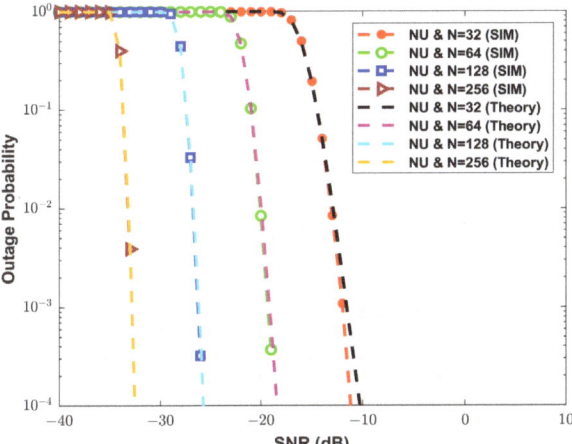

Figure 9. Comparison of RIS-AP-FNOMA NU outage probability by varying N.

The sum capacity (b/s/Hz) of the RIS-AP-FNOMA is shown in Figure 10 for different N in RIS. The sum capacity for all N increases as the transmit SNR increases. At SNR of -10 dB, the sum capacities are 6.5 b/s/Hz, 8.5 b/s/Hz, 10.5 b/s/Hz and 12.5 b/s/Hz when $N = 32$, $N = 64$, $N = 128$ and $N = 256$, respectively. When optimal powers are assigned, there is an improvement in the sum capacity over the sub-optimal power assignment for lower SNR. At higher SNR, the optimal and sub-optimal methods have essentially identical sum capacities.

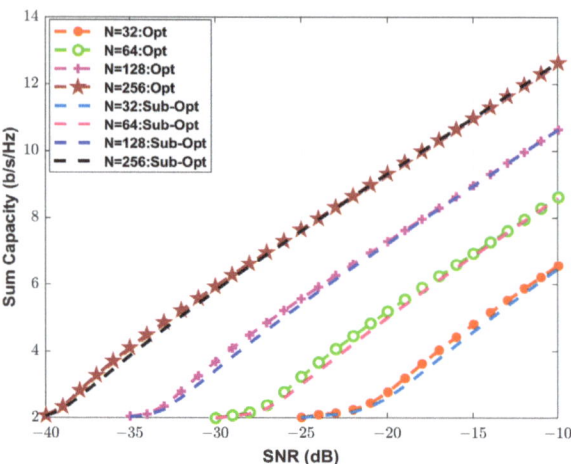

Figure 10. Sum capacity (b/s/Hz) of RIS-AP-FNOMA for optimal and sub-optimal power assignments and varying N.

For optimal and sub-optimal power assignments, the sum capacities (b/s/Hz) of FNOMA, RIS-AP-FNOMA, and RIS-SR-FNOMA systems are analyzed in Figure 11. The sum capacities of the RIS-AP-FNOMA and RIS-SR-FNOMA systems are calculated for the number of passive elements $N = 32$. The FNOMA system has reasonable sum capacities for positive values of SNR, whereas the RIS-SR-FNOMA and RIS-AP-FNOMA systems have good sum capacities, even for negative SNR values. The array and diversity gains via RIS-assisted communication result in an increase in capacity. With higher SNR values of RIS-AP-FNOMA and RIS-SR-FNOMA systems, the sum capacity difference between optimal and sub-optimal power assignments decreases. The RIS-AP-FNOMA system has a slightly higher sum capacity compared with the RIS-SR-FNOMA system. When optimal power allocation is employed at RIS-AP-FNOMA and FNOMA systems, the approximate sum capacities of 13.2 b/s/Hz and 5 b/s/Hz are achieved, respectively, for an SNR of 10 dB. The RIS-AP-FNOMA system has a 62% higher sum capacity than the FNOMA system.

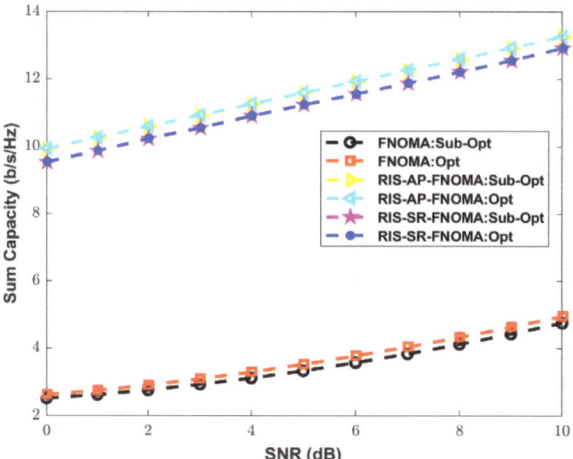

Figure 11. Sum capacity (b/s/Hz) comparison of FNOMA, RIS-SR-FNOMA and RIS-AP-FNOMA for optimal and sub-optimal power assignments.

7. Conclusions

The analytical outage probability expressions for RIS-SR-FNOMA and RIS-AP-FNOMA systems are derived in this paper. For larger numbers of reflecting elements, there is a close match between the MC simulations and analytical curves. The FU outage performance is superior to that of NU in both RIS-SR-FNOMA and RIS-AP-FNOMA systems. The outage performance for NU and FU improves as the elements in RIS increase. The optimal powers for NU and FU are also determined to maximize the sum capacity and satisfy the QoS constraints of both users. The sum capacities of RIS-SR-FNOMA and RIS-AP-FNOMA are clearly superior to FNOMA. Even with negative SNR values, the RIS-SR-FNOMA and RIS-AP-FNOMA systems can provide higher sum capacities. Over sub-optimal power assignments, the optimal power assignment maximizes the sum capacity. In terms of outage and sum capacity, RIS-AP-FNOMA is marginally better than RIS-SR-FNOMA. FNOMA paired with RIS, it may be argued, performs better in terms of outage and sum capacity. As a result, RIS-assisted NOMA will be a viable alternative for constructing next-generation networks that can handle massive connections. As a future work, the proposed model can be modified for uplink communication. The proposed system can be extended for ordered NOMA and cooperative NOMA.

Author Contributions: The manuscript was written through the contributions of all authors. V.B.K., P.G.S.V. and S.J.T. were responsible for the conceptualization of the topic; article gathering and sorting were carried out by V.B.K., A.L.I., F.R.C.S., P.G.S.V., S.J.T., D.-T.D. and A.M.; resources, V.B.K., P.G.S.V., S.J.T. and A.M.; supervision, V.B.K., A.L.I., F.R.C.S., P.G.S.V., S.J.T. and D.-T.D.; validation, V.B.K., A.L.I., F.R.C.S., P.G.S.V., S.J.T. and D.-T.D. All authors have read and agreed to the published version of the manuscript.

Funding: The work of Agbotiname Lucky Imoize was supported in part by the Nigerian Petroleum Technology Development Fund (PTDF) and in part by the German Academic Exchange Service (DAAD) through the Nigerian–German Postgraduate Program under grant 57473408.

Institutional Review Board Statement: Not applicable.

Informed Consent Statement: Not applicable.

Data Availability Statement: All data are available from the corresponding author with a reasonable request.

Conflicts of Interest: The authors declare no conflict of interest.

Abbreviations

The following abbreviations are used in this manuscript:

5G	Fifth-Generation
6G	Sixth-Generation
AP	Access Point
AWGN	Additive White Gaussian Noise
BS	Base Station
CSI	Channel State Information
EM	Electro-Magnetic
FNOMA	Fixed NOMA
FU	Far User
LoS	Line-of-Sight
MIMO	Multiple Input-Multiple Output
MC	Monte Carlo
NOMA	Non-Orthogonal Multiple Access
NU	Near User
OMA	Orthogonal Multiple Access
RF	Radio Frequency

RIS	Reconfigurable Intelligent Surface
SIC	Successive Interference Cancellation
SINR	Signal-to-Interference plus Noise Ratio
SNR	Signal-to-Noise Ratio
SR	Smart Reflector
UAV	Unmanned Aerial Vehicle
UE	User Equipment

References

1. De Alwis, C.; Kalla, A.; Pham, Q.V.; Kumar, P.; Dev, K.; Hwang, W.J.; Liyanage, M. Survey on 6G frontiers: Trends, applications, requirements, technologies and future research. *IEEE Open J. Commun. Soc.* **2021**, *2*, 836–886. [CrossRef]
2. Chowdhury, M.Z.; Shahjalal, M.; Ahmed, S.; Jang, Y.M. 6G wireless communication systems: Applications, requirements, technologies, challenges, and research directions. *IEEE Open J. Commun. Soc.* **2020**, *1*, 957–975. [CrossRef]
3. Huang, C.; Zappone, A.; Alexandropoulos, G.C.; Debbah, M.; Yuen, C. Reconfigurable intelligent surfaces for energy efficiency in wireless communication. *IEEE Trans. Wirel. Commun.* **2019**, *18*, 4157–4170. [CrossRef]
4. Khaleel, A.; Basar, E. Phase shift-free passive beamforming for reconfigurable intelligent surfaces. *IEEE Trans. Commun.* **2022**, *70*, 6966–6976. [CrossRef]
5. Xu, J.; Yuen, C.; Huang, C.; Hassan, N.U.; Alexandropoulos, G.C.; Renzo, M.D.; Debbah, M. Reconfiguring wireless environments via intelligent surfaces for 6g: Reflection, modulation, and security. *Sci. China Inf. Sci.* **2023**, *66*, 130304. [CrossRef]
6. Peng, Z.; Weng, R.; Pan, C.; Zhou, G.; Renzo, M.D.; Swindlehurst, A.L. Robust transmission design for ris-assisted secure multiuser communication systems in the presence of hardware impairments. *IEEE Trans. Wirel. Commun.* **2023**, early access. [CrossRef]
7. Björnson, E.; Özdogan, Ö.; Larsson, E.G. Reconfigurable intelligent surfaces: Three myths and two critical questions. *IEEE Commun. Mag.* **2020**, *58*, 90–96. [CrossRef]
8. Renzo, M.D.; Ntontin, K.; Song, J.; Danufane, F.H.; Qian, X.; Lazarakis, F.; Rosny, J.D.; Phan-Huy, D.-T.; Simeone, O.; Zhang, R.; et al. Reconfigurable intelligent surfaces vs. relaying: Differences, similarities, and performance comparison. *IEEE Open J. Commun. Soc.* **2020**, *1*, 798–807. [CrossRef]
9. Björnson, E.; Özdogan, Ö.; Larsson, E.G. Intelligent reflecting surface versus decode-and-forward: How large surfaces are needed to beat relaying. *IEEE Wirel. Commun. Lett.* **2019**, *9*, 244–248. [CrossRef]
10. Zhou, S.; Xu, W.; Wang, K.; Renzo, M.D.; Alouini, M.-S. Spectral and energy efficiency of irs-assisted miso communication with hardware impairments. *IEEE Wirel. Commun. Lett.* **2020**, *9*, 1366–1369. [CrossRef]
11. Tan, X.; Sun, Z.; Jornet, J.M.; Pados, D. Increasing indoor spectrum sharing capacity using smart reflect-array. In Proceedings of the 2016 IEEE International Conference on Communications (ICC), Kuala Lumpur, Malaysia, 22–27 May 2016; pp. 1–6.
12. Pan, C.; Ren, H.; Wang, K.; Xu, W.; Elkashlan, M.; Nallanathan, A.; Hanzo, L. Multicell mimo communications relying on intelligent reflecting surfaces. *IEEE Trans. Wirel. Commun.* **2020**, *19*, 5218–5233. [CrossRef]
13. Peng, H.; Wang, L.-C.; Li, G.Y.; Tsai, A.-H. Long-lasting uav-aided ris communications based on swipt. In Proceedings of the 2022 IEEE Wireless Communications and Networking Conference (WCNC), Austin, TX, USA, 10–13 April 2022; pp. 1844–1849.
14. Bai, T.; Pan, C.; Deng, Y.; Elkashlan, M.; Nallanathan, A.; Hanzo, L. Latency minimization for intelligent reflecting surface aided mobile edge computing. *IEEE J. Sel. Areas Commun.* **2020**, *38*, 2666–2682. [CrossRef]
15. Cao, Y.; Lv, T.; Ni, W.; Lin, Z. Sum-rate maximization for multi-reconfigurable intelligent surface-assisted device-to-device communications. *IEEE Trans. Commun.* **2021**, *69*, 7283–7296. [CrossRef]
16. Yang, L.; Yang, J.; Xie, W.; Hasna, M.O.; Tsiftsis, T.; Renzo, M.D. Secrecy performance analysis of ris-aided wireless communication systems. *IEEE Trans. Veh. Technol.* **2020**, *69*, 12296–12300. [CrossRef]
17. Wang, H.; Zhang, Z.; Zhu, B.; Dang, J.; Wu, L.; Wang, L.; Zhang, K.; Zhang, Y. Performance of wireless optical communication with reconfigurable intelligent surfaces and random obstacles. *arXiv* **2020**, arXiv:2001.05715.
18. Mu, X.; Liu, Y.; Guo, L.; Lin, J.; Schober, R. Intelligent reflecting surface enhanced indoor robot path planning: A radio map-based approach. *IEEE Trans. Wirel. Commun.* **2021**, *20*, 4732–4747. [CrossRef]
19. Singh, S.K.; Agrawal, K.; Singh, K.; Clerckx, B.; Li, C.-P. Rsma for hybrid ris-uav-aided full-duplex communications with finite blocklength codes under imperfect sic. *IEEE Trans. Wirel. Commun.* **2023**, early access. [CrossRef]
20. Liaskos, C.; Nie, S.; Tsioliaridou, A.; Pitsillides, A.; Ioannidis, S.; Akyildiz, I. A new wireless communication paradigm through software-controlled metasurfaces. *IEEE Commun. Mag.* **2018**, *56*, 162–169. [CrossRef]
21. Renzo, M.D.; Debbah, M.; Phan-Huy, D.-T.; Zappone, A.; Alouini, M.-S.; Yuen, C.; Sciancalepore, V.; Alexandropoulos, G.C.; Hoydis, J.; Gacanin, H.; et al. Smart radio environments empowered by reconfigurable ai meta-surfaces: An idea whose time has come. *EURASIP J. Wirel. Commun. Netw.* **2019**, *2019*, 129. [CrossRef]
22. Basar, E.; Renzo, M.D.; Rosny, J.D.; Debbah, M.; Alouini, M.-S.; Zhang, R. Wireless communications through reconfigurable intelligent surfaces. *IEEE Access* **2019**, *7*, 116753–116773. [CrossRef]
23. Wu, Q.; Zhang, S.; Zheng, B.; You, C.; Zhang, R. Intelligent reflecting surface-aided wireless communications: A tutorial. *IEEE Trans. Commun.* **2021**, *69*, 3313–3351. [CrossRef]

24. Shi, W.; Xu, J.; Xu, W.; Renzo, M.D.; Zhao, C. Secure outage analysis of ris-assisted communications with discrete phase control. *IEEE Trans. Veh. Technol.* **2022**, *72*, 5435–5440. [CrossRef]
25. Yuan, X.; Zhang, Y.-J.A.; Shi, Y.; Yan, W.; Liu, H. Reconfigurable-intelligent-surface empowered wireless communications: Challenges and opportunities. *IEEE Wirel. Commun.* **2021**, *28*, 136–143. [CrossRef]
26. Guo, H.; Liang, Y.-C.; Chen, J.; Larsson, E.G. Weighted sum-rate maximization for reconfigurable intelligent surface aided wireless networks. *IEEE Trans. Wirel. Commun.* **2020**, *19*, 3064–3076. [CrossRef]
27. Agarwal, A.; Chaurasiya, R.; Rai, S.; Jagannatham, A.K. Outage probability analysis for noma downlink and uplink communication systems with generalized fading channels. *IEEE Access* **2020**, *8*, 220461–220481. [CrossRef]
28. Singh, S.; Bansal, M. Outage analysis of noma-based cooperative relay systems with imperfect sic. *Phys. Commun.* **2020**, *43*, 101219. [CrossRef]
29. Yang, Y.; Zheng, B.; Zhang, S.; Zhang, R. Intelligent reflecting surface meets ofdm: Protocol design and rate maximization. *IEEE Trans. Commun.* **2020**, *68*, 4522–4535. [CrossRef]
30. Ni, W.; Liu, X.; Liu, Y.; Tian, H.; Chen, Y. Resource allocation for multi-cell irs-aided noma networks. *IEEE Trans. Wirel. Commun.* **2021**, *20*, 4253–4268. [CrossRef]
31. Zheng, B.; Wu, Q.; Zhang, R. Intelligent reflecting surface-assisted multiple access with user pairing: Noma or oma. *IEEE Commun. Lett.* **2020**, *24*, 753–757. [CrossRef]
32. Guo, Y.; Qin, Z.; Liu, Y.; Al-Dhahir, N. Intelligent reflecting surface aided multiple access over fading channels. *IEEE Trans. Commun.* **2020**, *69*, 2015–2027. [CrossRef]
33. Fu, M.; Zhou, Y.; Shi, Y.; Letaief, K.B. Reconfigurable intelligent surface empowered downlink non-orthogonal multiple access. *IEEE Trans. Commun.* **2021**, *69*, 3802–3817. [CrossRef]
34. Mu, X.; Liu, Y.; Guo, L.; Lin, J.; Al-Dhahir, N. Exploiting intelligent reflecting surfaces in noma networks: Joint beamforming optimization. *IEEE Trans. Wirel. Commun.* **2020**, *19*, 6884–6898. [CrossRef]
35. Trigui, I.; Ajib, W.; Zhu, W.-P.; Renzo, M.D. Performance evaluation and diversity analysis of ris-assisted communications over generalized fading channels in the presence of phase noise. *IEEE Open J. Commun. Soc.* **2022**, *3*, 593–607. [CrossRef]
36. Singh, S.; Bansal, M. Outage analysis of cooperative noma based hybrid cognitive radio system with channel estimation errors. *Phys. Commun.* **2021**, *48*, 101404. [CrossRef]
37. Hemanth, A.; Umamaheswari, K.; Pogaku, A.C.; Do, D.-T.; Lee, B.M. Outage performance analysis of reconfigurable intelligent surfaces-aided noma under presence of hardware impairment. *IEEE Access* **2020**, *8*, 212156–212165. [CrossRef]
38. Yang, L.; Yuan, Y. Secrecy outage probability analysis for ris-assisted noma systems. *Electron. Lett.* **2020**, *56*, 1254–1256. [CrossRef]
39. Kumaravelu, V.B.; Imoize, A.L.; Soria, F.R.C.; Velmurugan, P.G.S.; Thiruvengadam, S.J.; Murugadass, A.; Gudla, V.V. Outage probability analysis and transmit power optimization for blind-reconfigurable intelligent surface-assisted non-orthogonal multiple access uplink. *Sustainability* **2022**, *14*, 13188. [CrossRef]
40. Arslan, E.; Kilinc, F.; Arzykulov, S.; Dogukan, A.T.; Celik, A.; Basar, E.; Eltawil, A.M. Reconfigurable intelligent surface enabled over-the-air uplink noma. *IEEE Trans. Green Commun. Netw.* **2022**, *7*, 814–826. [CrossRef]
41. Jadhav, H.K.; Kumaravelu, V.B. Blind ris aided ordered noma: Design, probability of outage analysis and transmit power optimization. *Symmetry* **2022**, *14*, 2266. [CrossRef]
42. Basar, E. Transmission through large intelligent surfaces: A new frontier in wireless communications. In Proceedings of the 2019 European Conference on Networks and Communications (EuCNC), Valencia, Spain, 18–21 June 2019; pp. 112–117.

Disclaimer/Publisher's Note: The statements, opinions and data contained in all publications are solely those of the individual author(s) and contributor(s) and not of MDPI and/or the editor(s). MDPI and/or the editor(s) disclaim responsibility for any injury to people or property resulting from any ideas, methods, instructions or products referred to in the content.

Article

The 6G Ecosystem as Support for IoE and Private Networks: Vision, Requirements, and Challenges

Carlos Serôdio [1,2,3], José Cunha [1,4], Guillermo Candela [4], Santiago Rodriguez [4], Xosé Ramón Sousa [4] and Frederico Branco [1,5,*]

[1] Department of Engineering, School of Sciences and Technology, Universidade de Trás-os-Montes e Alto Douro, 5000-801 Vila Real, Portugal; cserodio@utad.pt (C.S.); jcunha@optaresolutions.com (J.C.)
[2] Center ALGORITMI, Universidade do Minho, Campus de Azurém, 4800-058 Guimarães, Portugal
[3] CITAB, Universidade de Trás-os-Montes e Alto Douro, 5000-801 Vila Real, Portugal
[4] Optare Solutions, Parque Tecnológico de Vigo, 35315 Vigo, Spain; gcandela@optaresolutions.com (G.C.); srodriguez@optaresolutions.com (S.R.); xrsousa@optaresolutions.com (X.R.S.)
[5] INESC TEC—Institute for Systems and Computer Engineering, Technology and Science, 4200-465 Porto, Portugal
* Correspondence: fbranco@utad.pt

Citation: Serôdio, C.; Cunha, J.; Candela, G.; Rodriguez, S.; Sousa, X.R.; Branco, F. The 6G Ecosystem as Support for IoE and Private Networks: Vision, Requirements, and Challenges. *Future Internet* 2023, 15, 348. https://doi.org/10.3390/fi15110348

Academic Editors: Alessandro Raschellà and Michael Mackay

Received: 26 August 2023
Revised: 15 October 2023
Accepted: 24 October 2023
Published: 25 October 2023

Copyright: © 2023 by the authors. Licensee MDPI, Basel, Switzerland. This article is an open access article distributed under the terms and conditions of the Creative Commons Attribution (CC BY) license (https://creativecommons.org/licenses/by/4.0/).

Abstract: The emergence of the sixth generation of cellular systems (6G) signals a transformative era and ecosystem for mobile communications, driven by demands from technologies like the internet of everything (IoE), V2X communications, and factory automation. To support this connectivity, mission-critical applications are emerging with challenging network requirements. The primary goals of 6G include providing sophisticated and high-quality services, extremely reliable and further-enhanced mobile broadband (feMBB), low-latency communication (ERLLC), long-distance and high-mobility communications (LDHMC), ultra-massive machine-type communications (umMTC), extremely low-power communications (ELPC), holographic communications, and quality of experience (QoE), grounded in incorporating massive broad-bandwidth machine-type (mBBMT), mobile broad-bandwidth and low-latency (MBBLL), and massive low-latency machine-type (mLLMT) communications. In attaining its objectives, 6G faces challenges that demand inventive solutions, incorporating AI, softwarization, cloudification, virtualization, and slicing features. Technologies like network function virtualization (NFV), network slicing, and software-defined networking (SDN) play pivotal roles in this integration, which facilitates efficient resource utilization, responsive service provisioning, expanded coverage, enhanced network reliability, increased capacity, densification, heightened availability, safety, security, and reduced energy consumption. It presents innovative network infrastructure concepts, such as resource-as-a-service (RaaS) and infrastructure-as-a-service (IaaS), featuring management and service orchestration mechanisms. This includes nomadic networks, AI-aware networking strategies, and dynamic management of diverse network resources. This paper provides an in-depth survey of the wireless evolution leading to 6G networks, addressing future issues and challenges associated with 6G technology to support V2X environments considering presenting +challenges in architecture, spectrum, air interface, reliability, availability, density, flexibility, mobility, and security.

Keywords: 6G; IoT; IoE; private networks; V2X

1. Introduction

The evolution of wireless communication has been marked by transformative leaps, each ushering in new paradigms of connectivity and interaction. Today, we face a new revolution, i.e., a new frontier. The emergence of sixth-generation (6G) technology promises to reshape connectivity and transcend the boundaries of its predecessors, unlocking unprecedented capabilities and enabling a plethora of applications that will change our perception of lifestyle, society, and business in ways that were once confined to the realm of "wishful thinking".

The forthcoming mobile network generation, 6G, is poised to address novel and innovative challenges. It is envisioned as a self-contained artificial intelligence ecosystem, moving from a human-centric paradigm to a dual human- and machine-centric focus. It is expected that 6G will usher in near-instant, seamless wireless connectivity that knows no bounds [1].

Anticipated as the enabler for a globally connected ecosystem, 6G is poised to realize comprehensive connectivity. At the heart of 6G's advancements lies edge intelligence (EI), a pivotal technology that amalgamates artificial intelligence (AI) with mobile multiple-access edge computing (MEC). This fusion unlocks the latent potential of intelligent, data-centric service at the edge. Furthermore, the integration of edge technology is imperative for the success of 6G, as it enables the convergence of cloud capabilities with intelligent devices in the proximity.

Expanding upon the foundation of 5G, the evolution to 6G is set to profoundly influence the progression of communication development's intelligence. This evolution encompasses intelligent, deep, holographic, and ubiquitous connectivity [2]. In the standardization processes and procedures of 5G networks, three distinct scenarios were identified in the initial stages: enhanced mobile broadband (eMBB), ultra-reliable and low-latency communications (URLLC), and massive machine-type communications (mMTC). These scenarios served as key foundations for establishing the design guidelines of 5G technologies.

Sixth-generation (6G) technology promises to profoundly enhance communication networks, with the ambitious goal of establishing a worldwide connection using sustainable approaches, all geared towards the ultimate aim of enriching the quality of life.

The horizon of mobile communications and internet technologies is witnessing advancements that transcend current scientific boundaries. Complex concepts such as automated driving, augmented and virtual reality, and mMTC demand an elevated mobile infrastructure for successful implementation [3].

Many applications, because of 6G, will be redefined and restructured: the landscape of technology will be reshaped with the transformation of the internet of things (IoT) into the internet of everything (IoE), marking the onset of numerous innovative technologies: intelligent internet of medical things (IIoMT), intelligent industrial internet of everything (IIIoE) like the intelligent grid (EC-IoT SC: edge computing iot-based smart grid) [4]. This will transform the transition from smart to intelligent, i.e., with AI capabilities within 6G, the IoE will evolve smart devices into intelligent entities. These devices will authentically operate with AI-driven capabilities, enabling them to predict, make decisions, and share their experiences with other intelligent devices [5].

The advent of 6G is poised to profoundly influence the evolution of communication development's intelligence process, encompassing intelligent, extensive, deep, holographic, and ubiquitous connectivity.

Future time-critical applications' demands on 6G communication technology encompass very high bandwidth (≥ 1 Tbps), very high operating frequencies (≥ 1 THz), very low latency times (≤ 1 ms), extremely high reliability (10^{-9}), high mobility (≥ 1000 km/h), and wavelengths within the range of ≤ 300 µm [5]. It will be a paradigm shift in time-critical applications, entirely dependent on communication technology.

While the prospects of 6G communication technology bring forth many challenges and complexities, worldwide deployment is expected in 2030 [6,7]. Promising enhanced coverage and mobility through satellite communication, 6G technology highlights a crucial gap in the current landscape—poor rural coverage, the absence of data rates exceeding 1 Tbps, and the necessity for exceptional reliability and extremely low latency.

This inherent disparity requires a delicate balance so as not to compromise the quality of the system and services, nor affect user satisfaction. The International Telecommunication Union (ITU), in its Recommendation ITU-T P.10/G, defines two approaches to quality assessment: one is the measure of quality of service (QoS), and the other is the measure of quality of experience (QoE) [8]. Typically, within a communication system, the communication quality, and media signal quality components are concerned with users' perceptions of how effectively the system supports communication. It specifically emphasizes the quality attributes associated with aspects of communication. Within network and communication applications, QoS represents an evaluative measure of service quality provided by the network. This network-centric gauge assesses the quality of data transmission in communication networks. QoS measurement encompasses metrics evaluating the key performance indicators (KPIs) of a communication system. QoS indicator values are anticipated through an analytical model of the overall telecommunications system's performance, considering known parameters of user behavior and the technical characteristics of the telecommunications network [9,10]. However, there are other definitions of QoS, such as that used by the Internet Engineering Task Force (IETF), where QoS characterizes the performance of functional services in network layer models. This paper adopts an approach that defines the characteristics of both a network-centric system and an end-to-end system. Quality of experience (QoE), in which the latter serves as the benchmark for high quality, and driven by user-centric communications, addressing the whole user experience. QoE refers to the extent of user satisfaction or dissatisfaction with an application or service. The assessment, representation, prediction, and utilization of QoE play a crucial role in evaluating the overall performance of the relationship between the user and the system or service. This process hinges on various dimensions, including user experience, technology, context, environment, application, resources, and network QoS impairments [11,12].

This will be realized through augmented reality, virtual reality, holographic communications, and the tactile internet, which necessitate very high data rates coupled with exceptionally low latency.

Discussions and research on 6G requirements are abundant [13–15], and multiple viewpoints and approaches propose different ways to meet these demands. Some proposals go towards exploring potential applications encompassing mobile broadband and low latency (MBBLL), massive broadband machine-type (mBBMT), and massive low-latency machine-type (mLLMT) communications [16]. Others emphasize issues such as further-enhanced mobile broadband (feMBB), extremely reliable and low-latency communications (ERLLC), umMTC, long-distance and high-mobility communications (LDHMC), and extremely low-power communications (ELPC) [17]. Still, others are also concerned with the following features: ubiquitous mobile ultra-broadband (uMUB), ultra-high-speed with-low-latency communications (uHSLLC), and ultra-high-data density (uHDD) [18].

Built upon an open network platform, 6G is poised to facilitate service-centric network slicing management on demand. This capability empowers service providers and industry-specific markets to swiftly deploy novel services as required.

Furthermore, incorporating AI algorithms for network monitoring and surveillance, data-driven business decisions, preventive maintenance, fraud detection, and robust blockchain-based security systems for data validation are also of utmost significance within the core of 6G.

Moreover, AI technology holds the potential to enable the dynamic orchestration and management of networks, caching, and computing resources, thereby enhancing the effectiveness of forthcoming network generations. Another crucial trend revolves around robust, endogenous network security spanning physical and network layers. Industry sectors such as cloud-based virtual reality (VR), IoT industrial automation, cellular vehicle-to-everything (C-V2X), digital twin body area networks, energy-efficient wireless network management and control, and federated learning systems collectively stand as driving forces, significantly propelling the advancement of 6G wireless communication networks.

The 5G Automotive Association (5GAA) is a collaborative initiative bringing together the automotive and telecommunications industries, driven by the overarching objective of expediting the worldwide implementation of C-V2X technology. This endeavor represents the initial stride towards realizing a seamlessly integrated intelligent transportation system that leverages the capabilities of 5G connectivity and beyond. The 5GAA has formulated a comprehensive framework, delineating various usage scenarios, methodological approaches, illustrative instances, and stipulated service-level requisites that are being followed by the industry and will continue its evolution towards 6G. In recent years, the automotive industry has witnessed the emergence of several pioneering applications rooted in C-V2X technologies. Furthermore, a continuum of such applications is anticipated in the ensuing years, poised to elucidate novel capabilities and augment the repertoire of connected vehicles. These forthcoming C-V2X use cases are poised to exert substantial influence, encompassing domains such as safety enhancement, vehicular operational management, vehicular software update (a particularization of the previous), convenience augmentation, autonomous driving, vehicular platooning, traffic optimization, ecological sustainability, and sociocultural integration [14]. We also have some use cases related to local hazard and traffic information, hazard information collection sharing, basic safety, intersection safety, sensor sharing, and tele-operated driving (ToD) including AVP [19]. This paper, we will dive into two of these use cases: (i) vehicle operations management (i.e., vehicular software update, one of its particularizations) and (ii) the cooperative adaptive cruise control (CACC) use case regarding safety [20].

In the 2024–2030 roadmap, 5GAA considers different types of V2X communication types (depending on the destination entity) in use cases that intend to achieve [19]:

- *V2X (Vehicle-to-Everything Communication)*: V2X represents a comprehensive set of communication protocols developed under the 3GPP framework. The cellular-V2X (C-V2X) paradigm encompasses all V2X technologies standardized by 3GPP. As per the 5GAA documentation, the imminent maturation of 5G-V2X is anticipated to establish a global standard specifically tailored for automotive applications within the 3GPP 5G framework. This encompasses network-centric (Uu mode) and direct (PC5/Slidelink) communication modalities, with the potential of operating in conjunction or independently of LTE-V2X. It supports advanced vehicular functionalities and maintains previously established message types, ensuring seamless service continuity.
- *V2P (Vehicle-to-Pedestrian Communication)*: The emphasis on vulnerable road user (VRU) applications has been accentuated due to the escalating incidents involving pedestrians and cyclists. The 3GPP framework is being adapted to seamlessly integrate with contemporary smartphones and connected consumer devices. The current C-V2X specifications facilitate direct communication between vehicles, pedestrians, cyclists, and motorcyclists. As delineated in the 3GPP Rel. 17, future enhancements are geared towards optimizing power efficiency of C-V2X for handheld consumer devices, ensuring longevity and bi-directional communication efficacy.
- *Vehicle-to-Vehicle (V2V) Communication*: V2V encapsulates protocols that facilitate direct information exchange between vehicles, enabling them to share data regarding their operational state and immediate environment.
- *Vehicle-to-Infrastructure (V2I) Communication:* Recent legislative developments, such as the German Automated Driving (AD) L4 regulation, underscore the significance of V2I communication in the realm of autonomous driving. This legislation facilitates the deployment of AD L4 vehicles on predefined routes, contingent upon the presence of robust connectivity. Such regulatory frameworks pave the way for initiating automated valet parking (AVP) services, which relies intrinsically on a connected infrastructure and V2I communication modalities.
- *Vehicle-to-Network (V2N) Communication:* V2N refers to communication between a vehicle and a cellular or wireless network infrastructure. This paradigm enables vehicles to access cloud services, receive real-time traffic and road condition updates, and connect to remote servers for software updates or advanced driving analytics. Essentially, V2N facilitates the integration of vehicles into the broader IoT ecosystem, allowing them to leverage network-based resources for enhanced functionality and safety. Mobile operators have spectrum requirements to deliver advanced automotive V2N services efficaciously. Specifically, a minimum of 50 MHz of service-agnostic low-band spectrum (<1 GHz) is necessitated for V2N functionalities in rural topogra-

phies. Concurrently, a minimum of 500 MHz of service-agnostic mid-band spectrum (1 to 7 GHz) is imperative to meet the demands of high-capacity, urban advanced automotive V2N services.
- *Vulnerable Road User (VRU):* The VRU complex interactions scenario delineates a situation wherein a VRU communicates its intent before crossing a thoroughfare. Subsequent vehicular acknowledgments reassure the VRU of the safety of the maneuver. As the VRU traverses, continuous communication with stationary vehicles ensures vehicular awareness of the VRU's position and trajectory. The global emphasis on VRU applications is accentuated by the potential of cellular-V2X (C-V2X) to mitigate incidents involving pedestrians and cyclists. The 3GPP framework is evolving to ensure compatibility with contemporary communication devices, facilitating direct vehicular communication with pedestrians, cyclists, and motorcyclists.

Some of the V2X use cases, technological advancements, and evaluations that can be considered are the following [19]:
- *Evolution of 5G-V2X:* After its initial definition in the Rel. 14 with LTE-V2X and post the introduction of Rel.16, 3GPP has been meticulously defining the C-V2X direct communication protocols (PC5) predicated on the 5G NR radio access technology (RAT). This encompasses innovations such as truncated symbols to minimize latency, feedback channels to augment reliability, and an expanded capacity to support diverse transmission modes, including unicast, multicast, and broadcast. Regional variations may manifest in deployment strategies, potentially operating with or devoid of LTE-V2X.
- *Power Optimization for Direct Communication:* The burgeoning focus on VRU applications necessitates advancements in C-V2X to pre-emptively address potential incidents involving pedestrians and cyclists. The 3GPP framework is evolving to ensure compatibility with the latest generation of smartphones and connected devices. Current specifications facilitate direct vehicular communication with pedestrians, cyclists, and motorcyclists. Subsequent enhancements, as outlined in 3GPP Rel. 17, are poised to refine power consumption metrics of C-V2X, particularly for battery-dependent handheld devices.
- *Advancements in Mobile Network Positioning:* The automotive sector is currently probing the potential of 5G NR precise positioning to bolster position accuracy, especially in regions with compromised GNSS coverage. This initiative is pivotal for autonomous vehicular operations and V2X safety protocols. Certain autonomous vehicular applications necessitate stringent position accuracy metrics. In such scenarios, 5G NR is being assessed as a potential component of sensor fusion systems, supplementing GNSS and its corrective algorithms to enhance positional accuracy.

This survey and comprehensive analysis explore the significant advancements introduced by 6G technology, comparing them to preceding 5G technologies. It assesses crucial aspects like data rate speed, system capacity, latency, and additional enhancements such as optimal coverage for very high-mobility, mobile edge computing, augmented reality (AR) facilitation, and enhanced connection reliability. Additionally, the paper delves into the pivotal enabling technologies essential for 6G support development environments based on V2X, evaluating feasibility, advantages, challenges and, consequently, implementation solutions.

This paper is organized as follows: Section 1 provides a concise overview of 6G technology, emphasizing key features and the V2X roadmap. Additionally, Section 2 reviews the cellular systems evolution from 1G to 5G, while Section 3 presents the background and ongoing evolution of 6G. Section 4 examines the requirements and enabling technologies of 6G, and Section 5 explores the broad applications of 6G, detailing its impact on healthcare, high-performance precision agriculture, intelligent transportation systems, and logistics and supply chains. In Section 6, the focus shifts to the impact of 6G communications infrastructure and technology on supporting the V2X applications addressing critical evaluation, challenges for the future and implementation solutions. Finally, Section 7 offers a comprehensive conclusion.

2. From 1G to 5G

The evolution of cellular wireless communications generations (#G) refers to significant changes in the infrastructure design architecture, speed, technology, bandwidth, and spectrum. Each generation introduces new standards, capabilities, techniques, and innovative or disruptive features that differentiate it from its predecessors [21]. The mobile generations have progressed in phases, with major milestones in 1981, 1992, 2001, 2010, and 2020, marking the advent of 1G, 2G, 3G, 4G, and 5G, respectively [22].

Throughout these evolutionary phases, several factors have undergone significant improvements. These include data speed, network service reliability, cost-effectiveness, network capacity enhancement, increased availability of network functions, energy-efficient design frameworks, cognition, security, and coverage [22]. These advancements have paved the way for developing more efficient and powerful mobile communication technologies, ultimately benefiting users, and expanding the capabilities of mobile devices and networks.

The evolution of inter-network services has brought about various changes in communication technology, from circuit-switching to packet-switching. Originally initiated with narrowband in 2G, the evolution advanced to broadband in 3G, ultra-broadband in 4G, and ultimately culminated in the wireless world wide web capabilities of 5G. These advancements have significantly impacted data transmission bandwidth, providing users with faster and more efficient communication experiences [23,24].

In the early stages, 1G utilized simple analogue assembly for communication, which later evolved to 2G and 3G, employing a 25 MHz bandwidth spectrum. The bandwidth was then expanded, reaching 100 MHz in 4G networks. The ambitious goal of 5G is to utilize an even broader spectrum, ranging from 30 GHz to 300 GHz, to establish communication networks with unprecedented capabilities [22].

These developments in bandwidth have been crucial in enabling the growth in both the quantity and complexity of advanced and complex services and applications that demand higher data rates and lower latency, i.e., they are time-critical, ultimately transforming how we connect and communicate in the modern world.

Over the past few decades, network speeds have experienced a gradual but significant transformation. The initial 1G networks offered a modest data transmission capacity of 2 Kbps, which saw a slight increase in 2G, reaching 64 Kbps. Subsequent advancements in 3G led to a remarkable boost in speed, providing up to 8 Mbps, and this progress continued with 4G networks offering speeds of up to 50 Mbps [25,26].

During this period, multiplexing and spectrum algorithms also experienced notable changes. In 1G, frequency division multiple access (FDMA) was the key multiplexing technique, while 2G adopted time division multiple access (TDMA), and 3G relied on wideband code division multiple access (W-CDMA). As 4G networks emerged, they utilized orthogonal frequency division multiplexing (OFDM), MIMO, and IoT-based schemes in their network operations [27–30].

With the advent of 5G, the standardization of new technologies has taken center stage: 5G networks incorporate extended LTE and various cutting-edge radio technologies, such as cmWave, mmWave, massive MIMO (mMIMO), radio access network (RAN), URLLC, mMTC, and extended mobile broadband services (eMBB) [22,31]. These innovations in 5G promise to revolutionize communication, offering unprecedented speeds and capacities that will power a new era of connectivity and enable a wide range of applications, from lightning-fast data transfers to reliable and ultra-low-latency services for critical systems and massive IoT deployments.

2.1. The First Generation (1G Analogue Technology)

During the first generation of mobile technology (1980–1990), data rates ranged from 1 Kbps to 2.8 Kbps, employing a circuit switch for communication. This era utilized analog phone service as its output technology, with a bandwidth of 40 MHz and a frequency range between 800 and 900 MHz, supporting only voice calls. The communication technique used during this time was FDMA [21].

Although it marked the initial steps in mobile communication, the first generation faced several limitations. Call quality was relatively low, and energy consumption was high. Users experienced poor voice connections, limited data capacity, a deficiency in security measures, and an unreliable transfer process [21,25]. Despite these drawbacks, the first generation laid the foundation for future advancements, paving the way for more sophisticated and capable mobile networks in subsequent generations.

2.2. The Second Generation (2G Digital Technology)

The foundation of 2G technology relies on the global system for mobile communications (GSM), primarily referred to as groupe special mobile, which was introduced in Finland in 1991. These networks marked a significant shift from analogue to digital cellular systems, providing substantial improvements over their predecessors, including enhanced standards and increased security [21].

The technologies of 2G marked the transition from analogue to digital communication networks, introducing encrypted services and data capabilities alongside voice services. This era brought features like SMS, and multimedia messaging services (MMS). Text messages were digitally encoded in the 2G realm, guaranteeing user privacy and data confidentiality during communication.

The advantage of digital encryption in 2G lies in its ability to protect data from being understood by unintended recipients. Three distinct types of 2G mobile techniques are available: FDMA, TDMA/GSM, and code division multiple access (CDMA). Each technique has different operational methods, characteristics, and terms [21,32]. These advancements in 2G technology laid the groundwork for further improvements and paved the way for more sophisticated mobile communication systems in subsequent generations. In the back-end, this involved migrating away from a connection-oriented, public-switched telephone network to a packet-oriented network. Other functionalities allowed for structuring the network into a hierarchy that enabled mobility through handovers and roaming.

As in 2G, voice was the dominant service, the evaluation of user perception about performance and quality of service depended on the average opinion score (MOS). This subjective test was widely used in traditional telephone networks [33].

Following the advent of 2G, a subsequent iteration emerged known as 2.5G, a combination of 2G technology with general packet radio service (GPRS) and a set of novel attributes and functionalities. While retaining the foundational architecture of its predecessor, the 2.5G system embraced packet switching, departing from the circuit switching exclusive to prior generations and an IP-based core network. This evolution facilitated a surge in data transfer speeds, peaking at 144 kbps, propelled by advanced modulation techniques (GMSK and 8-PSK), a new encoding scheme (MCS-1 to MCS-9), and slot aggregation. The essential technologies characterizing this phase encompassed GPRS, and the enhanced data rate for GSM evolution (EDGE) was designated as 2.75G [34].

EDGE surpasses GPRS by accommodating three times the data subscribers or tripling the data rate for an individual user, achieved through a swift and economical implementation. Adding EDGE-capable transceivers and software is the sole requisite, aligning with WCDMA through the GERAN (GSM EDGE radio access network) standardization. Achieving data rates of up to 384 Kbps (downlink) and 60 Kbps (uplink), this system also supported functionalities like SMS, MMS, voice communication, and peer-to-peer (P2P) networking. EDGE aims to amplify system capacity for real-time and best-effort services, positioning itself as a foundational step towards 3G evolution and potential parity with other 3G technologies [34].

2.3. The Third Generation (3G)

In 2000, the 3rd Generation Partnership Project (3GPP) introduced the 3G mobile communication system, recognized as universal mobile telecommunications systems (UMTS) in Europe. The ITU-T refers to this standard as International Mobile Telecommunications-2000 (IMT2000), while, in the United States, it is called CDMA2000 [35].

The third generation of mobile transmission systems represents a significant leap forward, offering impressive speeds, to date, of up to 144 kbps up to 2 Mpps and beyond, ideal for high-speed mobile access and data transfer with internet protocol services. Certainly, 3G encompasses enhancements over its predecessors, focusing on features like "high-speed transmission, multimedia access, and global roaming capabilities" [21], improved QoS, and better voice call quality [35].

One of the primary applications of 3G is its widespread use in mobile phones and handheld devices, serving as a reliable means to connect these devices to internet protocol suite networks. This enables users to make voice and video calls, transfer data, and browse the web easily. The multimedia potential of 3G is evident, supporting full video streaming, video conferencing, and seamless internet access [36].

Data transmission in 3G networks is facilitated through a technology known as packet switching, which efficiently handles data packets, allowing for efficient data transfer. On the other hand, voice calls are handled using circuit switching for clarity and reliability. This modern communication process has evolved significantly over the past era, revolutionizing how we connect and communicate, and unlocking a world of possibilities for multimedia applications and seamless connectivity [21]. Exemplified by WCDMA, C2K, time-division synchronous CDMA (TD-SCDMA), and worldwide interoperability for microwave access (WiMAX), 3G has facilitated an array of data services encompassing video calls, internet access, and mobile television. Concurrently, there was a transformation in the network core toward the IP multimedia subsystem (IMS), introducing a perspective of data-switched communications using the session initiation protocol (SIP). This shift strengthened the connection between cellular network cores and the broader internet, enabling portable mobility across various radio interfaces.

The emergence of technologies like WCDMA, high-speed uplink/downlink packet access (HSUPA/HSDPA), and evolution-data only (EV-DO) led to the introduction of an intermediate wireless communication generation known as 3.5G, offering data rates ranging from 5 to 30 Mbps [34].

The transition in user engagement perception within 3G networks has altered the landscape of service evaluation in network management. Initially, network management and performance were contingent on quality of service (QoS) metrics, considering factors like delay, instability, and call drop rate. However, with 3G facilitating the integration of voice and multimedia content, the assessment of both the system and services now incorporates metrics rooted in quality of experience (QoE) [33].

2.4. The Fourth Generation (4G)

The introduction of 4G mobile communication in the late 2000s marked a significant advancement with its IP-based network framework. The primary goal of 4G innovations was to offer high-quality, high-capacity, cost-effective, and minimal-effort security administration services to voice, data, multimedia, and internet applications through IP services. This approach aimed to standardize all IP addresses, creating a unified platform for various technologies developed up to that point. It can support speeds ranging between 100 Mbps in mobile and 1 Gbps in nomadic mode, and it is all-IP with heterogeneous networks where multiple radio access technologies (RATs) or RANs interoperate since 4G networks deliver unparalleled performance [21]. The services of 4G include MMS, high-definition and mobile TV, digital video broadcasting (DVB), voice over IP (VoIP), multimedia on demand (MoD), gaming, and video chat [37].

To access the 4G mobile network, the user equipment must be equipped with multimodal capabilities to choose the most suitable wireless destination system intelligently. Terminal mobility played a crucial role in achieving the vision of wireless service anytime, anywhere, enabling seamless automatic roaming across different wireless networks (vertical handover, RAT handover). The 4G technology seamlessly integrated various existing and future wireless techniques, including MIMO antenna architecture, OFDM, the all-internet protocol (IP), Multi-carrier code-division multiple access (MC-CDMA), large area synchronous code-division multiple access (LAS-CDMA), network local multipoint distribution system (LMDS), reconfigurable systems, and the cognitive radio/network, providing users with the freedom to move and continuously roam between different technologies [3,21,38]. MIMO and OFDM technologies enable the reception and transmission capabilities of 4G. These technologies have alleviated network congestion by accommodating a more significant number of users through MIMO.

Long-term evolution (LTE) and WiMAX emerged as prominent 4G technologies. These innovative advancements played a crucial role in defining the 4G landscape and introducing novel communication prospects [21,39]. With smartphones and tablets becoming widespread, mobile communications have claimed a central role, providing substantial data throughput within 4G networks. Simultaneously, the transformative influence of accompanying information and communications technologies (ICTs) has been instrumental in reshaping society.

These modifications enabled the establishment of a fully packet-switched core, achieving speeds of up to 300 Mbps in the downlink (utilizing $4 \times$ communications through four multiple-input multiple-outputs (MIMOs) with a 20 MHz allocation). The evolved packet core (EPC) played a pivotal role in creating a fully IP-based cellular network with mobility and billing management across various radio interfaces.

The 4G, known as LTE-advanced, witnessed substantial enhancements over LTE, particularly in access layer technology, resulting in a significant improvement in downlink rates (up to 1 Gbps). LTE-A facilitated the effective distribution of multimedia resources among the eNodeB, the evolved packet core (EPC), and content provider through multimedia broadcast multicast services (eMBMS). This innovation laid the groundwork for a novel business model founded on the LTE radio architecture [10].

Japan conducted the first successful field test of the fourth-generation technology in 2005, demonstrating its potential and setting the stage for the widespread adoption of 4G networks. The emergence of 4G technology revolutionized the mobile communication landscape, offering faster data rates and better performance and paving the way for more advanced services and applications in the mobile world.

An essential insight gleaned from the evolution is the emphasis on enhancing the mobile user experience by improving data rates. This shift involves aligning quality of experience (QoE) with a quality of service (QoS)-based approach in network management, distinct from isolated user perception considerations [33].

2.5. The Fifth Generation (5G)

In the realm of 5G research, there is a strong focus on advancing the "Worldwide Wireless Web (WWWW)," dynamic ad hoc wireless networks (DAWN), and other traditional wireless communication. Some of the most crucial techniques driving 5G technologies include 802.11 wireless local areas networks (WLAN), wireless metropolitan networks in urban areas (WMAN), ad hoc wireless personal area networks (WPAN), and other wireless networks to support digital communications. The introduction of 5G features has empowered portable devices with AI capabilities, unlocking new possibilities [21,39,40].

The wireless networks of 5G have brought about revolutionary technological concepts that bridge the gap between traditional IT domains and communication networks. Key innovations like cloudification and softwarization of networking technologies have enabled the deployment of a new range of use cases, services, and applications in wireless networks. From the physical layer's mMIMO to the application layer's machine learning (ML) technologies, 5G has significantly enhanced network capacities and capabilities. Despite these remarkable advancements, 5G still faces challenges in meeting the demands of emerging services like the IoE, primarily due to the intrinsic limitations within 5G systems [41,42]. During the initial deployment phase of 5G networks, operators and device manufacturers predominantly embrace the 3GPP 5G new radio (NR) standard, particularly in densely populated urban regions [43].

NR 5G enables mmWave spectrum access (24 to 100 GHz range), supplementing the initial sub-6 GHz spectrum commonly shared with 4G networks. The 20 Gbps requirement represents a substantial stride toward eMBB, alongside mMTC and URLLC. The advent of mMTC addresses the increasing reliance on IoT applications and aligns with IMT-2020 specifications for dense connectivity and low power consumption [33].

Operating within the 2–6 GHz spectra, the corresponding 5G network harnesses both mmWave and mMIMO technologies, albeit network densification initiatives might experience delays due to specific factors. Network slicing functionality plays a varying role in 5G mission-critical applications. The spectrum of services that benefit from 5G includes internet protocol television (IPTV), high-definition video streaming (HD-VS), high-speed mobility services, as well as foundational VR and augmented reality (AR) offerings.

Overall, 5G offers a high data transfer speed, very low latency, energy efficiency, and extensive connectivity. Its core services encompass eMBB to prioritize high throughput, capacity, and spectral efficiency; mMTC to deal with energy efficiency and massive connectivity; and URLLC to offer high reliability and low latency, to account for supporting diverse services [35,44]. To enhance user experience and network performance advanced technologies like mmWave, mMIMO, and device-to-device (D2D) communication are utilized. These innovations bolster both QoS and QoE for users [45].

Within 5G networks, softwarization facilitates the seamless instantiation of services across the entire network, ensuring resource allocation harmony and stability. This is supported by a two-tier cloud computing hierarchy, specifically the cloud edge, which divides physical network resources for various services such as eMBB, mMTC, and URLLC. The 5G core incorporates a network data analysis function (NWDAF) to address the growing reliance on resource sharing. This function plays a pivotal role in managing the increasing complexity of the network, particularly in executing autonomous policies or intent-based management [33].

The pursuit of 5G technology continues to push the boundaries of what is possible in wireless communication, and ongoing research aims to address the evolving requirements of an increasingly connected and data-driven world.

To meet the evolving demands for improved performance, portability, interoperability, elasticity, flexibility, reliability, scalability, and spectral and energy efficiency, the progression of mobile networks necessitates a software-driven approach [3,46], so the 5G core's softwarization capability allows the partitioning of functions into a layered architecture, showcasing remarkable flexibility. Key phases include virtualization—network function virtualization (NFV), service migration, orchestration, and service automation—like service function chaining (SFC) combined with software defined networking (SDN) [47], empowering network operators to maintain cost-effectiveness by minimizing both operational expenses (OPEX) and capital expenditures (CAPEX) [48], shaping the path to 5G and subsequent mobile paradigms [3]. As core and backhaul components of forthcoming mobile networks shift through software transformation, techniques like ultra-dense networks, mMIMO, and high-frequency communication play vital roles in enhancing wireless access networks. These advancements led to 5G's impressive 1000-fold capacity increase over its predecessor [3,40]. Key performance requirements for 5G encompass data rates of 1 to 10 Gbps, 1 ms RTT latency, heightened capacity for numerous connected devices via wide bandwidth channels, exceptional availability, pervasive connectivity, and a substantial 90% reduction in energy consumption to enhance battery life [3].

The 5G-PPP project introduces a comprehensive five-layered structure comprising infrastructure, network/control, orchestration, business, and services to establish the functional architecture of 5G. Within this framework, the orchestration layer is distributed across the other layers, and the services layer extends from the business layer [49,50]. The infrastructure layer embodies the RAN connectivity aspect, featuring RATs like non-orthogonal multiple access (NOMA), mMIMO, and coordinated multi-Point (CoMP) transmission to facilitate interface with high-data-capacity small-cells, and mmWave technologies. The control layer oversees network management, while the business layer is responsible for managing network and business services [3,51,52].

Nonetheless, the services offered by 5G are insufficient to effectively tackle the evolving needs of various applications, including health technologies and emergency scenarios. In the realm of health services, 5G plays a role by establishing internet connectivity for internet of medical things (IoMT) devices such as wearables and wireless body area networks (WBAN), along with internet of bio-nano things (IoBNT) via mMTC. It also facilitates superior video quality for telemedicine and AR/VR through eMBB, while simultaneously supporting unmanned aerial vehicles (UAV), unmanned ground vehicles (UGV), and autonomous vehicles through URLLC. Nevertheless, these technologies still have some limitations regarding privacy and security, ubiquitous communications in locations with poor infrastructure, connectivity for ultra-dense IoMT devices, and highly reliable and low-latency communications [44,53].

The 5G technologies offer ultra-reliable, low-latency communications. Still, its short-packet, sensing-based URLLC features hinder ultra-reliable, low-latency services with data-intensive applications like AR, mixed-reality (MR), and VR. The growing number of internet of everything applications calls for integrating communication, sensing, control, and computing functionalities, which are often neglected in the 5G context [18].

Recent progress enables the utilization of ML for tasks like radio-frequency (RF) signal processing, spectrum analysis, and RF spectrum mapping [54,55]. This integration of AI offers substantial support for precise capacity predictions, automated coverage optimization, efficient network resource scheduling, and network slicing.

Ongoing initiatives in 5G networks focus on developing standardized mappings of quality of experience (QoE) to network performance indicators. A notable challenge lies in transitioning from a management perspective rooted in quality of service (QoS) to one centered on QoE. The QoS viewpoint, being restrictive, confines network management to performance metrics like flow or packet priority, delay, jitter, bandwidth, etc., providing users with information about DiffServ/IntServ. Therefore, it remains crucial to further articulate the assumptions linked with QoE in a more comprehensive manner aligned with the functionalities and services provided by 5G [33].

The deployment of 5G networks will occur progressively, with the initial phase involving a modification in the radio interface. This involves linking 5G NR to the 4G network's EPC, termed the non-standalone phase. In the standalone phase, 5G NR will connect to the 5G core, enabling a dual-interface phone to execute handovers (or roaming) between the two networks.

eMBMS utilizes MIMO technology to deliver multicast/broadcast media content, ensuring a superior quality of experience (QoE), including high-definition video streaming for consumers. The introduction of 5G NR brings novel functionalities aimed at enhancing QoE, incorporating the integration of network slicing, edge computing, and 5G QoS Flow concepts [10].

3. Background and Current Development of 6G

The upcoming sixth-generation communications networks are poised to make a monumental leap beyond the capabilities of 5G, driven by the ever-evolving requirements of future services and societies. This transformative shift will revolve around processes that are data-centric, intelligent, and automated [56]. The progress of disruptive technologies across diverse domains will come together to meet the requirements of emerging applications and use cases [42].

The 5G Infrastructure Association (5GIA) envisions the next system generation, 6G, operating with flexible and on-demand infrastructure for mobile telecommunications systems [1]. It is anticipated that 6G will address various challenges and create an ecosystem deeply intertwined with artificial intelligence. The architecture of 6G should be sufficiently flexible and efficient, facilitating the integration and self-aggregation of connectivity and computing capabilities dynamically, heterogeneous types of resources of diverse elements such as a network of networks, joint communication and sensing, terrestrial and non-terrestrial networks, and novel AI-driven capabilities, including also local and distributed computing resources. The 6G framework is envisioned as a resource-as-a-service (RaaS), extending beyond bandwidth, time, power, and space considerations, emphasizing the imperative of optimizing infrastructure as a flexible and configurable resource tailored to meet distinct service demands. Furthermore, with the capabilities of dynamic network infrastructure management and service orchestration mechanism together, artificial intelligence (AI)-aware networking approaches, 6G can be viewed as an infrastructure-as-a-service (IaaS) [57,58]. The 5GPPP Architecture Working Group [59] states that to obtain its full potential, 6G needs to be AI- and computation-pervasive, which calls for the 6G architecture to be data-driven to enhance the optimization of its air interface—spanning physical layer setup, mobility management, resource allocation, and QoS guarantee, achieving a powerful and robust distributed AI platform, i.e., approaching the 6G network as AI-as-a-service (aIaaS). Because it is generally accepted that 6G systems necessitate the development of a strategy for the delivery and dissemination of services through a cloud-based framework to users and 6G applications [60], it is proposed that this objective can be achieved through an expanded interpretation of existing cloud-based service orchestration concepts, allowing for the organization and integration of diverse services to cater to the requirements of all types of 6G user applications, i.e., seeing 6G architecture as everything-as-a-service (EaaS).

The architects of the 6G network strive to supplant wired connections, ensuring reliability across diverse connectivity scenarios. These scenarios span from stationary, isolated devices to dynamic mobile groups, all of which necessitate seamless communication both among themselves and direct connectivity to the primary network. In other words, 6G is poised to build upon the techniques of the 5G systems while introducing advanced components such as enhanced RAT, terahertz (THz) communication [61,62] with abundant spectrum resources, molecular networking concepts, and integrated aerial and inter-terrestrial networks, urban air mobility (UAM), UAV, high-altitude platform stations (HAPS) and satellites of systems in low earth orbit (LEO) and geostationary orbit (GEO) [31,63–65], uncoordinated networks and the co-existence of RF—FM, TV, WiFi, visible light communication (VLC), energy-efficiency, and communication environment intelligence, ambient backscatter communication (AmBC) for energy savings, symbiotic communication radio, reconfigurable intelligent surface (RIS) for non-line-of-sight (nLoS) scenarios, a holistic security paradigm, physical layer security (PLS), and blockchain (BC) [66,67]. RIS equipped with computing resources seems to be a promising solution to dynamically reconfigure physical parameters for enhancing wireless system design and optimization. Their adaptability allows for improved signal propagation, channel modeling and acquisition, and creating intelligent radio environments that are advantageous for 6G innovative applications, i.e., the electromagnetic environment can be reshaped as needed.

Envisioned as a remarkable platform, 6G aims to integrate diverse network policies, devices, and algorithms, fostering cognitive-aware, user-centric mobile operations and mitigation strategies [16].

It is expected that 6G will demand an extensive spectrum allocation to support future mobile operations. Unlike the current range of existing 5G bands, which relies on mMIMO orchestration, which falls within the 1–30 GHz range, 6G is projected to rely on cell-free m-MIMO and utilize a spectrum extending from IR and visible light and 30–300 GHz, mmWave, or even beyond, THz wave, for its operations and for delivering efficient user-centric services [5,13,68].

The development of novel access methods is imperative to support extensive multiple access techniques in 6G. Among the noteworthy approaches from the literature review, we can underscore delta-orthogonal multiple access (D-OMA), filter bank multi-carrier (FBMC), and sparse code multiple access (SCMA). The D-OMA strategy leverages distributed large CoMP concepts, facilitating NOMA transmission through partially overlapping sub-bands within NOMA clusters [69]. SCMA prioritizes overall sum rates in cloud radio access network (C-RAN) scenarios, employing single-input single-output (SISO) systems and a low-complexity algorithm that considers individual user QoS, user association, and power constraints [70]. FBMC, compared to conventional OFDM systems, boasts diminished spectral side-lobes, granting it the capability for asynchronous transmission [71].

Novel breakthroughs in terahertz and optical communications will be crucial in unlocking unprecedented data transfer and communication speeds. Additionally, cell-less or poor coverage areas through integrated terrestrial satellite access technologies [72] will ensure seamless connectivity across vast areas, extending the reach of communication networks to remote and challenging locations [42].

The advent of 6G technology is set to profoundly reshape the landscape of communication progress, encompassing intelligent, deep, holographic, and pervasive connectivity, thus profoundly shaping the evolution of the intelligence process within communication [2].

Distributed end-user terminal-based AI [46,73] will bring intelligence and decision-making capabilities closer to the user, enabling personalized and context-aware services. Moreover, the integration of distributed ledger technologies (DLTs) [74] will enhance security, transparency, and efficiency in data handling and transactions across the network to fulfill the needs of emerging applications [42]. On the other hand, AI holds the potential to [4] enhance handover operation performance by considering network deployments and geographic conditions; optimize network planning by determining base station (BS) locations; lower network energy consumption; forecast, identify, and facilitate self-healing of network irregularities; predict channel coding for more extensive bit sequences, establishing resilient synchronization to meet 6G prerequisites, facilitating mobile positioning in nLoS environments with multiple paths, conducting non-linear and non-stationary channel estimation, and implementing adaptive, RT mMIMO beamforming to represent pivotal ML applications within the physical layer. DLT technologies drive the urgency for an intelligent self-organizing network (SON) capable of managing network operations, resources, and optimizations. So 6G will have to guarantee the transition from traditional SON, which adapts functions automatically to environment states, to a self-sustaining network (SSN). This SSN concept ensures continuous maintenance of key performance indicators (KPIs) within the intricate and dynamic environments spawned by diverse 6G application domains [75]. With regard to the 6G cellular network, the integration of connected robotics and autonomous systems (CRAS) and DLTs devices will necessitate the obligatory incorporation of SON and SSN. These mechanisms will be pivotal in governing network operations, resource allocation, and optimization.

As these diverse technologies converge, sixth-generation networks will usher in a new era of interconnectedness, empowering forthcoming services and societies with cutting-edge capabilities and revolutionizing how we interact, communicate, and utilize data. The journey towards 6G is set to push the boundaries of communication technology, shaping a more intelligent, efficient, and connected world. In short, 6G is poised to emerge as an authentic AI-driven communication network, imbuing the whole system with self-awareness, autonomous computation, and the capability to make independent decisions in various scenarios.

The potential of 6G lies in providing network performance that surpasses the limits perceivable by human senses. Quality of experience (QoE) is inherently connected to quality of service (QoS) measurements, and the state of the network is intertwined with and influences user experience. However, a crucial challenge is to shift the perspective from considering the network as the primary determinant in assessing QoE [33].

4. The Requirements of 6G

The emergence of 5G has ushered in remarkable technological achievements, distinguished by exceptional transmission speeds, minimal latency, efficient power usage, and a wide-reaching connectivity capability. This innovation stands ready to serve many purposes, from individual consumers to various sectors and industries. This transformative progress takes form through three central scenarios: eMBB, mMTC, and URLLC [2,76,77].

It is anticipated that 6G will attain data rates of 1 TBPS or higher. Diverging from the two-dimensional communication structure of 5G and B5G, 6G will adopt a three-dimensional approach encompassing time, space, and frequency. Emerging technologies like edge computing, AI-aware, cloud computing, and blockchain will support this novel paradigm. The communication network of 6G is projected to be seamlessly integrated and omnipresent [78].

Envisioned as a comprehensive solution, 6G is poised to expand coverage extensively, spanning device-to-device, terrestrial, and satellite communications. The overarching objective is to fuse computation, navigation, and sensing within the communication network. Furthermore, in the core of security, 6G aims to address safeguarding, secrecy, and privacy of the vast amounts of big data generated by countless smart devices [79].

The architecture of the 6G communication network must address challenges stemming from the constrained computation capacity of mobile devices. A potential solution is offloading computation tasks to more potent devices or servers. The network demands hyper-fast data rates and ultra-low latency to facilitate real-time computation task offloading.

The specifications for the end-to-end latency, radio delay, and processing in 6G are defined as $\leq$1 ms and $\leq$10 ns, respectively, ensuring real-time communication. Additionally, 6G is positioned as an authentic AI-driven communication technology [14]. The integration of satellite technology will be fundamental to 6G's capabilities. Furthermore, intelligent radio (IR) is anticipated to replace NR-Lite [80].

Anticipated to bring about a fully interconnected global environment, 6G is projected to establish a heterogeneous network that encompasses ground, air, space, maritime, and underwater communications. Enhanced by AI capabilities, artificial intelligence (AI)-driven communications will develop in a way that "the 6G is about the 6th sense" [81]; the network entities within 6G will possess the ability to perceive and dissect multi-dimensional data, thereby enabling the effortless interlinking of terrestrial devices and onboard systems. The incorporation of pervasive artificial intelligence allows the achievement of large-scale network automation. In the age of 6G, each edge device is anticipated to be connected to the internet and regularly employ AI software. Many AI applications rely on data, raising concerns about the security and privacy of the collected information [82].

The autonomous management capability of 6G systems is improved to meet diverse application requirements, such as MBBLL, mBBMT, and mLLMT communications [16,83]. Furthermore, other proposals indicate that the path to this evolution will also pass through the focus on feMBB, ERLLC, umMTC, LDHMC, and ELPC [17]. The upcoming 6G service classes of uMUB, uHSLLC, and uHDD stem from eMBB, URLLCs, and mMTC, mobile broadband reliable low-latency communication (MBRLLC), massive URLLC (mURLLC), human-centric services (HCS), multi-purpose services (MPS) [18,75]. As the spectrum of requirements continues to broaden, 6G envisions the rise of more sophisticated service categories that are shaped by clustering applications with comparable needs, such as big communications (BigCom), secure ultra-reliable low-latency communications (SuRLLC), unconventional data communications (UCDC), and three-dimensional integrated communications (3D-InteCom) [84]. These classes, respectively, provide extensive coverage and performance across diverse domains; ultrahigh rates with low latency, and high data density with ultra-reliability.

These technologies enhance robust communication infrastructure, ensuring ultra-massive connectivity, extreme reliability, and connection continuity, enabling pervasively intelligent, reliable, scalable, flexible, adaptable, and secure terrestrial wireless. Hence, 6G systems require a cellular communication redesign that offers exceptional flexibility, surpassing the existing scope through three key strategies: (i) leveraging various sensing mechanisms, including artificial intelligence (AI), to comprehend diverse facets of the communication network and environment, (ii) improving or revolutionizing technology options, and (iii) achieving optimal resource utilization by considering real-world sensing capabilities alongside awareness.

Quality, performance, and alignment with the specifications of 6G communication systems are evaluated by establishing key performance indicators (KPIs). These KPIs are currently in the process of formulation and finalization by entities like the ITU Telecommunication Standardization Sector (ITU-T) and various industry stakeholders. Although still under development, the existing literature points to several overarching areas often taken into account [66]:

- *Data Rate and Capacity:* associated with system throughput. Measures of how much data can be transferred within a given time interval, reflecting the high-speed, high-capacity, peak and experienced spectral efficiency, maximum channel bandwidth, traffic capacity per geographic coverage area, and connection density. Must be fulfilled at 95% of all user locations. QoS and QoE will manage trade-offs between data transmission capacity or spectral efficiency and other concurrent metrics like energy efficiency and service latency.
- *Latency:* Defines the end-to-end latency and jitter, aiming for ultra-low latency to enable delay-sensitive real-time applications.
- *Reliability:* Defined by the metric for the duration of uninterrupted operation of infrastructure, and related to the orchestration and management of networks, ensuring robust and dependable communication, especially for critical applications like remote surgery or autonomous vehicles.
- *Energy Efficiency:* Focus on reducing energy consumption to prolong device battery life and promote sustainability.
- *Coverage:* Ubiquitous mobile ultra-broadband will be available everywhere, extending connectivity to remote and underserved areas, potentially through satellite networks.
- *Spectral Efficiency:* Maximizing data transmission over limited frequency bands.
- *Mobility Support:* Seamless communication while moving at high speeds, such as in high-speed trains or vehicles.
- *Connection Density:* Accommodating a high, or even a massive, number of devices within a certain geographic area is important for the IoT.
- *Security and Privacy:* Implementing strong security procedures to protect users and data.
- *Sustainability:* Ensuring that 6G networks and devices are environmentally sustainable and minimize their ecological footprint.

A 6G network requires a service-based end-to-end (E2E) architecture with key roles played by software-defined networking (SDN), network function virtualization (NFV), and network slicing. These technologies enhance network programmability, enabling the creation of multiple logical networks on a shared physical infrastructure. Anticipated benefits include higher data rates, improved spectral and energy efficiency, broader coverage, wide bandwidths, extremely high reliability, ultra-low latency, and dynamic QoS management across all network segments. Dynamic QoS management is crucial for flexible network resource utilization. However, common SDN implementations often statically provide required QoS through resource reservation based on predefined rules in forwarding engines, mapping packets into existing queues with assigned priorities [85,86].

4.1. Network Architecture

In the future, networks are expected to integrate diverse RAN technologies, including macro and small cells with high-capacity short-range links. The extensive use of AI/ML is foreseen to enhance network performance as a service across applications, impacting air interface design, data processing, network architecture, and management for superior performance. The 6G era will bring a new network architecture paradigm, decomposing the system into platform, functions, orchestration, and specialization for increased efficiency. The convergence of RAN and core networks aims to reduce complexity, while dynamic offloading and flexible instantiation of sub-networks drive increased specialization. Future scenarios rely on a flexible, scalable, secure, and reliable transport network accommodating distributed and centralized/cloud RAN with AI-powered programmability. The 6G network-of-networks will cover various scales of physical and virtual networks to address local and specialized needs [59].

The technology of 6G must be prepared to enable the IoE, ensuring connectivity for multiple smart devices across its communication network, including every smart device, from small and compact gadgets like smartwatches and smartphones to expansive applications such as mobile healthcare, robotics, and vehicular communications systems. The IoE, eMBB, and mMTC services will intricately link these devices to one or more interfaces of wireless networks based on different technologies equipped with numerous access points (APs) or base stations (BS) that will be strategically positioned in high-density or ultra-dense configurations within the 6G network, generating overlapping coverage areas, which results in a need for the management and efficiency in frequency spectrum allocation, management and minimization of interference, handoff efficiency, and the use of transmission multiplexing or transmission coordination. All this results in a distributed, cell-less massive MIMO network topology. The infrastructure must ensure access to cloud computing services or multi-access edge computing to support services.

Assuming that the 6G data-rate requirement is about 1 Tbps [83] to enable applications like [6] smart cities, smart electric cars, smart healthcare, and virtual/augmented reality, among others, the system must be focused on QoE and provide an extremally high data-rate and low latency. To achieve QoE, it needs low latency, which will be obtained through small data packets and reliable transmission served by efficient forward error correction (FEC) schemes, high-level diversity channels, efficient control algorithms, neighbor-discovery algorithms, and efficient MAC protocol over a flat network architecture [14]. To increase reliability, 6G must enhance the URLLC of 5G to obtain ERLLC.

The requirements grow exponentially for the transition from 5G to 6G. Many features of 6G may be constrained or hampered by the current underdeveloped technology that could dramatically evolve 5G technology to 6G. Indeed, the network's optimal utilization can be achieved through softwarization. Substantial enhancements are imperative within software-defined radio (SDR), SDN, and NFV of 5G technology to attain the objectives of 6G. For instance, as 6G is a truly ubiquitous and distributed AI-driven communication technology, from the physical layer to the application layer, AI will have to be deployed in all 5G layers [48,87]. Softwarization, cloudization, virtualization, and slicing remain crucial attributes of autonomous networks. Consequently, SDN, NFV, and NS continue to constitute a significant toolkit for shaping the design of 6G. The synergy of AI-enabled with SDN/NFV/NS culminates in dynamic and zero or self-network orchestration, optimization, and administration. AI-enabled network orchestration adeptly manages network infrastructure, and slices and harmonizes diverse radio access technologies, resulting in liquid networks catering to ever-evolving service needs. AI-enabled network optimization continuously monitors KPIs in real time, swiftly adapting network parameters to ensure an exceptional QoE.

In 6G, native-AI will significantly influence the network's physical layer, enhancing tasks such as estimation or prediction of channel conditions, modulation classification, adaptative coding, and security [54,88]. Deep reinforcement learning will be employed for resource allocation at the data link layer [89], while the transport layer will see the application of algorithms for route computation and intelligent traffic prediction [16]. The design of 6G should aim for a genuine convergence of communication and computing, enabling users' diverse devices to tap into the network's available computational resources effortlessly.

The H2020 EU-funded Hexa-X proposes an architecture based on three layers: infrastructure, network service, and application [59]. The infrastructure layer, which provides physical resources to host network service and application layer, incorporates network RAN, network CN, and transport networks based on radio equipment like non-virtualized radio functions such as radio units (RUs), distributed units (DU), and BS, switches, routers, communication links, data centers, and cloud infrastructure. Based on the new features of RAN enhancements, it enables a high data rate, extremely low latency, high reliability, availability, high capacity, affordable coverage, high energy efficiency, high localization accuracy, and integrated sensing functionalities. Within the framework of 6G architecture, a diverse array of (sub)network solutions converge to form a comprehensive network of networks. This dynamic structure possesses the innate ability to conform to novel topologies readily and flexibly, effectively addressing the demands for exceptional performance and extensive global service coverage.

The 6G network service layer is designed with a foundation in the cloud and microservice-based technology, utilizing services that span from the central cloud to the far edges, encompassing devices beyond the RAN. This expansion of microservices across network functions, operations, and applications lays the groundwork for a softwarised, AI-driven, and efficient 6G architecture. To create an intelligent network, support for AI in 6G and AIaaS is crucial, alongside advancements in programmability and network automation. Embracing a cloud-native approach further simplifies RAN and CN architectures, reducing complexity by eliminating redundant processing points for specific messages and minimizing duplication of functionalities among functions. In the era of 6G, there is a significant and anticipated focus on merging the functionalities of both 5G RAN and its core components. This consolidation aims to streamline functional elements, culminating in a core-less RAN structure that offers enhanced precision in the user plane [64]. Cloud-native technologies will be crucial in establishing edge-based cloudlets, enabling seamless communication between applications and functions. This capability will serve many interconnected assets while accommodating dynamic and flexible mesh topologies to deal with the highly heterogeneous network of devices and technologies, encompassing variations in both hardware and software.

Security and privacy mechanisms are intrinsic components of the comprehensive architecture, impacting every network layer along with the management and orchestration domain [59].

Pursuing the elevated spectrum and energy efficiency mandates the integration of novel air interface and communication technologies. This encompasses the adoption of new waveforms, diversified multiple-access methods, advanced channel encoding techniques, multi-antenna technologies, and the strategic amalgamation of these diverse approaches. Concurrently, evolution necessitates innovative network architectures. These include paradigms like SDN and NFV, dynamic network slicing (DNS), service-based architecture (SBA), cognitive service architecture (CSA), and cell-free (CF) architectures.

The 5GPPP Architecture Working Group proposes an architecture based on a multidimensional approach, with five horizontal layers [59]: infrastructure and environment, user plane network functions, control plane network functions, the management plane, and vertical service providers. It has a vertically designated orchestration profile which deals with responsibilities related to: the network intelligent stratum, security stratum, sensing stratum and network stratum. The network intelligence stratum coordinates functions across the entire network, managing network functions intelligently and autonomously through data and analytics gathered from the infrastructure and environment layer. The security stratum oversees all cybersecurity and data privacy aspects throughout the network, coordinating functions across planes and domains, up to the vertical service provider by distributed data and AI/ML pipelines, with automated closed-loop network operations and orchestration to meet end-to-end service KPIs.

The cloudification trend is anticipated to persist in 6G, introducing innovative network designs, such as cloud-optimized procedures that involve network functions (NFs) capable of accessing network information with minimal hierarchical interactions [90].

AI is projected to optimize 6G communication and operate as AI-as-a-service across various network entities and layers of the radio stack. The potential applications of AI include optimizing the physical layer, mobility algorithms, network management, QoS, and more. As 6G approaches, the trend involves deeply integrating AI as a fundamental enabler for communication, influencing the behavior and communication of network components, in contrast to its role in previous generations as a tool for parameter optimization.

4.2. Spectrum

The realm of 6G spectrum management can be distinguished into two primary categories of challenges: the efficient reuse of spectrum and the adoption of either novel spectrum bands or innovative transmission technologies. For the reuse part, techniques similar to 5G can be used, sharing temporally underutilized spectrum to maintain the availability and reliability [5], or communications can be conducted using cognitive radio (CR) techniques [73] and, in this case, the devices can access a shared or underused spectrum using interference detection and allocation management mechanisms. Another innovative technique of spectrum sharing is symbiotic radio (SR), which supports and bolsters intelligent and diverse wireless networks while enhancing the effectiveness of spectrum sharing in a mutualistic and competitive way [91,92]. The efficiency of THz signals can be enhanced through spectrum reuse and sharing strategies. Among the techniques available for spectrum sharing and reuse, CR stands as a notable example. When considering spectrum sharing, temporally underutilized or unlicensed spectrum upholds availability and dependability. A novel SR technique has emerged to facilitate intelligent and diverse wireless networks.

The promise is that 6G will be based on THz communications, meaning high-frequency communication and a high data rate. However, the THz signal could be either a pulse or continuous type, but 6G transmission needs a continuous wave THz signal, which is very difficult to generate and comes at the expense of greater complexity in antenna/transmitter design. This presents a paradox as generating THz signals is costly, whereas 6G asserts to provide low-cost communication services.

However, other communication techniques are being considered: VLC uses light-emitting diodes (LEDs) to achieve high-frequency (HF) bands [93]. Nonetheless, VLC has some constraints in terms of coverage and noise interference [94], whereby its application within confined spaces devoid of interference from other light sources. Molecular communication [64,65], whose signals are biocompatible, has low energy consumption because needs low power to obtain the signal as well as for transmission, and can support high data rates [95]. In quantum communication, based on the application of quantum principles, information is encoded and stored in a quantum state (utilizing photons or quantum particles) and cannot be retrieved or copied without causing changes to the data, making it a major challenge for them to be accessible by unauthorized entities. This approach offers notable benefits, including robust security, high data rates, and efficient long-range transmission capabilities. However, this technique is still at an embryonic stage [95]. Overall, 6G offers an intelligent eco-system enabling a wireless propagation environment with active signal transmission and reception and an all-spectrum reconfigurable dynamic spectrum access [66]. A comprehensive hyperspectral and full-spectral system is anticipated, encompassing a spectrum ranging from visible light, microwave, mmWave, and terahertz frequencies to laser-based free-space optical communication.

5. Use Cases and Applications

Leveraging the power of current and upcoming wireless networks, 6G holds immense potential to enable a wide range of applications, particularly for energy-efficient devices reliant on symbiotic communication. This is especially pertinent in regions densely populated with passive sensors, offering effective harnessing of their capabilities. Additionally, 6G's role extends to serve various sectors such as building and factory automation, manufacturing, e-health, intelligent transport systems (ITS), smart and precision agriculture, surveillance, and the smart grid. These applications are vital components of Industry 4.0, anticipated to drive profound paradigm shifts.

5.1. Healthcare

Envisioned as a catalyst for progress in healthcare, 6G technology is poised to revolutionize robotic-assisted surgery, telemedicine, and integrate interconnected devices for deep-body implants. These medical applications necessitate the seamless collection and transmission of continuous health data, predominantly supported by low-power, battery-operated wireless devices, and sensors.

Wireless data transfer in medical devices, facilitated by active radios, can substantially deplete battery life. However, these devices have the potential to harness the signals of pre-existing wireless systems, such as WiFi APs found in hospitals or residential environments, to ensure reliable communication without draining power. Additionally, medical devices often transmit data to centralized servers, necessitating a localized network gateway. In the context of using symbiotic radio solutions, medical devices can effectively transmit their information online via WiFi, further streamlining the communication process [44,96].

Holographic teleportation emerges as the inherent evolution from AR and VR-based solutions. It stands apart by functioning within a genuine three-dimensional domain and harnessing all five senses—sight, hearing, touch, smell, and taste—to deliver an unparalleled immersive experience. This advancement finds diverse applications, particularly in advanced healthcare, encompassing remote diagnosis, telemedicine and surgery, high-resolution sensing for distant exploration, and lifelike video conferencing. However, 6G must evolve in a way that guarantees very high throughput (Tbps) and ultra-low latencies (<1ms), which can be obtained in the new design of eMBB and URLLC [66].

Current transport network architecture is ill-equipped to handle the required ≤ 1 ms latency, which requires a profound re-evaluation of network design. The solution will involve virtualizing the existing fiber infrastructure, facilitated by modern SDN and virtualization techniques and methodologies. Simultaneously, the main functions of the network will be structured in a microservices architecture capable of dynamic activation.

5.2. High-Performance Precision Agriculture

The synergy between environmental data collection and agriculture finds realization within an IoT-driven ecosystem. In precision farming, IoT devices and sensors are strategically positioned on plants, such as within intelligent greenhouses, to facilitate data acquisition. The paramount requirements for these devices include compact size, energy efficiency to enable ultra-dense deployment, and prolonged operational longevity [91].

Existing communication technologies for wireless sensor networks, for example, IEEE 802.15.4-based protocols, are energy-intensive and large, so they can be combined with nano UAVs or UGVs to support real-time and high-performance precision farming applications for online crop or soil monitoring tasks. Creating this communications scenario, focused on symbiotic communications and ubiquitous wireless access, between traditional WSNs, cellular and UAVs, or UGVs can improve active radios' energy efficiency and operating time, countering the usual coverage gaps in rural areas [66,97].

5.3. Intelligent Transport Systems

The field of transportation is experiencing transformative growth through integrating information and communication technologies into ITS. Innovations such as autonomous driving, remote driving, collision prevention, driver assistance, and mobility management actively enhance road safety and curtail accidents. Using sensors permits these systems to gather and analyze environmental data to enact essential measures. Additionally, this data is exchanged with neighboring vehicles and infrastructure through communication technologies like IEEE 802.11p and C-V2X, further advancing the ITS landscape. In vehicular networks, battery-powered IoT sensors and devices play a crucial role by transmitting active radio signals for data exchange. The increasing scale of transportation systems worldwide anticipates a substantial proliferation of sensors, leading to heightened demand for frequent data transmission.

Consequently, the forthcoming ITS landscape necessitates communication radios with power efficiency and advanced resource management capabilities. Using a symbiotic scenario, intelligent transportation systems (ITS) can be elevated, leveraging the cooperative potential of C-V2X and IEEE 802.11p networks, promoting communication efficiency regarding spectrum utilization and energy consumption [91]. Vehicles will possess genuine

AI-driven capabilities, learning from real-world experiences facilitated by the truly real-time communication prowess of 6G. Integrating such communications becomes paramount within the framework of 6G, as they lay the foundation for ensuring high-reliability and low-latency interactions and the secure exchange of massive driving data and the surrounding environment [98]. Applications such as autonomous driving, vehicle-to-vehicle (V2V), and V2X or integrating numerous sensors on upcoming vehicle models may lead to a collective data rate of 1 Gb/s. This data capacity can be harnessed for V2V and V2X interactions.

5.4. Intelligent Industrial Automation

Founded on the principles of supply chain management and optimization, autonomous machinery, additive manufacturing processes, data analytics, and the IoT, Industry 4.0 [99] has ignited the shift toward industrial automation. Conversely, the emerging Industry X.0 paradigm [100] aims to synergize industrial automation's diverse facets by integrating artificial intelligence. Interconnected factories are central to this vision as crucial hubs of significant big data, pivotal for guiding decision-making processes. Thus, it can be expected that future factories will require assured high-throughput connectivity for thousands of devices, frequently with sub-millisecond latency.

Enabled by symbiotic technology, the deployment of industrial IoT facilitates real-time monitoring, predictive maintenance, automation, and the realization of smart factory systems, revolutionizing manufacturing processes for enhanced efficiency, productivity, and scalability, with symbiotic connections with diverse radio systems, combining a variety of manufacturing processes, thereby raising efficiency and scalability to a comprehensive level, and ensuring the safety of safety-critical systems and operators. This kind of solution allows the digitization and automation of the manufacturing industry, promoting efficient, intelligent, and sustainable practices [67,91].

Intelligent driving and industrial transformations drive essential 6G needs, culminating in uMUB, uHSLLC, and uHDD service categories. These emerging services necessitate holistic communication, sensing, and computation integration, inspiring the fusion of photonics and AI [18].

The URLLC service classes encompass a wide range of use cases within upcoming ITS, future industrial facilities, and the management of unmanned swarms of aerial vehicles or robots. Within the realm of ITS, the integration of sensors, cameras, radars, AI/ML, and V2X technologies finds prominence. V2X assumes a pivotal role by furnishing AI-equipped vehicles with contextual information from smart roads, automated highways, and intelligent autonomous intersections.

5.5. Logistics and Supply Chains

Symbiotic technology enhances communication and operational efficiency in logistics and supply chain management. This frequently entails the incorporation of RFID tags into products, enabling efficient tracking and streamlined management for improved outcomes.

This kind of solution could be valuable for RT asset location and tracking and inventory management within warehouses, utilizing existing WiFi APs to identify and oversee inventory for indoor applications or outdoor real-time shipment tracking using the cellular network [91].

6. The 6G Network Infrastructure to Manage V2X Application Lifecycles

This section explores the evolution and potential of vehicular ad hoc networks (VANETs) in a 6G network environment, emphasizing the incorporation of air and space networks to ensure seamless vehicle communication across global locations. We delve into vehicle-to-everything (V2X) communications, exploring the developments from vehicle-to-infrastructure (V2I) and vehicle-to-vehicle (V2V) communications, towards a broader spectrum of interaction within the vehicular network. The section further discusses the technical demands posed by the integration of numerous sensors in contemporary vehicles and proposes advancements in 6G to accommodate these demands. Critical evaluations of three use cases and a proposal of implementation strategies and future work in the 6G-V2X domain are also presented.

As autonomous driving technology and automotive applications advance, the existing infrastructure and geographical coverage of ground networks might fall short of meeting the demands of future vehicular ad hoc networks (VANETs). In 6G, it is expected that VANETS will evolve beyond ground-based limitations and expand into a comprehensive 3D network encompassing a space–air–ground network. The incorporation of air and space networks will ensure seamless vehicle communication across global locations, addressing the limitations posed by ground-based networks [101]. The 6G VANET primarily consists of vehicles and surrounding infrastructure elements, including BSs, buildings, traffic lights, streetlamps, and more, each equipped with computing and communication capabilities. Within this setup, vehicles can communicate with all intelligent nodes in the 3D vehicular network, a communication paradigm referred to as V2X communications.

Initially, onboard units (OBUs) were integrated into vehicles, enabling direct communication with stationary roadside units (RSUs) via vehicle-to-infrastructure (V2I) wireless connections or between vehicles using V2V links. In the contemporary landscape, advancements in the automotive industry have allowed cars to exchange data with a broader spectrum of entities, including pedestrians' handheld devices, bicycles, ground stations (GNs), UAVs, and more. This evolution is achieved through V2X communication, enabling vehicles to engage and communicate with their surrounding environment [102].

Current vehicles are outfitted with an extensive array of up to 200 sensors, such as video and infrared cameras, automotive radars, light detection, and ranging systems—including RADAR and LIDAR, along with global positioning systems, as well as others—all demanding significantly elevated data rates up to 1 Gbps, which is well beyond the capability of digital short-range communication (DSRC), so using 6G they can be served by bands below 6 GHz for high reliability and mmWave bands to achieve Gbps low data rate latency, sharing a mobile edge compute (MEC) through a uRRLC network [103,104].

V2X adaptation enhances ITS, focusing on vehicular networks (VNs) within the 5G landscape. MEC or similar edge paradigms are essential for V2X applications due to their need for ultra-low latency and reliability [87,105–107]. The 3GPP-defined connected vehicle technology improves safety, reduces congestion, senses vehicle behavior, and supports vehicular services by offloading computational tasks to roadside BSs or infrastructure, enabling data-connected autonomous driving with reduced latency [3]. AI edge intelligence is implemented using AI/ML algorithms to deal with data and services in edge nodes.

Given the extensive implementation and deployment of service-oriented 5G networks, research is now focusing on the intelligence-driven 6G to enable a fully connected world, particularly emphasizing edge intelligence [108,109]. Therefore, 6G presents an integrated framework encompassing communication networks, artificial intelligence, and mobile MEC. MEC, an evolution of previous edge computing technologies [106,110,111], has emerged as a paradigm shift by decentralizing some functions from centralized mobile cloud computing (MCC) and placing them closer to edge devices within the RAN. It means that MEC is focused on communication originating from mobile devices like 5G terminals and IoT devices within the immediate environment. MEC was designed with mobile communication as its primary consideration. This approach delivers efficient services for computation-intensive or latency-critical tasks, striking a balance between uploading data to a central cloud server and processing it on resource-constrained mobile devices [106,112]. Challenges like propagation delay, i.e., ultra-low latency, network congestion, optimal performance, connectivity feasibility and reliability, scalability, robust security, and privacy concerns, all while facilitating high-speed communication and computations, are effectively tackled through well-designed AI-MEC schemes [113,114].

V2X is a crucial enabler for autonomous vehicles, potentially significantly enhancing road safety and traffic efficiency [115]. Within this context, C-V2X emerges as a standardized V2X solution specified by 3GPP. C-V2X offers communication capabilities with low latency, very high reliability, and a high data rate. It caters to various communication scenarios, encompassing V2V, vehicle-to-pedestrian, vehicle-to-infrastructure, and vehicle-to-cloud interactions. The 3GPP-defined MEC architecture is adaptable for V2X applications. MEC servers can be positioned within the cellular network or at the roadside, linked to the network—a decision influenced by business models and policies. MEC enables C-V2X to facilitate cooperative perception, computing, and decision-making for autonomous vehicles.

Vehicle density is a key aspect in V2X communications, especially considering the crucial nature of managing and facilitating communication in environments with varying vehicle densities. In the realm of 6G V2X communications, the network infrastructure must exhibit proficiency in handling high-density scenarios. This entails ensuring low-latency and reliable communication even in heavily populated vehicular networks. Additionally, positioning accuracy stands paramount in V2X communications. It is essential to ensure safe and effective interaction among vehicles and between vehicles and infrastructure. As we progress into the age of 6G, there is a pressing need to enhance localization accuracy to accommodate the stringent demands of various V2X use cases, especially those pivotal for safety and autonomous driving.

Another dimension of challenges revolves around interoperability (Table 1). Ensuring diverse systems, perhaps originating from different manufacturers or developers, can work cohesively is a significant hurdle. The 6G V2X communication framework should ideally promote interoperability, facilitating seamless interaction among disparate systems and technologies. Furthermore, navigating through and complying with various regional and global regulations and standards becomes imperative. The 6G framework must ensure that V2X communications are compliant and standardized, adhering to regulatory requisites and promoting global operability.

Table 1. Present Situation and Proposed Changes in 6G V2X Communications.

Aspect	Present Situation	Proposed Changes
Use Case Descriptions and Roadmaps	Currently, the focus is on developing and describing use cases for V2X communications, as documented across multiple volumes and white papers by 5GAA	Proactively, the focus may pivot towards the enhancement and progression of cellular vehicle-to-everything (C-V2X) use cases, delving deeper into facets such as autonomous vehicular navigation and the direct communication interface between vehicular units and network infrastructures.
Technical Requirements and Challenges	The dominant narrative highlights an array of technical prerequisites and obstacles inherent in the deployment of V2X communications.	For forthcoming 6G implementations, a meticulous elucidation of specific technical enablers and strategies to address identified challenges is imperative.
Regulations and Standards	The current dialogue touches upon compliance with regional and global regulations and standards, ensuring that V2X communications are standardized.	The future discourse could delve deeper into how 6G can navigate through and ensure adherence to evolving regulations and standards.
Interoperability	Presently, interoperability among systems from diverse manufacturers or developers is acknowledged as a significant challenge.	Looking ahead, outlining specific strategies, technologies, or frameworks to enhance interoperability in 6G V2X communications will be vital

Diving deeper into use cases, enhancing safety aspects through V2X communications might involve scenarios like collision avoidance and emergency vehicle warning. These use cases necessitate reliable and rapid communication facilitated by 6G. Vehicle operations management pertains to managing vehicle operations effectively through V2X communications and primarily focuses on use cases related to fleet management and vehicle diagnostics. On the convenience front, V2X communication involves use cases related to parking management and infotainment services, necessitating high data rates and low-latency communication in the 6G era. Furthermore, facilitating autonomous driving through V2X communication brings forth use cases related to cooperative maneuvering and autonomous navigation, demanding stringent communication reliability and accuracy in 6G networks.

As AI's rapid integration accelerates, the evolution of autonomous functionalities and vehicle intelligence becomes increasingly evident. Thus, the next-generation C-V2X technology should establish a comprehensive solution to foster collaboration among essential stakeholders within an ITS.

Several technology challenges and corresponding solutions have been documented, and some issues deserve more attention and resolution (Table 1), such as [116]:

- C-V2X architecture, spectrum, and air interface: C-V2X needs to introduce mMIMO, VLC, THz, and radar communications to enable reliable sensing and V2X communication to support cooperation among ITS players.
- Handover control, efficient network discovery/selection: The high mobility of vehicles gives rise to frequent handovers, leading to multiple transitions between points of attachment (PoA) in conventional systems, known as vertical handovers, and these events could present a considerable challenge in terms of resource allocation, resulting in notable overhead and latency. When a vehicle transits from an RSU-covered area to a BS-covered region, or vice versa, data is transferred using distinct PoAs with varying access control protocols. The use of cell-free communications, characterized by the absence of cell borders, has the potential to facilitate continuous vehicle mobility with the help of machine learning-assisted techniques [102].

6.1. Vehicle Operations Management

Vehicle operations management in C-V2X is an example of a use case focused on leveraging C-V2X to enhance and optimize vehicle operations within a connected environment. Vehicle operations management is an intelligent platform utilizing C-V2X communication to coordinate and improve various driving and vehicle performance aspects.

The Vehicle Operations Management use case can be split into several steps:

1. Traffic and Coordination: The vehicle operations management system receives real-time traffic information and communicates with other vehicles and traffic infrastructure through C-V2X. It optimizes routes and adjusts speeds to enhance traffic flow.
2. Collision Prevention: Using C-V2X data, the vehicle operations management system detects potential collision situations with other vehicles and alerts the driver. It takes actions such as speed adjustment to avoid collisions.
3. Emergency Response: Vehicle operations management employs C-V2X to alert nearby vehicles and emergency services about the situation in emergencies. This improves response times and road safety.
4. Fleet Optimization: In commercial fleets, vehicle operations management uses C-V2X to track vehicle locations, monitor efficiency, and coordinate routes and maintenance schedules.
5. Dynamic Traffic Light Control: Using C-V2X, the vehicle operations management system communicates with traffic lights to optimize their timing based on traffic conditions, reducing congestion, and improving travel efficiency.
6. Parking Assistance: Through C-V2X, the vehicle operations management system guides drivers to available parking spaces, simplifying parking search and enhancing traffic flow.
7. Remote Maintenance and Software Updates: Utilizing C-V2X, the vehicle operations management system conducts real-time remote diagnostics and sends software updates without requiring a physical workshop visit.

A. Critical Evaluation

Feasibility in 6G: 6G's capabilities to support a vast array of IoT devices and ensure high-reliability communication lay a robust foundation for advanced vehicle operations management. With features such as network slicing, 6G can allocate dedicated network resources to manage vehicle operations efficiently and reliably.

Advantages: Implementing 6G would facilitate enhanced real-time monitoring, control, and optimization of vehicle fleets, thereby improving logistical operations and reducing operational costs.

Challenges: Ensuring secure and consistent communication across various geographic locations and terrains presents a significant hurdle, alongside managing the voluminous data generated by vehicle fleets.

B. Implementation Solutions

Technical Framework: Develop a 6G-enabled IoT framework where vehicles continuously communicate operational data to a centralized management system, facilitating real-time monitoring and decision-making.

Addressing Challenges: Implement advanced cybersecurity protocols and utilize machine learning algorithms to process and analyze the data efficiently.

Practical Considerations: Explore aspects such as initial setup costs, adapting existing vehicles to the new system, and training personnel to manage the 6G-enabled operations management systems.

6.2. Over-the-Air (OTA) Software Updates

Regarding the last step of vehicle operations management, we have the particularization of vehicle software update, which encompasses the over-the-air (OTA) software updates that represent a process in which software enhancements are transmitted remotely from a cloud-based server via a cellular connection to a connected vehicle. The primary objective is to furnish the vehicle's software systems with new features and updates, and it represents a paradigm shift in how vehicles receive software upgrades, eliminating the need for physical interventions and ensuring timely updates. This mechanism enhances vehicle performance and features and addresses potential vulnerabilities, ensuring robust vehicular cybersecurity. These updates encompass potential modifications to any software governing the vehicle's physical components or electronic signal processing systems. In practice, OTA updates predominantly impact user interfaces, such as infotainment screens, navigation systems, and vehicle maps. The execution of OTA updates empowers continuous enhancement and upkeep of a vehicle's performance and features. The necessity for physical visits to repair or service centers is obviated by leveraging advanced data analytics and automated, remote service delivery. Two user stories are associated with the OTA scenario:

- Scheduled Updates: In this scenario, users can schedule updates during off-peak hours or when the vehicle is not in use, ensuring minimal disruption.
- Incremental Updates: Rather than fetching the complete software package, vehicles exclusively retrieve the modifications from the previous version, resulting in quicker update times and decreased data usage.

Considering different variables like current and predicted future network coverage, number of surrounding vehicles impacting the available bandwidth, remaining battery life, available storage, and others, the vehicular operations management system can decide to schedule the update according to off-peak hours, prioritize the updates based on urgency, have redundancy mechanisms ensuring continuous operation and implement robust and encryption and authentication protocols that guarantees the security of OTA updates., Additionally, this technological evolution in updates allows vehicle manufacturers to rejuvenate and refine their products continuously remotely. Notably, the effectiveness of the firmware over-the-air (FOTA) process hinges significantly on C-V2X technology, which facilitates efficient and scalable wireless communication between vehicles and software management platforms.

OTA software updates, as a component of vehicle operations management, highlight the significance of ongoing software improvements in the automotive sector. As vehicles become more interconnected and reliant on software, these methods guarantee peak performance and security.

A. *Critical Evaluation*

Feasibility in 6G: The advent of 6G and its inherent capabilities, such as eMBB and URLLC, pave the way for efficient OTA software updates in vehicular networks. The expansive bandwidth of 6G facilitates the rapid transmission of large software update files, ensuring vehicles receive pertinent updates in a timely manner.

Advantages: Using 6G for OTA updates ensures that vehicles are always equipped with the latest software features and security patches, enhancing functionality and safeguarding against potential vulnerabilities.

Challenges: Key challenges encompass ensuring the integrity and security of software updates, managing the simultaneous update of numerous vehicles without overwhelming the network, and ensuring that updates are installed and implemented successfully without inducing system errors.

B. *Implementation Solutions*

Technical Framework: Implement a cloud-based vehicle management system that leverages the 6G network to transmit OTA updates securely and efficiently. Vehicles could be equipped with a system that checks for updates during non-operational hours, downloads, and installs them autonomously while ensuring that the new software is compatible and stable.

Addressing Challenges: Employ end-to-end encryption for data transmission to ensure security. Implement a robust testing and validation process for new software updates to ensure compatibility and stability. Additionally, schedule updates during off-peak hours to manage network load effectively.

Practical Considerations: The practicality of implementing OTA updates via 6G also hinges on regulatory compliance, ensuring that software updates adhere to vehicular safety and operational standards, and managing user perceptions and trust regarding autonomous updates.

6.3. Cooperative Adaptive Cruise Control (CACC)

Cooperative adaptive cruise control (CACC) represents a pivotal advance in vehicular communication, aiming to enhance safety and driving convenience. It is a sophisticated vehicular communication mechanism that seeks to bridge the gap between the host vehicle (HV) and the leading vehicle (remote vehicle—RV). By ensuring a safe and adaptive distance, CACC paves the way for smoother vehicular maneuvers and anticipates undetectable behaviors, such as sudden accelerations or decelerations. The CACC use case is versatile, with applicability spanning across various terrains and settings, including urban, rural, and highway environments. The primary objective of the HV in the CACC scenario is to modulate its speed efficiently, aligning its reactions to the behaviors of the RV. Notably, this function retains its efficacy even when not all vehicles ahead can communicate status messages. Two user stories are associated with the CACC scenario:

- ACC with Status Messages: Incorporating status messages from surrounding vehicles into the existing adaptive cruise control (ACC) framework facilitates enhanced behavioral adaptation.
- ACC with Control Information: This variant of ACC leverages specific control messages from the RV's system, offering preliminary insights into acceleration or deceleration patterns, thereby refining ACC's adaptability.

The defined service level requirements associated with the CACC scenario are the following:

- Range: The practical operational distance is determined to be 800 m, considering vehicle speeds and the possible gaps between vehicles.
- Data Transmission: Vehicles are required to regularly transmit kinematic and positional data, with an average data size of 300 bytes.
- Vehicle Density: The system is engineered to accommodate a wide range of traffic scenarios, supporting densities of up to 10,000 vehicles per square kilometer.
- Positional Accuracy: The focus is on precise longitudinal positioning, with a defined accuracy threshold of 0.5 m ($X\sigma$).
- Standardization and Regulation: To establish inter-vehicle distances, the CACC framework requires compatibility among various original equipment manufacturers (OEMs), standardized protocols, and regulatory supervision.

The CACC use case highlights the transformative power of V2X communication in reshaping vehicle safety and the driving experience. As vehicle networks become increasingly complex, such innovations will be crucial in influencing the trajectory of ITS in the future.

A. *Critical Evaluation:*

Feasibility in 6G: CACC leverages V2V communication, and 6G, with its URLLC and high-mobility communication capabilities, can ensure that vehicles exchange data in real-time, enabling cooperative decision-making even at high speeds.

Advantages: Implementing CACC via 6G could enhance road safety, optimize traffic flow, and contribute to a more pleasant driving experience by reducing the burden on the driver.

Challenges: Developing algorithms that can manage diverse and dynamic traffic scenarios while ensuring that communication between vehicles is not only fast but also exceedingly reliable is crucial.

B. *Implementation Solutions:*

Technical Framework: Establish a system where vehicles utilize 6G to communicate data regarding speed, distance, and road conditions to each other, employing AI algorithms to make cooperative decisions regarding speed adjustments and lane changes.

Addressing Challenges: Ensure that the AI algorithms are robust enough to manage varied traffic scenarios and implement redundant communication channels to enhance reliability.

Practical Considerations: Address issues related to user adoption, update current vehicular communication systems to be 6G-compatible, and navigate regulatory compliance related to autonomous driving features.

6.4. Technical Requirements, Challenges and Future Work

In the pursuit of implementing 6G-enabled V2X applications, a meticulous analysis of technical requirements is paramount. The network infrastructure demands a robust architecture capable of supporting the voluminous data generated by vehicular and IoT devices, ensuring ultra-low latency and reliable connectivity, which are vital for real-time decision-making and data transmission in V2X applications. When it comes to hardware, vehicles need to be equipped with 6G-compatible communication modules, sophisticated sensors, and potent computing capabilities. Concurrently, the network infrastructure must be fortified with advanced base stations and edge computing devices to proficiently manage 6G connectivity.

The software realm necessitates the development of efficient communication protocols and intelligent algorithms to optimize data processing and manage communications effectively in V2X applications. Security encompasses another pivotal facet, demanding end-to-end data security through comprehensive encryption and secure data transmission protocols. Network security measures need to be fortified to thwart cyber-attacks and unauthorized access, ensuring the safety and integrity of the network and data.

Interoperability stands as a cornerstone to facilitate seamless communication between devices from different manufacturers, necessitating adherence to industry standards and the uniformity of communication protocols.

Embarking on the 6G journey introduces a spectrum of challenges. Network reliability stands out prominently, wherein ensuring continuous and steadfast connectivity, particularly in geographically challenging areas, becomes crucial. Upholding data integrity during transmission also becomes vital to prevent data corruption and ensure the reliability of communicated information. Scalability emerges as another formidable challenge, necessitating the network and V2X systems to efficiently manage increasing connected vehicles and data volumes.

Delving into security and privacy, safeguarding user and vehicle data, and protecting the network against cyber threats is paramount to uphold user trust and regulatory compliance. The implementation cost looms as a significant hurdle, entailing substantial investments in establishing 6G infrastructure and adapting vehicles to be 6G-compatible. Regulatory compliance further complicates the implementation, as V2X applications must adhere to strict safety and data protection standards.

To navigate through the elucidated challenges, adopting edge computing can be pivotal, enabling data processing closer to the source, thereby alleviating latency and bandwidth usage. Network slicing could be employed to dedicate network resources for specific V2X applications, ensuring consistent performance. Robust cybersecurity measures, such as advanced encryption and intrusion detection systems, need to be at the forefront to safeguard against cyber threats.

As we gaze into the future, enhancing the AI capabilities of V2X systems to adeptly manage complex scenarios and decision-making will be crucial. Further research into exploring alternative network technologies and architectures could pave the way for the evolution and enhancement of 6G V2X applications.

7. Conclusions

Ultimately, 6G is a pivotal communication technology poised to unlock many novel innovations. This article comprehensively explores the essential parameters of 6G technology, revealing substantial challenges that must be surmounted to realize these desired benchmarks and fulfill the envisioned potential. Wireless networks based on 6G promise to deliver a substantial increase in QoS while also emphasizing sustainability. This assurance is underpinned by a new architectural paradigm shift around existing and emerging spectrum technologies such as THz, VLC, molecular, and quantum communication. This paradigm also encompasses integrating terrestrial and non-terrestrial networks, fostering intelligent connections made possible by pervasive AI, and bolstering the network's protocol stack framework.

V2X scenarios are challenging, and the use cases presented highlight the transformative potential of V2X communication in reshaping the automotive industry. As the industry moves forward, addressing potential challenges, including cybersecurity risks and network bandwidth limitations, ensuring universal applicability across diverse terrains and settings will be imperative.

The presented vehicular operations management (VOM) system, leveraging C-V2X communication technology, underscores the paradigm shift toward a more connected and intelligent vehicular ecosystem. The system enhances driving experiences and optimizes vehicle performance and safety, presenting a holistic vehicular management.

As a subset of VOM, introducing OTA software updates represents a significant advancement in vehicular maintenance, eliminating the need for physical interventions and ensuring vehicles are always equipped with the latest software enhancements and security patches. This not only augments vehicle performance but also fortifies vehicular cybersecurity.

The effectiveness of both the OTA updates and CACC hinges significantly on C-V2X technology. This technology facilitates efficient and scalable wireless communication, making it indispensable for the future of vehicular operations and establishing C-V2X as the backbone.

CACC, as a sophisticated vehicular communication mechanism, plays a pivotal role in enhancing safety and driving convenience. Ensuring a safe and adaptive distance between vehicles paves the way for smoother vehicular maneuvers, potentially reducing traffic congestion and accidents.

Some future Implications must be considered as vehicles become increasingly interconnected and reliant on software. The methods and systems discussed will guarantee optimal vehicle performance, safety, and user convenience. The continuous evolution and refinement of these systems will shape the future of transportation, making it more efficient, safe, and user-centric.

The need for standardization and regulatory oversight, especially in frameworks like CACC, cannot be overstated. As vehicular communication systems become more intricate, ensuring compatibility among various original equipment manufacturers (OEMs) and defining inter-vehicle distances will be paramount.

The presented systems and use cases highlight the transformative power of V2X communication in reshaping the automotive sector. As the industry progresses, addressing potential challenges, including cybersecurity threats and network bandwidth limitations, and ensuring universal applicability across diverse terrains and settings will be imperative.

The bottom-up approach in designing and implementing 5G needs a shift towards considering the requirements of future applications as a cornerstone for successful 6G infrastructure. High-demand verticals, like vehicular applications, will be crucial in establishing the primary performance requirements for future 6G deployments.

In conclusion, 6G is positioned to bring about a revolutionary transformation across various domains, establishing itself as a paradigm-shifting technology with profound impacts.

Author Contributions: Conceptualisation, C.S. and J.C.; methodology, C.S.; investigation: C.S., J.C., G.C., S.R. and X.R.S.; writing—original draft, C.S., J.C. and G.C.; writing—review and editing, C.S., J.C. and F.B.; supervision, F.B.; funding acquisition, F.B. All authors have read and agreed to the published version of the manuscript.

Funding: This research received no external funding.

Data Availability Statement: The data presented in this study are available upon request from the corresponding author. The data are not publicly available due to institutional indications.

Conflicts of Interest: Author José Cunha is a full time employee with the role of Software Architect at Company Optare Solutions. Author Guillermo Candela is a full time employee with the role of Analyst/Developer at Company Optare Solutions. Author Santiago Rodriguez is a full time employee with the roles of R&D Manager and Software Architect at Company Optare Solutions. Author Xosé Ramón Sousa is a full time employee with the roles of R&D Director and Software Architect at Company Optare Solutions and is a company partner of Company Optare Solutions. The authors declare no conflict of interest.

References

1. Bernardos, C.J.; Uusitalo, M.A. *European Vision for the 6G Network Ecosystem*; Zenodo: Genève, Switzerland, 2021.
2. Lu, Y.; Zheng, X. 6G: A Survey on Technologies, Scenarios, Challenges, and the Related Issues. *J. Ind. Inf. Integr.* **2020**, *19*, 100158. [CrossRef]
3. Ranaweera, P.; Jurcut, A.; Liyanage, M. MEC-Enabled 5G Use Cases: A Survey on Security Vulnerabilities and Countermeasures. *ACM Comput. Surv.* **2022**, *54*, 1–37. [CrossRef]
4. Samsung Electronics. *6G: The Next Hyper-Connected Experience for All*; Samsung Electronics: Suwon-Si, Republic of Korea, 2020; p. 46.
5. Chen, S.; Liang, Y.-C.; Sun, S.; Kang, S.; Cheng, W.; Peng, M. Vision, Requirements, and Technology Trend of 6G: How to Tackle the Challenges of System Coverage, Capacity, User Data-Rate and Movement Speed. *arXiv* **2020**, arXiv:2002.04929. [CrossRef]
6. Nayak, S.; Patgiri, R. 6G Communications: A Vision on the Potential Applications. *arXiv* **2020**, arXiv:2005.07531. [CrossRef]
7. Mukherjee, A.; Mukherjee, P.; De, D.; Dey, N. QoS-aware 6G enabled ultra low lateny edge-asisted Iternet of Drone Things for real-time stride analysis. *Comput. Electr. Eng.* **2021**, *95*, 107438. [CrossRef]

8. ITU. *Vocabulary for Performance, Quality of Service and Quality of Experience*; P Series & G Series; ITU: Geneva, Switzerland, 2017; p. 50.
9. ITU. *Guidelines on Regulatory Aspects of Quality of Service*; E.800-series—Supplement 9; ITU: Geneva, Switzerland, 2021; p. 22.
10. Nasralla, M.M.; Khattak, S.B.A.; Ur Rehman, I.; Iqbal, M. Exploring the Role of 6G Technology in Enhancing Quality of Experience for M-Health Multimedia Applications: A Comprehensive Survey. *Sensors* **2023**, *23*, 5882. [CrossRef]
11. Poryazov, S.A.; Saranova, E.T.; Andonov, V.S. Overall Model Normalization towards Adequate Prediction and Presentation of QoE in Overall Telecommunication Systems. In Proceedings of the 2019 14th International Conference on Advanced Technologies, Systems and Services in Telecommunications (TELSIKS), Nis, Serbia, 23–25 October 2019; pp. 360–363.
12. ITU. *Quality of Experience (QoE) Requirements for Real-Time Multimedia Services over 5G Networks*; ITU: Geneva, Switzerland, 2022; p. 31.
13. Elmeadawy, S.; Shubair, R.M. 6G Wireless Communications: Future Technologies and Research Challenges. In Proceedings of the 2019 International Conference on Electrical and Computing Technologies and Applications (ICECTA), Ras Al Khaimah, United Arab Emirates, 19–21 November 2019; pp. 1–5.
14. Nayak, S.; Patgiri, R. 6G Communication: Envisioning the Key Issues and Challenges. *EAI Endorsed Trans. Internet Things* **2021**, *6*, 166959. [CrossRef]
15. Akyildiz, I.F.; Kak, A.; Nie, S. 6G and Beyond: The Future of Wireless Communications Systems. *IEEE Access* **2020**, *8*, 133995–134030. [CrossRef]
16. Gui, G.; Liu, M.; Tang, F.; Kato, N.; Adachi, F. 6G: Opening New Horizons for Integration of Comfort, Security, and Intelligence. *IEEE Wirel. Commun.* **2020**, *27*, 126–132. [CrossRef]
17. Zhang, Z.; Xiao, Y.; Ma, Z.; Xiao, M.; Ding, Z.; Lei, X.; Karagiannidis, G.K.; Fan, P. 6G Wireless Networks: Vision, Requirements, Architecture, and Key Technologies. *IEEE Veh. Technol. Mag.* **2019**, *14*, 28–41. [CrossRef]
18. Zong, B.; Fan, C.; Wang, X.; Duan, X.; Wang, B.; Wang, J. 6G Technologies: Key Drivers, Core Requirements, System Architectures, and Enabling Technologies. *IEEE Veh. Technol. Mag.* **2019**, *14*, 18–27. [CrossRef]
19. 5GAA. A Visionary Roadmap for Advanced Driving Use Cases, Connectivity Technologies, and Radio Spectrum Needs. Available online: https://5gaa.org/content/uploads/2023/01/5gaa-white-paper-roadmap.pdf (accessed on 24 August 2023).
20. 5GAA. C-V2X Use Cases and Service Level Requirements Volume III. Available online: https://5gaa.org/content/uploads/2023/01/5gaa-tr-c-v2x-use-cases-and-service-level-requirements-vol-iii.pdf (accessed on 24 August 2023).
21. Nawaz, F.; Ibrahim, J.; Junaid, M.; Kousar, S.; Parveen, T. A Review of Vision and Challenges of 6G Technology. *Int. J. Adv. Comput. Sci. Appl.* **2020**, *11*, 643–649. [CrossRef]
22. Ray, P.P. A Perspective on 6G: Requirement, Technology, Enablers, Challenges and Future Road Map. *J. Syst. Archit.* **2021**, *118*, 102180. [CrossRef]
23. Gui, G.; Huang, H.; Song, Y.; Sari, H. Deep Learning for an Effective Nonorthogonal Multiple Access Scheme. *IEEE Trans. Veh. Technol.* **2018**, *67*, 8440–8450. [CrossRef]
24. Kato, N.; Fadlullah, Z.M.; Mao, B.; Tang, F.; Akashi, O.; Inoue, T.; Mizutani, K. The Deep Learning Vision for Heterogeneous Network Traffic Control: Proposal, Challenges, and Future Perspective. *IEEE Wirel. Commun.* **2017**, *24*, 146–153. [CrossRef]
25. Goyal, P.; Sahoo, A.K. A Roadmap towards Connected Living: 5G Mobile Technology. *IJITEE* **2019**, *9*, 1670–1685. [CrossRef]
26. Tezergil, B.; Onur, E. Wireless Backhaul in 5G and Beyond: Issues, Challenges and Opportunities. *IEEE Commun. Surv. Tutor.* **2022**, *24*, 2579–2632. [CrossRef]
27. Wang, D.; Wang, M.; Zhu, P.; Li, J.; Wang, J.; You, X. Performance of Network-Assisted Full-Duplex for Cell-Free Massive MIMO. *IEEE Trans. Commun.* **2020**, *68*, 1464–1478. [CrossRef]
28. Hu, Y.; Ge, H.; Wang, H.; Wang, D. Spectral Efficiency of Network-Assisted Full-Duplex for Cell-Free Massive MIMO System Under Pilot Contamination. *IEEE Access* **2021**, *9*, 110826–110841. [CrossRef]
29. Li, J.; Chen, L.; Zhu, P.; Wang, D.; You, X. Satellite-Assisted Cell-Free Massive MIMO Systems with Multi-Group Multicast. *Sensors* **2021**, *21*, 6222. [CrossRef]
30. Huang, S.; Ye, Y.; Xiao, M.; Poor, H.V.; Skoglund, M. Decentralized Beamforming Design for Intelligent Reflecting Surface-Enhanced Cell-Free Networks. *IEEE Wirel. Commun. Lett.* **2021**, *10*, 673–677. [CrossRef]
31. Ghosh, A.; Maeder, A.; Baker, M.; Chandramouli, D. 5G Evolution: A View on 5G Cellular Technology Beyond 3GPP Release 15. *IEEE Access* **2019**, *7*, 127639–127651. [CrossRef]
32. Sah, H.N. A Brief History of Mobile Generations and Satellite Wireless Communication System. *J. Emerg. Technol. Innov. Res. (JETIR)* **2017**, *4*, 1211–1216.
33. Taha, A.-E.M. Quality of Experience in 6G Networks: Outlook and Challenges. *J. Sens. Actuator Netw.* **2021**, *10*, 11. [CrossRef]
34. Halonen, T.; Romero, J.; Melero, J. *GSM, GPRS and EDGE Performance: Evolution Towards 3G/UMTS*, 2nd ed.; John Wiley & Sons Ltd.: Hoboken, NJ, USA, 2003; ISBN 978-0-470-86694-8.
35. Khiadani, N. The Development of Mobile Communications in 5G and 6G. *mjtd* **2021**, *10*, 87–95. [CrossRef]
36. Nawaz, S.J.; Sharma, S.K.; Mansoor, B.; Patwary, M.N.; Khan, N.M. Non-Coherent and Backscatter Communications: Enabling Ultra-Massive Connectivity in 6G Wireless Networks. *IEEE Access* **2021**, *9*, 38144–38186. [CrossRef]
37. Park, Y.; Park, T. A Survey of Security Threats on 4G Networks. In Proceedings of the 2007 IEEE Globecom Workshops, Washington, DC, USA, 26–30 November 2007; pp. 1–6.

38. Gawas, A.U. An Overview on Evolution of Mobile Wireless Communication Networks: 1G–6G. *Int. J. Recent Innov. Trends Comput. Commun.* **2015**, *3*, 3130–3133.
39. Bariah, L.; Mohjazi, L.; Muhaidat, S.; Sofotasios, P.C.; Kurt, G.K.; Yanikomeroglu, H.; Dobre, O.A. A Prospective Look: Key Enabling Technologies, Applications and Open Research Topics in 6G Networks. *IEEE Access* **2020**, *8*, 174792–174820. [CrossRef]
40. Ren, J.; Zhang, D.; He, S.; Zhang, Y.; Li, T. A Survey on End-Edge-Cloud Orchestrated Network Computing Paradigms: Transparent Computing, Mobile Edge Computing, Fog Computing, and Cloudlet. *ACM Comput. Surv.* **2020**, *52*, 1–36. [CrossRef]
41. Ramezanpour, K.; Jagannath, J. Inrelligent zero trust archicteture for 5G/6G networks: Principles, challenges, and role of machine learning in the contet of O-RAN. *Comput. Netw.* **2022**, *217*, 109358. [CrossRef]
42. Ahmad, I.; Rodriguez, F.; Huusko, J.; Seppänen, K. On the Dependability of 6G Networks. *Electronics* **2023**, *12*, 1472. [CrossRef]
43. Parkvall, S.; Dahlman, E.; Furuskar, A.; Frenne, M. NR: The New 5G Radio Access Technology. *IEEE Comm. Stand. Mag.* **2017**, *1*, 24–30. [CrossRef]
44. Janjua, M.B.; Duranay, A.E.; Arslan, H. Role of Wireless Communication in Healthcare System to Cater Disaster Situations Under 6G Vision. *Front. Comms. Net.* **2020**, *1*, 610879. [CrossRef]
45. Yang, H.; Alphones, A.; Xiong, Z.; Niyato, D.; Zhao, J.; Wu, K. Artificial-Intelligence-Enabled Intelligent 6G Networks. *IEEE Netw.* **2020**, *34*, 272–280. [CrossRef]
46. Sekaran, R.; Patan, R.; Raveendran, A.; Al-Turjman, F.; Ramachandran, M.; Mostarda, L. Survival Study on Blockchain Based 6G-Enabled Mobile Edge Computation for IoT Automation. *IEEE Access* **2020**, *8*, 143453–143463. [CrossRef]
47. Hantouti, H.; Benamar, N.; Taleb, T.; Laghrissi, A. Traffic Steering for Service Function Chaining. *IEEE Commun. Surv. Tutor.* **2019**, *21*, 487–507. [CrossRef]
48. Fitzek, F.H.P.; Seeling, P. Why We Should not Talk about 6G. *arXiv* **2020**, arXiv:2003.02079. [CrossRef]
49. Khan, R.; Kumar, P.; Jayakody, D.N.K.; Liyanage, M. A Survey on Security and Privacy of 5G Technologies: Potential Solutions, Recent Advancements, and Future Directions. *IEEE Commun. Surv. Tutor.* **2020**, *22*, 196–248. [CrossRef]
50. Foukas, X.; Patounas, G.; Elmokashfi, A.; Marina, M.K. Network Slicing in 5G: Survey and Challenges. *IEEE Commun. Mag.* **2017**, *55*, 94–100. [CrossRef]
51. Bhatia, V.; Swami, P.; Sharma, S.; Mitra, R. Non-Orthogonal Multiple Access: An Enabler for Massive Connectivity. *J. Indian Inst. Sci.* **2020**, *100*, 337–348. [CrossRef]
52. Elbayoumi, M.; Kamel, M.; Hamouda, W.; Youssef, A. NOMA-Assisted Machine-Type Communications in UDN: State-of-the-Art and Challenges. *IEEE Commun. Surv. Tutor.* **2020**, *22*, 1276–1304. [CrossRef]
53. Ahad, A.; Tahir, M.; Yau, K.-L.A. 5G-Based Smart Healthcare Network: Architecture, Taxonomy, Challenges and Future Research Directions. *IEEE Access* **2019**, *7*, 100747–100762. [CrossRef]
54. O'Shea, T.J.; West, N. Radio Machine Learning Dataset Generation with GNU Radio. In Proceedings of the 6th GNU Radio Conference, Boulder, CO, USA, 12–16 September 2016; Volume 1.
55. Zong, B.; Zhang, X.; Li, X.; Wang, J.; Zhang, S. Photonics Defined Radio—A New Paradigm for Future Mobile Communication of B5G/6G. In Proceedings of the 6th International Conference on Photonics, Optics and Laser Technology, SCITEPRESS—Science and Technology Publications, Funchal, Portugal, 25–27 January 2018; pp. 155–159.
56. Qadir, Z.; Le, K.N.; Saeed, N.; Munawar, H.S. Towards 6G Internet of Things: Recent Advances, Use Cases, and Open Challenges. *ICT Express* **2023**, *9*, 296–312. [CrossRef]
57. Barmpounakis, S.; Alonistioti, N.; Alexandropoulos, G.C.; Kaloxylos, A. Dynamic Infrastructure-as-a-Service: A Key Paradigm for 6G Networks and Application to Maritime Communications. *ITU J-FET* **2022**, *3*, 326–341. [CrossRef]
58. Gran, A.; Lin, S.-C.; Akyildiz, I.F. Towards Wireless Infrastructure-as-a-Service (WIaaS) for 5G Software-Defined Cellular Systems. In Proceedings of the 2017 IEEE International Conference on Communications (ICC), Paris, France, 21–25 May 2017; pp. 1–6.
59. Bahare, M.K.; Gavras, A.; Gramaglia, M.; Cosmas, J.; Li, X.; Bulakci, Ö.; Rahman, A.; Kostopoulos, A.; Mesodiakaki, A.; Tsolkas, D.; et al. The 6G Architecture Landscape—European Perspective. In *5G Infrastructure Public-Private-Partnership*; Zenodo: Genève, Switzerland, 2023. [CrossRef]
60. Taleb, T.; Benzaïd, C.; Lopez, M.B.; Mikhaylov, K.; Tarkoma, S.; Kostakos, P.; Mahmood, N.H.; Pirinen, P.; Matinmikko-Blue, M.; Latva-Aho, M.; et al. 6G System Architecture: A Service of Services Vision. *ITU J-FET* **2022**, *3*, 710–743. [CrossRef]
61. Harter, T.; Füllner, C.; Kemal, J.N.; Ummethala, S.; Steinmann, J.L.; Brosi, M.; Hesler, J.L.; Bründermann, E.; Müller, A.-S.; Freude, W.; et al. Generalized Kramers–Kronig Receiver for Coherent Terahertz Communications. *Nat. Photonics* **2020**, *14*, 601–606. [CrossRef]
62. Guerboukha, H.; Shrestha, R.; Neronha, J.; Fang, Z.; Mittleman, D.M. Conformal Leaky-Wave Antennas for Wireless Terahertz Communications. *Commun. Eng.* **2023**, *2*, 17. [CrossRef]
63. Arnold, M.; Hoydis, J.; ten Brink, S. *Novel Massive MIMO Channel Sounding Data Applied to Deep Learning-Based Indoor Positioning*; VDE VERLAG GmbH: Berlin, Germany, 2019; ISBN 978-3-8007-4862-4.
64. Viswanathan, H.; Mogensen, P.E. Communications in the 6G Era. *IEEE Access* **2020**, *8*, 57063–57074. [CrossRef]
65. Farsad, N.; Yilmaz, H.B.; Eckford, A.; Chae, C.-B.; Guo, W. A Comprehensive Survey of Recent Advancements in Molecular Communication. *IEEE Commun. Surv. Tutor.* **2016**, *18*, 1887–1919. [CrossRef]
66. Xu, H.; Klaine, P.V.; Onireti, O.; Cao, B.; Imran, M.; Zhang, L. Blockchain-enabled resource management and sharing for 6G communications. *Digit. Commun. Netw.* **2020**, *3*, 261–269. [CrossRef]

67. Zhang, W.; Qin, Y.; Zhao, W.; Jia, M.; Liu, Q.; He, R.; Ai, B. A Green Paradigm for Internet of Things: Ambient Backscatter Communications. *China Commun.* **2019**, *16*, 109–119. [CrossRef]
68. Elayan, H.; Amin, O.; Shubair, R.M.; Alouini, M.-S. Terahertz Communication: The Opportunities of Wireless Technology beyond 5G. In Proceedings of the 2018 International Conference on Advanced Communication Technologies and Networking (CommNet), Marrakech, Morocco, 2–4 April 2018; pp. 1–5.
69. Al-Eryani, Y.; Hossain, E. The D-OMA Method for Massive Multiple Access in 6G: Performance, Security, and Challenges. *IEEE Veh. Technol. Mag.* **2019**, *14*, 92–99. [CrossRef]
70. Farhadi Zavleh, A.; Bakhshi, H. Resource Allocation in Sparse Code Multiple Access-based Systems for Cloud-radio Access Network in 5G Networks. *Trans. Emerg. Tel. Tech.* **2021**, *32*, e4153. [CrossRef]
71. Zhao, J.; Townsend, P. Fast Channel Estimation and Equalization Scheme for Offset-QAM OFDM Systems. *Opt. Express* **2019**, *27*, 714. [CrossRef] [PubMed]
72. Zhu, X.; Jiang, C. Integrated Satellite-Terrestrial Networks Toward 6G: Architectures, Applications, and Challenges. *IEEE Internet Things J.* **2022**, *9*, 437–461. [CrossRef]
73. Mathew, A. Artificial Intelligence and Cognitive Computing for 6G Communications & Networks. *Int. J. Comput. Sci. Mob. Comput.* **2021**, *10*, 26–31.
74. Krummacker, D.; Veith, B.; Lindenschmitt, D.; Schotten, H.D. DLT Architectures for Trust Anchors in 6G. *Ann. Telecommun.* **2023**, *78*, 551–560. [CrossRef]
75. Saad, W.; Bennis, M.; Chen, M. A Vision of 6G Wireless Systems: Applications, Trends, Technologies, and Open Research Problems. *IEEE Netw.* **2020**, *34*, 134–142. [CrossRef]
76. Ji, H.; Park, S.; Yeo, J.; Kim, Y.; Lee, J.; Shim, B. Ultra-Reliable and Low-Latency Communications in 5G Downlink: Physical Layer Aspects. *IEEE Wirel. Commun.* **2018**, *25*, 124–130. [CrossRef]
77. Lee, D.; Camacho, D.; Jung, J.J. Smart Mobility with Big Data: Approaches, Applications, and Challenges. *Appl. Sci.* **2023**, *13*, 7244. [CrossRef]
78. Katz, M.; Matinmikko-Blue, M.; Latva-Aho, M. 6Genesis Flagship Program: Building the Bridges Towards 6G-Enabled Wireless Smart Society and Ecosystem. In Proceedings of the 2018 IEEE 10th Latin-American Conference on Communications (LATINCOM), Guadalajara, Mexico, 14–16 November 2018; pp. 1–9.
79. Kazmi, S.H.A.; Hassan, R.; Qamar, F.; Nisar, K.; Ibrahim, A.A.A. Security Concepts in Emerging 6G Communication: Threats, Countermeasures, Authentication Techniques and Research Directions. *Symmetry* **2023**, *15*, 1147. [CrossRef]
80. Letaief, K.B.; Chen, W.; Shi, Y.; Zhang, J.; Zhang, Y.-J.A. The Roadmap to 6G: AI Empowered Wireless Networks. *IEEE Commun. Mag.* **2019**, *57*, 84–90. [CrossRef]
81. Wild, T.; Viswanathan, H. Building a Network with a Sixth Sense. In *Envisioning a 6G Future*; Nokia Bell Labs: New York, NY, USA, 2023.
82. Kaushik, H. Shifting Towards 6G from 5G Wireless Networks—Advancements, Opportunities and Challenges. *JECNAM* **2022**, *2*, 20–29. [CrossRef]
83. Zhang, S.; Xiang, C.; Xu, S. 6G: Connecting Everything by 1000 Times Price Reduction. *IEEE Open J. Veh. Technol.* **2020**, *1*, 107–115. [CrossRef]
84. Dang, S.; Amin, O.; Shihada, B.; Alouini, M.-S. What Should 6G Be? *Nat. Electron.* **2020**, *3*, 20–29. [CrossRef]
85. Bojović, P.D.; Malbašić, T.; Vujošević, D.; Martić, G.; Bojović, Ž. Dynamic QoS Management for a Flexible 5G/6G Network Core: A Step toward a Higher Programmability. *Sensors* **2022**, *22*, 2849. [CrossRef] [PubMed]
86. Javed, F.; Antevski, K.; Mangues-Bafalluy, J.; Giupponi, L.; Bernardos, C.J. Distributed Ledger Technologies for Network Slicing: A Survey. *IEEE Access* **2022**, *10*, 19412–19442. [CrossRef]
87. Siriwardhana, Y.; Porambage, P.; Liyanage, M.; Ylianttila, M. AI and 6G Security: Opportunities and Challenges. In Proceedings of the 2021 Joint European Conference on Networks and Communications & 6G Summit (EuCNC/6G Summit), Porto, Portugal, 8–11 June 2021; pp. 616–621.
88. Hamamreh, J.M.; Furqan, H.M.; Arslan, H. Classifications and Applications of Physical Layer Security Techniques for Confidentiality: A Comprehensive Survey. *IEEE Commun. Surv. Tutor.* **2019**, *21*, 1773–1828. [CrossRef]
89. Kato, N.; Mao, B.; Tang, F.; Kawamoto, Y.; Liu, J. Ten Challenges in Advancing Machine Learning Technologies toward 6G. *IEEE Wirel. Commun.* **2020**, *27*, 96–103. [CrossRef]
90. Ericson, M.; Condoluci, M.; Rugeland, P.; Wanstedt, S.; Abad, M.S.H.; Haliloglu, O.; Saimler, M.; Feltrin, L. 6G Architectural Trends and Enablers. In Proceedings of the 2021 IEEE 4th 5G World Forum (5GWF), Montreal, QC, Canada, 13–15 October 2021; pp. 406–411.
91. Janjua, M.B.; Arslan, H. A Survey of Symbiotic Radio: Methodologies, Applications, and Future Directions. *Sensors* **2023**, *23*, 2511. [CrossRef]
92. Liang, Y.-C.; Zhang, Q.; Larsson, E.G.; Li, G.Y. Symbiotic Radio: Cognitive Backscattering Communications for Future Wireless Networks. *arXiv* **2020**, arXiv:2007.01506. [CrossRef]
93. Khan, L.U. Visible Light Communication: Applications, Architecture, Standardization and Research Challenges. *Digit. Commun. Netw.* **2017**, *3*, 78–88. [CrossRef]

94. Chedup, S.; Subba, B.; Dorji, S.; Perera, T.D.P.; Rajaram, A.; Jayakody, D.N.K. Visible Light Energy Harvesting in Modern Communication Systems. In Proceedings of the International Conference on Electrical, Electronics, Computer, Communication, Mechanical and Computing (EECCMC), Tamil Nadu, India, 28–29 January 2018; pp. 252–257.
95. Huang, T.; Yang, W.; Wu, J.; Ma, J.; Zhang, X.; Zhang, D. A Survey on Green 6G Network: Architecture and Technologies. *IEEE Access* **2019**, *7*, 175758–175768. [CrossRef]
96. Mao, Z.; Hu, F.; Ling, Z.; Li, S. Bidirectional Intra-Network Mutual Ambient Backscatter Communications in Distributed Wireless Wearable Measurement Networks. *Measurement* **2021**, *183*, 109863. [CrossRef]
97. Tokekar, P.; Hook, J.V.; Mulla, D.; Isler, V. Sensor Planning for a Symbiotic UAV and UGV System for Precision Agriculture. *IEEE Trans. Robot.* **2016**, *32*, 1498–1511. [CrossRef]
98. Cheng, N.; Lyu, F.; Chen, J.; Xu, W.; Zhou, H.; Zhang, S.; Shen, X. Big Data Driven Vehicular Networks. *IEEE Netw.* **2018**, *32*, 160–167. [CrossRef]
99. Suleiman, Z.; Shaikholla, S.; Dikhanbayeva, D.; Shehab, E.; Turkyilmaz, A. Industry 4.0: Clustering of Concepts and Characteristics. *Cogent Eng.* **2022**, *9*, 2034264. [CrossRef]
100. Abood, D.; Quilligan, A.; Narsalay, R. *Industry X.0: Combine and Conquer*; Accenture: Cebu, Philippines, 2017.
101. Guo, H.; Zhou, X.; Liu, J.; Zhang, Y. Vehicular Intelligence in 6G: Networking, Communications, and Computing. *Veh. Commun.* **2022**, *33*, 100399. [CrossRef]
102. Hussein, N.H.; Yaw, C.T.; Koh, S.P.; Tiong, S.K.; Chong, K.H. A Comprehensive Survey on Vehicular Networking: Communications, Applications, Challenges, and Upcoming Research Directions. *IEEE Access* **2022**, *10*, 86127–86180. [CrossRef]
103. Choi, J.; Va, V.; Gonzalez-Prelcic, N.; Daniels, R.; Bhat, C.R.; Heath, R.W. Millimeter Wave Vehicular Communication to Support Massive Automotive Sensing. *arXiv* **2016**, arXiv:1602.06456. [CrossRef]
104. He, R.; Schneider, C.; Ai, B.; Wang, G.; Zhong, Z.; Dupleich, D.A.; Thomae, R.S.; Boban, M.; Luo, J.; Zhang, Y. Propagation Channels of 5G Millimeter-Wave Vehicle-to-Vehicle Communications: Recent Advances and Future Challenges. *IEEE Veh. Technol. Mag.* **2020**, *15*, 16–26. [CrossRef]
105. Porambage, P.; Gur, G.; Osorio, D.P.M.; Liyanage, M.; Gurtov, A.; Ylianttila, M. The Roadmap to 6G Security and Privacy. *IEEE Open J. Commun. Soc.* **2021**, *2*, 1094–1122. [CrossRef]
106. Mao, Y.; You, C.; Zhang, J.; Huang, K.; Letaief, K.B. A Survey on Mobile Edge Computing: The Communication Perspective. *IEEE Commun. Surv. Tutor.* **2017**, *19*, 2322–2358. [CrossRef]
107. Mach, P.; Becvar, Z. Mobile Edge Computing: A Survey on Architecture and Computation Offloading. *IEEE Commun. Surv. Tutor.* **2017**, *19*, 1628–1656. [CrossRef]
108. Xiao, Y.; Shi, G.; Li, Y.; Saad, W.; Poor, H.V. Toward Self-Learning Edge Intelligence in 6G. *IEEE Commun. Mag.* **2020**, *58*, 34–40. [CrossRef]
109. Qi, W.; Li, Q.; Song, Q.; Guo, L.; Jamalipour, A. Extensive Edge Intelligence for Future Vehicular Networks in 6G. *IEEE Wirel. Commun.* **2021**, *28*, 128–135. [CrossRef]
110. Mazhelis, O. Costs of Using Hybrid Cloud Infrastructure: Towards a General Framework. In *Software Business*; Cusumano, M.A., Iyer, B., Venkatraman, N., Eds.; Lecture Notes in Business Information Processing; Springer: Berlin, Heidelberg, 2012; Volume 114, pp. 261–266. ISBN 978-3-642-30745-4.
111. Satyanarayanan, M.; Bahl, P.; Caceres, R.; Davies, N. The Case for VM-Based Cloudlets in Mobile Computing. *IEEE Pervasive Comput.* **2009**, *8*, 14–23. [CrossRef]
112. Cao, J.; Feng, W.; Ge, N.; Lu, J. Delay Characterization of Mobile-Edge Computing for 6G Time-Sensitive Services. *IEEE Internet Things J.* **2021**, *8*, 3758–3773. [CrossRef]
113. Wei, P.; Guo, K.; Li, Y.; Wang, J.; Feng, W.; Jin, S.; Ge, N.; Liang, Y.-C. Reinforcement Learning-Empowered Mobile Edge Computing for 6G Edge Intelligence. *arXiv* **2022**, arXiv:2201.11410. [CrossRef]
114. Gupta, R.; Reebadiya, D.; Tanwar, S. 6G-Enabled Edge Intelligence for Ultra-Reliable Low Latency Applications: Vision and Mission. *Comput. Stand. Interfaces* **2021**, *77*, 103521. [CrossRef]
115. Lien, S.-Y.; Deng, D.-J.; Lin, C.-C.; Tsai, H.-L.; Chen, T.; Guo, C.; Cheng, S.-M. 3GPP NR Sidelink Transmissions toward 5G V2X. *IEEE Access* **2020**, *8*, 35368–35382. [CrossRef]
116. You, X.; Wang, C.-X.; Huang, J.; Gao, X.; Zhang, Z.; Wang, M.; Huang, Y.; Zhang, C.; Jiang, Y.; Wang, J.; et al. Towards 6G Wireless Communication Networks: Vision, Enabling Technologies, and New Paradigm Shifts. *Sci. China Inf. Sci.* **2021**, *64*, 110301. [CrossRef]

Disclaimer/Publisher's Note: The statements, opinions and data contained in all publications are solely those of the individual author(s) and contributor(s) and not of MDPI and/or the editor(s). MDPI and/or the editor(s) disclaim responsibility for any injury to people or property resulting from any ideas, methods, instructions or products referred to in the content.

Article

Joint Beam-Forming Optimization for Active-RIS-Assisted Internet-of-Things Networks with SWIPT

Lidong Liu [1], Shidang Li [1,*], Mingsheng Wei [1], Jinsong Xu [2] and Bencheng Yu [3]

[1] School of Physics and Electronic Engineering, Jiangsu Normal University, Xuzhou 221116, China; 3020213425@jsnu.edu.cn (L.L.); weims@jsnu.edu.cn (M.W.)
[2] The JSNU-SPBPU Institute of Engineering, Jiangsu Normal University, Xuzhou 221116, China; casxjs2003@jsnu.edu.cn
[3] School of Information Engineering, Xuzhou Vocational College of Industrial Technology, Xuzhou 221140, China; lb18060015@cumt.edu.cn
* Correspondence: shidangli@jsnu.edu.cn

Citation: Liu, L.; Li, S.; Wei, M.; Xu, J.; Yu, B. Joint Beam-Forming Optimization for Active-RIS-Assisted Internet-of-Things Networks with SWIPT. *Future Internet* **2024**, *16*, 20. https://doi.org/10.3390/fi16010020

Academic Editors: Alessandro Raschellà and Michael Mackay

Received: 11 December 2023
Revised: 31 December 2023
Accepted: 4 January 2024
Published: 6 January 2024

Copyright: © 2024 by the authors. Licensee MDPI, Basel, Switzerland. This article is an open access article distributed under the terms and conditions of the Creative Commons Attribution (CC BY) license (https:// creativecommons.org/licenses/by/ 4.0/).

Abstract: Network energy resources are limited in communication systems, which may cause energy shortages in mobile devices at the user end. Active Reconfigurable Intelligent Surfaces (A-RIS) not only have phase modulation properties but also enhance the signal strength; thus, they are expected to solve the energy shortage problem experience at the user end in 6G communications. In this paper, a resource allocation algorithm for maximizing the sum of harvested energy is proposed for an active RIS-assisted Simultaneous Wireless Information and Power Transfer (SWIPT) system to solve the problem of low performance of harvested energy for users due to multiplicative fading. First, in the active RIS-assisted SWIPT system using a power splitting architecture to achieve information and energy co-transmission, the joint resource allocation problem is constructed with the objective function of maximizing the sum of the collected energy of all users, under the constraints of signal-to-noise ratio, active RIS and base station transmit power, and power splitting factors. Second, the considered non-convex problem can be turned into a standard convex problem by using alternating optimization, semi-definite relaxation, successive convex approximation, penalty function, etc., and then an alternating iterative algorithm for harvesting energy is proposed. The proposed algorithm splits the problem into two sub-problems and then performs iterative optimization separately, and then the whole is alternately optimized to obtain the optimal solution. Simulation results show that the proposed algorithm improves the performance by 45.2% and 103.7% compared to the passive RIS algorithm and the traditional without-RIS algorithm, respectively, at the maximum permissible transmitting power of 45 dBm at the base station.

Keywords: active reconfigurable intelligent surfaces; simultaneous wireless information and power transfer; iterative optimization; successive convex approximation

1. Introduction

Fifth-Generation Communication (5G) has significantly improved spectral efficiency, energy efficiency, and performance by utilizing different advanced technologies [1–3]. As an integral part of the smart connected society in 2030, Sixth-Generation Communication (6G) will provide an all-round performance superior to 5G and cater to emerging smart services and applications [4]. However, compared to 5G networks, 6G imposes higher requirements on various performance metrics [5,6], which require higher spectral efficiency [7], higher energy efficiency [8], and faster data rates [9]. To achieve these excellent performances, many emerging technologies have been proposed, including Reconfigurable Intelligent Surface (RIS). RIS has strong beam-pointing gains and can significantly reduce energy usage and hardware expenses. It has become a very competitive technical solution to the above challenges and has attracted widespread attention in industry and academia. [10–12].

The Reconfigurable Intelligent Surface (RIS) is a programmable structure that can change the electromagnetic properties of its own surface in real-time, making the direction of signal propagation change, which is expected to build a new paradigm of 6G intelligent programmable wireless environment [13]. MIMO, as a key physical layer technology currently used in 5G communications, inevitably generates communication blocking, and RIS can effectively solve the blocking problem in this communication process, which is not only energy-efficient but also highly cost-effective [14]. Its basic principle is to arrange adjustable panels on the surface of an outdoor building to reflect passive signals sent from the base station in any desired direction, thus intrinsically manipulating the propagation environment and achieving the goal of improving energy and spectral efficiency [15,16]. For RIS, there have been more research results [17–21]. For example, [17] investigated the electromagnetic and physical properties of RIS, and the authors developed a signal propagation attenuation model for wireless communication in free space after the inclusion of RIS, which is applicable in various scenarios, revealing that the signal propagation attenuation is not only related to the area of RIS, the distance from the transmitting end and the receiving end to the RIS, but also the direction of radiation between the antenna and the RIS unit, as well as the effect of the RIS's long-/short-range action. Ref. [18] focuses on the uplink of RIS-enabled multiuser MISO communication systems, and based on this, a channel estimation framework based on parallel factorization is proposed. Ref. [19] proposes a new concept of active RIS(A-RIS), which reduces the limitation of the "multipath fading" effect and solves the optimization problem of maximizing the summation rate in an A-RIS-assisted MU-MISO system. The physical implementation of the active RIS consists of two parts; first, the element has an internal phase-shift circuit which is responsible for changing the phase of the signal; in addition to this, each active RIS element is additionally equipped with an active reflection-type amplifier, which can amplify the reflected signals at the cost of affordable power consumption and hardware cost. Particularly, the reflection-type amplifier can be realized by many low-cost methods, such as current-inverting converter or asymmetric current mirror. Ref. [20] also points out that, unlike passive RIS (P-RIS), A-RIS can both change the direction of the signal and increase its strength. The "multiplicative fading" effect due to the presence of BS to RIS channels and RIS to User K channels is overcome, and the size of the RIS is drastically reduced. Ref. [21] added P-RIS and A-RIS to the same communication system, respectively, and after comparing them, it was discovered that the A-RIS system saves more power than the P-RIS system when the same performance is achieved.

The number of devices in 6G IoT communication has exploded, but the spectrum is becoming more and more scarce, and the energy is becoming more and more limited. To be able to effectively alleviate this problem, the Simultaneous Wireless Information and Power Transfer (SWIPT) technology came into being, which can effectively alleviate the spectrum and energy crisis [22,23]. Specifically, this technology can transmit signals to users while performing information decoding (ID) and energy harvesting (EH). Since signal receivers have different sensitivities, there are two typical receiver architectures in information and energy co-transmission systems, namely, the time splitting (TS) architecture, which uses time as the dividing factor, and the power splitting (PS) architecture [24], which uses power as the splitting factor. With the PS architecture, any user can use a power divider to split the power of the received signal into two parts in a specified ratio, one for ID and the other for EH [25]. Ref. [26] investigates multiuser MISO networks with simultaneous information and energy users under incomplete channel state information by optimizing the information beam and energy so that the weighted sum of the total harvested power is maximized. Further, [27] studied the power minimization problem under power splitting architecture and proposed two algorithms, optimal and suboptimal, with the suboptimal algorithm having lower complexity, and the results showed that the power splitting architecture can save the power loss of the system in a better way compared to the time splitting architecture. However, in the information and energy co-transmission communication system, the path loss determines the level of energy harvesting at the user end. To reduce the path loss, the energy-harvesting efficiency can be significantly improved by combining the RIS technology and multi-antenna technology using the dual beam-forming gain of the base station (BS) and RIS.

1.1. Related Work

There have been many research results on the combination of RIS technology and information and energy co-transmission technology [28–32]. For example, [28] investigated the base station radiant power minimization problem in SWIPT-based RIS-assisted MIMO communication networks in the hope of improving the energy utilization of the communication system to meet the needs of 6G green communication. Further, [29] investigates a multi-user RIS-assisted MISO communication network based on SWIPT and achieves base station (BS) transmits power minimization based on a nonlinear energy-harvesting model, generalizing the results in [27]. Ref. [30] proposed a novel RIS-enhanced SWIPT system based on an EMC framework, which improves energy efficiency by optimizing the impedance parameters of the RIS elements with the active-shaped beam at the base station. Ref. [31] investigated the problem of co-optimization of information rate and energy harvesting in a SWIPT-based RIS-assisted MISO communication network. To solve the problem, the optimal solution was obtained by using pricing-based, sequential, and alternating optimization methods. Ref. [32] combines RIS-assisted SWIPT technology with Unmanned Aerial Vehicle (UAV) technology and develops iterative algorithms using methods based on successive convex approximations and alternating optimization to maximize the minimum average achievable rate for multiple devices. However, due to the defect of P-RIS "multiplicative fading", the actual capacity gain that can be brought by the existing P-RIS is insignificant for typical communication scenarios with strong direct paths, which leads to a significant reduction in the energy harvested at the user end and the lack of existing research on the SWIPT-based multiuser RIS-assisted scheme for maximizing energy harvesting at the user end under MISO communication networks.

1.2. Motivation and Contribution

To solve the problem of low energy harvesting at the user end caused by path loss and "multiplicative fading" of P-RIS defects, this paper proposes a scheme to maximize the sum of energy harvesting at the user end under multi-antenna and multi-user scenarios for RIS-assisted multi-user MISO-SWIPT system. This ensures that the sum of the energy harvested by the user is maximized.

The main contributions of this paper are summarised as follows:

1. A communication scenario for transmitting information from multiple antennae to multiple users is considered, and a problem of jointly optimizing the BS beam direction vector, RIS phase shift matrix, signal amplitude enhancement coefficients, and power splitting factors to maximize the sum of energy harvesting at the user end is constructed under the constraints of maximum transmit power at the base station, power distribution ratio, and minimum signal to noise ratio at the user end. The problem is strongly coupled due to the entanglement of variables and requires further transformations.
2. To transform this non-convex problem into a standard convex problem, this paper uses the overall BCD algorithm to split the optimization problem into two optimization subproblems. First, we fix Θ and P to solve w_k, ρ_k, t_k. The optimization sub-objective is power reduced using Taylor series expansion, and then the non-convex problem is converted into a standard convex problem using semi-definite relaxation (SDR) and successive convex approximation (SCA). The optimal solution to the subproblem is obtained by continuous iterative optimization. Next, we fix w_k, ρ_k, t_k to solve Θ and P. After transforming the objective function into a convex problem via slack variables, the convex problem can be solved via semi-definite programming. The penalty-based technique is then used to ensure that the obtained solution satisfies the rank one constraint. However, the convex difference function obtained is not a standard convex

problem. We use successive convex approximations and Taylor series expansions to make it a standard convex problem. Then, iterative optimization is performed to obtain the optimal solution. Finally, the optimal solution of the initial optimization problem can be obtained by alternating the optimal solutions of the two optimization subproblems with iterative optimization.

3. Three benchmark scenarios were considered based on the optimization problem, and the simulation results demonstrate that the total sum of energy harvested at the user end is maximized with the assistance of A-RIS. Compared with the three benchmark scenarios, the total energy harvested by the user is significantly improved, and the algorithms remain converged after several iterations. In addition, this paper also demonstrates that the dynamic power splitting algorithm can better improve the sum of energy harvested by the user compared to the average power splitting algorithm.

1.3. Notation Note

All bold uppercase letters appearing in this manuscript represent matrices, and bold lowercase letters represent vectors. For a square matrix A, A^H, A^T, $\text{Tr}(A)$, $\|A\|_*$ and $\text{Rank}(A)$ denote its conjugate transpose, transpose, trace, trace paradigm, and rank, respectively. In addition, $A \succeq 0$ denotes that the square matrix is a semipositive definite matrix. The diagonalization operation of the matrix is denoted by $\text{diag}(\cdot)$. $\|\mathbf{x}\|$, $|\mathbf{x}|$, $\nabla_\mathbf{x} f(\mathbf{x})$, and $\mathbb{E}[\mathbf{x}]$ denotes the Euclidean paradigm, the absolute value, the gradient vector, and the expectation of x. A circularly symmetric complex Gaussian (CSCG) random vector is denoted as $\sim \mathcal{CM}(\mu, C)$, where C represents the covariance matrix and μ represents the mean value. $\mathbb{C}^{M \times N}$ indicates $M \times N$ dimensional complex matrices. $\mathcal{O}$ stands for the capital O symbol. The full names of all the abbreviations appearing in this paper are shown in Table 1.

Table 1. Abbreviation correspondence table.

Abbreviations	Full Name
5G	Fifth-Generation Communication
6G	Sixth-Generation Communication
RIS	Reconfigurable Intelligent Surface
MIMO	Multiple-Input Multiple-Output
MISO	Multiple-Input Single-Output
A-RIS	Active Reconfigurable Intelligent Surface
P-RIS	Passive Reconfigurable Intelligent Surface
SWIPT	Simultaneous Wireless Information and Power Transfer
ID	Information Decoding
EH	Energy Harvesting
TS	Time Splitting
PS	Power Splitting
BS	Base Station
UAV	Unmanned Aerial Vehicle
BCD	Block Coordinate Descent
CSCG	Circularly Symmetric Complex Gaussian
SDR	Semi-Definite Relaxation
SCA	Successive Convex Approximation
SDP	Semi-Definite Program

1.4. Organization

The remaining paper is presented as follows. In Section 2, the system model of Multi-user MISO A-RIS-assisted SWIPT system is first established and the optimization problem is formulated. Section 3 presents the overall algorithm and the computational complexity analysis. Simulations are executed in Section 4. Section 5 arrives at the conclusions of this paper.

2. System Models and Problem Modeling

In this paper, we study a multi-user, multi-input, single-output PS-SWIPT network model in which RIS is introduced as an aid, as can be seen in Figure 1, which consists of a BS, RIS, and k single-input channels of users, where the BS has M input channels and the RIS has N reflector units. The set of users is defined as $\mathcal{K} = \{1, \cdots, K\} (\forall k \in \mathcal{K})$. The set of array cells for RIS is $\mathcal{N} = \{1, \cdots, N\} (\forall n \in \mathcal{N})$. Let $G \in \mathbb{C}^{N \times M}$ denote the flat fading channel gain of the BS-RIS, $h_{b,k} \in \mathbb{C}^{M \times 1}$ denote the flat fading channel gain of the BS-the user k, and $h_{r,k} \in \mathbb{C}^{N \times 1}$ denote the flat fading channel gain of the RIS-user k. All channels experience quasi-static flat gradient fading that remains constant over several symbols [33]. Then the signal transmitted from the BS can be described as

$$x = \sum_{i=1}^{K} w_i s_i, \tag{1}$$

where $w_i \in \mathbb{C}^{M \times 1}, \forall i \in \mathcal{K}$ represents the beam-former and s_i denotes the information symbol of user i satisfying $\mathbb{E}\left[|s_i|^2\right] = 1, i \in \mathcal{K}$. In this way, the reflected signal of a P-RIS with N reflective elements can be written as

$$r = \Theta x, \tag{2}$$

where $\Theta = \text{diag}\left(e^{j\theta_1}, e^{j\theta_2}, \ldots, e^{j\theta_N}\right)$, $\theta_N \in [0, 2\pi)$ denotes the reflection coefficient matrix of the RIS, and x denotes the signal transmitted from the base station (BS).

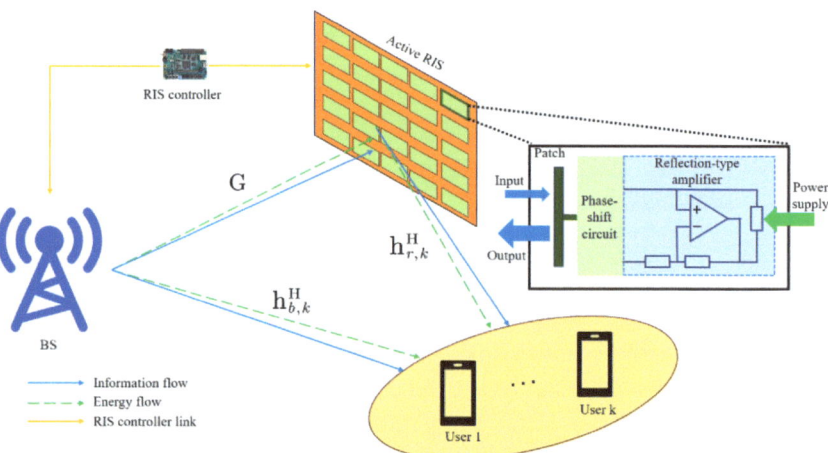

Figure 1. Multi-user MISO A-RIS-assisted SWIPT system.

If assisted by an RIS containing N reflective elements, the communication link can be strengthened, resulting in an increase in the energy power available to the user. If the base station (BS) transmits a signal strong enough to propagate through free space directly to a single user k without being blocked or reflected *en route*, the role of P-RIS becomes negligible due to the "multipath fading" effect. To maximize the sum of the energy collected by all users in the communication area in any case, this paper adopts A-RIS to solve this problem. The biggest difference between A-RIS and P-RIS is that A-RIS can amplify the reflected signals, and compared with the traditional relay, A-RIS is smaller in size and more flexible in layout. The output signal of the incident signal after reflection that occurs through the A-RIS can be written as

$$r = P\Theta x + P\Theta v + \nu, \tag{3}$$

where $P = \text{diag}(p_1, \ldots, p_N) \in \mathbb{R}^{N \times N}$ represents the A-RIS amplification factor matrix with all elements greater than 1, $P\Theta v$ represents the dynamic noise at the A-RIS, and v represents the static noise at the A-RIS. In addition, $v \sim \mathcal{CN}(0_N, \sigma_v^2 I_N)$ is only related to the device noise and input noise inherent in the A-RIS, whereas the static noise v is not related to P and can therefore be disregarded.

In the base station (BS) to the A-RIS channel, the signal received at the A-RIS can be represented as

$$\tilde{r} = P\Theta G \sum_{i=1}^{K} w_i s_i + P\Theta v. \tag{4}$$

In an A-RIS to single user k channel, the signal received by the user k can be described as

$$y_k = \sum_{i=1}^{K} h_k^H w_i s_i + h_k^H P\Theta v + z_k, \forall k, \tag{5}$$

where $h_k^H = h_{r,k}^H P\Theta G + h_{b,k}^H$ represents the total channel gain from the base station to user k, and $z_k \sim \mathcal{CN}(0, \sigma_k^2)$ represents the complex Gaussian noise received at user k. At this point, the base station (BS) uses the available time and frequency resources to transmit signals to all single users, and the energy power received by the user is divided into two parts ID and EH. We set $\rho_k \in (0,1)$ as the PS ratio, where part ρ_k is used for ID, so the decoded signal from user k can be described as

$$y_k^{ID} = \sqrt{\rho_k} y_k + n_k, \tag{6}$$

where $n_k \sim \mathcal{CN}(0, \delta_k^2)$ is the additional noise generated by the signal processing circuitry of the single user k when performing information decoding. Part $1 - \rho_k$ is used for EH, so the energy-harvesting signal of user k can be expressed as

$$y_k^{EH} = \sqrt{1 - \rho_k} y_k. \tag{7}$$

Based on this, the signal-to-noise ratio at a single user k can be expressed as

$$\text{SINR}_k = \frac{\left|h_k^H w_k\right|^2}{\sum_{\substack{i=1 \\ i \neq k}}^{K} \left|h_k^H w_i\right|^2 + \sigma_v^2 \|h_{r,k}^H P\Theta\|^2 + \sigma_k^2 + \frac{\delta_k^2}{\rho_k}}, \forall k. \tag{8}$$

For the energy-harvesting (EH) circuit, this paper adopts the linear model from the literature [34], whose linear input power is denoted by P_k^L. The energy harvested at user k can then be described as

$$P_k^L = \eta_k (1 - \rho_k) \left(\sum_{i=1}^{K} \left|h_k^H w_i\right|^2 + \sigma_v^2 \|h_{r,k}^H P\Theta\|^2 \right), \forall k, \tag{9}$$

where $\eta_k \in [0,1]$ represents the energy conversion efficiency of user k. In this paper, we assume that the energy conversion efficiency of all users is 100%, i.e., $\eta_k = 1$.

After modeling the signal and energy, the sum of energy harvesting at the user end is maximized by co-optimizing the base station beam-former, the PS ratio, and the RIS phase shift/amplification factor, a problem that can be described as

$$(P1): \underset{w_k, \Theta, P, \rho_k}{\text{maxmize}} f_1 = \sum_{k=1}^{K} P_k^L, \tag{10}$$

$$\text{s.t.} \frac{\left|\mathbf{h}_k^H \mathbf{w}_k\right|^2}{\sum_{\substack{i=1 \\ i \neq k}}^K \left|\mathbf{h}_k^H \mathbf{w}_i\right|^2 + \sigma_v^2 \|\mathbf{h}_{r,k}^H P\Theta\|^2 + \sigma_k^2 + \frac{\delta_k^2}{\rho_k}} \geqslant \gamma_k, \tag{11}$$

$$\sum_{i=1}^K \|P\Theta \mathbf{G}\mathbf{w}_i\|^2 + \sigma_v^2 \|P\Theta\|^2 \leqslant p_{\max}, \tag{12}$$

$$\sum_{k=1}^K \|\mathbf{w}_k\|_2^2 \leqslant P_B, \forall k, \tag{13}$$

$$0 < \rho_k < 1, \forall k,. \tag{14}$$

where (10) is the sum of energy collected by the user, and the optimization objective in this paper is to maximize it. Equation (11) is the signal-to-dry noise ratio constraint for user k, and γ_k is the minimum signal-to-dry noise ratio threshold required for user k. Equation (12) denotes the reflected power constraint of the A-RIS, and $p_{\max}$ is the maximum reflected power threshold of the A-RIS. Equation (13) denotes the radiant power constraint of the BS, and P_B is the maximum radiant power threshold of the BS. Equation (14) represents the PS factor scaling constraint. Since the variables are entangled with each other and strongly coupled, the problem (P1) is non-convex and cannot be solved directly using the software CVX, so the next step is to turn the problem (P1) into a convex problem.

3. Proposed Algorithm

To transform the problem (P1) from a non-convex to a convex problem, the variable t_k is introduced below, so (P1) can be rewritten in the following form:

$$(\text{P2}): \underset{\mathbf{w}_k, \Theta, P, \rho_k, t_k}{\text{maxmize}} f_2 = \sum_{k=1}^K t_k^2, \tag{15}$$

$$\text{s.t.} \frac{\left|\mathbf{h}_k^H \mathbf{w}_k\right|^2}{\sum_{\substack{i=1 \\ i \neq k}}^K \left|\mathbf{h}_k^H \mathbf{w}_i\right|^2 + \sigma_v^2 \|\mathbf{h}_{r,k}^H P\Theta\|^2 + \sigma_k^2 + \frac{\delta_k^2}{\rho_k}} \geqslant \gamma_k, \tag{16}$$

$$\sum_{i=1}^K \|P\Theta \mathbf{G}\mathbf{w}_i\|^2 + \sigma_v^2 \|P\Theta\|^2 \leqslant p_{\max}, \tag{17}$$

$$\sum_{k=1}^K \|\mathbf{w}_k\|_2^2 \leqslant P_B, \forall k, \tag{18}$$

$$P_k^L \geqslant t_k^2, \forall k, \tag{19}$$

$$0 < \rho_k < 1, \forall k. \tag{20}$$

The problem (P2) is not a convex problem because the variables are entangled with each other and there is a strong coupling relationship, so it cannot be solved by CVX, the most popular method for solving convex problems. To solve this problem, the optimization objective is first Taylor's first-order expansion, due to the strong coupling relationship between the variables, and then we use the overall BCD algorithm. After first fixing the RIS phase matrix Θ and the signal strength increase coefficient P, Semidefinite Relaxation (SDR) and Successive Convex Approximation (SCA) are used to optimize the base station (BS) beam-former w, the PS ratio ρ_k and t_k, iterating until convergence. The converged base station (BS) beam-former w, and PS ratio ρ_k and t_k are used as known quantities to design the RIS phase matrix Θ and signal strength increase coefficient P. The outputs of the last two components are optimized iteratively with each other until convergence.

3.1. Optimizing w_k, ρ_k, t_k Given Θ and P

Since Θ and P appear as products in problem (P2), we define $Y = P\Theta$ such that optimizing Θ and P is equivalent to optimizing the RIS precoding matrix of $Y = P\Theta = \text{diag}(p_1 e^{j\theta_1}, \cdots, p_N e^{j\theta_N})$. Next, the optimization objective (15) is transformed into a first-order function using the following lemma.

Lemma 1 (Taylor series expansion formula). *Assuming that the function $f(x)$ has a derivative of order n on some closed interval $[a, b]$ containing x_0 and a derivative of order $(n + 1)$ on the open interval (a, b), the following equation holds for any point x on the closed interval $[a, b]$ [35]:*

$$f(x) = \frac{f(x_0)}{0!} + \frac{f'(x_0)}{1!}(x - x_0) + \frac{f''(x_0)}{2!}(x - x_0)^2 + \cdots + \frac{f^n(x_0)}{n!}(x - x_0)^n + R_n(x), \quad (21)$$

where $R_n(x) = o((x - x_0)^n)$ represents the remainder term of the Taylor series expansion formula, which can be ignored in the conversion since it is an infinitesimal term. A Taylor first-order expansion of t_k^2 using Lemma 1 above gives

$$t_k^2 = t_{k_0}^2 + 2t_{k_0}(t_k - t_{k_0}). \quad (22)$$

In addition to this, this paper defines $W_k = w_k w_k^H$ and $H_k = h_k h_k^H \ \forall k$ so that (15) can be transformed into the following form:

$$(P3): \underset{w_k, \rho_k, t_k}{\text{maximize}} \ f_3 = \sum_{k=1}^{K} t_{k_0}^2 + 2t_{k_0}(t_k - t_{k_0}). \quad (23)$$

For (16), we define $\tilde{\sigma} = \sigma_k^2 + \frac{\delta_k^2}{\rho_k}$. The following process can be obtained by shifting terms:

$$\frac{\left|h_k^H w_k\right|^2}{\gamma_k} - \sum_{\substack{i=1 \\ i \neq k}}^{K} \left|h_k^H w_i\right|^2 \geqslant \sigma_v^2 \|h_{r,k}^H P\Theta\|^2 + \tilde{\sigma},$$

$$\frac{\text{Tr}\left(h_k^H h_k w_k^H w_k\right)}{\gamma_k} - \sum_{\substack{i=1 \\ i \neq k}}^{K} \text{Tr}\left(h_k^H h_k w_i^H w_i\right) \geqslant \sigma_v^2 \|h_{r,k}^H P\Theta\|^2 + \tilde{\sigma},$$

$$\frac{\text{Tr}(H_k W_k)}{\gamma_k} - \sum_{\substack{i=1 \\ i \neq k}}^{K} \text{Tr}(H_k W_i) \geqslant \sigma_v^2 \|h_{r,k}^H P\Theta\|^2 + \tilde{\sigma} \quad (24)$$

For (17) and (18), there is the following process due to $\|A\| = \sqrt{\text{Tr}(A^H A)}$:

$$\sum_{i=1}^{K} \|YGw_i\|^2 + \sigma_v^2 \|Y\|^2 \leqslant p_{\max},$$

$$\sum_{i=1}^{K} \text{Tr}\left(YGW_i G^H Y^H\right) + \sigma_v^2 \|Y\|^2 \leqslant p_{\max} \quad (25)$$

$$\sum_{i=1}^{K} \text{Tr}\left(w_k w_k^H\right) \leqslant P_B, \forall k,$$

$$\sum_{i=1}^{K} \text{Tr}(W_k) \leqslant P_B, \forall k, \qquad (26)$$

For (19), due to $P_k^L = \eta_k(1-\rho_k)\left(\sum_{i=1}^{K}\left|h_k^H w_i\right|^2 + \sigma_v^2 \|h_{r,k}^H P\Theta\|^2\right), \forall k$, the following process is assumed to be $\eta_k = 1$ for all users:

$$(1-\rho_k)\left(\sum_{i=1}^{K}\left|h_k^H w_i\right|^2 + \sigma_v^2 \|h_{r,k}^H P\Theta\|^2\right) \geqslant t_k^2, \forall k,$$

$$\sum_{i=1}^{K}\left|h_k^H w_i\right|^2 + \sigma_v^2 \|h_{r,k}^H P\Theta\|^2 \geqslant \frac{t_k^2}{(1-\rho_k)}, \forall k, \qquad (27)$$

$$\sum_{i=1}^{K}\left|h_k^H h_k w_i w_i^H\right|^2 + \sigma_v^2 \|h_{r,k}^H Y\|^2 \geqslant \frac{t_k^2}{(1-\rho_k)}, \forall k,$$

$$\sum_{i=1}^{K} \text{Tr}(H_k W_i) + \sigma_v^2 \|h_{r,k}^H Y\|^2 \geqslant \frac{t_k^2}{(1-\rho_k)}, \forall k. \qquad (28)$$

For (20), due to the use of SDR and SCA optimization methods, the rank-one constraints are to be relaxed on the original constraints, which can be expressed as

$$0 < \rho_k < 1, W_k \succeq 0, \forall k. \qquad (29)$$

To make (P3) a convex problem, we relax the rank-one constraints. The optimization objective of (P2) is to find the maximum value of t_k^2, which can be equated to finding the maximum value at the minimum point t_{k_0} in the function t_k^2. After expanding it with Taylor's first-order series, it is a first-order linear function, which can be solved efficiently by CVX as the same constraints as in (P3), and the solution obtained by substituting t_k as a new t_{k_0} repeats the process of solving and iterating until convergence, which leads to the final w_k, ρ_k, t_k. These solutions have a unique rank and can be proved by solving the KKT condition using the Lagrangian dyadic method [36].

3.2. Optimizing P, Θ Given w_k, ρ_k, t_k

After solving the problem (P3), the next step is to find suitable P and Θ so that they satisfy the constraints of (P2), and we define $\theta = \left(p_1 e^{j\theta_1}, \cdots, p_N e^{j\theta_N}\right)^H \in \mathbb{C}^{N \times 1}$. To make the problem easier to deal with, we use the variables $a_{k,i} = h_{b,k}^H w_i$ and $\theta^H b_{k,i} = h_{r,k}^H YGw_i$, where $Z_k = \text{diag}\left(h_{r,k}^H\right)\text{diag}(h_{r,k}), \forall k \in \mathcal{K}, Q_k = \text{diag}(Gw_k)(\text{diag}(Gw_k))^H$, and $b_{k,i} = \text{diag}\left(h_{r,k}^H\right)Gw_i$. This way, the optimization problem (P4) can be obtained via the following steps.

For (P2), due to $h_k^H = h_{r,k}^H P\Theta G + h_{b,k}^H$, (16) can be rewritten by the following process:

$$h_k^H = h_{r,k}^H YG + h_{b,k}^H$$

$$\left|h_k^H w_k\right|^2 = \left|h_{r,k}^H YGw_k + h_{b,k}^H w_k\right|^2 = \left|\theta^H b_{k,k} + a_{k,k}\right|^2$$

$$\sum_{\substack{j=1\\j\neq k}}^{K}\left|h_k^H w_j\right|^2 = \sum_{\substack{j=1\\j\neq k}}^{K}\left|h_{r,k}^H YGw_j + h_{b,k}^H w_j\right|^2 = \sum_{\substack{j=1\\j\neq k}}^{K}\left|\theta^H b_{k,j} + a_{k,j}\right|^2$$

$$\sigma_v^2 \|h_{r,k}^H P\Theta\|^2 = \sigma_v^2 \left(p_1 e^{j\theta_1}, \cdots, p_N e^{j\theta_N}\right) \text{diag}\left(h_{r,k}^H\right)\text{diag}(h_{r,k})\left(p_1 e^{j\theta_1}, \cdots, p_N e^{j\theta_N}\right)^H.$$

$$\sigma_v^2 \|\mathbf{h}_{r,k}^H \mathbf{P}\Theta\|^2 = \sigma_v^2 \theta^H Z_k \theta$$

$$\frac{|\theta^H b_{k,k} + a_{k,k}|^2}{\sum_{\substack{j=1 \\ j \neq k}}^{K} |\theta^H b_{k,j} + a_{k,j}|^2 + \sigma_v^2 \theta^H Z_k \theta + \widetilde{\sigma}_k} \geq \gamma_k. \tag{30}$$

For (17), it can be rewritten by the following process:

$$\sum_{i=1}^{K} \|\mathbf{P}\Theta \mathbf{G}\mathbf{w}_i\|^2 = \sum_{i=1}^{K} \left(p_1 e^{j\theta_1}, \cdots, p_N e^{j\theta_N}\right) \operatorname{diag}(\mathbf{G}\mathbf{w}_i)(\operatorname{diag}(\mathbf{G}\mathbf{w}_i))^H \left(p_1 e^{j\theta_1}, \cdots, p_N e^{j\theta_N}\right)^H,$$

$$\sum_{i=1}^{K} \|\mathbf{P}\Theta \mathbf{G}\mathbf{w}_i\|^2 = \sum_{i=1}^{K} \theta^H Q_i \theta,$$

$$\sigma_v^2 \|\mathbf{P}\Theta\|^2 = \sigma_v^2 \left(p_1 e^{j\theta_1}, \cdots, p_N e^{j\theta_N}\right) \left(p_1 e^{j\theta_1}, \cdots, p_N e^{j\theta_N}\right)^H,$$

$$\sigma_v^2 \|\mathbf{P}\Theta\|^2 = \sigma_v^2 \theta^H \theta,$$

$$\sum_{i=1}^{K} \theta^H Q_i \theta + \sigma_v^2 \theta^H \theta \leq p_{\max}. \tag{31}$$

For (27), since $\mathbf{h}_k^H = \mathbf{h}_{r,k}^H \mathbf{P}\Theta \mathbf{G} + \mathbf{h}_{b,k}^H$, it can be rewritten by the following process:

$$\sum_{j=1}^{K} \left|\mathbf{h}_k^H \mathbf{w}_j\right|^2 = \sum_{j=1}^{K} \left|\mathbf{h}_{r,k}^H \mathbf{Y}\mathbf{G}\mathbf{w}_j + \mathbf{h}_{b,k}^H \mathbf{w}_j\right|^2$$

$$\sum_{j=1}^{K} \left|\mathbf{h}_k^H \mathbf{w}_j\right|^2 = \sum_{j=1}^{K} \left|\theta^H b_{k,j} + a_{k,j}\right|^2$$

$$\sigma_v^2 \|\mathbf{h}_{r,k}^H \mathbf{P}\Theta\|^2 = \sigma_v^2 \left(p_1 e^{j\theta_1}, \cdots, p_N e^{j\theta_N}\right) \operatorname{diag}\left(\mathbf{h}_{r,k}^H\right) \operatorname{diag}(\mathbf{h}_{r,k}) \left(p_1 e^{j\theta_1}, \cdots, p_N e^{j\theta_N}\right)^H,$$

$$\sigma_v^2 \|\mathbf{h}_{r,k}^H \mathbf{P}\Theta\|^2 = \sigma_v^2 \theta^H Z_k \theta$$

$$\sum_{j=1}^{K} \left|\theta^H b_{k,j} + a_{k,j}\right|^2 + \sigma_v^2 \theta^H Z_k \theta \geq \frac{t_k^2}{1 - \rho_k}, \tag{32}$$

Thus, (P3) is transformed into (P4) as follows:

$$(\text{P4}): \text{Find}\, \theta, \tag{33}$$

(P4) is not a convex problem because it contains quadratic inequality constraints, and to turn it into a solvable convex problem, the SDR technique is used. Introducing variables $\widetilde{\theta} = \begin{bmatrix} \theta^T & 1 \end{bmatrix}^T \in \mathbb{C}^{(N+1) \times 1}$ and $S_{k,j} = \begin{bmatrix} b_{k,j} b_{k,j}^H, & b_{k,j} a_{k,j}^H; & b_{k,j}^H a_{k,j}, & 0 \end{bmatrix}, \forall i \in \mathcal{K}$, $T = \widetilde{\theta}\widetilde{\theta}^H \in \mathbb{C}^{(N+1) \times (N+1)}$ can be defined, which requires $T \succeq 0$ and T to satisfy the rank one constraint. After relaxing the rank one constraints, (P5) can be obtained by rewriting it in this way:

$$\left|\theta^H b_{k,k} + a_{k,k}\right|^2 = \theta^H b_{k,k} \theta b_{k,k}^H + \theta^H b_{k,k} a_{k,k}^H + \theta b_{k,k}^H a_{k,k} + a_{k,k} a_{k,k}^H$$

$$\left|\theta^H b_{k,k} + a_{k,k}\right|^2 = \text{Tr}(S_{k,k}T) + |a_{k,k}|^2$$

$$\left|\theta^H b_{k,j} + a_{k,j}\right|^2 = \text{Tr}\left(S_{k,j}T\right) + |a_{k,j}|^2$$

$$\theta^H Z_k \theta = \text{Tr}\left(\widetilde{Z}_k T\right)$$

$$\frac{\text{Tr}(S_{k,k}T) + |a_{k,k}|^2}{\gamma_k} - \sum_{\substack{j=1 \\ j \neq k}}^{K} \text{Tr}\left(S_{k,j}T\right) - \sigma_v^2 \text{Tr}\left(\widetilde{Z}_k T\right) \geq \tilde{o}_k, \tag{34}$$

$$\theta^H Q_i \theta = \text{Tr}\left(\widetilde{Q}_k T\right)$$

$$\theta^H \theta = \text{Tr}(T)$$

$$\sum_{i=1}^{K} \text{Tr}\left(\widetilde{Q}_k T\right) + \sigma_v^2 \text{Tr}(T) \leq p_{\max}, \tag{35}$$

$$\sum_{j=1}^{K} \text{Tr}\left(S_{k,j}T\right) + |a_{k,j}|^2 + \sigma_v^2 \text{Tr}\left(\widetilde{Z}_k T\right) \geq \frac{t_k^2}{1 - \rho_k}. \tag{36}$$

In this way, the optimization problem (P4) is transformed into finding a suitable T as follows:

$$(P5): \text{Find } T, \tag{37}$$

$$T \succeq 0, \tag{38}$$

where $\widetilde{Q}_k$ and $\widetilde{Z}_k$ in (35) and (36) have zero rows and zero columns more than the other matrices. After the transformation of (P5) into an SDP problem, we can use CVX software (version 3.0) to solve this convex problem. Due to the SDR technique, the resulting solution does not satisfy the rank-one constraint. To obtain a solution with only a unique rank, a penalty-based approach can be used. The rank one constraint can be described in the following equivalent form:

$$\|T\|_* - \|T\|_2 \leq 0.$$

For any given $T \in \mathbb{H}^{m \times n}$, the following equation holds if and only if the rank of T is 1:

$$\|T\|_* = \sum_i \sigma_i \geq \|T\|_2 = \max_i \{\sigma_i\},$$

where σ_i is the ith singular value of T. After adding the rank-one constraint, (P5) can be rewritten in the following form:

$$(P6): \min_{T} \frac{1}{2\mu}(\|T\|_* - \|T\|_2) \tag{39}$$

$$\text{s.t.} \frac{\text{Tr}(S_{k,k}T) + |a_{k,k}|^2}{\gamma_k} - \sum_{\substack{j=1 \\ j \neq k}}^{K} \text{Tr}\left(S_{k,j}T\right) - \sigma_v^2 \text{Tr}\left(\widetilde{Z}_k T\right) \geq \tilde{o}_k, \tag{40}$$

$$\sum_{i=1}^{K} \text{Tr}\left(\widetilde{Q}_k T\right) + \sigma_v^2 \text{Tr}(T) \leq p_{\max}, \tag{41}$$

$$\sum_{j=1}^{K} \text{Tr}\left(S_{k,j}T\right) + \left|a_{k,j}\right|^2 + \sigma_v^2 \text{Tr}\left(\widetilde{Z}_k T\right) \geq \frac{t_k^2}{1-\rho_k}, \tag{42}$$

$$T \succeq 0, \tag{43}$$

where μ is the penalty factor, and only when the value of μ reaches a very small value does (P6) obtain a solution with only a unique rank. It is worth noting that (P6) is non-convex because its optimization objective function is the subtraction of two convex functions, which does not guarantee that the resulting difference is necessarily convex. This problem can be solved by using the SCA technique. Using Taylor series expansion to represent $\Psi(T)$, its first-order expansion can be used in place of $\|T\|_2$, and this is the global minimum since $\Psi(T)$ is a convex function and its first-order expansion is as follows:

$$\Psi(T) \geq \Psi(T^i) + \text{Tr}\left(\nabla_T^H \Psi(T^i)(T - T^i)\right) \triangleq \widetilde{\Psi}(T), \tag{44}$$

where $\nabla_T \|T^i\|_2 = \nabla_T u_1^H T^i u_1 = \nabla_T \text{Tr}(T^i u_1 u_1^H) = u_1 u_1^H$. Inside u_1 is the eigenvector, which corresponds to the largest eigenvalue of T^i. (P6) already has an optimization objective function inside and hence is a feasibility problem; any solution that satisfies the constraints and has a unique rank is optimal. Therefore, we can add additional optimization variables to this so that the optimal solution obtained can have better performance. Therefore, it is decided to optimize the SINR and harvest energy boundaries while satisfying the constraint of having a unique rank. To obtain the optimal solution, two new relaxation variables τ_k and Δ_k are introduced as "SINR residuals" and "energy harvesting residuals", respectively, and with the introduction of the additional new variables (P6) can be rewritten as follows:

$$(P7): \underset{T,\tau_k,\Delta_k}{\text{minimize}} f_4 = \frac{1}{2\mu}\left(\|T\|_* - \widetilde{\Psi}(T)\right) - \sum_{k=1}^{K}(\alpha \tau_k + \beta \Delta_k), \tag{45}$$

$$\text{s.t.} \frac{\text{Tr}(S_{k,k}T) + |a_{k,k}|^2}{\gamma_k + \tau_k} - \sum_{\substack{j=1 \\ j \neq k}}^{K} \text{Tr}\left(S_{k,j}T\right) - \sigma_v^2 \text{Tr}\left(\widetilde{Z}_k T\right) \geq \widetilde{\sigma}_k, \tag{46}$$

$$\sum_{j=1}^{K} \text{Tr}\left(S_{k,j}T\right) + \left|a_{k,j}\right|^2 + \sigma_v^2 \text{Tr}\left(\widetilde{Z}_k T\right) \geq \frac{t_k^2}{1-\rho_k}, \tag{47}$$

$$T \succeq 0, \tag{48}$$

$$\tau_k, \Delta_k \geq 0, \forall k, \tag{49}$$

The flowchart of the overall algorithm proposed in this paper is shown in Figure 2.

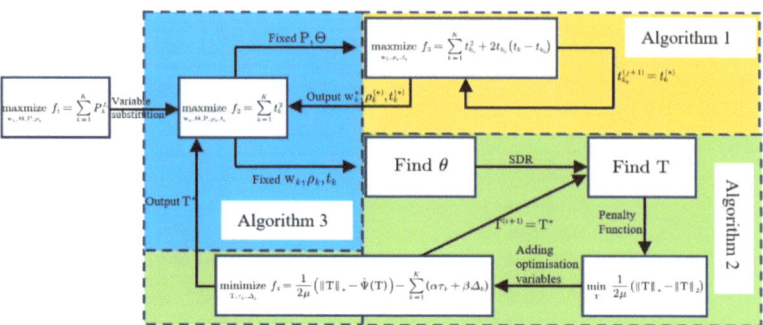

Figure 2. Flowchart of the overall algorithm (As shown in Algorithms 1–3).

Algorithm 1 Set the maximum number of iterations $L_{\max}$, $j = 0$, fix T, initialize $t_{k_0}^{(0)}$.

(1) while $j \leqslant L_{\max}$ do
(2) Solve P(3), output $w_k^{(*)}, \rho_k^{(*)}, t_k^{(*)}$, update $w_k^{(j+1)} = w_k^{(*)}, \rho_k^{(j+1)} = \rho_k^{(*)}, t_{k_0}^{(j+1)} = t_k^{(*)}$
(3) Let $j = j + 1$
(4) end while
(5) Output $w_k^{(*)}, \rho_k^{(*)}, t_k^{(*)}$

Algorithm 2 Set the maximum number of iterations $L_{\max}$, $i = 0$, fix T, initialize w_k, ρ_k.

(1) while $i \leqslant L_{\max}$ do
(2) Calculation of $\widetilde{\Psi}(T)$ according to (8)
(3) Solve P(7), output $\{T^*\}$, update $\{T^{(i+1)}\} = \{T^*\}$
(4) Let $i = i + 1$
(5) end while
(6) Output $\{T^*\}$

Algorithm 3 Set the maximum number of iterations $L_{\max}$, $l = 0$, and initialize $T = T^{(0)}$.

(1) while $l \leqslant L_{\max}$ do
(2) Given $T^{(l)}$ solves P(3) and outputs $\{w_k^l, \rho_k^{(l)}\}$
(3) Given $\{w_k^l, \rho_k^{(l)}\}$ solves P(7), output $\{T^{(l+1)}\}$ according to Algorithm 2 and update $\{T^{(l+1)}\} = \{T^*\}$
(4) Let $l = l + 1$
(5) end while
(6) Output $\{T^*\}$

Remark 1 (Complexity Analysis). *The overall complexity of the proposed BCD algorithm (Algorithm 3) arises from two components: Algorithm 1 for solving subproblem 1 and Algorithm 2 for solving subproblem 2. In each iteration of the BCD algorithm (Algorithm 3), we independently address problems (23) and (45). To illustrate the complexity related to Algorithm 1, which addresses the convex problem (23), its algorithmic complexity can be expressed as*

$$\mathcal{O}_1 = I_1 \cdot \mathcal{O}\left(\sqrt{KM}\left(K^3 M^2 + K^2 M^3\right) \log \frac{1}{\epsilon_1}\right),$$

where ϵ_1 represents the given solution accuracy, I_1 denotes the number of iterations before convergence, K is the total number of users, and M is the number of antennae. The algorithmic complexity for solving the SDP problem (45) with Algorithm 2 can be expressed as

$$\mathcal{O}_2 = I_2 \cdot \mathcal{O}\left(\left((3K+1)\left(N^{3.5} + 3KN^{2.5}\right)\right)\log\frac{1}{\epsilon_2}\right),$$

where ϵ_2 represents the given solution accuracy, I_2 denotes the number of iterations before convergence, K is the total number of users, and N is the dimension of the semidefinite cone. In summary, the overall complexity of the BCD algorithm (Algorithm 3) is given by

$$\mathcal{O}_3 = I_3(\mathcal{O}_1 + \mathcal{O}_2),$$

where I_3 represents the total number of iterations executed by Algorithm 3.

4. Simulation Results and Discussion

To validate the reliability of the proposed energy-harvesting sum maximization algorithm at the user end, this paper compares the proposed energy-harvesting sum maximization algorithm at the user end with three benchmark scenario algorithms, respectively, which are designed as follows: (1) A-RIS-assisted using average power splitting algorithm ($\rho_k = 0.5$); (2) P-RIS-assisted algorithm; and (3) traditional RIS-assisted algorithm without RIS. The propagation loss model $L(d) = C_0\left(\frac{d}{D_0}\right)^{-\kappa}$ is used in this paper, where $C_0 = -30$ dB denotes the propagation loss at $D_0 = 1$ m, d denotes the link distance, and κ represents the propagation loss index. The propagation loss indices from the base station to the RIS and the user are assumed to be $\kappa_{BI} = 3$ and $\kappa_{BU} = 3$, respectively, and the propagation loss index from the RIS to the user is assumed to be $\kappa_{IU} = 2.2$. It is assumed that all channels G, $h_{b,k}$, $h_{r,k}$ undergo flat-terrain attenuation and maintain stability over time. The other parameters of the proposed energy-harvesting sum maximization algorithm at users are set as follows: the number of reflective units of the RIS $N = 12$; the number of base station input channels $M = 20$; the number of users $K = 4$; the maximum number of iterations $L_{max} = 200$; the minimum signal-to-dryness-noise ratio required for each user $\gamma_k = 10$ dB; the maximum radiant power of the A-RIS $p_{max} = 10$ mW; the maximum radiant power of the base station antennae $P_B = 20$ W; the noise power $\sigma_k^2 = -80$ dBm, $\delta_k^2 = -80$ dBm, $\sigma_v^2 = -80$ dBm; and the penalty factor $\mu = 5 \times 10^{-7}$.

Figure 3 illustrates the convergence curves of the proposed algorithm for maximizing the sum of energy harvesting at the user's location under different channel conditions. Channel 1 represents the BS-user K channel, channel 2 represents the BS-Passive RIS-user K channel, and channel 3 represents the BS-A-RIS-user K channel. From Figure 3, it can be observed that the proposed algorithm for maximizing the sum of energy harvesting at the user's location can reach a stable value relatively quickly after 2–3 iterations, demonstrating good convergence. The stable value of the proposed algorithm under Channel 1 conditions is 35.1% higher than that under Channel 2 conditions. This improvement is attributed to the A-RIS's ability to provide additional transmit power to enhance signal strength, overcoming the drawback of substantial signal degradation due to the passive RIS's inherent "multiplicative fading". As a result, the user receives more energy, leading to a larger sum of harvested energy at the user's location. Furthermore, the stable value of the proposed algorithm under Channel 2 conditions is 67.5% higher than that under Channel 3 conditions. This is because the P-RIS can adjust its reflection array phase to change the transmission beam direction of the base station antenna, thereby enhancing the transmission efficiency of the beam. As a result, the user receives more energy, and the proposed algorithm for maximizing the sum of energy harvesting at the user's location harvests more energy.

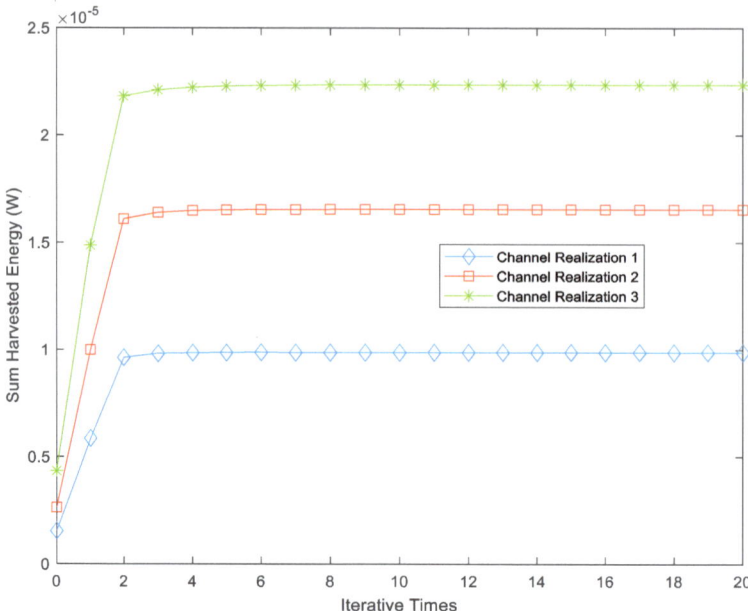

Figure 3. Convergence of the proposed algorithm for maximizing energy harvesting at the user end.

Figure 4 illustrates the variation in total energy collected at the user's location under different transmission scenarios as the maximum allowable transmit power of the base station changes. This encompasses considerations for the number of reflecting elements in the RIS and the number of antennae at the base station. The graph reveals that with an increase in the base station's maximum allowable transmit power, there is a corresponding rise in the total energy collected at the user's location for all algorithms. In comparison to the P-RIS-assisted algorithm, the A-RIS-assisted algorithm, employing dynamic power splitting, demonstrates gains of 36.5% and 45.2% when the base station's maximum allowable transmit power is set at 40 dBm and 45 dBm, respectively. This improvement is attributed to the A-RIS's ability to not only manipulate the phase of the reflected signal but also amplify its transmit power, overcoming the significant signal power decay resulting from dual-path loss. The P-RIS-assisted algorithm achieves gains of 48.7% and 40.3% when the base station's maximum allowable transmit power is 40 dBm and 45 dBm, respectively. This is owing to the P-RIS's capacity to achieve a high-array gain of the reflected beam by adjusting the phase of the reflected signal. Compared to traditional RIS-assisted algorithms without an RIS, the P-RIS-assisted algorithm provides gains of 48.7% and 40.3% when the base station's maximum allowable transmit power is 40 dBm and 45 dBm, respectively. Furthermore, in terms of power splitting algorithms, both under A-RIS assistance, the dynamic power splitting algorithm outperforms the average power splitting algorithm ($\rho_k = 0.5$), resulting in increases of 21.7% and 23.5% in the total energy collected at the user's location when the base station's maximum allowable transmit power is set at 40 dBm and 45 dBm, respectively. This is due to the dynamic power splitting algorithm offering greater optimization flexibility, allowing more power to be split to enhance the total energy collected at the user's location, consequently leading to a higher energy harvest.

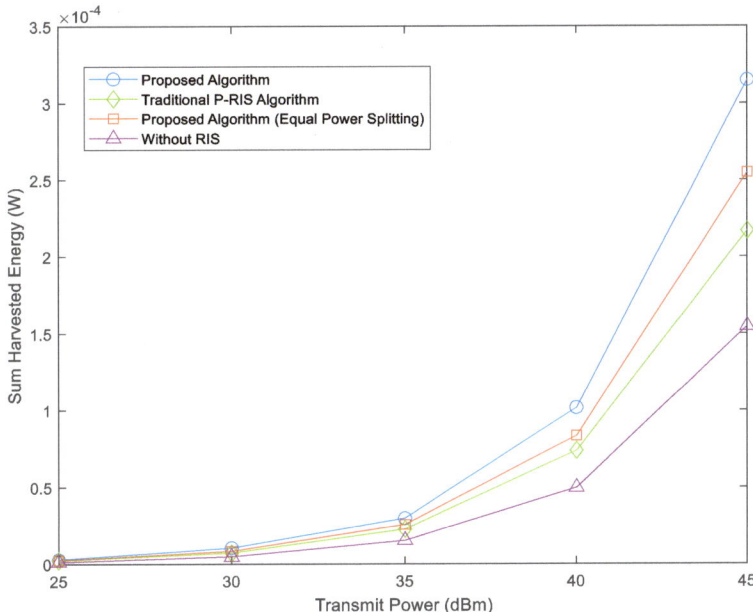

Figure 4. Relationship between the total energy collected at the user end and the maximum radiant power of the BS.

Figure 5 plots the comparison curves of the total energy collected by the user for several different algorithms with different numbers of base station transmitting antennae, where RIS has 12 reflective units, i.e., N = 12. As can be seen from Figure 5, the total energy collected by the user under several algorithms increases accordingly after the increase in the base station input channel M. The main reason for this is that the transmitting beamwidth of the BS is fixed, and with the increase in the base station input channel, the transmitting beamwidth of each antenna becomes narrower, which increases the additional array gain, and the available degrees of freedom of the system increases, and the performance improves consequently, and the total amount of energy collected at the user end under the various algorithms increases as well. Also, since the A-RIS has a feature that the P-RIS does not have, i.e., the enhancement of the transmitted power of the reflected signals, it allows for an increase in the power of the received signals at the user end, which results in more power being used for energy harvesting (EH); thus, the A-RIS-assisted energy-harvesting algorithm improves the sum of the energy harvested at the user end as compared to the P-RIS-assisted energy-harvesting algorithms. In addition to this, the use of the dynamic power partitioning algorithm is very effective in improving the total energy collected by the user; this is because the dynamic power partitioning algorithm improves the degree of freedom of the optimization so that more power can be used to improve the total energy collected at the user end. Compared to the average power splitting algorithm ($\rho_k = 0.5$), the dynamic power splitting algorithm is used to improve the total energy collected by the user by 23.1% at the number of input channels M = 12.

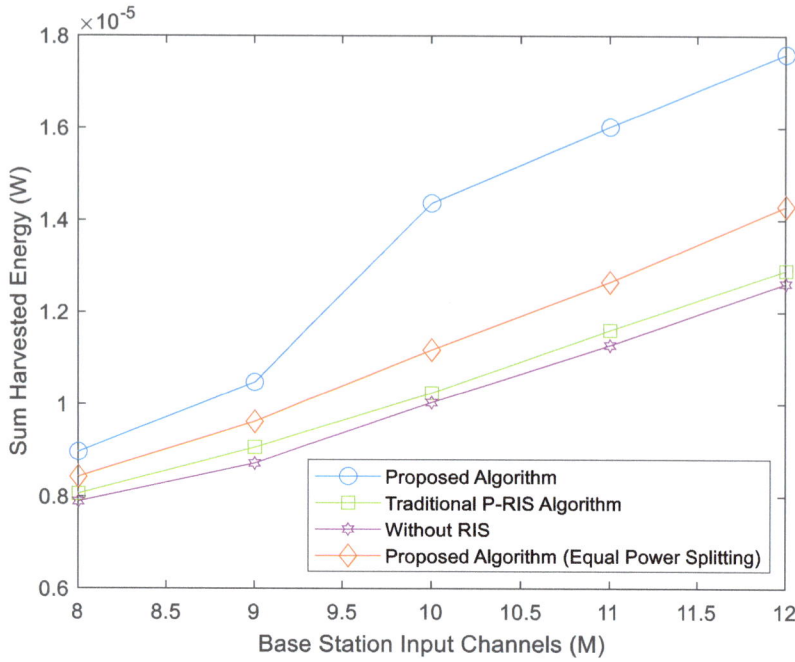

Figure 5. Relationship between the total energy collected at the user end and the number of antennae.

To evaluate the effect of different numbers of reflection units on the performance of each algorithm, Figure 6 shows the effect of different numbers of reflection units on the total energy collected from the user under each algorithm, where the number of input channels at the base station is M = 20. It can be observed from Figure 6 that there is no relationship between the total energy collected from the user and the reflection units for the traditional algorithm without RIS assistance, mainly because the RIS has been removed from the algorithm. This led to no change in the total energy captured by the user as the number of reflection units increased. With the increase in the number of reflection units, the energy collected by the user of the proposed three algorithms, namely, the energy-harvesting algorithm with dynamic power splitting assisted by A-RIS, the energy-harvesting algorithm with average power splitting ($\rho_k = 0.5$) assisted by A-RIS, and the energy-harvesting algorithm assisted by P-RIS, increases and the performance of the algorithms is also enhanced. This finding also laterally verifies that configuring more reflection units can increase the reflection path from the base station to the user, further expanding the multipath propagation and making the received array gain at the user end larger, and by optimizing the RIS phase shift, the received signal power at the user end is enhanced so that more power is used to boost the total energy collected at the user end. In addition, as shown in Figure 6, when using the energy-harvesting algorithm assisted by the A-RIS, the total energy collected by the user is further increased because the A-RIS amplifies the signal strength, and the total energy collected at the user end can be effectively increased compared to the use of the P-RIS.

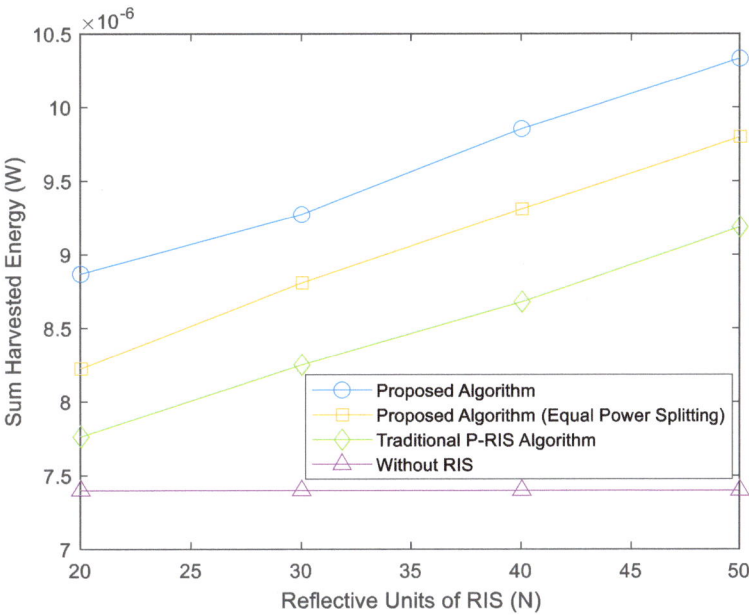

Figure 6. Relationship between the total energy collected at the user end and the number of RIS reflector units.

Figure 7 shows the variation curves of the energy collection performance of several different algorithms at the user end for different user-required minimum signal-to-dry-noise ratio γ_{min}, where the number of reflector units of RIS is N = 12 and the number of base station input channels is M = 20. It can be seen from Figure 7 that with the increase in the user-required sub-minimum signal-to-dry noise ratio γ_{min}, the user's energy collection of several algorithms decreases correspondingly, and the total energy collected decreases accordingly. The main reason for this phenomenon is that to satisfy the more stringent user minimum SINR γ_{min} constraint, the base station antenna (BS) needs to allocate more power to the user for information decoding (ID), which results in less power left to be allocated for energy harvesting (EH), resulting in lower energy harvested from the user. It can also be seen that due to the presence of dual path losses, the sum of energy harvested by the user by the P-RIS-assisted energy-harvesting algorithm does not differ significantly compared to the conventional RIS-assisted energy-harvesting algorithm without RIS-assisted energy harvesting. However, since the dynamic power splitting energy-harvesting algorithm with A-RIS assistance proposed herein can give full play to the advantage that A-RIS can amplify the reflected signal radiant power, it can overcome the defect of the "multiplicative fading" of P-RIS so that the sum of energy harvested at the user end can be improved. Further, the dynamic power partitioning algorithm increases the degree of freedom of the optimization so that more power is available for energy harvesting (EH), resulting in more energy harvested by the user. The sum of energy harvested at the user end with the dynamic power splitting algorithm is improved by 70.1% compared to the energy-harvesting algorithm with average power splitting ($\rho_k = 0.5$) assisted by A-RIS when the minimum required signal-to-dry noise ratio $\gamma_{min} = 2$ dB at the user end is satisfied.

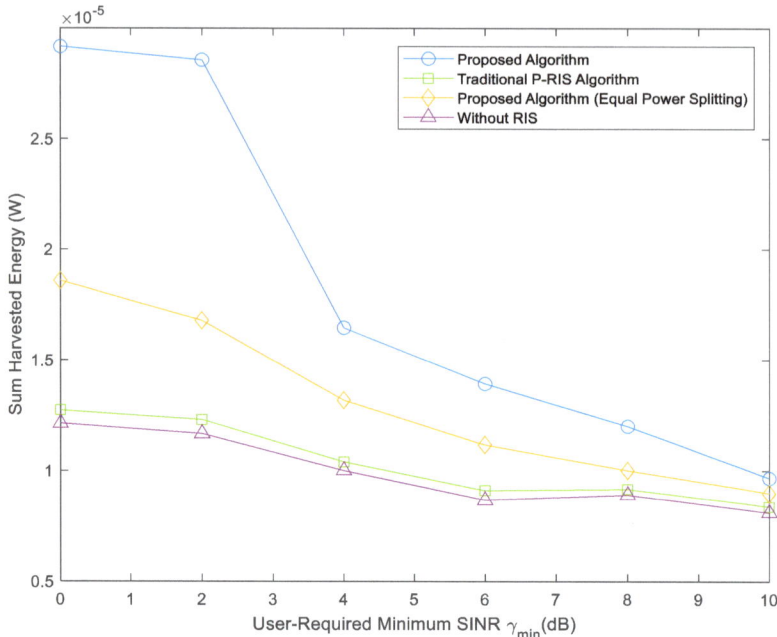

Figure 7. Relationship between the total energy collected at the user end and the minimum signal-to-noise ratio at the user end.

5. Conclusions

This paper investigates how to solve the problem of the shortage of energy harvested by users in communication systems based on the multi-user MISO system model using the A-RIS-assisted SWIPT technique, which can significantly improve the sum of energy harvested by users. In this paper, the problem of maximizing the sum of energy harvested by the user is established under the constraints of the minimum signal-to-dry noise ratio required by the user, the maximum power of active RIS, the maximum power of the base station, and the PS ratio. The algorithm for maximizing the sum of energy captured by the user is proposed through the joint optimization of the BS beam-former, power splitting factor, RIS phase matrix, and signal strength increase. For the proposed optimization problem, Algorithms 1–3 are used to transform the original problem into a convex problem which is first solved by local iterations, and finally, the whole is optimized alternatively. The numerical values show that the proposed algorithm has good convergence. At the maximum allowable radiant power of 40 dBm and 45 dBm at the base station, the total energy captured by the user using the A-RIS-assisted algorithm is improved by 48.7% and 40.3%, respectively, compared to the P-RIS-assisted algorithm. In addition, with A-RIS assistance, the use of the dynamic power splitting algorithm improves the system degrees of freedom by 21.7% and 23.5% of the total energy collected by the user compared to the use of the average power splitting algorithm ($\rho_k = 0.5$), respectively.

Author Contributions: Conceptualization, L.L., S.L., M.W., J.X. and B.Y.; methodology, L.L., S.L. and M.W.; software, L.L. and S.L.; validation, L.L., S.L. and J.X.; formal analysis, L.L., S.L. and B.Y.; data curation, J.X. and B.Y.; writing—original draft preparation, L.L.; writing—review and editing, S.L.; funding acquisition, S.L. All authors have read and agreed to the published version of the manuscript.

Funding: This work was supported in part by the Chunhui plan international cooperation project of China Education Ministry under Grant 202201406, in part by the key research and development plan of Xuzhou under Grant KC20027 and Grant KC18079, and in part by college students' innovative entrepreneurial training plan program under Grant 20221032006Z.

Data Availability Statement: Data are contained within the article.

Conflicts of Interest: The authors declare no conflicts of interest.

References

1. Xu, Y.J.; Xie, H.; Li, D.; Hu, R.Q. Energy-Efficient Beamforming for Heterogeneous Industrial IoT Networks With Phase and Distortion Noises. *IEEE Trans. Ind. Inform.* **2022**, *18*, 7423–7434. [CrossRef]
2. Xu, Y.J.; Gui, G.; Gacanin, H.; Adachi, F. A Survey on Resource Allocation for 5G Heterogeneous Networks: Current Research, Future Trends, and Challenges. *IEEE Commun. Surv. Tutor.* **2021**, *23*, 668–695. [CrossRef]
3. Wang, D.M.; Zhang, C.; Du, Y.Q.; Zhao, J.N.; Jiang, M.; You, X.H. Implementation of a Cloud-Based Cell-Free Distributed Massive MIMO System. *IEEE Commun. Mag.* **2020**, *58*, 61–67. [CrossRef]
4. Zhang, Z.Q.; Xiao, Y.; Ma, Z.; Xiao, M.; Ding, Z.G.; Lei, X.F.; Karagiannidis, G.K.; Fan, P.Z. 6G Wireless Networks: Vision, Requirements, Architecture, and Key Technologies. *IEEE Veh. Technol. Mag.* **2019**, *14*, 28–41. [CrossRef]
5. Wang, C.X.; You, X.H.; Gao, X.Q.; Zhu, X.M.; Li, Z.X.; Zhang, C.; Wang, H.M.; Huang, Y.M.; Chen, Y.F.; Haas, H.; et al. On the Road to 6G: Visions, Requirements, Key Technologies, and Testbeds. *IEEE Commun. Surv. Tutor.* **2023**, *25*, 905–974. [CrossRef]
6. Hong, E.K.; Lee, I.; Shim, B.; Ko, Y.C.; Kim, S.H.; Pack, S.; Lee, K.; Kim, S.; Kim, J.H.; Shin, Y.; et al. 6G R&D Vision: Requirements and Candidate Technologies. *J. Commun. Netw.* **2022**, *24*, 232–245.
7. Younes, M.; Desombre, P.; Louet, Y. Trade-off between spectral and energy efficiency in THz frequency bands for 6G. In Proceedings of the 2022 1st International Conference on 6G Networking (6GNet), Paris, France, 6–8 July 2022; pp. 1–5.
8. Shen, S.; Yu, C.; Zhang, K.; Ni, J.; Ci, S. Adaptive and dynamic security in AI-empowered 6G: From an energy efficiency perspective. *IEEE Commun. Stand. Mag.* **2021**, *5*, 80–88. [CrossRef]
9. Jiang, W.; Han, B.; Habibi, M.A.; Schotten, H.D. The road towards 6G: A comprehensive survey. *IEEE Open J. Commun. Soc.* **2021**, *2*, 334–366. [CrossRef]
10. Gao, Z.N.; Xu, Y.J.; Wang, Q.Z.; Wu, Q.Q.; Li, D. Outage-Constrained Energy Efficiency Maximization for RIS-Assisted WPCNs. *IEEE Commun. Lett.* **2021**, *25*, 3370–3374. [CrossRef]
11. Ji, T.T.; Hua, M.; Li, C.G.; Huang, Y.M.; Yang, L.X. A Robust IRS-Aided Wireless Information Surveillance Design With Bounded Channel Errors. *IEEE Wirel. Commun. Lett.* **2022**, *11*, 2210–2214. [CrossRef]
12. Xu, Y.J.; Xie, H.; Wu, Q.Q.; Huang, C.W.; Yuen, C. Robust Max-Min Energy Efficiency for RIS-Aided HetNets With Distortion Noises. *IEEE Trans. Commun.* **2022**, *70*, 1457–1471. [CrossRef]
13. Zainud-Deen, S.H. Reconfigurable Intelligent Surfaces For Wireless Communications. In Proceedings of the 2022 39th National Radio Science Conference (NRSC), Cairo, Egypt, 29 November–1 December 2022; p. 342.
14. Pan, C.H.; Ren, H.; Wang, K.Z.; Kolb, J.F.; Elkashlan, M.; Chen, M.; Di Renzo, M.; Hao, Y.; Wang, J.Z.; Swindlehurst, A.L.; et al. Reconfigurable Intelligent Surfaces for 6G Systems: Principles, Applications, and Research Directions. *IEEE Commun. Mag.* **2021**, *59*, 14–20. [CrossRef]
15. Basar, E.; Di Renzo, M.; De Rosny, J.; Debbah, M.; Alouini, M.S.; Zhang, R. Wireless Communications Through Reconfigurable Intelligent Surfaces. *IEEE Access* **2019**, *7*, 116753–116773. [CrossRef]
16. Di Renzo, M.; Zappone, A.; Debbah, M.; Alouini, M.S.; Yuen, C.; de Rosny, J.; Tretyakov, S. Smart Radio Environments Empowered by Reconfigurable Intelligent Surfaces: How It Works, State of Research, and The Road Ahead. *IEEE J. Sel. Areas Commun.* **2020**, *38*, 2450–2525. [CrossRef]
17. Tang, W.K.; Chen, M.Z.; Chen, X.Y.; Dai, J.Y.; Han, Y.; Di Renzo, M.; Zeng, Y.; Jin, S.; Cheng, Q.; Cui, T.J. Wireless Communications With Reconfigurable Intelligent Surface: Path Loss Modeling and Experimental Measurement. *IEEE Trans. Wirel. Commun.* **2021**, *20*, 421–439. [CrossRef]
18. Wei, L.; Huang, C.W.; Alexandropoulos, G.C.; Yuen, C.; Zhang, Z.Y.; Debbah, M. Channel Estimation for RIS-Empowered Multi-User MISO Wireless Communications. *IEEE Trans. Commun.* **2021**, *69*, 4144–4157. [CrossRef]
19. Zhang, Z.J.; Dai, L.L.; Chen, X.B.; Liu, C.H.; Yang, F.; Schober, R.; Poor, H.V. Active RIS vs. Passive RIS: Which Will Prevail in 6G? *IEEE Trans. Commun.* **2023**, *71*, 1707–1725. [CrossRef]
20. Khoshafa, M.H.; Ngatched, T.M.N.; Ahmed, M.H.; Ndjiongue, A.R. Active Reconfigurable Intelligent Surfaces-Aided Wireless Communication System. *IEEE Commun. Lett.* **2021**, *25*, 3699–3703. [CrossRef]
21. Zhi, K.D.; Pan, C.H.; Ren, H.; Chai, K.K.; Elkashlan, M. Active RIS Versus Passive RIS: Which is Superior With the Same Power Budget? *IEEE Commun. Lett.* **2022**, *26*, 1150–1154. [CrossRef]
22. Lu, W.D.; Si, P.Y.; Liu, X.; Li, B.; Liu, Z.L.; Zhao, N.; Wu, Y. OFDM Based Bidirectional Multi-Relay SWIPT Strategy for 6G IoT Networks. *China Commun.* **2020**, *17*, 80–91. [CrossRef]
23. Lu, W.D.; Si, P.Y.; Huang, G.X.; Han, H.M.; Qian, L.P.; Zhao, N.; Gong, Y. SWIPT Cooperative Spectrum Sharing for 6G-Enabled Cognitive IoT Network. *IEEE Internet Things J.* **2021**, *8*, 15070–15080. [CrossRef]
24. Song, K.; Nie, M.Y.; Jiang, J.; Li, C.G.; Yin, Y.F. On the Secrecy for Relay-Aided SWIPT Internet of Things System With Cooperative Eavesdroppers. *IEEE Access* **2021**, *9*, 28204–28212. [CrossRef]
25. Krikidis, I. SWIPT in 3-D Bipolar Ad Hoc Networks With Sectorized Antennas. *IEEE Commun. Lett.* **2016**, *20*, 1267–1270. [CrossRef]

26. Wen, Z.G.; Guo, Z.M.; Beaulieu, N.C.; Liu, X.Q. Robust Beamforming Design for Multi-User MISO Full-Duplex SWIPT System With Channel State Information Uncertainty. *IEEE Trans. Veh. Technol.* **2019**, *68*, 1942–1947. [CrossRef]
27. Jang, S.; Lee, H.; Kang, S.; Oh, T.; Lee, I. Energy Efficient SWIPT Systems in Multi-Cell MISO Networks. *IEEE Trans. Wirel. Commun.* **2018**, *17*, 8180–8194. [CrossRef]
28. Yaswanth, J.; Singh, S.K.; Singh, K.; Flanagan, M.F. Energy-Efficient Beamforming Design for RIS-Aided MIMO Downlink Communication With SWIPT. *IEEE Trans. Green Commun. Netw.* **2023**, *7*, 1164–1180. [CrossRef]
29. Zargari, S.; Hakimi, A.; Tellambura, C.; Herath, S. Multiuser MISO PS-SWIPT Systems: Active or Passive RIS? *IEEE Wirel. Commun. Lett.* **2022**, *11*, 1920–1924. [CrossRef]
30. Ma, R.; Tang, J.; Zhang, X.; Wong, K.-K.; Chambers, J.A. Energy Efficiency Optimization for Mutual-Coupling-Aware Wireless Communication System based on RIS-enhanced SWIPT. *IEEE Internet Things J.* **2023**, *10*, 19399–19414. [CrossRef]
31. Mohamed, A.; Zappone, A.; Di Renzo, M. Bi-Objective Optimization of Information Rate and Harvested Power in RIS-Aided SWIPT Systems. *IEEE Wirel. Commun. Lett.* **2022**, *11*, 2195–2199. [CrossRef]
32. Liu, Y.; Han, F.X.; Zhao, S.J. Flexible and Reliable Multiuser SWIPT IoT Network Enhanced by UAV-Mounted Intelligent Reflecting Surface. *IEEE Trans. Reliab.* **2022**, *71*, 1092–1103. [CrossRef]
33. Zargari, S.; Khalili, A.; Wu, Q.Q.; Mili, M.R.; Ng, D.W.K. Max-Min Fair Energy-Efficient Beamforming Design for Intelligent Reflecting Surface-Aided SWIPT Systems With Non-Linear Energy Harvesting Model. *IEEE Trans. Veh. Technol.* **2021**, *70*, 5848–5864. [CrossRef]
34. Wu, Q.Q.; Zhang, R. Weighted Sum Power Maximization for Intelligent Reflecting Surface Aided SWIPT. *IEEE Wirel. Commun. Lett.* **2020**, *9*, 586–590. [CrossRef]
35. Xue, L.; Wang, C.; Shen, Y.; Gong, X. Sum Secrecy Rate Maximization for IRS-Aided SWIPT System with Artificial Noise. In Proceedings of the 2023 IEEE 13th International Conference on CYBER Technology in Automation, Control, and Intelligent Systems (CYBER), Qinhuangdao, China, 11–14 July 2023; pp. 169–174.
36. Shi, Q.J.; Liu, L.; Xu, W.Q.; Zhang, R. Joint Transmit Beamforming and Receive Power Splitting for MISO SWIPT Systems. *IEEE Trans. Wirel. Commun.* **2014**, *13*, 3269–3280. [CrossRef]

Disclaimer/Publisher's Note: The statements, opinions and data contained in all publications are solely those of the individual author(s) and contributor(s) and not of MDPI and/or the editor(s). MDPI and/or the editor(s) disclaim responsibility for any injury to people or property resulting from any ideas, methods, instructions or products referred to in the content.

Article

Exploring Universal Filtered Multi Carrier Waveform for Last Meter Connectivity in 6G: A Street-Lighting-Driven Approach with Enhanced Simulator for IoT Application Dimensioning

Véronique Georlette [1,*,†], Anne-Carole Honfoga [1,2], Michel Dossou [2] and Véronique Moeyaert [1]

1 Electromagnetism and Telecommunication Department, University of Mons, 7000 Mons, Belgium; anne-carole.honfoga@umons.ac.be or annecarole.honfoga@uac.bj (A.-C.H.); veronique.moeyaert@umons.ac.be (V.M.)
2 LETIA, Polytechnic School of Abomey-Calavi, University of Abomey-Calavi, Abomey-Calavi 01 BP 2009, Benin; dossoumichel@gmail.com
* Correspondence: verogeorlette@gmail.com or veronique.georlette@umons.ac.be
† Current address: Department of Electrical and Computer Engineering, University of Illinois, Chicago, IL 60607, USA.

Abstract: In the dynamic landscape of 6G and smart cities, visible light communication (VLC) assumes critical significance for Internet of Things (IoT) applications spanning diverse sectors. The escalating demand for bandwidth and data underscores the need for innovative solutions, positioning VLC as a complementary technology within the electromagnetic spectrum. This paper focuses on the relevance of VLC in the 6G paradigm, shedding light on its applicability across smart cities and industries. The paper highlights the growing efficiency of lighting LEDs in infrastructure, facilitating the seamless integration of VLC. The study then emphasizes VLC's robustness in outdoor settings, demonstrating effective communication up to 10 m. This resilience positions VLC as a key player in addressing the very last meter of wireless communication, offering a seamless solution for IoT connectivity. By introducing a freely available open-source simulator combined with an alternative waveform, UFMC, the study empowers researchers to dimension applications effectively, showcasing VLC's potential to improve wireless communication in the evolving landscape of 6G and smart cities.

Keywords: visible light communication (VLC); 6G; IoT applications; smart cities; wireless communication; last meter connectivity; open-source simulator; application dimensioning; outdoor VLC communication; efficient lighting LEDs

1. Introduction

The anticipated sixth generation of wireless communication technology, 6G, represents a paradigm shift in connectivity, aiming to surpass the capabilities of its predecessor, 5G. Envisioned as a transforming force, 6G seeks to provide ultra-fast data rates, incredibly low latency, and unparalleled connectivity, fostering innovations that extend beyond conventional wireless communication boundaries [1]. The technology envisions a seamless integration of diverse communication paradigms, including terahertz frequencies, new waveforms, edge computing, holographic communications, and advanced artificial intelligence [2]. The overarching goal is to create an ecosystem where connectivity is not just pervasive but also intelligent and adaptive to the diverse needs of users. In the pursuit of 6G, the emphasis on continuous innovation becomes paramount. The optimization of resources, efficient spectrum utilization, and sustainable practices are integral aspects that drive the evolution of 6G. Embracing innovation is crucial not only for achieving unprecedented levels of performance but also for addressing the evolving demands of a connected world, ensuring that technological advancements contribute to a more resource-efficient and sustainable future.

In that context, the terahertz (THz) band emerges as a promising domain with its vast bandwidth and exceptionally high data rates [3], offering robust support for diverse 6G applications, including wireless data centers [4], ultra-short-distance communications, and other novel scenarios. Optical wireless communications (OWCs) harness various bands within the optical spectrum, comprising infrared (IR), visible light, and ultraviolet (UV) bands, presenting nearly thousands of terahertz of untapped spectral resources. Notably, the visible light band shows several merits, including its eco-friendliness, cost-effectiveness, freedom from spectrum regulation, heightened security, and immunity to electromagnetic interference [5,6]. Particularly in settings where radio frequency (RF) communications encounter limitations, OWCs demonstrate substantial application potential, giving rise to a range of optical communication technologies such as visible light communications (VLC), light fidelity (Li-Fi), optical camera communications (OCC), free space optical (FSO) communications, and light detection and ranging (LiDAR), all being more than relevant for 6G.

In the pursuit of 6G technologies, it is imperative to recognize that not all applications demand ultra-high data rates but mainly robustness. In that context, considerations for IoT applications, dedicated industrial use cases, and certain vehicular communications underscore the importance of diverse communication solutions. VLC emerges as a pertinent technology [7]. Unlike bandwidth-intensive applications, VLC offers a balanced and resource-efficient approach for different types of scenarios. Integrating VLC into the portfolio of 6G technologies holds particular relevance for smart cities and industries. Its adaptability, low power consumption, and suitability for specific use cases align seamlessly with the varied communication needs in urban environments and industrial settings. By acknowledging the nuanced requirements of different applications, 6G can position itself as a holistic and inclusive technological ecosystem where innovations like VLC contribute to the optimization of resources and the realization of a technologically advanced yet tailored connectivity landscape.

The potential applications of visible light communication (VLC) within the 6G technology landscape are diverse and strategically aligned with the demands of contemporary urban and industrial scenarios, as depicted in Figure 1. Each sector, starting with automotive, exemplifies the adaptability of VLC to meet specific communication needs. In the automotive domain, VLC can leverage LED headlights for vehicle-to-vehicle (V2V) communication, facilitating short warnings and creating communication daisy chains in heavy traffic conditions [8]. Similarly, private and office spaces benefit from consumer-oriented Li-Fi products, offering internet connectivity through visible or infrared lights [9]. Smart cities stand to gain from VLC's capacity to relieve RF spectrum usage outdoors, providing alternative communication for local, line-of-sight, and short-distance applications [10]. The smart industry sector, including factory automation and logistics, witnesses the potential of VLC in optimizing wireless connectivity within industrial warehouses [11]. Deploying free space optical (FSO) communication as a backhauling system in cities characterized by towering skyscrapers offers a high-capacity and wireless solution for data transmission across urban landscapes [12,13]. The military sector explores the secure, non wall-penetrating nature of VLC, potentially replacing wired communication means for local applications [14]. Healthcare applications leverage VLC for remote health monitoring, aligning with smart health strategies in smart cities [15]. Finally, underwater communication, a traditionally challenging domain, sees VLC's potential to achieve communications in harsh turbulent conditions [16]. This paper critically analyzes and provides the essential tools for integrating VLC communication in short-distance scenarios within urban and industrial settings, contributing to the dynamic landscape of 6G technologies.

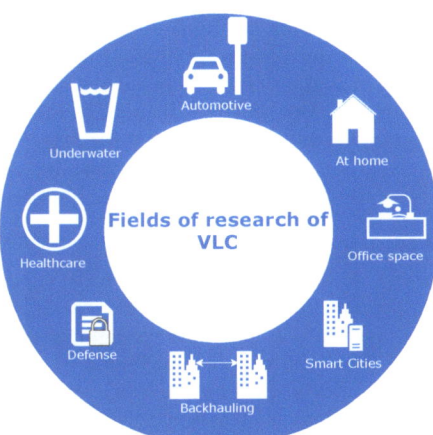

Figure 1. A few examples of related 6G VLC fields of research.

In the evolution from 5G to 6G, the incorporation of novel waveforms emerges as a pivotal consideration. While 5G's development was encumbered by material limitations, 6G signifies a phase of unconstrained exploration. A central tenet of 6G's objectives lies in augmenting spectral throughput, particularly for IoT applications. This trajectory may initiate with a transition from the prevailing orthogonal frequency-division multiplexing (OFDM) standards, thereby paving the path for potential migration towards universal filtered multi carrier (UFMC) for enhanced efficiency. Indeed, UFMC has several benefits for 6G applications. UFMC has better spectral efficiency, lower sensitivity to synchronization errors (compared to OFDM) [17], can be resilient to the Doppler effect in some cases [18], which is relevant for applications with mobility, and finally, has more flexibility in the filters used for pulse-shaping [19]. Taking into account the advantages of VLC and its growing interest for 6G combined with the promising future of UFMC for 6G, combining both seems a relevant study. To summarize, this paper presents the combination of VLC, which is a technology that has been foreseen as promising for 6G among optical wireless communication technologies [20], and UFMC.

This study delves into the strategic utilization of visible light communication (VLC) as a means of short-range communication within urban and industrial environments. By concentrating on scenarios where ultra-high data rates are non-essential, the investigation explores VLC's pragmatic applications in optimizing communication resources.The prior research, such as studies examining VLC's efficacy in industrial automation or urban infrastructure monitoring, furnishes invaluable insights [21]. This study advances this domain by proposing a methodology for calculating indoor and outdoor VLC channels, augmenting the existing body of knowledge. Additionally, it offers a comprehensive suite of open-source tools for designing and simulating VLC scenarios, accessible via the Github platform. Leveraging these resources, the study advocates for simulating VLC communications in a tailored smart city scenario using the UFMC waveform, assessing performance metrics such as bit error rate and spectral efficiency. The promising outcomes position UFMC-VLC technology as a prospective component of future 6G systems. Through this endeavor, the study seeks to expedite the integration of VLC within the broader spectrum of 6G technologies, fostering an adaptive framework conducive to smart city and industrial applications.

The study begins by establishing the relevance of VLC as a communication resource for scenarios where ultra-high data rates are not paramount. Emphasizing the significance of diverse communication solutions, the paper positions VLC as a tailored and efficient option for specific applications within smart cities and industries. Subsequently, attention is directed towards the introduction of an open-source simulator designed to provide researchers with fundamental tools for designing and simulating VLC scenarios. The simulator serves as a versatile platform, enabling the modeling and analysis of VLC communication systems in various urban and industrial environments. The paper then presents insightful results derived from simulations using innovative modulation schemes such as UFMC, a general and enhanced version of OFDM, showcasing the practicality and efficacy of integrating VLC in short-distance communications. Finally, a concluding section synthesizes the findings, emphasizing the role of VLC within the 6G landscape, and underscores the importance of continued exploration and innovation in optimizing communication resources for diverse applications in urban and industrial domains.

2. Materials and Methods

In the realm of visible light communication (VLC), even in outdoor environments, the optical power propagation from emitter to receiver is profoundly influenced by the specific scenario. Given that VLC operates with light, obstacles pose a significant challenge, acting as disruptors to communication. Additionally, reflections in the environment can have varying effects, either adding up constructively to the signal or introducing noise-like contribution at the receiver [22]. Recognizing these factors, smart city applications capitalizing on VLC could strategically align with scenarios where these requirements are inherently met, where there is mainly line of sight (LoS). This is particularly possible and advantageous for applications such as IoT, urban Li-Fi or OCC, vehicle-to-vehicle (V2V) communication, vehicle-to-infrastructure (V2I) communication, communication among drones, and various supplementary scenarios illustrated in Figure 2.

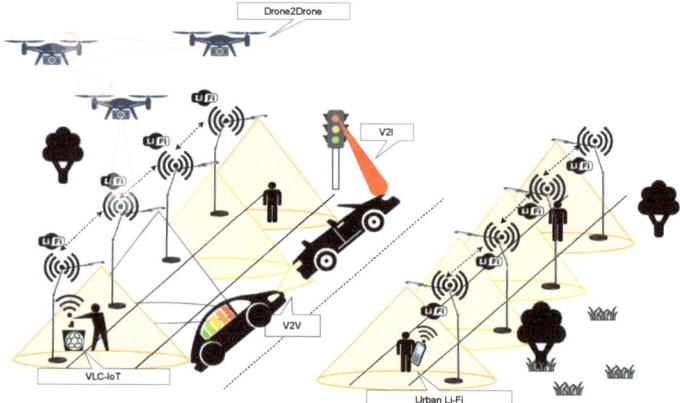

Figure 2. Potential applications of VLC in Smart Cities.

Moving beyond the scenario considerations, it is essential to understand that while VLC utilizes LEDs for communication, the diversity of LEDs introduces a range of parameters within the emitter itself. Each LED functions akin to an antenna, possessing a distinct radiation pattern that delineates how the power consumed by the LED is distributed through space in an angular manner [23]. Notably, LEDs employed in different applications exhibit unique radiation patterns. For instance, LEDs designed for indoor lighting, also called Lambertian emitters, disperse light evenly in the room [24], while car headlights, street lights, and industrial lighting each carry their distinctive angular radiation signatures [21,25]. Figure 3 shows a plane representation of the radiation pattern of a Lambertian emitter for three different half power angles (on the left side of the figure) and a NIKKON streetlight (on the right side of the figure). A Lambertian emitter has a uniaxial symmetry to the radiation pattern and its half-power angle parameter gives it directionality. Two perpendicular planes of the streetlight 3-D radiation pattern are represented on the right side of the figure. It can be seen that there is no axial symmetry and a preferred direction in the radiation of light power.

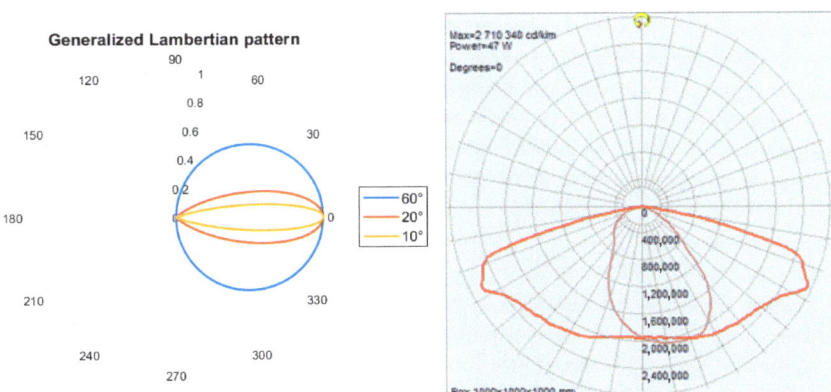

Figure 3. (**left**) Lambertian LED emitter and (**right**) real radiation pattern of a streetlight [26].

This paper underscores the nuanced interplay between the materials employed in visible light communication (VLC) systems, the configuration setup, and the surrounding environment. Recognizing the distinctiveness of each LED and its crucial positioning relative to the receiver in diverse scenarios, this paper introduces a simulator designed to empower end users to define these pivotal parameters. In its primary phase, the simulator allows users to intricately characterize the LED properties and spatial arrangement, considering the unique features of each light emitter. Additionally, it facilitates the assessment of communication performance under an innovative modulation scheme, UFMC. Notably, the simulator, also meant for outdoor communication, extends its functionality relative to the baseline literature to incorporate environmental factors, allowing users to specify the quantity of particles in the air and consequently identify optical power loss attributable to atmospheric presence. While a more comprehensive exploration of these atmospheric effects can be found in our earlier work [21], this paper concentrates on highlighting the simulator's versatility and the pertinence of VLC within the 6G paradigm. Figure 4 shows how both simulators work together to study a scenario. The MATLAB simulator focuses on generating the point-to-point communication data stream, and the Python channel simulator takes into account the path loss computation of the communication. The two combined give us communication performance metrics of a point in space in a scenario.

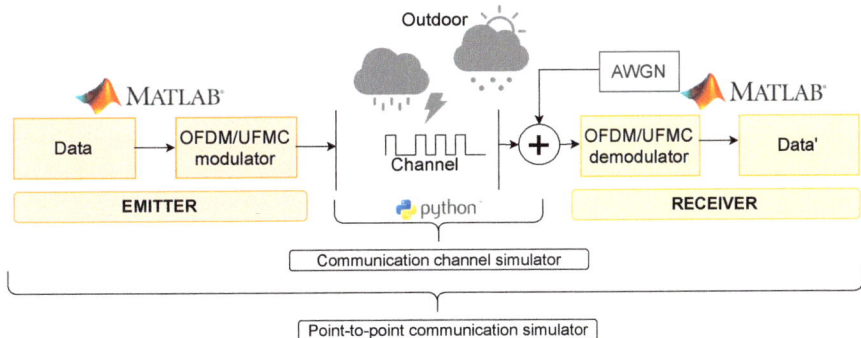

Figure 4. Representation of the concatenation of both simulators.

The subsequent section delineates the simulator's key features and presents the primary outcomes obtained while employing the UFMC modulation scheme in regards to OFDM performance.

2.1. The Channel Simulator

The material employed in this study comprises a communication channel simulator crafted using Python. Initially, the foundation for this simulator drew inspiration from a primary version based on MATLAB, as documented in reference [27]. Our improved Python simulator not only operates on an open-source platform but also brings novel simulation parameters. These enhancements encompass the introduction of an innovative smoke model, the integration of 3-D graphical representations, increased flexibility for customizing simulation "room" parameters or outdoor configuration, and the consideration of authentic lamp radiation patterns.

The channel simulator presented in this study can be found on Github [28]. It empowers users to incorporate radiation measurements provided by light fixture manufacturers, typically available in formats such as the redIlluminating Engineering Society (IES) or EULUMDAT [29]. These files encompass comprehensive information about the light fixture, its characteristics, and the associated radiation pattern. Users can integrate these data into the simulator for precise simulation in each specific situation, enhancing the accuracy and realism of VLC performance assessments. The simulator has, for example, been applied in various smart city or concrete industrial use cases in the past [21].

The present simulator is an enhanced version of our previous work where the communication simulator was upgraded to include several modulation schemes such as orthogonal frequency division multiplexing (OFDM) and universal frequency multi carrier (UFMC), together with the introduction of performance measures.

Figure 5 explains the simulated environment and the basic principle of the simulator. The aim of the simulator is to assess the optical power distribution of a VLC system in a scenario under study. To do so, the software creates first a virtual three-dimensional room where the axes' origin is in the center. Here, the light is in the center of the ceiling, and the reception plane is located at the same distance from the origin as the emitter but in the negative application of the Cartesian coordinate system. Then, several parameters can be set such as the presence of walls or not, their reflection coefficients, and the position of the emitter in the virtual room. Afterward, the reception plane where the communication coverage needs to be assessed is set. It should be noted that the tilting of the emitting light or receiver is not taken into account. As mentioned before, only the scenarios that can benefit from a major part of LoS are considered here. The walls are subdivided into a matrix of unit surfaces to assess the quantity of power coming from the LED and then acts as a Lambertian point source. The ground being also subdivided in unit cells enables the computation of the portion of optical power reaching the receiver at each cell of the receiver's plane cell.

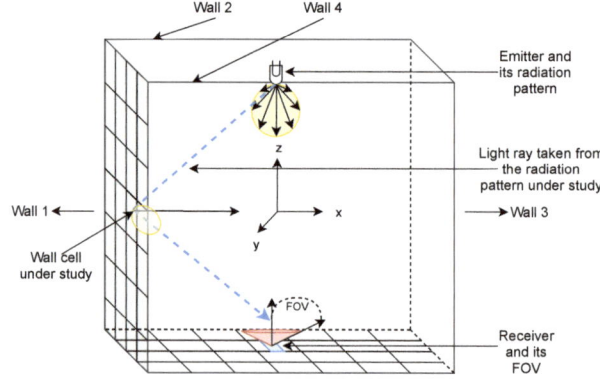

Figure 5. 3-D environment simulated when using the software-wall can be made transparent to take into account outdoor scenarios or the presence of windows.

In the scope of this paper, a scenario where a light source is hanging on a wall was chosen to study the performances of the UFMC modulation scheme. Figure 6 shows (left) the setup under study where the light source is enlightening the pedestrian under it and its connected device, as well as (middle and right) the resulting optical power coverage map. To be as close to reality as possible, a 47 W streetlight NIKKON MURAS with a light temperature of 4000 K was selected. Its corresponding IES file was obtained from the Lumsearch website, as referenced in [26]. This file contains the light's name and radiation pattern, defined by a table using the two angles C and Gamma. The IES file encompasses data for 13 azimuth angles (ranging from 0 to 360 degrees with a 30-degree interval) and 181 elevation angles (ranging from 0 to 180 degrees with a 1-degree increment). The luminous flux value per solid angle (measured in candela or lumens per steradian) is provided for each pair of angles to construct the radiation pattern. Its radiation pattern is represented in Figure 7. The non-axial symmetry is clearly visible.

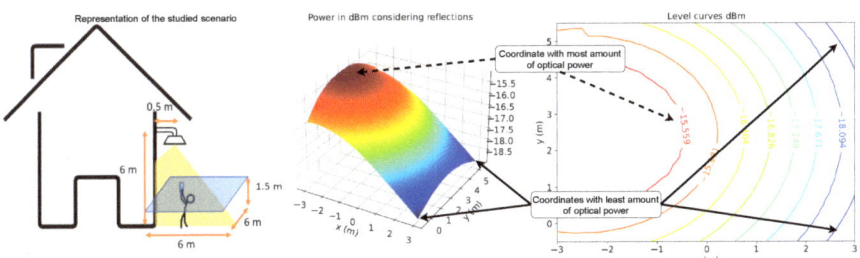

Figure 6. 3-D environment simulated when using the channel simulator for the NIKKON streetlight hanging on a wall.

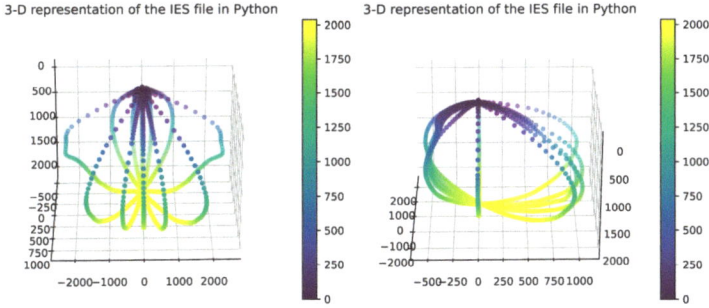

Figure 7. Raw point cloud of the IES file of the real radiation pattern of a streetlight for two points of view.

Due to the power map (right side of Figure 6), it is possible to choose a location in space where the UFMC performance should be quantified. For a user positioned under a streetlight of 6 m high with the end-device at a height of 1.5 m, the signal is the strongest at the closest point to the streetlight as opposed to the corner of the space under study. The coordinate with the strongest optical power and the two coordinates with the weakest optical power are represented in Figure 6. In the remainder of this paper, we assume that the user is located at the ideal location.

2.2. The Communication Simulator

Now that the point in space where the UFMC performance is studied is set, the communication channel simulator gives the information of the amount of optical power received and can also give us the information about the channel's impulse response (CIR). The CIR is a key parameter to assess the available coherence bandwidth and is defined according to the delay between the LoS main peak (the first ray reaching the receiver) and the second peak (the reflected ray on a wall) reaching the receiver. Given that the light wave travels at the speed of light, and the measures of the scenario, if the LoS ray of light arrives at a time of 1.5×10^{-8} and the first reflection (due to the proximity of the wall to the light) is approximately 1.53×10^{-8}, the difference between both rays, the main signal and its reflection, gives place to a bandwidth of approximately 3000 MHz, which is more than enough for the envisioned scenario (See Equation (1)). Thus, the available coherence bandwidth is sufficient to apply the flat channel hypothesis.

$$BW = \frac{1}{\Delta t} = \frac{1}{0.03 \times 10^{-8}} = 33.33 \times 10^8 \text{ Hz} \qquad (1)$$

Furthermore, OFDM for VLC has been standardized in ITU G.9991 standard [30], and the framework of this standard was chosen in this paper to generate the waveforms. The standard proposes a set of parameters for bandwidths of 50, 100, or 200 MHz, which fit our scenario well given the available bandwidth computed above. Using the parameters of the G.9991 standard chosen is thus consistent.

A point-to-point communication simulator as illustrated in Figure 4 is used in this study. Both OFDM and UFMC modulation schemes are implemented in this simulator to estimate the system's performance in terms of bit error rate (BER) and spectral efficiency (bit/s/Hz). The paper's use of OFDM simulation is interesting, especially as it is widely standardized. What sets it apart is comparing OFDM with UFMC, a 5G candidate waveform that was not selected. Furthermore, the inclusion of a realistic lamp pattern adds originality to the study. This section highlights the key parameters for OFDM and UFMC that were studied. On top of the use of UFMC, the originality of this study is the use of realistic LED optical spatial distributions and real photodiode models in the scenario under study. The rest of this section describes the working principles of UFMC and how to generate a VLC compatible signal, namely, a real-valued and positive signal. It then presents the various key parameters used in the simulation.

2.2.1. UFMC Principles

Figure 8 shows the functional blocs of UFMC adapted to VLC. As OFDM has widely been studied and standardized, its working principles are not reiterated in this paper. The interested reader can find information about it at the following reference [31]. The input data of UFMC are also complex symbols resulting from an IQ in-phase and quadrature (IQ) symbol mapping method just like OFDM. In UFMC, the total bandwidth is first divided into B sub-bands. The filtering operation in UFMC is carried out per sub-band (cf Figure 8). The data from each sub-band undergo an IFFT operation, and the Chebyshev filter (of length L) is applied in the time domain on each sub-band. To be compatible with VLC, OFDM uses the Hermitian symmetry (HS) property to make it real-valued by making the data symbols transmitted on positive frequencies the complex conjugates of those on negative frequencies. As opposed to OFDM, it is more difficult to apply the HS to UFMC signals to make it a real-valued signal. Since the filter stage is after the IFFT, it does not make sense to add HS as in OFDM. Adding an extra IFFT stage before sending on the transmission channel does not solve the problem either. Therefore, a juxtaposition method is used instead to have a real-valued signal HS-free UFMC signal, as suggested in [32] (cf Figure 9). A zero-padding technique is applied on each received symbol of length $(N + L - 1)$ at the receiver side to reach a sample number equal to twice ($2N$) the subcarrier number N used at the emission. This operation is followed by the FFT and the down-sampling technique for data recovery.

The OFDM and UFMC data are generated thanks to a MATLAB program that can also be found in our Github [28]. The constraint of the VLC technology is using a real and positive signal to modulate the LED's current. This implies that the two modulations, developed in the framework of RF transmission, require adequate changes to fulfill these constraints. The juxtaposition method has been chosen to have a real-valued signal, and a constant bias is added to have a positive-valued signal. The juxtaposition method consists of generating a conventional complex signal (OFDM or UFMC) and juxtaposing all the real parts and all the imaginary parts of the complex numbers forming the desired symbols in the time domain to obtain a real-valued signal. The mechanism of juxtaposition is illustrated in Figure 9.

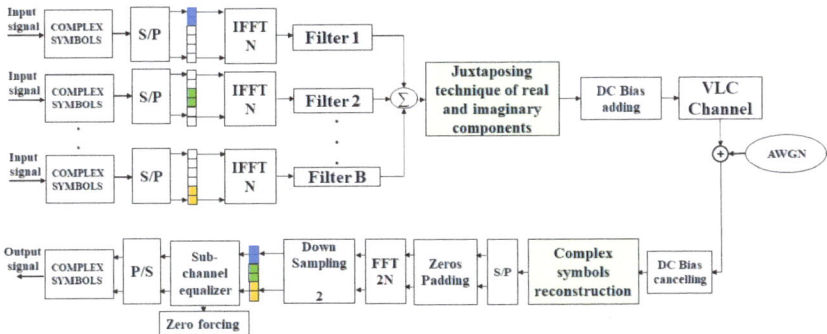

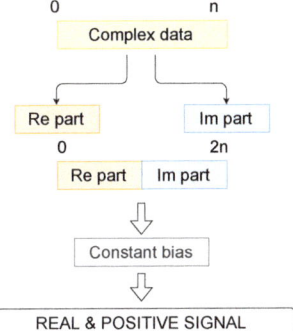

Figure 8. Schematic of a UFMC communication system applied to VLC communication.

Figure 9. Representation of the juxtaposition mechanism on complex data.

2.2.2. Key Parameters for the Simulations

The parameters that OFDM and UFMC modulations have in common are the number of bits per subcarrier m, the number of subcarriers N, the total number of symbols generated for the simulations N_{symb}, and the number of bits coded per subcarrier $bitsPerSubCarrier$. In this paper, several sizes of QAM modulation were used to encode bits. They are the 2-QAM (also called binary phase shift keying (BPSK)), 4-QAM (also called quadrature phase shift keying (QPSK)) and 16-QAM. For OFDM, the size of the guard interval (GI) is often proportional to N. Logically, the important parameters of the UFMC scheme are the number of sub-bands $N_{subband}$ (B^{th} filter in Figure 8), the number of subcarriers per subband $SubbandSize$, the side-lobe attenuation $slobeAtten$, the type of filter used $FilterType$ and the filter's length $filterLen$.

The strategy followed to generate the UFMC waveform was to adopt the OFDM parameters of the ITU G.9991 standard [30]. It proposes a set of 256, 512, or 1024 subcarriers for bandwidths of 50, 100, or 200 MHz, respectively. As we target as a first step the lowest bit rates and simplest settings, it was decided to work with 256 subcarriers for both modulation schemes. The GI suggested in the standard for 256 subcarriers (N) is $\frac{N}{32}$.

The parameters for UFMC were subsequently adapted to have a similar comparison base. This involved setting the number of effective subcarriers to N 256, employing 21 sub-bands, each containing 12 subcarriers, and using a Chebyshev filter length (L) of 19, approximately twice the size of the guard interval (GI). To calculate the bit error rate (BER),

10,000 symbols were generated, leading to the results.

3. Results

3.1. General Observations

The first step was to validate if the Hermitian symmetry and the juxtaposition methods are comparable in terms of performance. As only OFDM is able to perform both techniques, Figure 10 represents the result for OFDM with a simple back to back communication. As expected, both techniques behave the same way, and the juxtaposition method can indeed replace the Hermitian symmetry.

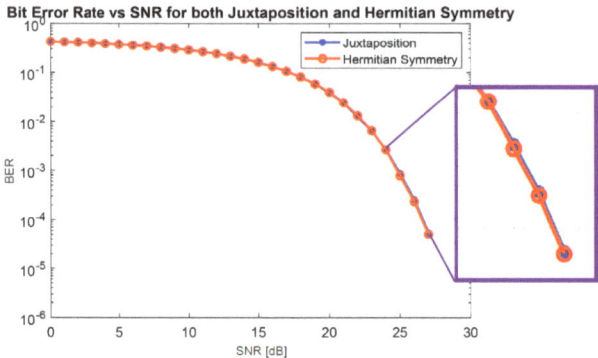

Figure 10. The use of juxtaposition or Hermitian Symmetry for OFDM.

Even though the use of a constant bias is a necessity to have a real and positive valued signal on the LED for both OFDM and UFMC, it is, however, an extra source of power consumed. Figure 11 shows a UFMC communication taking place with a direct current (DC) bias of 0.5 and without a DC bias with BPSK modulation per subcarrier. A bias of 0.5 normalized unit is chosen, as the UFMC waveform is generated in a normalized way in the simulator. Thus, adding 0.5 on all the values necessarily makes the signal positive.

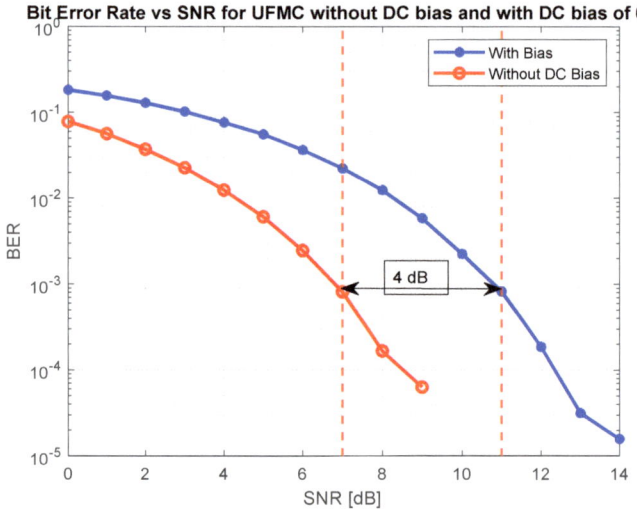

Figure 11. Comparison between UFMC/BPSK modulations with or without DC Bias.

It can be seen that there is a shift between the two curves, introducing a penalty of approximately 4 dB in SNR for the use of the bias. The advantage with VLC is that this extra power is not wasted but essential for the room to be lit. On the other hand, when infrared lighting devices are used, the question sometimes arises as to the relevance of Li-Fi in infrared, as this extra DC bias is not used to light the room and could be considered wasted power. However, there are other methods of making a signal positive in OFDM, from clip-OFDM, which uses only the odd carrier, to other more sophisticated forms [31]. To the best of our knowledge, these have not yet been explored in the scientific literature for UFMC. In terms of computational complexity, as UFMC requires more computational steps compared to OFDM due to the filtering stages, a physical implementation of a UFMC communication on an electronic board would consume more power than OFDM. Indeed, the power consumed by programming boards is proportional to the number of computations it is required to do. Furthermore, it is easy to understand that the use of optical OFDM or UFMC is less spectrally efficient due to the Hermitian symmetry condition or the juxtaposition of real and imaginary data. Indeed, both techniques require at least twice the resources to send the desired information compared to the RF version. Nevertheless, VLC still is interesting where RF cannot reach.

3.2. Comparison of OFDM and UFMC

The parameters for OFDM are derived from the G.9991 standard, utilizing 256 subcarriers. To ensure a consistent basis for comparison, the parameters for UFMC were then adjusted. This adjustment includes the use of 256 effective subcarriers, organized into 24 sub-bands, each containing 12 subcarriers, with a filter length (L) of 19.

A set of 10,000 symbols was generated to produce the results presented in Figure 12. The DC bias is set to 0.5, and the graph illustrates the trends for DC-OFDM and DC-UFMC in terms of BER as a function of SNR.

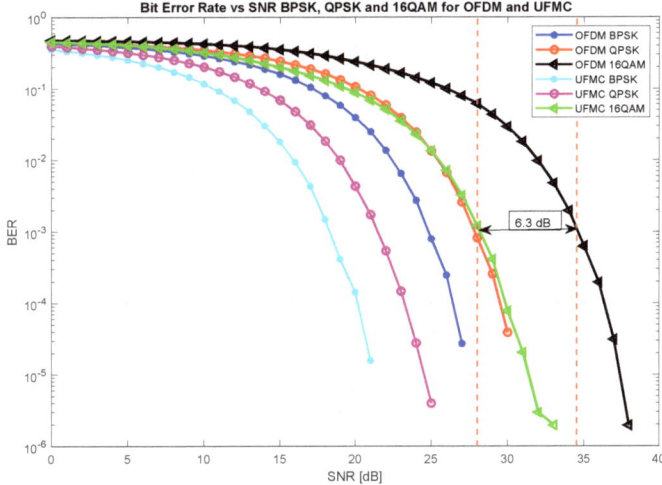

Figure 12. UFMC and OFDM performance for different constellation sizes with a DC bias of 0.5.

It can be observed that in general, the UFMC performs better than the OFDM. The difference between the QPSK and 16-QAM for both modulation techniques is the same and is approximately 6 dB of penalty. The observed 6 dB enhancement in UFMC, attributed to its superior spectral efficiency compared to OFDM, may effectively offset the 4 dB loss incurred due to the introduced DC bias. This means that UFMC needs 6 dB of power less than OFDM to achieve the same performance. Furthermore, as we saw the necessity of the 4 dB additional power to make the signal real-valued, this 6 dB gain makes UFMC more energy efficient than its OFDM counterpart. Consequently, the implementation of DC-UFMC demonstrates a significantly improved performance compared to DC-OFDM.

Due to the analytical computation of the relative spectral efficiency gain between OFDM and UFMC, its result highlights a gain of 16% when the UFMC is used instead of OFDM. To compute this value, the results of the following work were used [33]. The spectral efficiency of UFMC compared to OFDM is defined in Equation (2).

$$P_{OFDM-UFMC} = 100 \left(1 - \frac{M_{OFDM}}{M_{UFMC} + (N_{FFT} GI)}\right) \quad (2)$$

where M_{OFDM} is the number of effective subcarriers, M_{UFMC} is the effective number of UFMC subcarriers, N_{FFT} is the total number of subcarriers, and GI is the number of subcarriers used as GI. The effective number of subcarriers refers to those used to carry the data. In terms of complexity, the filtering stage in UFMC is more constitutionally intensive than OFDM. Further studies should be carried on to quantify it, but the most important fact is laid down. Nevertheless, some studies have been carried out to make UFMC's level of complexity the same as OFDM. For example, lightweight IFFT can be introduced in the UFMC transmitter, combining both finite impulse response (FIR) or CIR in our work, and the poly-phase filter structure could be the way to reduce the computational complexity of the transmitter [34]. This is an interesting perspective to further prove that UFMC can improve the performance significantly.

These promising results increase the relevance of UFMC-VLC for 6G application. The efficient spectrum usage of UFMC allows more devices to connect simultaneously without interference. It also enables faster and more reliable data transmission to the end-user or IoT application. This translates to quicker response times for smart city services such as traffic management, emergency response systems, V2V communications, etc. On the end-user point of view, this means seamless connectivity, whether they are accessing smart city services through smartphones, IoT devices, or other gadgets. Furthermore, the utilization of the existing infrastructure such as LED streetlights for data transmission makes VLC a sustainable and energy-efficient solution for smart cities. By utilizing VLC for communication purposes, cities can reduce energy consumption while simultaneously providing connectivity to residents and visitors.

4. Conclusions

In conclusion, the relevance of visible light communication (VLC) in the 6G era is underlined by its application versatility in various scenarios. From facilitating communication between vehicles in smart cities to enabling connectivity in outdoor spaces, VLC proves instrumental in addressing the evolving communication landscape. This paper aims to contribute to the understanding and optimization of VLC systems through the introduction of open-source tools. These tools assess the optical power distribution, allowing researchers to configure scenarios by specifying parameters like space size, wall presence, and reflective properties. The methodology incorporates realistic LED radiation patterns, enhancing scenario precision, visualization of 3D-curves, and evaluating power loss. The second part delves into multi carrier modulation schemes, OFDM and UFMC. The adaptations for UFMC in VLC are explored, revealing a superior performance compared to OFDM. The computed relative spectral efficiency gain demonstrates a 16% improvement with UFMC to be balanced by the increased computational complexity, particularly the filtering stage, that still has to be studied. On a practical note, the paper reflects the relevance of VLC in the 6G communication technologies landscape, as well as the integration of UFMC.

Author Contributions: Conceptualization, V.G., M.D. and V.M.; data curation, V.G. and A.-C.H.; formal analysis, V.G. and A.-C.H.; funding acquisition, V.M.; investigation, V.G. and A.-C.H.; methodology, V.G., A.-C.H. and V.M.; project administration, M.D. and V.M.; resources, V.G.; software, V.G. and A.-C.H.; supervision, M.D. and V.M.; validation, V.G.; visualization, V.G. and A.-C.H.; writing—original draft, V.G.; writing—review and editing, V.G., M.D. and V.M. All authors have read and agreed to the published version of the manuscript.

Funding: This research was funded by the project Wal-e-Cities, a research project supported by the European Regional Development Fund (ERDF) of the European Union and also BEL6GICA (https://www.6G.be accessed on 19 March 2024) is supported by FOD 'Economie, K.M.O., Middenstand en Energie' of Belgium and "The APC was funded by BEL6GICA".

Data Availability Statement: All the codes can be found at: https://github.com/veroniquegeorlette/VLC_channel_modeling_python (accessed on 19 March 2024).

Conflicts of Interest: The authors declare no conflicts of interest. The funders had no role in the design of the study; in the collection, analyses, or interpretation of data; in the writing of the manuscript; or in the decision to publish the results.

References

1. Banafaa, M.; Shayea, I.; Din, J.; Azmi, M.H.; Alashbi, A.; Daradkeh, Y.I.; Alhammadi, A. 6G mobile communication technology: Requirements, targets, applications, challenges, advantages, and opportunities. *Alex. Eng. J.* **2023**, *64*, 245–274. [CrossRef]
2. Shen, L.H.; Feng, K.T.; Hanzo, L. Five facets of 6G: Research challenges and opportunities. *ACM Comput. Surv.* **2023**, *55*, 1–39. [CrossRef]
3. Wang, C.X.; You, X.; Gao, X.; Zhu, X.; Li, Z.; Zhang, C.; Wang, H.; Huang, Y.; Chen, Y.; Haas, H.; et al. On the road to 6G: Visions, requirements, key technologies and testbeds. *IEEE Commun. Surv. Tutor.* **2023**, *25*, 905–974. [CrossRef]
4. Rommel, S.; Raddo, T.R.; Monroy, I.T. Data center connectivity by 6G wireless systems. In Proceedings of the 2018 Photonics in Switching and Computing (PSC), Limassol, Cyprus, 19–21 September 2018; pp. 1–3.
5. Chi, N.; Zhou, Y.; Wei, Y.; Hu, F. Visible light communication in 6G: Advances, challenges, and prospects. *IEEE Veh. Technol. Mag.* **2020**, *15*, 93–102. [CrossRef]
6. Chowdhury, M.Z.; Shahjalal, M.; Hasan, M.K.; Jang, Y.M. The role of optical wireless communication technologies in 5G/6G and IoT solutions: Prospects, directions, and challenges. *Appl. Sci.* **2019**, *9*, 4367. [CrossRef]
7. Pei, J.; Li, S.; Yu, Z.; Ho, L.; Liu, W.; Wang, L. Federated Learning Encounters 6G Wireless Communication in the Scenario of Internet of Things. *IEEE Commun. Stand. Mag.* **2023**, *7*, 94–100. [CrossRef]
8. Noor-A-Rahim, M.; Liu, Z.; Lee, H.; Khyam, M.O.; He, J.; Pesch, D.; Moessner, K.; Saad, W.; Poor, H.V. 6G for vehicle-to-everything (V2X) communications: Enabling technologies, challenges, and opportunities. *Proc. IEEE* **2022**, *110*, 712–734. [CrossRef]
9. Arfaoui, M.A.; Soltani, M.D.; Tavakkolnia, I.; Ghrayeb, A.; Assi, C.M.; Safari, M.; Haas, H. Measurements-based channel models for indoor LiFi systems. *IEEE Trans. Wirel. Commun.* **2020**, *20*, 827–842. [CrossRef]
10. Mishra, P.; Singh, G. 6G-IoT Framework for Sustainable Smart City: Vision and Challenges. In *Sustainable Smart Cities: Enabling Technologies, Energy Trends and Potential Applications*; Springer: Berlin/Heidelberg, Germany, 2023; pp. 97–117.
11. Almadani, Y.; Plets, D.; Bastiaens, S.; Joseph, W.; Ijaz, M.; Ghassemlooy, Z.; Rajbhandari, S. Visible light communications for industrial applications—Challenges and potentials. *Electronics* **2020**, *9*, 2157. [CrossRef]
12. Singh, H.; Miglani, R.; Mittal, N.; Singh, H.; Kaur, J.; Gupta, A. Development of a cost-effective optical network based on free space optical (FSO) and optical fiber links for enabling smart city infrastructure: A hybrid approach. *Opt. Fiber Technol.* **2023**, *81*, 103544. [CrossRef]
13. Elamassie, M.; Uysal, M. Free Space Optical Communication: An Enabling Backhaul Technology for 6G Non-Terrestrial Networks. *Photonics* **2023**, *10*, 1210. [CrossRef]
14. Kumar, S.; Sharma, N. Emerging Military Applications of Free Space Optical Communication Technology: A Detailed Review. In Proceedings of the Journal of Physics: Conference Series, Manipal, India, 28–30 October 2021; Volume 2161, p. 012011.
15. Kharche, S.; Kharche, J. 6G Intelligent Healthcare Framework: A Review on Role of Technologies, Challenges and Future Directions. *J. Mob. Multimed.* **2023**, *19*, 603–644. [CrossRef]
16. Majlesein, B.; Geldard, C.T.; Guerra, V.; Rufo, J.; Popoola, W.O.; Rabadan, J. Empirical study of an underwater optical camera communication system under turbulent conditions. *Opt. Express* **2023**, *31*, 21493–21506. [CrossRef] [PubMed]
17. Liu, Q.; Kai, G. An effective preamble-based CFO synchronization for UFMC systems. In Proceedings of the 2018 10th International Conference on Communications, Circuits and Systems (ICCCAS), Chengdu, China, 22–24 December 2018; pp. 484–488.
18. D'Andrea, C.; Buzzi, S.; Fresia, M.; Wu, X. Doppler-resilient universal filtered multicarrier (dr-ufmc): A beyond-otfs modulation. In Proceedings of the 2023 Joint European Conference on Networks and Communications & 6G Summit (EuCNC/6G Summit), Gothenburg, Sweden, 6–9 June 2023; pp. 150–155.
19. Adoum, B.A.; Zoukalne, K.; Idriss, M.S.; Ali, A.M.; Moungache, A.; Khayal, M.Y. A comprehensive survey of candidate waveforms for 5G, beyond 5G and 6G wireless communication systems. *Open J. Appl. Sci.* **2023**, *13*, 136–161. [CrossRef]

20. Amakawa, S.; Aslam, Z.; Buckwater, J.; Caputo, S.; Chaoub, A.; Chen, Y.; Corre, Y.; Fujishima, M.; Ganghua, Y.; Gao, S.; et al. White Paper on RF Enabling 6G—Opportunities and Challenges from Technology to Spectrum. 2021. Available online: https://biblio.ugent.be/publication/8704523 (accessed on 19 March 2024).
21. Georlette, V.; Bette, S.; Brohez, S.; Pérez-Jiménez, R.; Point, N.; Moeyaert, V. Outdoor visible light communication channel modeling under smoke conditions and analogy with fog conditions. *Optics* **2020**, *1*, 259–281. [CrossRef]
22. Raj, R.; Jaiswal, S.; Dixit, A. On the effect of multipath reflections in indoor visible light communication links: Channel characterization and BER analysis. *IEEE Access* **2020**, *8*, 190620–190636. [CrossRef]
23. Moreno, I.; Sun, C.C. Modeling the radiation pattern of LEDs. *Opt. Express* **2008**, *16*, 1808–1819. [CrossRef]
24. Bhalerao, M.V.; Sumathi, M.; Sonavane, S. Line of sight model for visible light communication using Lambertian radiation pattern of LED. *Int. J. Commun. Syst.* **2017**, *30*, e3250. [CrossRef]
25. Memedi, A.; Tsai, H.M.; Dressler, F. Impact of realistic light radiation pattern on vehicular visible light communication. In Proceedings of the GLOBECOM 2017–2017 IEEE Global Communications Conference, Singapore, 4–8 December 2017; pp. 1–6.
26. NIKKON Lighting Datasheet 45W LED STREET LANTERN MURA S NIKKON (3000K). 2024. Available online: https://luminaires.dialux.com/fr/article/Z4uKfIZtRYKEYL-xqyHFNQ (accessed on 22 March 2024).
27. Ghassemlooy, Z.; Popoola, W.; Rajbhandari, S. Optical Sources and Detectors. In *Optical Wireless Communications: System and Channel Modelling with MATLAB*; Springer Series in Optical Sciences; Springer: Berlin/Heidelberg, Germany, 2019; Chapter 2.2, pp. 39–52.
28. Georlette, V. VLC Channel Modeling in Python. Version 1. 2023. Available online: https://doi.org/10.5281/zenodo.8154407 (accessed on 19 March 2024).
29. IES Library IES Library. Make Better Render with Real-World-Lighting. 2023. Available online: https://ieslibrary.com/ (accessed on 19 March 2024).
30. ITU-T Telecommunication Standardization Sector of ITU. G.9991: High Speed Indoor Visible Light Communication Transceiver—System Architecture, Physical Layer and Data Link Layer Specification. 2019. Available online: https://www.itu.int/rec/T-REC-G.9991/en (accessed on 19 March 2024).
31. Zhang, X.; Babar, Z.; Petropoulos, P.; Haas, H.; Hanzo, L. The evolution of optical OFDM. *IEEE Commun. Surv. Tutor.* **2021**, *23*, 1430–1457. [CrossRef]
32. Chintala, V.D.; Sundru, A. Hermitian symmetry free direct current optical-universal filtered multicarrier with companding techniques for intensity modulation/direct detection systems. *Opt. Eng.* **2020**, *59*, 096104.
33. Honfoga, A.C.; Dossou, M.; Moeyaert, V. Performance comparison of new waveforms applied to DVB-T2 transmissions. In Proceedings of the 2020 IEEE International Symposium on Broadband Multimedia Systems and Broadcasting (BMSB), Paris, France, 27–29 October 2020; pp. 1–6.
34. Guo, Z.; Liu, Q.; Zhang, W.; Wang, S. Low complexity implementation of universal filtered multi-carrier transmitter. *IEEE Access* **2020**, *8*, 24799–24807. [CrossRef]

Disclaimer/Publisher's Note: The statements, opinions and data contained in all publications are solely those of the individual author(s) and contributor(s) and not of MDPI and/or the editor(s). MDPI and/or the editor(s) disclaim responsibility for any injury to people or property resulting from any ideas, methods, instructions or products referred to in the content.

Article

Microservice-Based Vehicular Network for Seamless and Ultra-Reliable Communications of Connected Vehicles

Mira M. Zarie [1,2], Abdelhamied A. Ateya [1,3,*], Mohammed S. Sayed [1,4], Mohammed ElAffendi [3] and Mohammad Mahmoud Abdellatif [1,2]

1. Department of Electronics and Communications Engineering, Zagazig University, Zagazig 44519, Egypt; mira.mohsen@bue.edu.eg (M.M.Z.); mohammed.sayed@ejust.edu.eg (M.S.S.); mohammad.abdellatif@bue.edu.eg (M.M.A.)
2. Department of Electrical Engineering, Faculty of Engineering, The British University in Egypt, Cairo 11837, Egypt
3. EIAS Data Science Lab, College of Computer and Information Sciences, Prince Sultan University, Riyadh 11586, Saudi Arabia; affendi@psu.edu.sa
4. Department of Electronics and Communication Engineering, Egypt-Japan University of Science and Technology, Alexandria 21934, Egypt
* Correspondence: aateya@psu.edu.sa

Abstract: The fifth-generation (5G) cellular infrastructure is expected to bring about the widespread use of connected vehicles. This technological progress marks the beginning of a new era in vehicular networks, which includes a range of different types and services of self-driving cars and the smooth sharing of information between vehicles. Connected vehicles have also been announced as a main use case of the sixth-generation (6G) cellular, with ultimate requirements beyond the 5G (B5G) and 6G eras. These networks require full coverage, extremely high reliability and availability, very low latency, and significant system adaptability. The significant specifications set for vehicular networks pose considerable design and development challenges. The goals of establishing a latency of 1 millisecond, effectively handling large amounts of data traffic, and facilitating high-speed mobility are of utmost importance. To address these difficulties and meet the demands of upcoming networks, e.g., 6G, it is necessary to improve the performance of vehicle networks by incorporating innovative technology into existing network structures. This work presents significant enhancements to vehicular networks to fulfill the demanding specifications by utilizing state-of-the-art technologies, including distributed edge computing, e.g., mobile edge computing (MEC) and fog computing, software-defined networking (SDN), and microservice. The work provides a novel vehicular network structure based on micro-services architecture that meets the requirements of 6G networks. The required offloading scheme is introduced, and a handover algorithm is presented to provide seamless communication over the network. Moreover, a migration scheme for migrating data between edge servers was developed. The work was evaluated in terms of latency, availability, and reliability. The results outperformed existing traditional approaches, demonstrating the potential of our approach to meet the demanding requirements of next-generation vehicular networks.

Keywords: distributed edge computing; software-defined networks; VANETs; 5G; fog computing; microservices

Citation: Zarie, M.M.; Ateya, A.A.; Sayed, M.S.; ElAffendi, M.; Abdellatif, M.M. Microservice-Based Vehicular Network for Seamless and Ultra-Reliable Communications of Connected Vehicles. *Future Internet* 2024, *16*, 257. https://doi.org/10.3390/fi16070257

Academic Editors: Alessandro Raschellà and Michael Mackay

Received: 24 June 2024
Revised: 10 July 2024
Accepted: 15 July 2024
Published: 19 July 2024

Copyright: © 2024 by the authors. Licensee MDPI, Basel, Switzerland. This article is an open access article distributed under the terms and conditions of the Creative Commons Attribution (CC BY) license (https://creativecommons.org/licenses/by/4.0/).

1. Introduction

With the evolution of wireless devices, the Internet and communication systems have evolved rapidly. Thus, next-generation networks (NGN), including sixth-generation (6G) networks, are expected to support novel applications and meet new requirements [1]. The vehicular network is a highly promising network that is expected to provide reliable communication infrastructure for vehicles. The introduction of the fifth-generation (5G) technology brings innovative solutions for vehicular communications, with significant consequences for the transportation sector [2]. Connected vehicles, which serve as the foundation for intelligent transportation systems, are one of the most prominent applications of 5G technology and are expected to be a main part of the 6G networks. The upcoming 6G networks are expected to support ultra-high mobility; thus, enabling vehicular communication with the announced requirements of such networks is a big demand. This new paradigm, i.e., vehicular networks, includes a wide range of services to enable autonomous vehicles and facilitate data interchange between vehicles, infrastructure, and the cloud. Such systems promise increased safety, improved traffic management, and a better driving experience [3].

Forced by the recent advances in vehicles and embedded smart tools including wireless sensors, onboard computers, global positioning system (GPS), antenna, radar, and data storage solutions, vehicular networks have attracted academics and industry. Nowadays, the evolution of vehicles is to convert the traditional vehicles that supply basic services to smart vehicles that provide advanced services, achieving higher road safety and an easier life. VANT is a mobile ad hoc network (MANT) where vehicles act as mobile nodes or routers. This aims to acquire two types of communication: immediate communication between vehicles (V2V) and vehicle-to-everything (V2X), which provides communication between vehicles, roadside fixed infrastructure, and other network parts [4]. In VANT, each vehicle contains an onboard unit (OBU) that contains the radio transceiver to enable communication between vehicles and roadside units (RSUs).

According to the International Telecommunication Union (ITU), vehicular networks in the 6G (IMT2030) era must provide full coverage, ultra-high reliability, availability, ultra-low delay, and significant system flexibility. Specifically, delivering end-to-end latency as low as 1 millisecond, managing huge data flow, and supporting high-to-ultra-high mobility are significant problems that must be overcome [5,6]. Ultra-low latency communication (uRLLC) is required for numerous VANET scenarios and applications, including autonomous/safe driving. It is critical to think beyond the traditional structures of automotive networks to achieve these requirements [6]. Modern innovative technologies, including distributed edge computing, microservices, and software-defined networking (SDN), can greatly improve network performance. SDN provides a programmable network management architecture that improves flexibility and resource efficiency [7].

Distributed edge computing enables more efficient data processing and dissemination, improving the overall user experience in VANETs. It can speed up local data analytics and decision-making processes, allowing vehicles to respond instantly to changing conditions and events. In two ways, distributed edge computing can be deployed for vehicular networks: mobile edge computing (MEC) and fog computing [8]. Furthermore, MEC and fog enable offloading computationally intensive activities from vehicles, which frequently have limited processing capacity and energy resources. This offloading feature saves vehicle resources and ensures that programs that require a lot of computational power may still run smoothly and consistently [9].

MEC has arisen, providing cloud functionality at the edges of wireless networks. MEC significantly improves vehicular network performance by moving computational resources closer to the data source. This advancement allows vehicles to offload computationally heavy tasks to MEC servers with low latency. In the context of vehicular networks, MEC entails placing small-scale data centers or servers in important areas, such as base stations or RSUs, to execute functions that would normally need connection with a distant central cloud. This proximity dramatically reduces end-to-end latency, which is critical for real-time applications, including self-driving cars, collision avoidance, and high-definition mapping [10]. However, the complicated network environment and vehicles' intrinsic mobility pose issues typical offloading solutions frequently fail to meet.

Fog computing extends cloud computing to the network edge, distributing data processing instead of centralization. Fog computing in vehicular networks uses roadside equipment, traffic signals, and automobiles to process data closer to where it is created. This distributed strategy minimizes latency and boosts network resiliency [8]. Fog computing aids traffic management, smart parking, emergency response, and environmental monitoring in automotive networks. It provides instant insights and reactions for time-sensitive applications by processing data locally. Fog computing's distributed nature makes vehicular networks more scalable, allowing them to handle the large data flow from linked vehicles and smart infrastructure. It lessens the load on centralized data centers, improving network efficiency and sustainability [11].

SDN is a networking framework that isolates the control and data planes, allowing for programmable administration. SDN allows VANETs to be more adaptable and dynamic, which is necessary for controlling vehicular networks' mobility. It allows network administrators to apply policies, optimize traffic flow, and improve security through a centralized controller monitoring the entire network. Furthermore, SDN centralizes control to optimize routing patterns and manage network resources, decreasing congestion and improving network performance. SDN's programmability rapidly adapts to changing network conditions, which is essential for dependable communication in dynamic vehicle contexts. This adaptability helps advanced applications, including real-time traffic management, emergency vehicle prioritization, and adaptive streaming [12].

Microservice in VANET is a promising software design and implementation approach that offers many benefits. Microservices facilitate dividing intricate applications into more manageable, autonomous, and independently implemented and expanded parts. It provides higher flexibility, modularity, and scalability in designing and implementing VANET applications [13]. Microservices can also improve fault tolerance, reliability, performance, and efficiency. Additionally, microservices enable greater flexibility and modularity in designing and implementing VANET applications, allowing for easier customization to meet the specific needs of different use cases and environments. As VANET systems become more complex and diverse, microservices will become increasingly important for successfully deploying and operating VANET applications. Microservices offer a promising approach to developing VANET systems that can improve reliability, efficiency, and flexibility [14].

The handover and migration processes are critical operations in VANET that enable seamless communication between network infrastructure. The handover process is challenging due to high vehicle mobility, network topology changes, and maintaining service continuity during handovers. Effective handover and migration mechanisms are essential for reducing service disruption and improving the reliability and performance of VANET applications [15]. The migration process is also important for integrating different network technologies and architectures, enabling efficient resource utilization, and reducing service disruption during handovers [16]. Microservices can simplify the handover and migration process by decomposing applications into smaller, autonomous, separately scalable components.

This work addresses the challenges posed by the ultimate requirements of 6G networks to enable vehicular communications with ultra-high vehicle mobility. The work presents an architecture for vehicular networks using a microservices-based approach. This design addresses latency and reliability concerns, ensuring seamless communication and effective data management. The key contributions of this work include the following:

1. Developing a reliable vehicular network architecture based on the distributed edge computing paradigm. The proposed structure deploys edge computing in two linked levels: MEC and fog;
2. Proposing a novel microservice approach for vehicular applications that considers task prioritizing. The proposed algorithm allows for greater flexibility, modularity, and scalability in designing and implementing VANET applications;
3. Implementing an efficient offloading approach for the proposed VANET based on the proposed microservice algorithm. It is difficult to control the energy usage and system delay during the vehicle's movement and quick change in the channels and bandwidth in wireless communication systems. With the assistance of RSU, the MEC server helps vehicles offload the computing tasks to MEC linked to the cellular base

station. The offloading scheme effectively manages computational tasks between vehicles and edge servers, reducing latency and improving system energy efficiency;
4. Implementing a seamless handover approach to maintain seamless communication as vehicles move across different network coverage zones, ensuring uninterrupted service;
5. Developing an efficient migration scheme for efficient data transfer between edge servers, ensuring data availability and consistency across the network. The proposed migration approach uses the proposed microservice algorithm to facilitate task migration between edge servers;
6. Assessing the performance of the introduced microservice-based VANET regarding latency, availability, and reliability. Heterogeneous real-based simulation scenarios were considered for evaluating the proposed network and approaches.

2. Related Works

With the recent improvements in throughput and latency, cellular networks still face many failures and cannot provide the required reliable infrastructure for vehicular applications. This made the mobile network operators work hard to build a network that can be recovered automatically. Many proposed studies and solutions have been developed to enable VANET and its applications. This section summarizes the most related studies to our proposed VANET.

In [17], the authors provided a case study of independent vehicles that are foreseeable and trendy ways for vehicle expansion for the coming era. This type of vehicle requires uRLLC and the 5G cellular network among independent vehicles and its network infrastructure. The uRLLC supports the slicing solution for the network services and function for the vehicle network that is also offered by the 5G network for independent vehicles. This was all proven by a case study simulation, which proved that the slicing solution helps to develop the latency and reliability of the network system and ensures that uRLLC works well for vehicular network applications. Fakhar Abbas et al. [18] investigated the links among the VANETs affected by the high vehicle speed that causes quick breaks in these links. The authors proposed a new cluster-based routing scheme, i.e., an ad hoc multipath approach, that ensures the selection of maximum reliability links. Moreover, the authors optimized the proposed model using an ant colony optimizer (ACO). The ACO works to identify the best route path for the vehicles between the vehicle's links for VANETs represented in four quality of service (QoS) metrics, including reliability, end-to-end latency, throughput, and energy.

Ana Gómez-Andrades et al. [19] developed an automatic system diagnosis depending on self-organized maps (SOM) and Ward's hierarchical method. This helps in making the vehicular network more reliable and less costly. This system was tested using real LTE data to resolve its execution and match it with reference mechanisms. Andrei Vladyko et al. [20] presented a VANET system based on MEC that addresses the issues of high traffic density in automotive networks. The system provides an effective offloading method for vehicle traffic, considerably lowering the latency of data connection between vehicles and stationary RSUs. To assess the effectiveness of the developed VANET, the system was subjected to thorough simulation in a reliable setting. Furthermore, the system was experimentally tested, and the examinations verified that the system could effectively handle a large volume of traffic, minimize delays in communication, and offer a dependable solution for offloading in-vehicle networks.

The SDN-enabled vehicular network (SDN/VANET) provides full, real-time network management and monitoring. Yet, relying on a central control unit presents considerable obstacles, such as bottlenecks and controller failure. The distribution of the control scheme is a realistic option that poses important considerations regarding the deployment and the number of needed controllers. To address these problems, Azzedine Boukerche et al. [21] introduced an adaptive controller management technique for SDN/VANET. This technique used vehicle mobility density and delays to inform decision making. The authors used a split-and-merge clustering strategy that dynamically modifies the distribution of control units based on real-time network conditions. The proposed clustering solution's performance was tested with genuine mobility traces. The results showed that the suggested approach greatly decreases energy consumption, lowers latency, and balances network strain. These findings demonstrated the effectiveness of the developed adaptive controller management technique for improving the overall efficiency and performance of next-generation vehicular networks.

Furthermore, Noura Aljeri et al. [22] suggested an effective proactive controller deployment and assignment technique for 5G SDN/VANET. This technique uses predicted vehicle traffic flow and latency data to dynamically optimize controller location and assignment. The proposed solution took a proactive approach, anticipating changes in traffic patterns and network circumstances and adjusting controller placement and allocation accordingly. This is critical for sustaining low latency and balanced load distribution in the fast-changing environment of vehicle networks. The authors ran a performance study to validate the technique across various mobility scenarios indicative of real-world vehicular networks. They evaluated the developed system's performance regarding delay and controller load. The study compared the proactive clustering strategy to conventional and contemporary controller placement strategies. The developed solution beat previous strategies by preemptively adjusting to traffic flow estimates, reducing end-user latency, and preventing controller overload. This proactive strategy successfully manages vehicular networks' dynamic and heterogeneous character, resulting in consistent and reliable network performance.

Penglin Dai et al. [23] investigated a scenario for compute offloading in a MEC-assisted architecture, concentrating on three critical aspects: job upload coordination across many vehicles, task migration, and servers' heterogeneous processing capabilities. The authors created a cooperative computation offloading (CCO) problem and solved it using the probabilistic computation offloading (PCO) approach. This approach lets MEC servers schedule live tasks independently. The PCO approach changes the objective function into an augmented Lagrangian form before iteratively achieving the optimal solution utilizing a convex optimization framework. Furthermore, the authors created an extensive simulation, and the results confirmed the PCO's superiority across various scenarios, emphasizing its effectiveness in minimizing job completion delays and optimizing resource utilization in MEC-assisted vehicle networks.

Haixia Peng et al. [24] investigated multidimensional resource management in VANETs powered by MEC and unmanned aerial vehicles (UAVs). The authors aimed to optimize the spectrum, computation, and cache resources available at MEC-mounted base stations and UAVs. To achieve this, they formulated a resource optimization problem to be solved by a central controller. Given the lengthy time necessary to solve the optimization problem and the tight delay constraints of automotive applications, the authors employed reinforcement learning techniques. They created a solution using the deep deterministic policy gradient (DDPG) algorithm. The simulation findings showed that the technique outperformed random resource management, resulting in higher QoS satisfaction.

Ammar Muthanna et al. [25] presented an integrated architecture that addresses the issues of traffic density and network coverage in VANET. This design combines MEC and SDN technologies to improve network reliability and scalability, particularly in high-traffic environments. To boost network coverage, the authors used a device-to-device (D2D) clustering mechanism that connects orphan nodes, i.e., vehicles disconnected from the network. This clustering strategy ensures that even the most difficult network nodes remain connected, increasing coverage and reliability. The suggested architecture enables ultra-low latency applications since it provides a stable and adaptable framework. The architecture's performance improved significantly when tested under realistic settings and network scenarios. Specifically, the MEC/SDN-enabled vehicular network architecture reduced task blockage rates by up to 74% compared to the baseline implementation. These findings demonstrate the efficiency of the suggested method in controlling high traffic densities while maintaining consistent network coverage.

The complexity of VANET's environment and vehicles' intrinsic mobility pose issues typical offloading solutions frequently fail to meet. Bingxue Qiao et al. [26] suggested the heuristic task migration computation offloading (TMCO) scheme to address these challenges. Unlike old approaches, TMCO dynamically identifies the best spots for unloading jobs from moving vehicles, ensuring that activities are performed within tight timeframes. This approach considered both vehicle mobility and strict delay requirements. In this technique, a hash table was used to track the number of tasks given to each server, while a random function mimics the likelihood of job offloading. According to experimental results, the TMCO scheme outperformed standard full-offloading systems in latency by 10% on average. The reliability, availability, and security of exchanged data are among the numerous challenges of vehicular networks. Andrei Vladyko et al. [27] resolved the scientific challenge of creating a vehicle network structure that guarantees secure and correct data transmission in the V2X. They aimed to improve the safety of people using the roads by utilizing blockchain technology and MEC. The authors implemented an offloading model to manage traffic dispatching to the MEC efficiently. The system and the implemented subsystems and algorithms were evaluated in a dependable simulation environment across several scenarios. The simulations' results proved the system's efficiency.

Nirmin Monir et al. [28] developed a seamless handover mechanism for MEC-based V2X systems. The suggested approach successfully handles the handover as vehicles travel between adjacent RSUs on multilane bidirectional roadways. The system was implemented with MECs linked to the RSUs, considerably reducing installation time and speeding up the handover procedure. The MEC platform uses a MEC controller, which runs under the control scheme of an SDN controller in charge of network management. The implementation of the SDN paradigm ensures a smooth handover process. The MEC controller speeds up the handover process, increasing overall efficiency. The evaluation results confirmed the effectiveness and efficiency of the suggested plan.

Noura Aljeri et al. [29] offered a new methodology for estimating connectivity time in autonomous vehicular networks. The authors investigated the most accurate way to estimate the communication lifetime between automobiles and infrastructure units by using a variety of machine learning algorithms. They based their assessments on realistic mobility traces from the Cologne city dataset to ensure practical relevance and applicability. This dataset contains detailed and authentic vehicle movement patterns required for creating and testing the predictive algorithm in real-world scenarios. The suggested model combined a variety of machine learning methodologies, and each technique was tested for its accuracy and dependability in forecasting connectivity duration. The model considered various parameters influencing connectivity length, including vehicle speed, density, and traffic circumstances. Simulations and experiments demonstrated the efficiency of the proposed paradigm. The approach improved communication reliability in autonomous vehicle networks by precisely forecasting connectivity length, allowing for smoother and more efficient interactions between vehicles and infrastructure. Table 1 summarizes the features of the previously introduced related studies and compares these works with the proposed work to provide the novelty of the work.

Overall, 5G high-availability testing is an important step in ensuring that next-generation wireless networks satisfy the demanding needs of modern applications. This evaluation is based on robust modeling stages that include advanced mathematical frameworks [30]. Table 2 presents some of the most common methodologies that are particularly useful in addressing performance and availability challenges in designing 5G infrastructures. SRNs and MUGFs have been widely employed in the literature to simulate and examine the robustness of telecommunication networks, specifically those related to 5G technology. These approaches allow researchers to accurately measure the likelihood of network failures and understand how they affect the overall availability of the system. For instance, SRNs can represent different states of network components and the changes between these states caused by failures and repairs. MUGFs, on the other hand, enable the combination of many performance measures into a unified analytical framework, making it easier to conduct a thorough assessment of network reliability [31,32].

G/G/m queuing models are commonly employed in analyzing 5G architectures for performance evaluation, specifically in assessing latency. These models aid in comprehending the behavior of network traffic as it moves through different nodes, each with its unique service characteristics. The versatility of G/G/m models in supporting various arrival and service time distributions makes them well suited for representing the diverse and ever-changing nature of 5G traffic patterns. Research has demonstrated that the utilization of G/G/m models can offer valuable insights into identifying performance limitations and aid in devising strategies to reduce latency and enhance overall network performance [33].

Table 1. Main features of the existing related works.

Ref.	Key Technology					Handover	Migration	Evaluation	Metrics	Application
	Fog	MEC	SDN	AI/ML	Microservices					
[17]	x	√	x	x	x	x	x	Simulation	• Latency • Reliability • Accuracy	uRLLC
[18]	x	x	x	x	x	x	x	Simulation	• End-to-end latency • Reliability • Throughput • Energy consumption	General
[19]	√	√	x	√	x	x	x	Simulation/ Experimental	• False positive rate • False negative rate • Diagnosis error rate	Automatic diagnosis
[20]	√	√	x	x	x	x	x	Simulation	• Latency • Reliability • Availability • Network Security • Energy consumption	General
[34]	x	x	√	x	x	x	x	Simulation	• Delay • Reliability	General
[35]	x	x	√	x	x	x	x	Simulation	• Availability • Security	5G-enabled vehicular apps
[21]	x	x	√	x	x	x	x	Simulation	• Energy consumption • Latency • Load on network entities	General
[22]	x	x	√	x	x	x	x	Simulation	• Latency • Load on network entities	5G-enabled vehicular apps
[23]	x	√	x	x	x	x	√	Simulation	• Latency	General
[24]	x	√	x	x	x	x	x	Simulation	• Latency • Resources efficiency	UAV-assisted vehicular apps
[25]	x	√	√	x	x	x	x	-	-	General
[26]	x	√	x	x	x	√	√	Simulation	• Latency	General
[27]	x	√	x	x	x	x	x	Simulation	• Latency • Communication overhead • Availability	V2X applications
[28]	x	√	√	x	x	√	x	Simulation	• Latency • Reliability • Availability	General
[29]	x	x	√	√	x	x	x	Simulation	• Latency	General
Proposed	√	√	√	x	√	√	√	Simulation	• Latency • Availability • Reliability	General

Table 2. Most common methodologies that are particularly useful in addressing performance and availability challenges in designing 5G infrastructures [30–33].

Methodology	Description	Benefits	Applications	Limitations
Petri nets	Petri nets are graphical and mathematical modeling tools used to describe and analyze the flow of information in systems with concurrent processes.	It provides a visual and formal representation of system dynamics, making identifying and resolving bottlenecks easier.	In 5G networks, Petri nets can model and analyze the synchronization and resource sharing between different network components.	It can become complex and difficult to manage as the system size increases.
Fault tree analysis (FTA)	FTA is a top-down, deductive failure analysis that focuses on identifying the root causes of system failures.	Helps identify critical components whose failure would have significant impacts, thus guiding redundancy and maintenance planning.	FTA can be used to model the probability of different failure scenarios in 5G infrastructure, helping to design more resilient systems.	Requires detailed knowledge of the system architecture and failure modes.
Stochastic reward nets (SRNs)	SRNs are extensions of Petri nets (a place/transition net) that incorporate stochastic timing and reward structures to model and evaluate complex systems.	SRNs allow for a detailed and flexible representation of system behavior, capturing both the probabilistic nature of events and their rewards (or penalties).	In the context of 5G networks, SRNs can be used to assess system reliability and availability by modeling different states of network components and their failure/recovery processes.	The complexity of SRNs can lead to significant computational overhead, especially for large-scale 5G networks.
Monte Carlo simulation	Monte Carlo simulation uses random sampling and statistical modeling to estimate the behavior of a system.	Offers flexibility and can model complex systems that are difficult to analyze using traditional methods.	Monte Carlo simulations can evaluate the performance and reliability of 5G networks under various scenarios and uncertainties.	Requires significant computational resources and careful interpretation of results.
Multidimensional universal generating functions (MUGFs)	MUGFs provide a powerful framework for analyzing the performance and reliability of multi-state systems.	MUGFs offer a compact and efficient way to represent and compute the performance distribution of complex systems, making them suitable for high-dimensional problems.	MUGFs can be applied to model the availability of 5G infrastructure by evaluating the combined impact of multiple performance measures, such as bandwidth, latency, and reliability, in a unified manner.	Developing accurate MUGF models requires a deep understanding of the system's operational characteristics and dependencies.
G/G/m queuing models	G/G/m queuing models generalize traditional queuing theory by allowing for arbitrary arrival and service time distributions with multiple servers (m).	G/G/m models provide a flexible approach to analyzing the performance of network nodes under realistic traffic conditions, enabling the identification of bottlenecks and optimization opportunities.	These models are particularly useful for the characterization of latency in 5G networks, where traffic patterns can be highly variable and unpredictable.	Solving G/G/m models analytically can be complex, often necessitating numerical methods or simulations.

3. Proposed VANET

VANET supplies the process of interchanging data between vehicles. This takes place through several processes through communication links known as V2V communications or through vehicle-to-infrastructure (V2I), e.g., evolved node B (eNB) of long-term evolution (LTE). The V2X type also works on communication with the assistance of any components related to the IoT. Furthermore, the wireless heterogeneous networking that is built depends on all the 802.11p, Bluetooth, and various systems of the cellular network generations as well as the routing protocol that helps to build an efficient VANET. This section introduces the developed VANET and provides all network features and components.

3.1. System Structure

Figure 1 presents the proposed VANET network that deploys multiple technologies and interfaces to support heterogeneous vehicular applications. Heterogeneous wireless technologies can be used to build communication links between vehicles and RSUs. This kind of communication link is known for wireless access in the vehicular environment (WAVE). Passenger safety is verified with the help of WAVE communication. WAVE communication works to bring up-to-date information on vehicles and traffic flow. This offers a huge improvement in the competence of the management traffic system. The proposed VANET contains various entities, including OBU, RSU, and trusted authority (TA). Many applications that RSU accommodates aim to link with various network systems. OBU is available in every vehicle to gather helpful data about each vehicle, such as fuel, speed, acceleration, and other data. All information is then sent to any nearby vehicles with the help of the wireless network. The wired network is used to link between TA and RSU, knowing that all RSU are connected. TA is one of the main components of VANET, as it helps keep the VANET system working. Figure 2 presents the main components of the lower layer of the considered VANET.

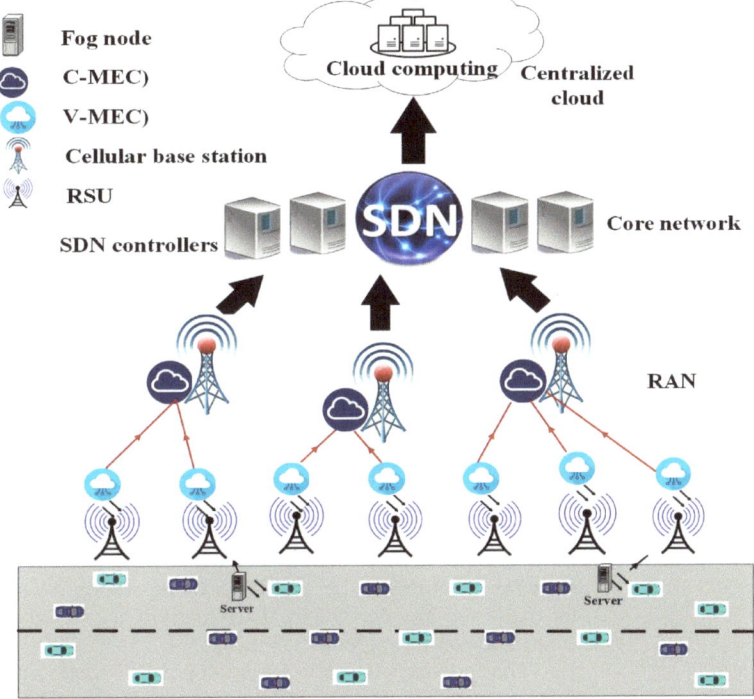

Figure 1. End-to-end structure of the proposed VANET.

The main features of these components are summarized as follows:
- RSU: RSU is situated in several locations along the roadsides. These locations include the parking regions or crossroads. This offers the vehicles domestic links for any crossing vehicles. The network devices inside the RSU depend on radio technology in IEEE 802.11P. This illustrates that these network devices are working to dedicate short-

range communication (DSRC). Besides this, RSU is useful to link different network systems with different network infrastructures;
- OBU: OBU is considered a global positioning system (GPS)-based tracking device available in each vehicle and offers vehicle data to transfer to RSU. Many electronic components are inside OBU, including IoT sensors, a resources command processor (RCP), an interface to users, and storage for read–write data to restore data. OBU's fundamental task is linking OBU with RSU or other OBUs. The radio transceiver of the OBU uses the IEEE 802.11p for wireless connection [36]. This connection with OBUs and RSUs takes place in message form. Furthermore, OBU gets its power from the vehicle's battery as well as the presence of several other components in each vehicle that work as an input for OBU, including the GPS, event data recorder (EDR), and forward and backward sensors;
- TA: TA's main duty is to control the VANET system, including the vehicle users, RSU, and OBU. It is also responsible for guaranteeing the VANET security administration.

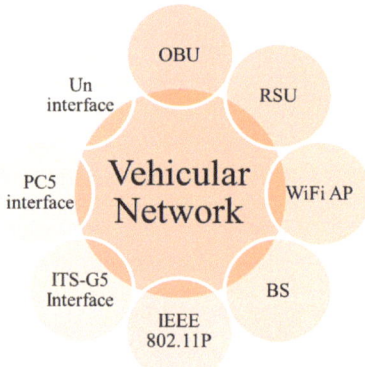

Figure 2. Main components of the lower level of the proposed VANET.

The proposed VANET deploys distributed edge computing at two tiers: fog computing (which represents the lower level) and MEC (which represents the higher level). Fog computing is considered an edge computing paradigm that helps the cloud computing network to enlarge its benefits and facilities among the network edges. It creates a link between the cloud and other smart devices that build all the links needed for the connection process. The difference between the cloud and the fog is that fog is assigned at the edges with less latency, while the cloud is more localized. Fog can send information, compute, save, stratify, and services for the end devices. VANET can meet its requirement by fog computing, for example, by decreasing the conjunction on the cloud and by fast reply to the important devices in addition to its capability to resolve the live data flow. The fog node can be represented in any device in the proposed VANET, including the infrastructure for roads and mobile vehicles. Each fog unit has all the facilities of network connections, stock, and computing units.

The proposed VANET also deploys MEC nodes into two levels. The first level represents the vehicular MECs (V-MECs), which are MEC servers connected to RSUs. The second level is made up of cellular MECs, which are MEC servers that are linked to eNBs (M-MECs). Using two MEC levels makes it easier to implement the proposed networking algorithms. The V-MEC uses our proposed handover and migration methods, which were introduced later, resulting in higher execution efficiency than standard systems. The introduction of distributed edge units makes it easier for V2X applications to meet the requisite QoS.

SDN is considered one of the gathering techniques that stands out among programmable networking technologies. SDN is a main part of the proposed VANET that can adapt to any alteration in the network topology. Besides its ability to realize the programmability portions related to the VANET control plane, it plays an important role in delivering novel services. SDN plays an important role in configuring network simplicity, computing, and new methods in network management.

Traditional VANET networks experience weak flexibility; however, deploying SDN for such networks achieves high flexibility. SDN can mirage between the data and the control plane and send the logical control starting from the node and ending to the central controller. Joining fog computing, MEC, and SDN helps cope with the challenges of the VANET system, including nonintelligence, inflexibility, and short connectivity. The SDN offers network behavior control while the fog computing transfers the position and service slots. The miraging between the SDN and fog helps lower delays and improves network resources. The integration of SDN guarantees a seamless process for the established handover method by maintaining a persistent TCP connection.

3.2. VANET Features and Interfaces

The VANET wireless network contains nodes distributed along the RSU or vehicles with high mobility. The network's infrastructure restricts access to it; however, it is highly dynamic and dependable and provides many services. The proposed VANET has the following features:

- Scalability and flexibility: Edge computing enables dynamic resource allocation based on current demand, maintaining optimal performance. SDN offers a flexible networking framework that can readily scale to support increasingly linked vehicles and devices;
- Low latency and real-time processing: Distributed edge computing brings computer resources closer to vehicles, dramatically lowering latency by processing data locally rather than depending on remote cloud servers. Edge nodes offer real-time analysis and speedy decision making, which benefits critical applications such as collision avoidance, traffic management, and autonomous driving;
- Enhanced network management and control: SDN provides centralized network control via a controller that governs data flows across the network, simplifying network management and increasing overall efficiency. SDN's programmability enables the customization and optimization of network policies and behaviors, which adapt to changing traffic conditions and application requirements;
- Improved security and privacy: SDN increases security by isolating essential network control functions from possible attackers. Edge computing enables local processing of sensitive data, reducing the need to send it across the network and improving privacy;
- Load balancing: SDN allows for sophisticated load balancing across the network, reducing congestion and assuring effective use of network resources;
- Resource optimization: Edge nodes can be dynamically deployed and scaled to meet real-time demand, ensuring that computational resources are used efficiently;
- Enhanced QoS: SDN prioritizes vital vehicular data, ensuring that high-priority communications, including emergency alarms, are delivered quickly. SDN facilitates smooth control over network traffic and enables consistent and reliable performance for various applications, from entertainment to safety-critical systems;
- Reduced backhaul traffic: Processing data at the edge reduces the amount of data that needs to be transported back to central servers, resulting in energy savings and lower backhaul traffic;
- Adaptive network topology: With SDN's centralized control, the network topology may be dynamically adjusted to accommodate vehicle mobility while maintaining robust communication links;
- Efficient resources management: SDN's ability to dynamically assign network resources based on demand contributes to energy conservation by preventing resource overprovisioning;

- Efficient handover implementation: The system can effectively manage handovers between RSUs by combining edge computing and SDN, assuring continuous connectivity and service for moving vehicles;
- Advanced data analytics and AI integration: Distributed edge nodes may execute complex data analytics close to the data source, delivering actionable insights in real time for applications such as traffic prediction and route optimization. Integrating AI and machine learning algorithms at the edge might help improve decision-making processes, including predictive maintenance and intelligent traffic management;
- Interoperability: SDN enables interoperability across various network protocols and standards, resulting in seamless communication across various automotive systems.

The proposed VANET supports many forms of communications, including V2V, V2I, vehicle-to-pedestrians (V2P), V2X, and cellular vehicle-to-everything (C-V2X) communications. Enabling such forms of communication provides efficient communication over the network, provides all kinds of vehicular applications, helps in traffic safety, and offers very well-authorized data in real time. In V2V communications, the high transmission rate and the low latency are among the main advantages. Vehicles can propagate beneficial data like braking for emergencies, detecting accidents, or traffic situations between vehicles. V2I works mainly to send data among vehicles and the network's infrastructure. Then, the vehicles improve the link with RSUs to interchange data with different networks, such as the Internet. Moreover, the V2I demands a wider bandwidth than V2V, making V2I more protected against any risks or attacks.

C-V2X significantly improves vehicular communications, providing reliable, robust, and low-latency communication capabilities. C-V2X increases road safety, traffic efficiency, and a variety of ITS applications by utilizing both direct and network-based communication. C-V2X is a communication technology specifically developed to offer connection for ITS. C-V2X, a 3GPP standard, enables direct and network-based communication across cellular networks. Using C-V2X, vehicles can communicate directly with each other, infrastructure, and pedestrians through the PC5 interface. This direct communication interface supports the frequency band of 5.9 GHz ITS allocated mainly for vehicular communications. C-V2X enables vehicles for cellular communication using the Uu interface, which was developed for next-generation NodeB (gNB) [37]. This interface provides access to cloud services, traffic information, and broader network resources.

Integrating fog and MEC computing with SDN brings control facilities to the network's edge. Instead of delivering data to a central controller, fog computing processes services and data at the network's edge. Low latency, location awareness, and enhanced QoS are just some advantages. We considered the MEC platform introduced in [28] for the proposed VANET. We considered a distributed control scheme, in addition to the centralized controller, to provide global intelligence. Each RSU deploys an SDN RSU controller (RSUC), which has a direct interface to the centralized scheme. This distributed scheme supports distributed edge computing and assists the MEC controller deployed in the considered MEC platform. The SDN controller controls the RSUC, which is also an SDN-enabled device. On the other hand, the SDN controller does not take full control of the network; instead, it gives policy information to the RSUC.

The RSUC decides on the exact conduct based on the policy information received and their local understanding. A fog orchestration layer is placed at the SDN architecture, and the operation is located at the SDN controller coordinates between RSUCs. The RSUC sends data to the SDN controller while also maintaining local storage. In the event of an emergency, RSUC serves the requests rather than sending them to the controller, resulting in a significant reduction in latency. This has raised the same worry about latency control, emphasizing the significance of an edge-up design with hierarchically distributed control and an edge layer. This is rather than a cloud-down approach (Internet-based SDVN) in terms of the use of radio resources.

4. Proposed Microservice-Based Scheme

Microservices are becoming increasingly popular in many industries, including the automotive sector, due to their ability to improve software systems' flexibility, scalability, and maintainability. Microservices can potentially revolutionize the design and operation of VANETs in the designed system. VANETs are networks that enable communication between vehicles, road infrastructure, and other devices in the transportation ecosystem. These networks are characterized by their dynamic and rapidly changing nature, which makes them challenging to design and operate. Microservices are tiny, self-contained, and loosely interconnected software elements that can be deployed and scaled autonomously, making them an important part of any designed network system. We considered microservices for the proposed VANET since they offer several benefits, including fault isolation, ease of maintenance, and the ability to handle large amounts of data. By adopting microservices in the designed VANET, it is possible to create modular and scalable systems that can handle the challenges of vehicular networks. Microservices can implement various services in the proposed VANET, including traffic monitoring, collision warning systems, and remote vehicle diagnostics.

Another important benefit of implementing microservices in the designed VANET is their ability to improve the QoS, which is a critical aspect of VANETs, as it affects the performance of safety-critical applications such as collision warning systems. Microservices can help to improve QoS by enabling dynamic scaling, fault tolerance, and load balancing. For example, microservices can be used to automatically scale up or down the processing power of a given service based on the current demand. This approach ensures the service can handle the current load while minimizing resource usage. The use of microservices in the proposed VANETs can enable new and innovative services that were previously impossible. For example, microservices can be used to implement new applications that rely on real-time data, such as traffic congestion monitoring or parking space detection. These services can be deployed as independent microservices that can be easily integrated into existing systems, reducing the time and cost of development.

Each microservice can be deployed and scaled independently, allowing for greater resource utilization and improved performance. This is particularly important in the proposed VANET, where resources are limited, and efficient use of these resources is critical for the success of VANET applications. By adopting microservices, it is possible to create modular and scalable systems that can handle the dynamic and rapidly changing nature of any VANETs. This approach allows for greater flexibility, modularity, and scalability in designing and implementing VANET applications. Algorithm 1 provides the proposed microservice scheme for the considered VANET.

Algorithm 1: Microservices model for vehicular applications

1: Initialize service type (T), service priority, microservices (M), and categories of microservice
2:     For (i = 1: T)
3:         Output: Define the service type
4:         Output: Define the service priority
5:     End for
6:     For (x = 1: M)
7:         Output: Define the microservice type
8:         Output: Define the microservice priority
9:     End for
10: End

The proposed microservices algorithm depends mainly on the task priority. The algorithm starts by prioritizing the received tasks according to their main applications. It works by first indicating the data priority, defining the application, and assigning binary values to each task. If it is a high priority, it takes the data and divides the data service into microservices. After this, the microservices are also numbered based on their priority, with the decision of which data or service must be sent first based on their priority number. This reduces the task load on the vehicle service. Based on task priority, it is now well known which task needs to be handled and which will be handled by the MEC service. The main steps of the proposed algorithm are introduced as follows:

- *Step 1:* The algorithm starts by initializing all the necessary parameters, including the service type, counter for the service priority (T), service priority, microservices, counter for the microservices priority (M), and categories of microservices;
- *Step 2:* We start a for-loop that starts from 1, which indicates a task with high priority, until T, which represents the counter for the service priority with less priority. Each step-in loop indicates the task "service type" and "service priority." When the loop is done, we move to step 3;
- *Step 3:* After defining the task priority and type, we divide each task into microservices and categorize each based on microservice and microservice priority. In this case, the for loop starts from 1, which is the high priority, to M, which represents the counter for the microservices priority. Each step-in loop indicates the task "microservice type" or "microservice priority".

5. Handover Scheme

VANET consists of vehicles traveling along roads or streets. Its main purpose is to improve vehicles' safety, comfort, reliability, and security on the road. However, one of the most significant challenges in designing VANET is the issue of handover (HO), which arises when a vehicle goes from one network region featured by an RSU to another region encompassed by a different RSU. Achieving seamless HO in VANET is complex because of the high vehicle mobility and the limited coverage of RSUs, which do not have overlapping signals. 5G technology can help provide enhanced characteristics that are well-suited for real-time video streaming and can be utilized in designing effective solutions for the HO problem. Any system must include a handover method to facilitate the transfer of active communication management between RSUs. For example, let us assume vehicle A is traveling from the coverage region of RSU_2 to RSU_1, whereas vehicle B is moving between the coverage of RSU_1 to RSU_2. After the handover procedure is finished, RSU_1 takes charge of communication management for vehicle A, while RSU_2 acquires responsibility for vehicle B. Two main categories of handover methods exist: inter-RSU handover and intra-RSU transfer [38].

Inter-RSU handover refers to the process in which a vehicle moves from one RSU to another, requiring a smooth transfer of communication duties to ensure uninterrupted connectivity. In contrast, intra-RSU handover refers to the process of a vehicle transitioning between various types of connections inside the same coverage area of an RSU, such as switching from V2V communication to vehicle-to-RSU (V2R) communication. Both types of handover approaches are crucial for guaranteeing efficient and dependable communication management in dynamic vehicle networks. Inter-RSU handover in VANET can be classified based on several criteria, one of which is the classification of handover into soft or hard HO. In hard handover, the link to the previous RSU is disconnected before connecting to the incoming RSU, while in soft handover, the link to the incoming RSU is established before the disconnection of the previous RSU [39].

The handover process in an SDN vehicular network is more intricate than in conventional cellular networks. Initially, the radio resources may be renegotiated with a new SDN controller. Secondly, flow tables must be updated to reflect the topology. Third, live migration and service redirection are required if a MEC is present, which adds even more complexity to the handover process. Lastly, the generation of the handover for multi-hop links and MEC services will occur concurrently. Each of these elements increases the difficulty of handover.

Trajectory prediction can be used to improve the handover process. This can assist in finishing flow table entry updates and service migration ahead of schedule. Learning-based methods are one way to tackle the problems of high mobility and handover. These techniques can be used to find possible trends that could lead to better load balancing and handover. For instance, reinforcement learning has been applied using base station context data such as vehicle speed, user count, and handover history.

Similarly, online probabilistic neural networks have been proposed to use the mobility information of the vehicles to predict the next serving access point. However, the complexity of creating an appropriate objective that simultaneously maximizes the performance makes these machine-learning (ML) algorithms difficult to use, particularly when energy consumption needs to be considered. SDN prioritizes security and privacy because of the possibility of unauthorized access or false information causing catastrophic mishaps. Security mechanisms must perform real-time authentication to avoid traffic congestion that could hinder SDN operation [40].

Smooth vehicle HO is essential in a system designed with 5G-VANET to minimize user interruptions. Nevertheless, frequent handovers can result from vehicles' high mobility, which presents a major obstacle in VANET. These difficulties show the importance of finding practical ways to deal with the HO issue in systems built for 5G-VANETs. Seamless communication between vehicles must be maintained without interruption when they move from one RSU to another, which is challenging due to the latency caused by handover.

5G-enabled vehicular networks offer a promising solution to enable real-time services in high-density urban areas. Existing HO solutions do not effectively address the most significant problems in VANET, such as reduced quality of connection and QoS performance degradation. Frequent HOs can also lead to unnecessary and excessive signaling, resulting in a signaling storm that consumes VANET resources and energy, ultimately leading to HO failure. Several critical factors contribute to HO failure in VANET, including mobility, communication interference, coverage regions, and traffic congestion. Addressing these problems is essential for designing effective HO solutions to improve the VANET's QoS [28].

The high-speed movement of vehicles on highways poses significant mobility challenges in the proposed layout of 5G-VANET networks. Addressing these mobility problems is critical for ensuring seamless vehicle communication and reducing HO failures in the proposed design 5G-VANET.

Many of the current HO solutions address the ideal situation of vehicles traveling on roads and being HO from one RSU to another. However, signal strength information has been the primary focus of ping-pong solutions in the literature, which may be inaccurate in environments with fluctuating signal strength. Increasing the HO margin, HO performance indicator, and time-to-trigger are examples of HO parameters that can be improved to reduce pointless HOs in 5G-VANET networks. Addressing these HO problems is crucial for ensuring seamless communication and reducing the frequency of HO failures in high-speed highway environments. By developing effective solutions to these HO problems, 5G-VANET networks can improve the quality and reliability of communication between vehicles and RSUs, ultimately enhancing the safety and efficiency of highway transportation.

One approach is to use advanced encryption techniques to secure communication between vehicles and RSUs. Another approach is to use frequency-hopping techniques to avoid jamming attacks by changing the transmitted signal's frequency in a pseudo-random pattern. Additionally, directional antennas can be used to minimize interference and improve signal quality in areas with high signal interference. ML algorithms can also be deployed to detect and prevent jamming attacks by analyzing the patterns of jamming signals. In summary, jamming and interference signals pose significant challenges in designed 5G-VANET networks and can negatively impact network performance and driver safety. Addressing these challenges requires the deployment of effective countermeasures such as advanced encryption techniques, frequency=hopping techniques, directional antennas, and ML algorithms. By mitigating the impact of jamming and interference signals, 5G-VANET networks can ensure the safety and reliability of vehicle communication, ultimately enhancing the efficiency and effectiveness of transportation on highways. For the proposed microservice-based VANET, we considered the HO scheme introduced in [28].

6. Proposed Migration Scheme

Migration is a critical aspect of any designed VANET, which refers to the process of moving from one network to another. VANETs enable communication between vehicles, road infrastructure, and other devices in the transportation ecosystem. Due to the dynamic and rapidly changing nature of VANETs, migration is essential to network design and operation. By enabling vehicles to maintain connectivity and access services as they move between different network environments, migration plays a vital role in ensuring the reliable and efficient operation of VANETs. One of the primary challenges of migration in designed VANETs is ensuring seamless and uninterrupted connectivity during the transition from one network to another. This is particularly important for safety-critical applications such as collision warning systems, which rely on continuous connectivity to operate effectively. Therefore, designing and implementing migration mechanisms in the designed system to ensure seamless connectivity is crucial for the safety and reliability of vehicular networks.

Another challenge of migration in VANETs is the potential loss of data during the transition from one network to another. This can occur due to network latency, packet loss, or other factors that may cause data loss during migration. Researchers have proposed several approaches to address this challenge to ensure data continuity during migration, such as caching, replication, and proactive handoff mechanisms. These approaches aim to reduce data loss and ensure critical data are available to the vehicle during migration. Moreover, migration in the proposed designed VANETs presents opportunities for innovation and new services. For example, the ability to migrate between different types of networks, such as cellular networks and dedicated short-range communication (DSRC) networks, enables the development of new services that rely on the strengths of each network type. This approach can improve the reliability, scalability, and efficiency of VANETs by leveraging the strengths of different network technologies.

In the designed VANET, the migration process is challenging because of the high vehicle mobility and the need to maintain service continuity during handovers. The migration process must consider several factors, including the vehicle's location, speed, direction, and communication requirements. Additionally, the migration process must be fast enough to ensure that the handover occurs without interruption in service. Furthermore, the migration process must be able to handle different types of services, such as infotainment, safety, and traffic management, which have varying requirements in terms of latency, bandwidth, and reliability. The migration process also critically integrates different network technologies and architectures, such as cellular networks, Wi-Fi, and ad hoc networks. This integration allows for the efficient utilization of network resources and the provision of high-quality services to vehicular users. The migration process in the proposed VANET must be designed to handle the dynamic nature of network environments, including changes in network topology, traffic load, and available bandwidth.

One of the most important benefits of an efficient migration process in a designed VANET is the reduction of service disruption during handovers. This is particularly important for safety-critical applications that require real-time communication such as collision avoidance and emergency response systems. The migration process must ensure that these applications continue to function seamlessly during handovers without any delay or loss of data. The migration process is a critical component in the designed VANET, enabling seamless transfer of services and data between different network infrastructures. The migration process must be fast, reliable, and efficient to ensure uninterrupted communication for vehicular users. It also plays a critical role in integrating different network technologies and architectures, reducing service disruption during handovers, and enabling safety-critical applications. Therefore, developing effective and efficient migration mechanisms is essential for the success of VANET and realizing its full potential for improving road safety, traffic efficiency, and passenger comfort. Algorithm 2 introduces the proposed migration scheme for the developed VANET. The algorithm is built based on our previously developed handover scheme proposed in [28].

Algorithm 2: Handover and migration algorithm

1:	Initialize SNR_1, SNR_2, SNR_3, Signal power of RSU
2:	Initialize positions x_i (i = 1, 2, 3, ..., n)
3:	If ($P > SNR_1$)
4:	Output: Dedicate parameter
5:	Output: Dedicate P RSU
6:	Else
7:	If ($P < SNR_1$) || ($P > SNR_2$)
8:	Output: Start inspection state phase
9:	Else
10:	If ($P < SNR_2$) || ($P > SNR_3$)
11:	Send a migration request to target MEC
12:	Initialize migration process
13:	Send task specification target MEC
14:	Receive migration response and time stamps
15:	Else
16:	Start the execution stage
17:	Migrate computing tasks
18:	Load to target MEC
19:	Move serving vehicle parameters to RSU
20:	End If
21:	End If
22:	End If
23:	End migration

The power indicates the vehicle's position with the RSU. The signal power for the RSU is denoted as P, and the signal-to-noise ratio (SNR) is calculated by dividing the signal RSU power value (P) by the noise power of the channel. The main steps of the proposed migration algorithm are summarized below:

- *Step 1:* First, the algorithm initializes all the parameters needed, including the SNR and P;
- *Step 2:* Then, it compares the P with the SNR1 (i.e., the first level of thresholds). If the P > SNR1, two actions will occur: The first is "dedicate the parameter", and the second is "dedicate P RSU". If not, it goes to step 3;
- *Step 3:* We have two possibilities if P is not greater than the SNR1. These possibilities are (P < SNR1 or P > SNR2). In this case, if either of the possibilities is true, the action is to "Start the inspection state phase". If not, then it goes to step 4;
- *Step 4:* If P is not smaller than SNR1 or greater than SNR2, then we have another two possibilities. These two possibilities are (P < SNR2 or P > SNR3). In this case, if either of the possibilities is true, the action is 4 steps. The first is "send migration request to target MEC", and second is "Initialize migration process". The third is "Send task specification to the target MEC", and fourth is "Receive migration response and time stamps". If not, it goes to step 5;
- *Step 5:* If P is not smaller than SNR2 or greater than SNR3, we have any other special condition. In this case, the action will be four steps. The first is "Start execution stage", the second is "Migrate computing task", the third is "Load target MEC", and the fourth is " Move serving vehicle parameters to RSU."

The proposed algorithm covers all possibilities during the handover and migration processes. The migration process takes place at the start of the handover algorithm.

7. Offloading Scheme

For the proposed VANET, we modified our proposed offloading scheme in [41]. The considered offloading model deploys three main offloading levels in addition to the local execution, and Figure 3 presents the main offloading levels in the proposed VANET. The local execution is represented as zero-level offloading, which illustrates an important mission of the end device's ability to process these tasks without the offloading procedure. This can occur based on obtainable resources offered by the end devices and QoS assigned for each task. The first level of offloading is exemplified in the fog computing server. The mission that cannot be carried out with the help of end devices is offloaded with the help of a suitable communication connection to the RSU's MEC. Depending on the recent obtainable resources at the fog server, the fog server admits or declines the offloading. If the recently obtainable resources of the fog server are not sufficient at that time to manage the offloading workloads, the workload is moved to the second level. The fog server offloads all workloads that cannot be managed to the dedicated RSU's MEC. The MEC unit can admit or decline the offloaded tasks depending on recent obtainable resources besides the QoS needed for these tasks.

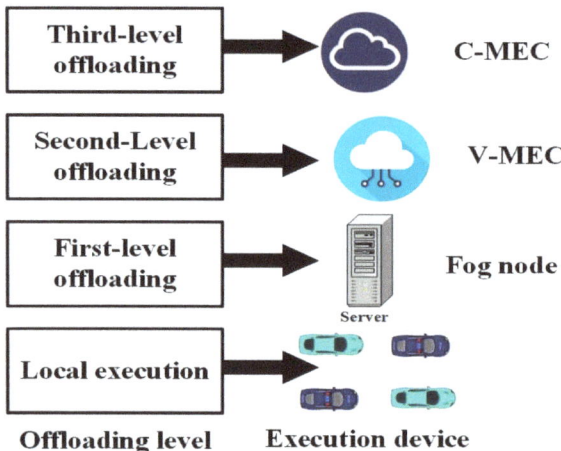

Figure 3. Considered offloading levels of the proposed microservice-based VANET.

The major offloading decisions are determined through the end devices based on their recent obtainable facilities, e.g., energy, storage, and processing, and the QoS time. Each device's programmed profile determines the size of the workload and the necessary number of processor cycles. The end device's decision engine implements hardware for the proposed offloading mechanism. It collects data from the program profile and data on the resources currently available from the resource's schedule. Additionally, the decision engine gets the maximum permitted time to process the computing work, which indicates the needed QoS time for the recent workload. The decision engine uses these variables to select the offloading. The decision engine initially determines how long it will take to complete the job locally at the vehicle and then decides how to offload in terms of energy and time.

The energy choice is made by comparing the vehicle's remaining energy after task execution with its threshold energy. The job is passed straight to the fog server if, following local execution, the vehicle's remaining energy is greater than that, provided that offloading is permitted. The execution time and QoS latency are compared to determine the time decision of offloading. The job is offloaded to the fog unit if the decision engine chooses to offload. When the fog server's decision engine receives an offloading request from a vehicle, it determines whether to execute the job internally or to move it to the next level. The decision engine of the fog server determines the execution time needed to complete the requested job before calculating the total time needed to complete it. The decision engine of the fog then determines the binary offloading energy and time decision values. After completing the desired job, leftover energy is compared to the energy threshold to determine the energy decision. The necessary QoS latency and the overall time needed to complete the requested job are compared to determine the time choice.

8. Simulation and Results

8.1. Simulation Setup

Considering various vehicular applications and scenarios, the proposed microservice-based framework was evaluated over NS-3 environments. The mobility of considered vehicles was achieved using the simulation of urban mobility (SUMO) platform. We used the ms-van3t platform available at [42]. We modified our previously proposed system model introduced in [43] and considered it for the proposed VANET. The vehicles' mobility was simulated to match highway conditions. Utilizing OpenFlow version 1.3, all essential SDN modules for the SDN controller and OpenFlow switches were integrated. The simulation topology was developed in accordance with the specifications outlined in Table 3. The simulation consisted of a five-kilometer-long, bidirectional, two-lane road with an RN87-like curvature. The traffic density (TD) parameters summarized in Table 3 were used to distribute vehicles along this road. Table 3 identifies the specifications of the used MEC servers and RSUs. It also displays the attributes of the fog nodes and the SDN network employed in the simulation. The road considered was covered by five RSUs, with a circular coverage of 0.5 km radius for each RSU. The system deployed five MEC units connected to RSUs, with the specifications introduced in Table 3. Each RUS coverage was served by five fog nodes distributed over the coverage area. Communication was carried out over the NR C-V2X using the platform introduced in [42].

Table 3. Parameters used during simulation.

Parameter	Value
Road	Length = 5 Km Direction: Bi-directional Lane: Two Curvature: RN87-like
RSU	Number = 5 Interface = NR C-V2X Radio transmission range = 500 m Max. transmission level = 20 dBm Packet transmission frequency = 10 Hz
Vehicles	Number (N) = $N \in \{200, 400, 600, 800\}$ TD = $TDv_i \in \{0.1, 0.2, 0.3\}$ veh/m Mobility (v) = $v_i \in \{30, 40, 50, 60, 70\}$ Km/h Interface = NR C-V2X
SDN	Service rate$_{Controller}$ = 30,000 req/sec OpenFlow version = 1.3 Average request rate$_{Switch}$ = ϵ [1500, 3000] Processing delay$_{Controller}$ = 0.5 µs Processing delay$_{Switch}$ = 5 µs
MEC	Number = 5 Placement = equidistant Processing ϵ [0.7, 2.5] GHz Max. workload = 10 Mbps Storage (RAM, HDD) = (4 × 2048 Mb, 256 Gb)
Fog	Number = 5 per RSU Processing ϵ [0.7, 1.4] GHz Storage (RAM, HDD) = (2048 Mb, 10 Gb)
Tasks	Streaming bandwidth ϵ [10, 2048] (Kb/S) App Category: I, II, III, IV

Heterogeneous computing tasks of different applications were considered during the simulation. These tasks were of different applications, including sensor data, image processing, V2V communications, video processing, and traffic management. The data were extracted from the datasets introduced in [44–48]. Various datasets were considered to cover a variety of computing tasks ranging from simple to complex tasks. The tasks were categorized into four main categories in terms of computing complexity as follows:

- Category (I): Very simple tasks, including sensor data;
- Category (II): Simple tasks, including workloads equivalent to processing simple images and websites;
- Category (III): Medium-complexity tasks, including 3D images and simple videos;
- Category (IV): High-complex tasks, including high-quality and 3D videos.

Tasks were randomly allocated to the considered vehicles, and the next task was assigned once the task was completed.

To investigate the influence of the growing traffic on the efficiency of the developed microservice-based VANET, we examined four different values for the total number of deployed vehicles. In addition, we analyzed the impact of varying levels of TD by assessing three distinct traffic density scenarios. The three TD scenarios provide additional insights into the impact of alterations in vehicle distribution on the VANET. These scenarios involved varying levels of TD, ranging from low to high, with each level correlating to different distances between vehicles and frequencies of interaction. The vehicles were placed along the route based on the traffic densities stated in Table 3.

Three main performance metrics were considered for evaluating the proposed micro service-based VANET: reliability, availability, and latency. The reliability of the proposed network was assessed by measuring the successfully received packets. The packet delivery ratio (PDR) was calculated for the proposed system and compared with other existing solutions. The system availability was assessed by measuring the number of blocked tasks (BT) among the assigned tasks to vehicles. The results were compared with other existing systems to indicate the performance improvement of the developed microservice-based VANET. The latency performance of the proposed network was assessed by calculating the performance improvement in latency of handling assigned computing tasks. The following equation was used to calculate the percentage improvement of latency compared with the traditional MEC VANETs.

$$\text{Latency improvement } (\%) = \frac{\text{Average latency}_{Traditional} - \text{Average latency}_{System(i)}}{\text{Average latency}_{Traditional}} \quad \forall\, i \in \mathbb{R} \quad (1)$$

8.2. Results

Figure 4 presents the average value of the obtained PDR for the three systems with the parameters provided in Table 4. The PDR was measured at different traffic densities and distances from the RSUs. The proposed microservice-based VANET (system 3) achieved higher PDR at the three considered traffic densities. With the increase in the TD, the PDR of the existing systems (system (1) and system (2)) was reduced compared with the proposed microservice model. This is mainly due to the deployment of microservices and the proposed migration scheme. Moreover, the PDR of the three systems was measured at different vehicle mobilities. Figure 5 presents the average PDR of the three systems at different vehicle velocities with the specifications presented in Table 5.

Table 4. Parameters for PDR measurements (Figure 4).

Parameter	Vehicle Velocity (v)	Number of Vehicles (N)	System (1)	System (2)	System (3)
Value	50 Km/h	400	Traditional VANET	System developed in [28]	Proposed microservice-based VANET

Table 5. Parameters for PDR measurements (Figure 5).

Parameter	Traffic Density (TD)	Number of Vehicles (N)	System (1)	System (2)	System (3)
Value	0.1 veh/m	400	Traditional VANET	System developed in [28]	Proposed microservice-based VANET

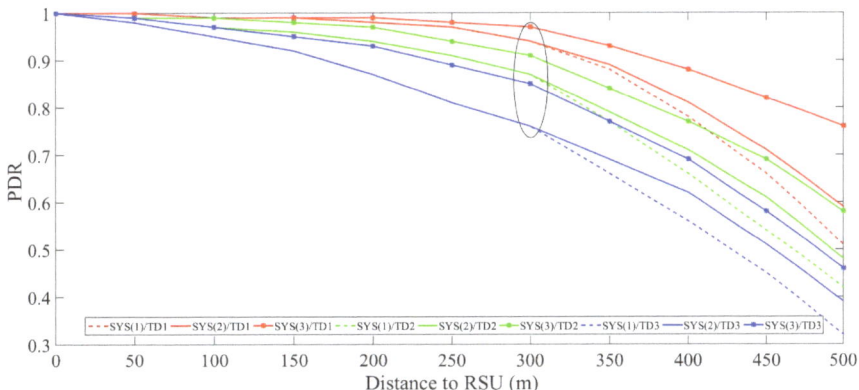

Figure 4. PDR at different TDs.

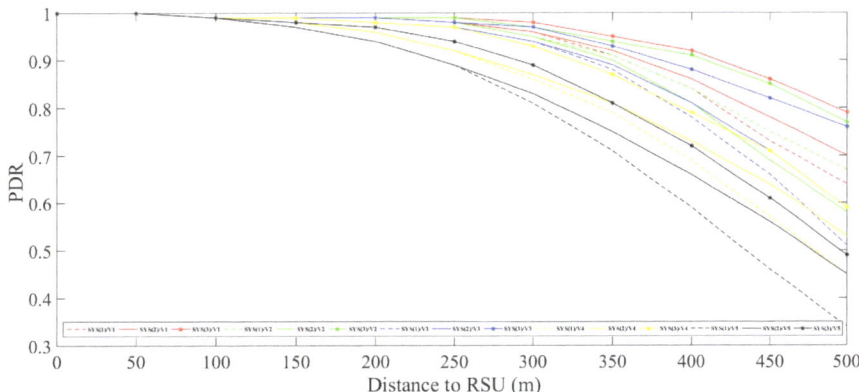

Figure 5. PDR at different vehicle mobility.

Figures 6–9 present the average performance of utilizing computing resources of vehicles, fog, and MEC nodes. This measure was considered to evaluate the performance of the proposed microservice and migration schemes. Also, this investigates the effectiveness of introducing the fog layer to VANETs. These figures measured the average resource utilization at different vehicle mobilities with the specifications introduced in Table 6. Each figure represents the results while simulating the systems with tasks from certain application categories. Figure 6 presents the average resource utilization of the four systems simulated using Category (I) tasks. The proposed model achieved lower utilization performance for this category of applications compared to other simulated systems. This is due to the plurality of available resources, e.g., fog and MEC, compared to the workloads required for processing. Since the assigned tasks are all sensor data that require low computing resources, this makes the resources of end devices, i.e., vehicles, enough to handle most of such tasks. However, with the increase in vehicle velocity, the performance of traditional systems degraded, and the performance of the proposed system increased.

Table 6. Simulation parameters for utilization efficiency measurements (Figures 6–9).

Parameter	Traffic Density (TD)	Number of Vehicles (N)	System (1)	System (2)	System (3)	System (4)
Value	0.1 veh/m	400	Traditional VANET	Traditional MEC-VANET	System developed in [28]	Proposed microservice-based VANET

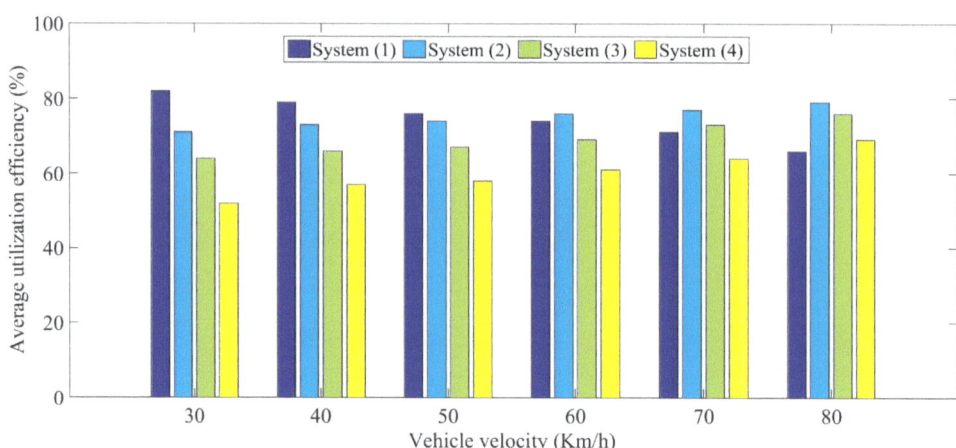

Figure 6. Average resource utilization efficiency at different vehicle mobility for Category (I) tasks.

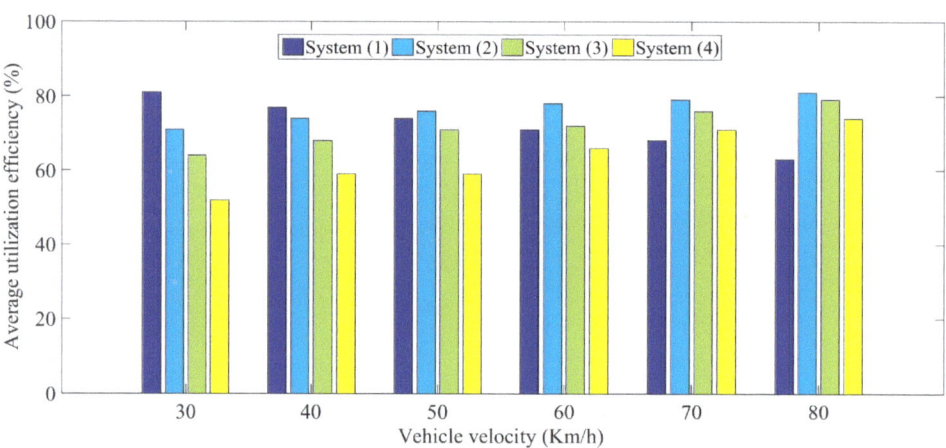

Figure 7. Average resource utilization efficiency at different vehicle mobility for Category (II) tasks.

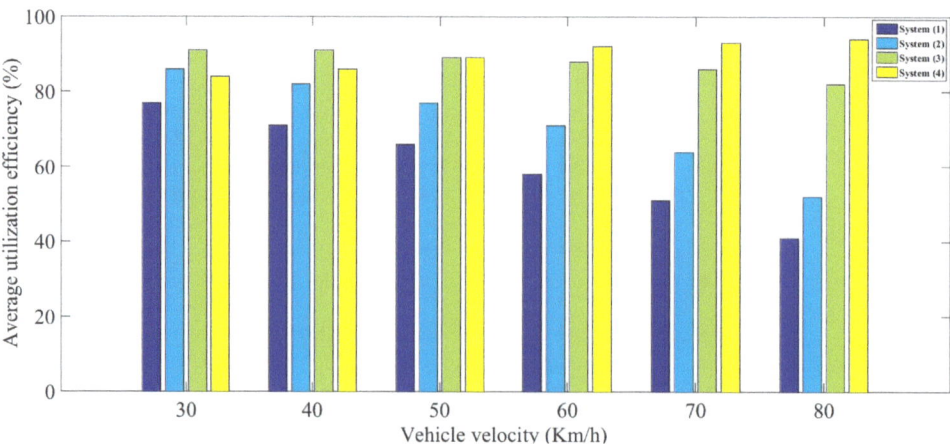

Figure 8. Average resource utilization efficiency at different vehicle mobility, for Category (III) tasks.

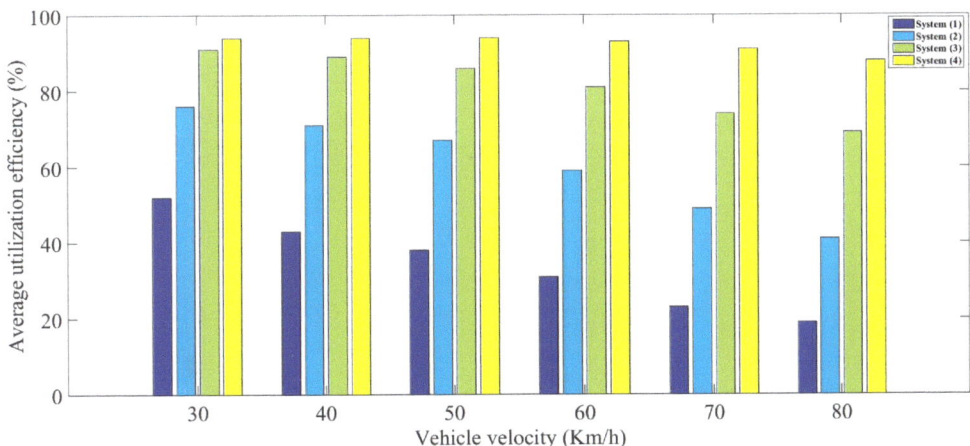

Figure 9. Average resource utilization efficiency at different vehicle mobility for Category (IV) tasks.

Figures 7 and 8 present the utilization efficiency for the four simulated systems when simulated using tasks from Category (II) and Category (III), respectively. With the increase in task complexity, moving from Category (I) to Category (II) and then to Category (III), the demands for higher computing resources and efficient use of such resources increase. The proposed microservice-based VANET achieved an average utilization of computing resources higher than other existing systems, mainly at high vehicle mobility. Also, this performance improvement increases in Figure 9, which provides the results of Category (IV). This is due to the complexity of tasks that need higher computing capabilities, achieved through introducing the fog layer and efficient use of resources, achieved using microservice and offloading approaches. Moreover, the proposed migration scheme increases efficiency in high vehicle mobilities.

Figures 10–13 present the resource utilization performance at different numbers of deployed vehicles, with the specifications introduced in Table 7. For tasks of Category (I), i.e., results introduced in Figure 10, the traditional VANET and traditional MEC-VANET provide efficient resources; however, the proposed system offers computing resources with capabilities higher than the system requires. This reduces the utilization efficiency in this case and for the Category (II) tasks introduced in Figure 11. For tasks of Categories (III and IV), the proposed system achieved higher utilization efficiency than other simulated systems, mainly for larger numbers of deployed vehicles. This can be interpreted in the same way as for Figures 8 and 9. Similarly, Figures 14–17 provide the obtained results of the resource utilization of the four simulated systems at different traffic densities for the specifications introduced in Table 8.

Table 7. Simulation parameters for utilization efficiency measurements (Figures 10–13).

Parameter	Traffic Density (TD)	Vehicle Velocity (v)	System (1)	System (2)	System (3)	System (4)
Value	0.1 veh/m	50 Km/h	Traditional VANET	Traditional MEC-VANET	System developed in [28]	Proposed microservice-based VANET

Table 8. Simulation parameters for utilization efficiency measurements (Figures 14–17).

Parameter	Number of Vehicles (N)	Vehicle Velocity (v)	System (1)	System (2)	System (3)	System (4)
Value	400	50 Km/h	Traditional VANET	Traditional MEC-VANET	System developed in [28]	Proposed microservice-based VANET

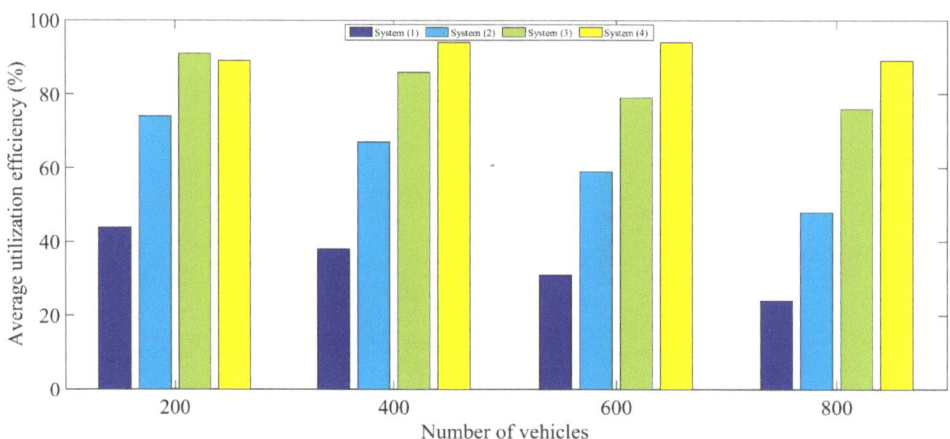

Figure 10. Average resource utilization efficiency at different numbers of vehicles for Category (I) tasks.

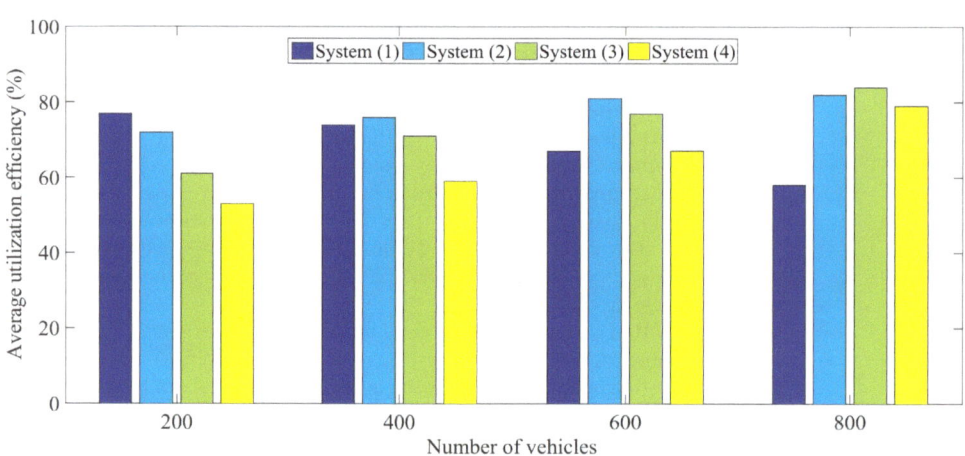

Figure 11. Average resource utilization efficiency at different numbers of vehicles for Category (II) tasks.

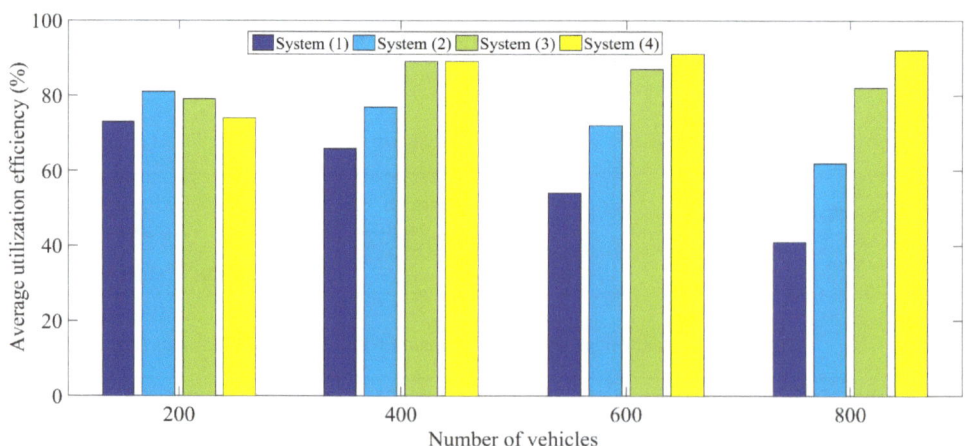

Figure 12. Average resource utilization efficiency at different numbers of vehicles for Category (III) tasks.

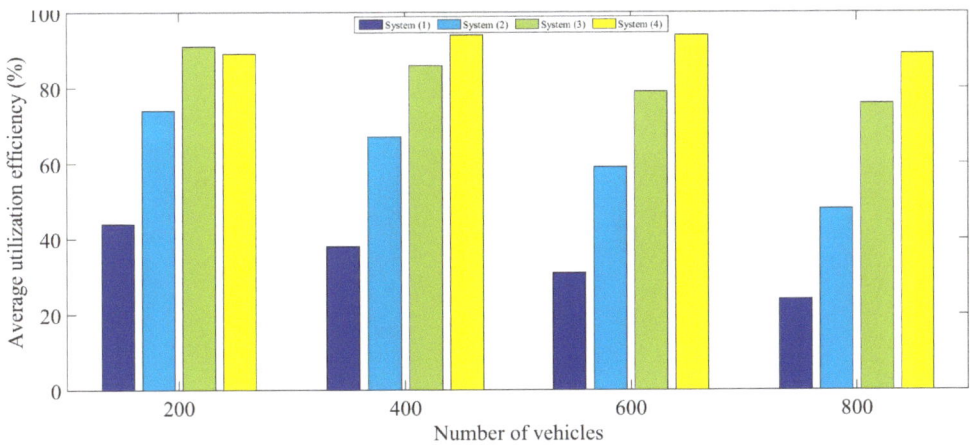

Figure 13. Average resource utilization efficiency at different numbers of vehicles for Category (IV) tasks.

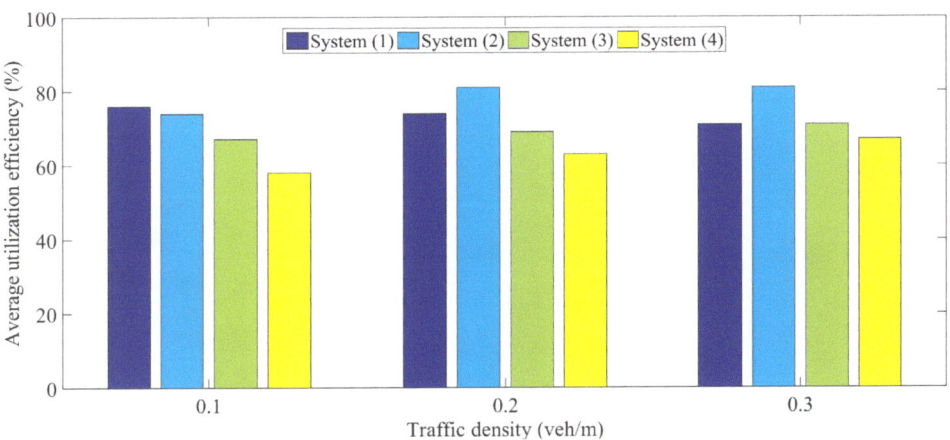

Figure 14. Average resource utilization efficiency at different TDs for Category (I) tasks.

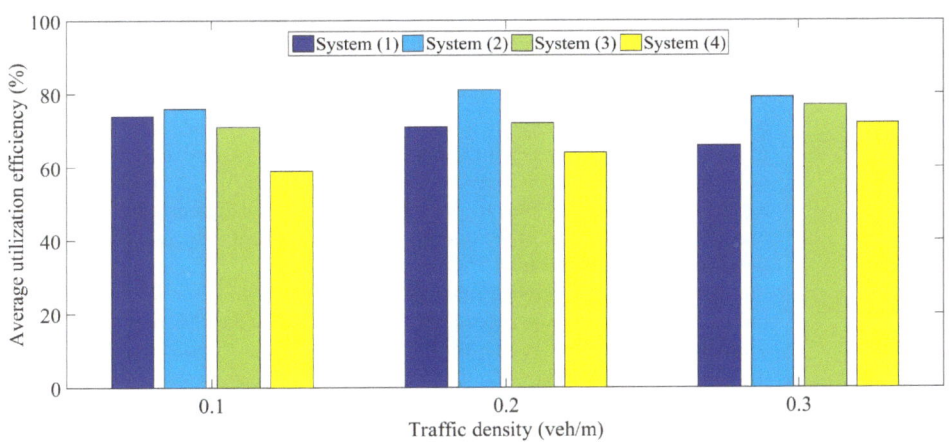

Figure 15. Average resource utilization efficiency at different TDs for Category (II) tasks.

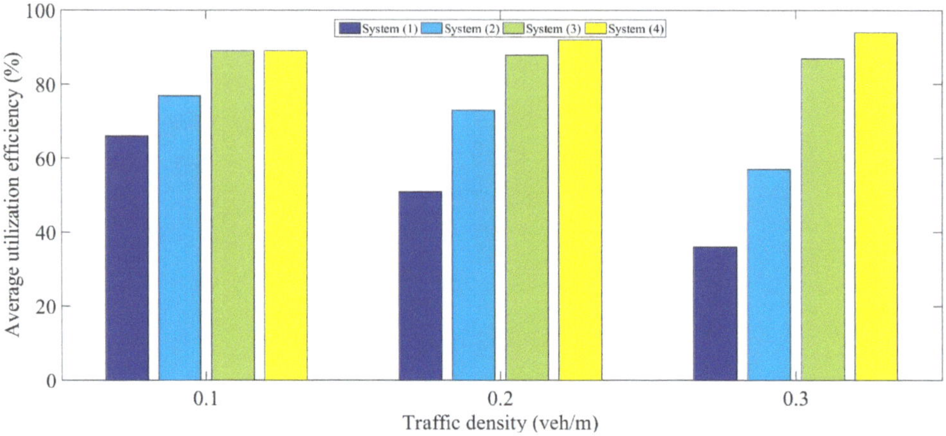

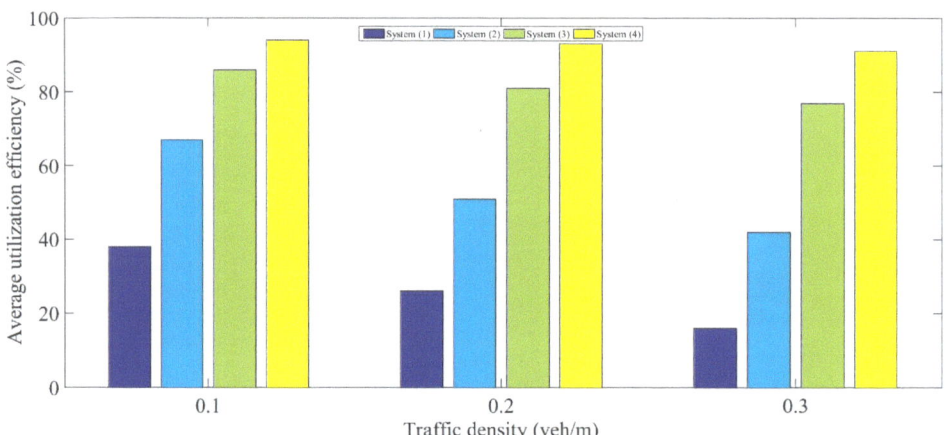

Figure 16. Average resource utilization efficiency at different TDs for Category (III) tasks.

Figure 17. Average resource utilization efficiency at different TDs for Category (IV) tasks.

To evaluate the availability of the proposed microservice-based VANET, the average number of the blocked tasks, i.e., tasks that cannot be handled during simulation due to unavailability of resources or other reasons, was measured. The developed and existing systems used for comparison were simulated with Categories (III and IV) tasks. We considered these categories and neglected the first two categories since these tasks have constraints regarding QoS time. Tasks of the first two categories require low computing resources and have little constraints in terms of QoS time. Figures 18–23 present the average percentage of BT (%BT) compared to the total number of assigned tasks during the simulation. Figures 18 and 19 present the average %BT at different vehicle mobilities for the specifications introduced in Table 9. The proposed model outperformed the existing systems for the two categories of applications. This is due to the introduction of microservices and the increase of available resources introduced by fog nodes. Moreover, the system achieved higher performance at higher mobilities due to the proposed migration scheme with the microservice approach.

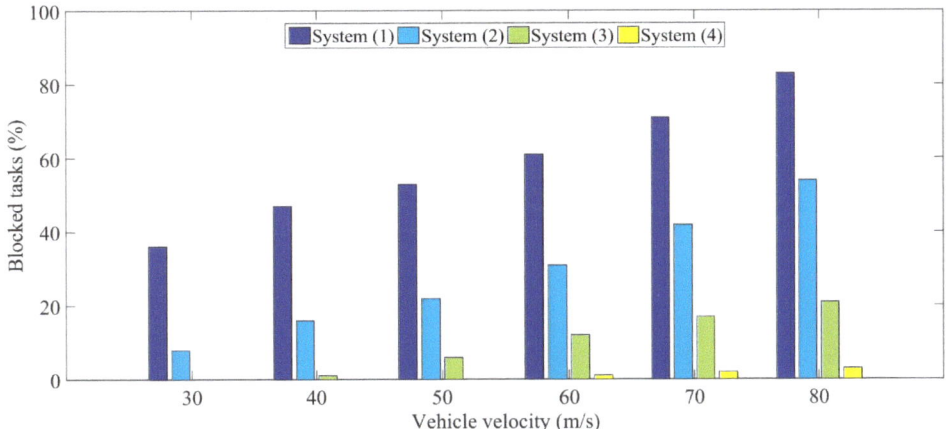

Figure 18. %BTs at different vehicle mobility for Category (III) tasks.

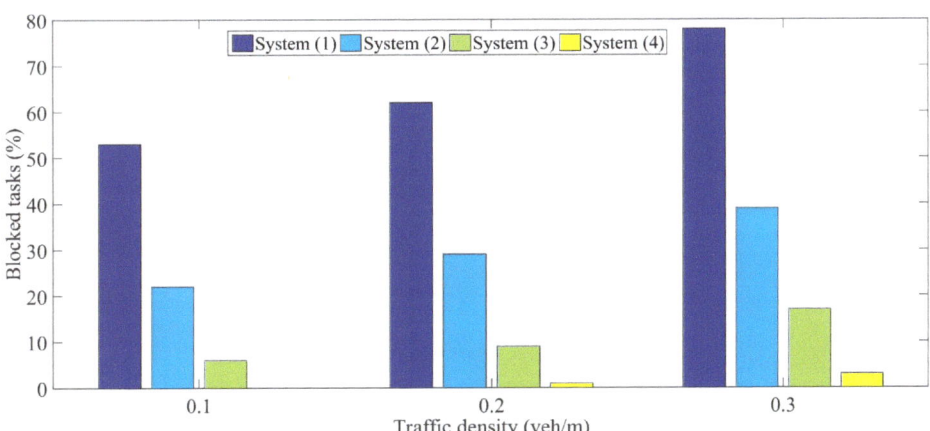

Figure 19. %BTs at different vehicle mobility for Category (IV) tasks.

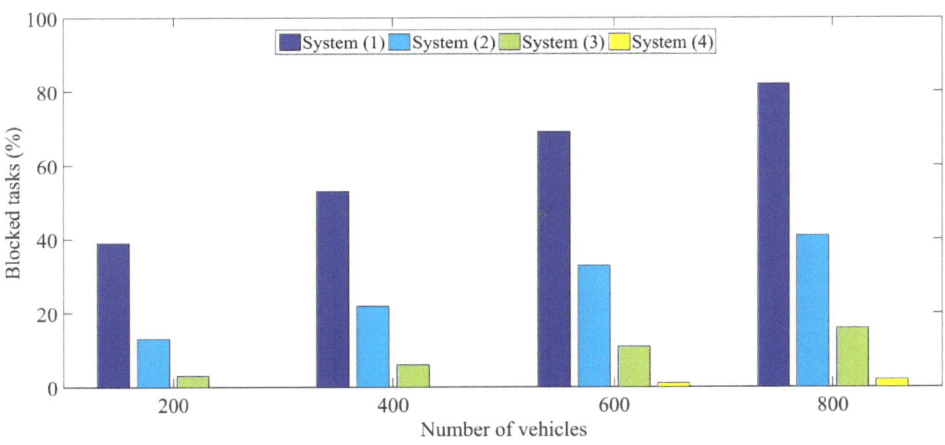

Figure 20. %BTs at different numbers of vehicles for Category (III) tasks.

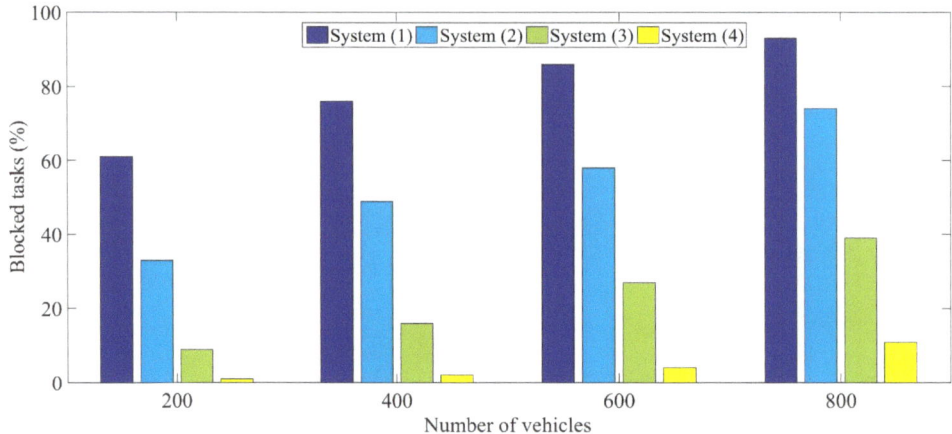

Figure 21. BTs at different numbers of vehicles for Category (IV) tasks.

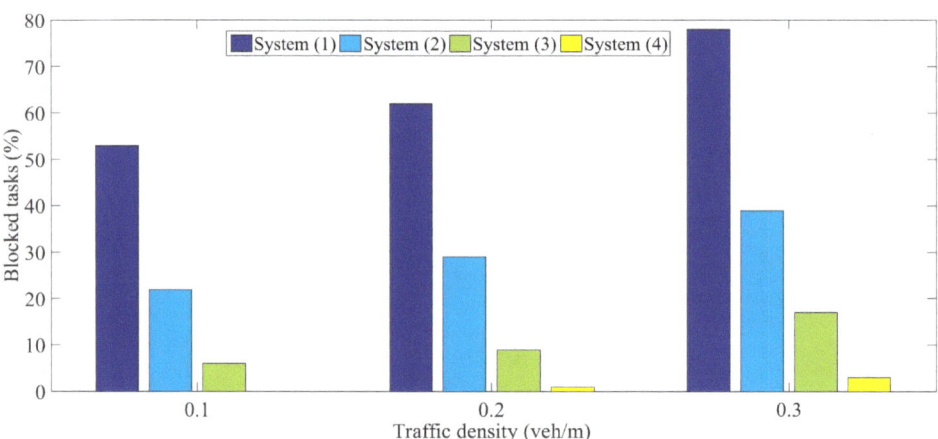

Figure 22. BTs at different TDs for Category (III) tasks.

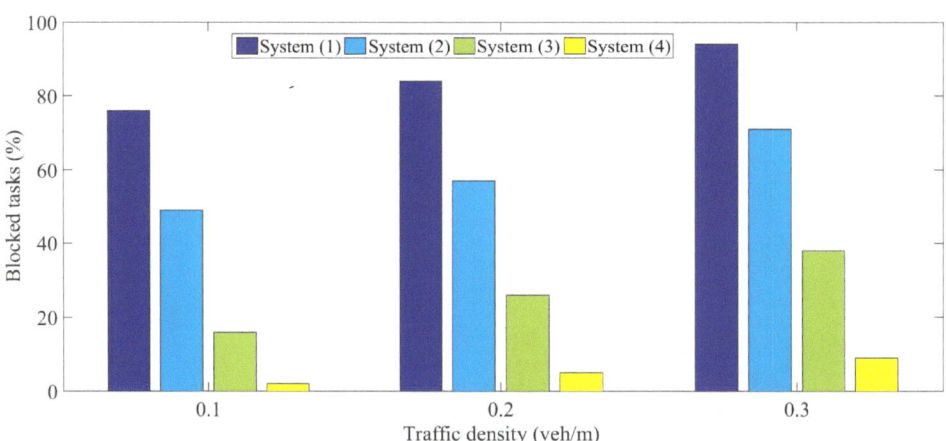

Figure 23. BTs at different TDs for Category (IV) tasks.

Table 9. Simulation parameters for the %BT measurements (Figures 18 and 19).

Parameter	Number of Vehicles (N)	Traffic Density (TD)	QoS Time (Category III) Tasks	QoS Time (Category IV) Tasks	System (1)	System (2)	System (3)	System (4)
Value	400	0.1 veh/m	10 ms	5 ms	Traditional VANET	Traditional MEC-VANET	System developed in [28]	Proposed microservice-based VANET

Figures 20 and 21 present the average %BT for different numbers of employed vehicles for the specifications introduced in Table 10. The proposed model outperformed the existing systems for the two categories of applications. This is mainly due to a higher number of deployed vehicles due to the introduction of microservice and the increase of available resources introduced by fog nodes. Similarly, Figures 22 and 23 present the average %BT at different traffic densities for the specifications introduced in Table 11.

Table 10. Simulation parameters for the %BT measurements (Figures 20 and 21).

Parameter	Vehicle Velocity (v)	Traffic Density (TD)	QoS Time (Category III) Tasks	QoS Time (Category IV) Tasks	System (1)	System (2)	System (3)	System (4)
Value	50 Km/h	0.1 veh/m	10 ms	5 ms	Traditional VANET	Traditional MEC-VANET	System developed in [28]	Proposed microservice-based VANET

Table 11. Simulation parameters for the %BT measurements (Figures 22 and 23).

Parameter	Vehicle Velocity (v)	Number of Vehicles (N)	QoS Time (Category III) Tasks	QoS Time (Category IV) Tasks	System (1)	System (2)	System (3)	System (4)
Value	50 Km/h	400	10 ms	5 ms	Traditional VANET	Traditional MEC-VANET	System developed in [28]	Proposed microservice-based VANET

The average latency for handling computing tasks was measured during the simulation. The performance improvement in terms of latency was calculated to the traditional MEC/VANET, using Equation (1). This performance measure was considered for the third and fourth categories of applications since the first and second application categories have no constraints in terms of latency. Figures 24 and 25 present the percentage improvement of the latency for the systems and specifications mentioned in Table 12. Figure 24 presents the performance improvement of latency for tasks of Category (III) of applications at different numbers of vehicles, and similarly, Figure 25 provides the results for tasks of Category (IV). The proposed system outperformed the existing systems and reduced the average latency required to handle computing tasks of Categories (III and IV).

Table 12. Simulation parameters for the percentage improvement of latency measurements (Figures 24 and 25).

Parameter	Vehicle Velocity (v)	Traffic Density (TD)	QoS Time (Category III) Tasks	QoS Time (Category IV) Tasks	System (2)	System (3)
Value	50 Km/h	0.1 veh/m	10 ms	5 ms	System developed in [28]	Proposed microservice-based VANET

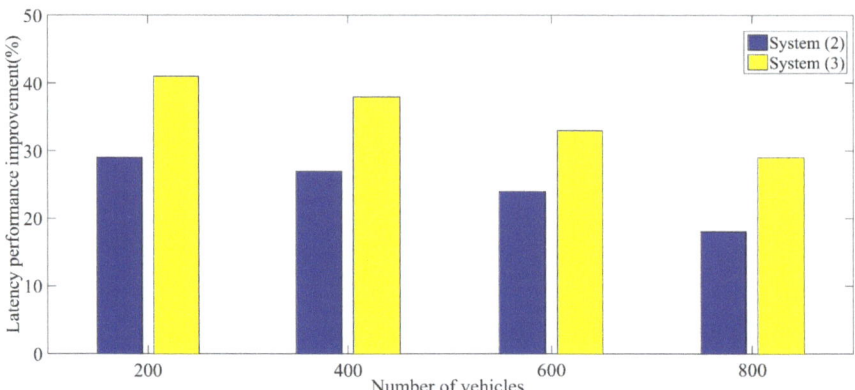

Figure 24. Latency performance improvement at different numbers of vehicles for Category (III) tasks.

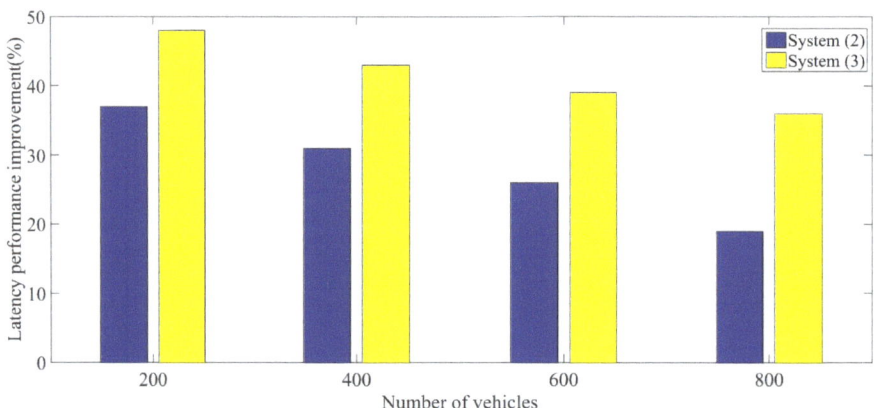

Figure 25. Latency performance improvement at different numbers of vehicles for Category (IV) tasks.

9. Conclusions

This work investigated the major challenges presented by VANETs' demanding needs, including extremely low latency, exceptional reliability, and seamless communications at high mobilities. It introduced a novel structure for VANETs based on fog computing, MEC, and microservices architecture. Utilizing this two-layer edge computing approach improves the network's capacity to handle computational activities and maintain minimal latency effectively. Introducing the microservice architecture with prioritizing tasks provided improved flexibility, modularity, and scalability in the design and implementation of automotive applications. An efficient offloading scheme was implemented to distribute the computing workload efficiently between vehicles and the two-level edge servers, resulting in a significant decrease in system delay, improved resource utilization efficiency, and higher network availability. In addition, a seamless migration scheme was developed and implemented with an efficient HO strategy to provide seamless communications with the intended QoS at high vehicle mobility. The proposed microservice-based VANET was simulated for heterogeneous real-based scenarios considering different TDs, different numbers of deployed vehicles, and different vehicle mobilities. The results indicated that the proposed system outperformed existing VANET systems regarding latency, availability, and reliability.

Author Contributions: Conceptualization, M.M.Z., A.A.A., M.M.A. and M.S.S.; methodology, M.M.Z., A.A.A., M.M.A., M.E. and M.S.S.; software, M.M.Z., A.A.A., M.M.A. and M.S.S.; formal analysis, M.M.Z., A.A.A., M.M.A. and M.S.S.; investigation, A.A.A., M.M.A. and M.S.S.; resources, A.A.A., M.M.A. and M.S.S.; writing—original draft preparation, M.M.Z., A.A.A., M.M.A. and M.S.S.; writing—review and editing, A.A.A., M.M.A., M.E. and M.S.S.; visualization, M.M.Z.; supervision M.S.S.; project administration, A.A.A.; funding, M.E. and A.A.A. All authors have read and agreed to the published version of the manuscript.

Funding: This research was funded by Prince Sultan University.

Data Availability Statement: The data are contained within the article and/or available from the corresponding author upon reasonable request.

Acknowledgments: The authors would like to acknowledge the support of Prince Sultan University for paying the article processing charges (APC) of this publication.

Conflicts of Interest: The authors declare no conflicts of interest.

References

1. Chaccour, C.; Saad, W.; Debbah, M.; Han, Z.; Poor, H.V. Less Data, More Knowledge: Building next Generation Semantic Communication Networks. *IEEE Commun. Surv. Tutor.* **2024**, 1–11. [CrossRef]
2. Hakak, S.; Gadekallu, T.R.; Maddikunta, P.K.R.; Ramu, S.P.; M, P.; De Alwis, C.; Liyanage, M. Autonomous Vehicles in 5G and beyond: A Survey. *Veh. Commun.* **2023**, *39*, 100551. [CrossRef]
3. Liu, W.; Hua, M.; Deng, Z.; Meng, Z.; Huang, Y.; Hu, C.; Song, S.; Gao, L.; Liu, C.; Shuai, B.; et al. A Systematic Survey of Control Techniques and Applications in Connected and Automated Vehicles. *IEEE Internet Things J.* **2023**, *10*, 21892–21916. [CrossRef]
4. Mahi, M.J.N.; Chaki, S.; Ahmed, S.; Biswas, M.; Kaiser, M.S.; Islam, M.S.; Sookhak, M.; Barros, A.; Whaiduzzaman, M. A Review on VANET Research: Perspective of Recent Emerging Technologies. *IEEE Access* **2022**, *10*, 65760–65783. [CrossRef]
5. Guo, H.; Zhou, X.; Liu, J.; Zhang, Y. Vehicular Intelligence in 6G: Networking, Communications, and Computing. *Veh. Commun.* **2022**, *33*, 100399. [CrossRef]
6. Javed, F.; Khan, Z.A.; Rizwan, S.; Shahzadi, S.; Chaudhry, N.R.; Iqbal, M. A Novel Energy-Efficient Reservation System for Edge Computing in 6G Vehicular Ad Hoc Network. *Sensors* **2023**, *23*, 5817. [CrossRef] [PubMed]
7. Nurkahfi, G.N.; Triwinarko, A.; Prawara, B.; Armi, N.; Juhana, T.; Syambas, N.R.; Mulyana, E.; Dogheche, E.; Dayoub, I. On SDN to Support the IEEE 802.11 and C-V2X Based Vehicular Communications Use-Cases and Performance: A Comprehensive Survey. *IEEE Access.* [CrossRef]
8. Behravan, K.; Farzaneh, N.; Jahanshahi, M.; Hosseini Seno, S.A. A Comprehensive Survey on Using Fog Computing in Vehicular Networks. *Veh. Commun.* **2023**, *42*, 100604. [CrossRef]
9. Wakgra, F.G.; Kar, B.; Tadele, S.B.; Shen, S.-H.; Khan, A.U. Multi-Objective Offloading Optimization in MEC and Vehicular-Fog Systems: A Distributed-TD3 Approach. *IEEE Trans. Intell. Transp. Syst.* **2024**, 1–13. [CrossRef]
10. Waheed, A.; Shah, M.A.; Mohsin, S.M.; Khan, A.; Maple, C.; Aslam, S.; Shamshirband, S. A Comprehensive Review of Computing Paradigms, Enabling Computation Offloading and Task Execution in Vehicular Networks. *IEEE Access* **2022**, *10*, 3580–3600. [CrossRef]
11. Hamdi, A.M.A.; Hussain, F.K.; Hussain, O.K. Task Offloading in Vehicular Fog Computing: State-of-the-Art and Open Issues. *Future Gener. Comput. Syst.* **2022**, *133*, 201–212. [CrossRef]
12. Nkenyereye, L.; Naik, R.P.; Jang, J.W.; Chung, W.Y. Software-Defined Small Cell-Linked Vehicular Networks: Architecture and Evaluation. *Electronics* **2023**, *12*, 304. [CrossRef]
13. Taha, M.B.; Alrabaee, S.; Choo, K.K.R. Efficient Resource Management of Micro-Services in Vanets. *IEEE Trans. Intell. Transp. Syst.* **2023**, *24*, 6820–6835. [CrossRef]
14. Alam, F.; Toosi, A.N.; Cheema, M.A.; Cicconetti, C.; Serrano, P.; Iosup, A.; Tari, Z.; Sarvi, M. Serverless Vehicular Edge Computing for the Internet of Vehicles. *IEEE Internet Comput.* **2023**, *27*, 40–51. [CrossRef]
15. Alkaabi, S.R.; Gregory, M.A.; Li, S. Multi-Access Edge Computing Handover Strategies, Management, and Challenges: A Review. *IEEE Access* **2024**, *12*, 4660–4673. [CrossRef]
16. Zakarya, M.; Gillam, L.; Khan, A.A.; Rana, O.; Buyya, R. ApMove: A Service Migration Technique for Connected and Autonomous Vehicles. *IEEE Internet Things J.* **2024**, 1. [CrossRef]
17. Ge, X. Ultra-Reliable Low-Latency Communications in Autonomous Vehicular Networks. *IEEE Trans. Veh. Technol.* **2019**, *68*, 5005–5016. [CrossRef]
18. Abbas, F.; Fan, P. Clustering-Based Reliable Low-Latency Routing Scheme Using ACO Method for Vehicular Networks. *Veh. Commun.* **2018**, *12*, 66–74. [CrossRef]
19. Gomez-Andrades, A.; Munoz, P.; Serrano, I.; Barco, R. Automatic Root Cause Analysis for LTE Networks Based on Unsupervised Techniques. *IEEE Trans. Veh. Technol.* **2016**, *65*, 2369–2386. [CrossRef]
20. Vladyko, A.; Khakimov, A.; Muthanna, A.; Ateya, A.A.; Koucheryavy, A. Distributed Edge Computing to Assist Ultra-Low-Latency VANET Applications. *Future Internet* **2019**, *11*, 128. [CrossRef]

21. Boukerche, A.; Aljeri, N. An Energy-Efficient Controller Management Scheme for Software-Defined Vehicular Networks. *IEEE Trans. Sustain. Comput.* **2022**, *7*, 61–74. [CrossRef]
22. Aljeri, N.; Boukerche, A. A Novel Proactive Controller Deployment Protocol for 5G-Enabled Software-Defined Vehicular Networks. *Comput. Commun.* **2022**, *182*, 88–97. [CrossRef]
23. Dai, P.; Hu, K.; Wu, X.; Xing, H.; Teng, F.; Yu, Z. A Probabilistic Approach for Cooperative Computation Offloading in MEC-Assisted Vehicular Networks. *IEEE Trans. Intell. Transp. Syst.* **2022**, *23*, 899–911. [CrossRef]
24. Peng, H.; Shen, X.S. DDPG-Based Resource Management for MEC/UAV-Assisted Vehicular Networks. In Proceedings of the 2020 IEEE 92nd Vehicular Technology Conference (VTC2020-Fall), Victoria, BC, Canada, 18 November–16 December 2020; IEEE: Piscataway, NJ, USA, 2020; pp. 1–6.
25. Muthanna, A.; Shamilova, R.; Ateya, A.A.; Paramonov, A.; Hammoudeh, M. A Mobile Edge Computing/Software-defined Networking-enabled Architecture for Vehicular Networks. *Internet Technol. Lett.* **2020**, *3*, e109. [CrossRef]
26. Qiao, B.; Liu, C.; Liu, J.; Hu, Y.; Li, K.; Li, K. Task Migration Computation Offloading with Low Delay for Mobile Edge Computing in Vehicular Networks. *Concurr. Comput.* **2022**, *34*, e6494. [CrossRef]
27. Vladyko, A.; Elagin, V.; Spirkina, A.; Muthanna, A.; Ateya, A. Distributed Edge Computing with Blockchain Technology to Enable Ultra-Reliable Low-Latency V2X Communications. *Electronics* **2022**, *11*, 173. [CrossRef]
28. Monir, N.; Toraya, M.M.; Vladyko, A.; Muthanna, A.; Torad, M.A.; El-Samie, F.E.A.; Ateya, A.A. Seamless Handover Scheme for MEC/SDN-Based Vehicular Networks. *J. Sens. Actuator Netw.* **2022**, *11*, 9. [CrossRef]
29. Aljeri, N.; Boukerche, A. Performance Evaluation of Communication Lifetime Prediction Model for Autonomous Vehicular Networks. In *PE-WASUN '23, Proceedings of the Int'l ACM Symposium on Performance Evaluation of Wireless Ad Hoc, Sensor, & Ubiquitous Networks, Montreal, QC, Canada, 30 October–3 November 2023*; ACM: New York, NY, USA, 2023.
30. Khan, Z.; Koubaa, A.; Benjdira, B.; Boulila, W. A Game Theory Approach for Smart Traffic Management. *Comput. Electr. Eng.* **2023**, *110*, 108825. [CrossRef]
31. Martins Maciel, P.R. *Performance, Reliability, and Availability Evaluation of Computational Systems, Volume I: Performance and Background*; Chapman & Hall/CRC: Philadelphia, PA, USA, 2023; ISBN 9781032295374.
32. De Simone, L.; Di Mauro, M.; Longo, M.; Natella, R.; Postiglione, F. Performability Assessment of Containerized Multi-Tenant IMS through Multidimensional UGF. In Proceedings of the 2022 18th International Conference on Network and Service Management (CNSM), Thessaloniki, Greece, 31 October–4 November 2022; IEEE: Piscataway, NJ, USA, 2022; pp. 145–153.
33. Simone, L.D.; Mauro, M.D.; Natella, R.; Postiglione, F. Performance and Availability Challenges in Designing Resilient 5G Architectures. *IEEE Trans. Netw. Serv. Manag.* **2024**, 1. [CrossRef]
34. Aljeri, N.; Boukerche, A. An Adaptive Traffic-Flow Based Controller Deployment Scheme for Software-Defined Vehicular Networks. In *MSWiM '20, Proceedings of the 23rd International ACM Conference on Modeling, Analysis and Simulation of Wireless and Mobile Systems, Alicante, Spain, 16–20 November 2020*; ACM: New York, NY, USA, 2020.
35. Garg, S.; Kaur, K.; Kaddoum, G.; Ahmed, S.H.; Jayakody, D.N.K. SDN-Based Secure and Privacy-Preserving Scheme for Vehicular Networks: A 5G Perspective. *IEEE Trans. Veh. Technol.* **2019**, *68*, 8421–8434. [CrossRef]
36. Fung, C.C.; Yogarayan, S.; Abdul Razak, S.F.; Azman, A. A Review Study of IEEE 802.11p on-Board Unit for V2X Deployment. In Proceedings of the 2023 11th International Conference on Information and Communication Technology (ICoICT), Melaka, Malaysia, 23–24 August 2023; IEEE: Piscataway, NJ, USA, 2023; pp. 165–171.
37. Kumar, D. Rammohan Revolutionizing Intelligent Transportation Systems with Cellular Vehicle-to-Everything (C-V2X) Technology: Current Trends, Use Cases, Emerging Technologies, Standardization Bodies, Industry Analytics and Future Directions. *Veh. Commun.* **2023**, *43*, 100638. [CrossRef]
38. Fernandez, Z.; Martin, A.; Perez, J.; Garcia, M.; Velez, G.; Murciano, F.; Peters, S. Challenges and Solutions for Service Continuity in Inter-PLMN Handover for Vehicular Applications. *IEEE Access* **2023**, *11*, 8904–8919. [CrossRef]
39. K, S.; Chinnasamy, C. Efficient VANET Handover Scheme Using SSDN by Incorporating Media Independent Handover Framework. *Measur. Sens.* **2023**, *26*, 100684. [CrossRef]
40. Khan, N.; bin Salleh, R.; Khan, Z.; Koubaa, A.; Hamdan, M.; Abdelmoniem, A.M. Ensuring Reliable Network Operations and Maintenance: The Role of PMRF for Switch Maintenance and Upgrades in SDN. *J. King Saud Univ.—Comput. Inf. Sci.* **2023**, *35*, 101809. [CrossRef]
41. Ateya, A.A.; Muthanna, A.; Koucheryavy, A.; Maleh, Y.; El-Latif, A.A.A. Energy Efficient Offloading Scheme for MEC-Based Augmented Reality System. *Clust. Comput.* **2023**, *26*, 789–806. [CrossRef]
42. Ms-Van3t. Available online: https://github.com/ms-van3t-devs/ms-van3t (accessed on 15 April 2024).
43. Ateya, A.A.; Vybornova, A.; Samouylov, K.; Koucheryavy, A. System Model for Multi-Level Cloud Based Tactile Internet System. In *Wired/Wireless Internet Communications, Proceedings of the 15th IFIP WG 6.2 International Conference, WWIC 2017, St. Petersburg, Russia, 21–23 June 2017*; Springer International Publishing: Cham, Switzerland, 2017; pp. 77–86. ISBN 9783319613819.
44. Cruz, S.; Aguiar, A. Cooperative Localization in Vehicular Networks Dataset 2020. Available online: https://ieee-dataport.org/open-access/cooperative-localization-vehicular-networks-dataset (accessed on 1 June 2024).
45. From Images to 3D Shapes (FI3S). Available online: https://www.kaggle.com/datasets/lehomme/from-images-to-3d-shapesfi3s (accessed on 20 April 2024).
46. TikTokDataset. Available online: https://www.kaggle.com/datasets/yasaminjafarian/tiktokdataset (accessed on 20 April 2024).

47. YouTube Faces with Facial Keypoints. Available online: https://www.kaggle.com/datasets/selfishgene/youtube-faces-with-facial-keypoints (accessed on 20 April 2024).
48. Google Scraped Image Dataset. Available online: https://www.kaggle.com/datasets/duttadebadri/image-classification (accessed on 20 April 2024).

Disclaimer/Publisher's Note: The statements, opinions and data contained in all publications are solely those of the individual author(s) and contributor(s) and not of MDPI and/or the editor(s). MDPI and/or the editor(s) disclaim responsibility for any injury to people or property resulting from any ideas, methods, instructions or products referred to in the content.

MDPI AG
Grosspeteranlage 5
4052 Basel
Switzerland
Tel.: +41 61 683 77 34

Future Internet Editorial Office
E-mail: futureinternet@mdpi.com
www.mdpi.com/journal/futureinternet

Disclaimer/Publisher's Note: The statements, opinions and data contained in all publications are solely those of the individual author(s) and contributor(s) and not of MDPI and/or the editor(s). MDPI and/or the editor(s) disclaim responsibility for any injury to people or property resulting from any ideas, methods, instructions or products referred to in the content.

www.ingramcontent.com/pod-product-compliance
Lightning Source LLC
LaVergne TN
LVHW072345090526
838202LV00019B/2482